POETICS

ARISTOTLE
POETICS

TRANSLATED AND WITH
CRITICAL NOTES BY
S. H. BUTCHER

*With a prefatory essay
"Aristotelian Literary Criticism"* by
JOHN GASSNER

Fourth Edition

DOVER PUBLICATIONS, INC.
MINEOLA, NEW YORK

Bibliographical Note

This Dover edition, first published in 1951, is an unabridged and unaltered republication of the 1911 edition of the translation originally published by the St. Martin's Press in 1894 under the title *Aristotle's Theory of Poetry and Fine Art*. This first American edition is published by special arrangement with the St. Martin's Press. A new Introduction, written by John Gassner specially for this Dover edition, is included.

International Standard Book Number

ISBN-13: 978-0-486-20042-2
ISBN-10: 0-486-20042-6

Library of Congress Catalog Card Number: 51-7282

Manufactured in the United States by LSC Communications
20042624   2019
www.doverpublications.com

PREFACE TO THE FIRST EDITION

THE present volume has grown out of certain chapters relating to the *Poetics* in the first edition of 'Some Aspects of the Greek Genius.' These chapters have been enlarged and partly re-written; and further questions, not touched on in the earlier volume, and bearing on Aristotle's theory of tragedy, are here discussed. A text and a translation of the *Poetics* are prefixed to the Essays.

It is just a hundred years since a critical text of the *Poetics* has been published in Great Britain. Tyrwhitt's edition, which appeared at Oxford in 1794, was, indeed, the work of an admirable scholar; but since that time much light has been thrown on almost every page of this treatise. And yet even to-day, after all the labours of German scholars, no editor can hope to produce a text which will not provoke dissent on the part of competent critics. For my own part, I find myself more frequently in agreement with William Christ on questions of reading, than with any previous editor. Susemihl, to whom every student of Aristotle is profoundly indebted, appears to me to carry conjecture too far, more especially in the transposition of sentences and the omission of words. On the other hand, Vahlen's adherence to the Parisian MS. (A^c) borders on superstition,—if one may dare so to speak of the critic who in a preeminent degree has contributed to the elucidation of the *Poetics*.

The superiority of the Parisian over all other extant MSS. is beyond dispute; still I cannot share the confidence with which the best editors now speak of it as the sole source from which the rest are derived. It is true there are no decisive passages by which the independent value of these latter can be established. But that some of them have an independent worth is rendered highly probable by two considerations. First, by the appearance in them of words which are omitted in A^c, but are necessary to complete the sense. The missing words are not unfrequently such as a copyist could hardly have supplied. Secondly, by the number of instances in which the true reading is hopelessly obscured in A^c, but preserved in some of the so-called 'apographa.' No ordinary scribe could have hit on such happy corrections. While doubting, however, whether A^c is indeed the archetype of all extant MSS., I have, for the sake of convenience, retained in the critical notes the usual abbreviation 'apogr.,' to denote any MS. or MSS. other than A^c.

The conjectures of my own which are admitted into the text are few in number. They will be found in iii. 3. 1448 a 33, xix. 3. 1456 b 8, xxiii. 1. 1459 a 17, xxiv. 10. 1460 a 35, xxv. 4. 1460 b 17, xxv. 14. 1461 a 27, xxv. 16. 1461 a 35.[1] The emendation in xxiii. 1, ἐνὶ μέτρῳ μιμητικῆς for ἐν μέτρῳ μιμητικῆς will, I hope, appear as plausible to others as it is convincing to myself. In ix. 5 (οὕτω τὰ τυχόντα ὀνόματα), though I have not altered the traditional reading, yet for reasons stated in note 1, p. 376, I suspect we ought to read οὐ τὰ τυχόντα ὀνόματα, and I venture to press this suggestion. In a certain number of passages I have bracketed words, hitherto retained by the editors, which I take to be glosses that have crept into the text. The passages are these—iii. 1. 1448 a 23, vi. 18. 1450 b 13, xvii. 1. 1455 a 27, xvii. 5. 1455 b 22.[2] But the detailed treatment of these and other questions of criticism and interpretation must be reserved for the more fitting pages of a commentary.

Fortunately, the general views of Aristotle on

---

[1] Of these the conjecture in iii. 3 is withdrawn in later editions; that in xxv. 14 gives place to <οἱονοῦν> (Tucker).

[2] In vi. 18 I read in ed. 2 τῶν λεγομένων (Gomperz) instead of [τῶν μὲν λόγων] of ed. 1, and in xvii. 5 ὅτι αὐτὸς (Bywater) for [τινὰς αὐτός]. In ed. 3, however, I returned to the MSS. reading in xvii. 5 : see infra, p. xxv.

Poetry and Art are not affected by the minor difficulties with which the *Poetics* abounds. Incomplete as our material is when all scattered references have been brought together, the cardinal points of Aristotle's aesthetic theory can be seized with some certainty. But his *Poetics* must be read in the light of his other writings; we must trace the links which connect his theory of Art with his philosophic system as a whole; we must discover the meaning he attaches to 'Imitation' as an aesthetic term,—a somewhat infelicitous term, it must be owned, inherited by him from his predecessors, but henceforth charged with a new meaning. Such an inquiry will dispel the vulgar notion that still survives in popular manuals, that by 'Imitation' Aristotle means a literal copy, a mere facsimile of the world of experience. The clue to his real thought is to be found in the assertion that Poetry is an expression of the 'universal'; that is, of the universal element in human life. In interpreting the full significance of this conception frequent reference will of necessity be made to the wider principles of the Aristotelian philosophy.

In the following pages I have attempted to bring out some of the vital connexions which are thus suggested between Aristotle's theory of Poetry and other sides of his comprehensive thought. In endeavouring to state his views and estimate their worth candidly and without exaggeration, I have not forgotten that Aristotle, more than any other writer, has suffered from the intemperate admiration of his friends. There have been periods when he was held to be infallible both in literature and in philosophy. A sovereign authority has been claimed for him by those who possessed no first-hand knowledge of his writings, and certainly were not equipped with sufficient Greek to interpret the text. A far truer respect would have been shown him had it been frankly acknowledged, that in his *Poetics* there are oversights and omissions which cannot be altogether set down to the fragmentary character of the book; that his judgments are based on literary models which, perfect as they are in their kind, do not exhaust the possibilities of literature; that many of his rules are tentative rather than dogmatic; that some of them need revision or qualification; that, for example, the requisites laid down in chap. xiii. for the character of the tragic protagonist would exclude from the first rank of art some of the noblest figures of the Greek drama,—Antigone, Clytemnestra, and possibly Prometheus. On the other hand, we may well wonder at the impartiality of mind, which lifted him above some, at least, of the limitations of his age, though he could not wholly emancipate himself from the external rules and usages of the Athenian theatre.

b

Above all we may admire his insight into the essential quality of Poetry as a concrete expression of the universal. To this result he was led by a penetrating analysis of the imaginative creations of Greece itself. Universality is, indeed, their characteristic note. The accidents of human nature seem here to fall into the background, while its larger lineaments are disengaged.

A list of the more important works which treat of the *Poetics* will be found on page xxxvii. I desire, however, here to mention the books which have chiefly aided me in the preparation of the Essays : E. Müller, *Geschichte der Kunst bei der Alten*, Breslau, 1834. Vahlen, *Beiträge zu Aristoteles' Poetik*, Wien, 1865. Teichmüller, *Aristotelische Forschungen*, Halle, 1869. Reinkens, *Aristoteles über Kunst*, Wien, 1870. Döring, *Die Kunstlehre des Aristoteles*, Jena, 1870. Bernays, *Zwei Abhandlungen über die Aristotelische Theorie des Drama*, Berlin, 1880. I owe, moreover, special and personal thanks to Prof. A. C. Bradley for valuable criticisms on my earlier volume, which I have here turned to account. I have reason also gratefully to acknowledge the singular care and skill displayed by Messrs. R. & R. Clark's Reader.

EDINBURGH, *November* 1894.

PREFACE TO THE SECOND EDITION

THE chief alterations in this edition, as compared
with the first, consist in the enlargement of the
Critical Notes, and a careful revision of the Translation. Minor changes and additions will be found
in the Essays. A third index also has been added
containing a list of the passages in Greek authors
referred to in the volume.

In making use of the mass of critical material
which has appeared in recent years, especially in
Germany, I have found it necessary to observe a
strict principle of selection, my aim still being
to keep the notes within limited compass. They
are not intended to form a complete *Apparatus
Criticus*, still less to do duty for a commentary.
I trust, however, that no variant or conjectural
emendation of much importance has been over-
looked.

Of my own conjectures, printed in the text of
the first edition, one or two appear to have carried
general conviction, in particular that in xxiii. 1.

Two have been withdrawn (see p. vii.). One, which I previously relegated to the notes, while putting in a plea for its acceptance in the preface, has since won the approval of many scholars, including the distinguished names of Professor Susemihl and Professor Tyrrell, and it is with some confidence that I now insert it in the text. I refer to οὐ (οὕτω MSS.) τὰ τυχόντα ὀνόματα in ix. 5. 1451 b 13, where the Arabic has 'names not given at random.' For the copyist's error cf. ix. 2. 1451 a 37 (= a 36 Bekk.), where Aᶜ has οὕτω, though οὐ τὸ rightly appears in the 'apographa': and for a similar omission of οὐ in Aᶜ cf. vi. 12. 1450 a 29, οὐ ποιήσει ὃ ἦν τῆς τραγῳδίας ἔργον, the indispensable negative being added in 'apographa' and found in the Arabic. The emendation not only gives a natural instead of a strained sense to the words τὰ τυχόντα ὀνόματα, but also fits in better with the general context, as I have argued at some length, pp. 376–9 (note).

Another conjecture of my own I have ventured to admit into the text. In the much disputed passage, vi. 8. 1450 a 12, I read <πάντες> ὡς εἰπεῖν for οὐκ ὀλίγοι αὐτῶν ὡς εἰπεῖν of the MSS., following the guidance of Diels and of the Arabic. I regard οὐκ ὀλίγοι αὐτῶν as a gloss which displaced part of the original phrase (see Critical Notes). As a parallel case I have adduced *Rhet*. i. 1. 1354 a

12, where οὐδὲν ὡς εἰπεῖν, the reading in the margin of Aᶜ, ought, I think, to be substituted in the text for the accepted reading ὀλίγον. The word ὀλίγον is a natural gloss on οὐδὲν ὡς εἰπεῖν, but not so, οὐδὲν ὡς εἰπεῖν on ὀλίγον.

In two other difficult passages the *Rhetoric* may again be summoned to our aid. In xvii. 1. 1455 a 27 I have (as in the first edition) bracketed τὸν θεατήν, the object to be supplied with ἐλάνθανεν being, as I take it, the poet, not the audience. This I have now illustrated by another gloss of a precisely similar kind in *Rhet.* i. 2. 1358 a 8, where λανθάνουσίν τε [τοὺς ἀκροατὰς] has long been recognised as the true reading, the suppressed object being not the audience but the rhetoricians.

Once more, in xxiv. 9. 1460 a 23, where Aᶜ gives the meaningless ἄλλου δέ, I read (as in the first edition) ἀλλ᾽ οὐδέ, following the reviser of Aᶜ. This reading, which was accepted long ago by Vettori, has been strangely set aside by the chief modern editors, who either adopt a variant ἄλλο δὲ or resort to conjecture, with the result that προσθεῖναι at the end of the sentence is forced into impossible meanings. A passage in the *Rhetoric*, i. 2. 1357 a 17 ff., appears to me to determine the question conclusively in favour of ἀλλ᾽ οὐδὲ . . . ἀνάγκη . . . προσθεῖναι. The passage runs thus:

ἐὰν γὰρ ᾖ τι τούτων γνώριμον, οὐδὲ δεῖ λέγειν· αὐτὸς γὰρ τοῦτο προστίθησιν ὁ ἀκροατής, οἷον ὅτι Δωριεὺς

στεφανίτην ἀγῶνα νενίκηκεν, ἱκανὸν εἰπεῖν ὅτι Ὀλύμπια
γὰρ νενίκηκεν, τὸ δ' ὅτι στεφανίτης τὰ Ὀλύμπια, οὐδὲ
δεῖ προσθεῖναι· γιγνώσκουσι γὰρ πάντες. The general
idea is closely parallel to our passage of the *Poetics*,
and the expression of it is similar, even the word
οὐδέ (where the bare οὐ might have been expected)
in the duplicated phrase οὐδὲ δεῖ λέγειν, οὐδὲ δεῖ
προσθεῖναι. One difficulty still remains. The subject to εἶναι ἢ γενέσθαι is omitted. To supply it
in thought is not, perhaps, impossible, but it is
exceedingly harsh, and I have accordingly in this
edition accepted Professor Tucker's conjecture,
ἀνάγκη <κἀκεῖνο> εἶναι ἢ γενέσθαι.

The two conjectures of my own above mentioned
are based on or corroborated by the Arabic. I
ought to add, that in the Text and Critical Notes
generally I have made a freer use than before of
the Arabic version (concerning which see p. 4).
But it must be remembered that only detached
passages, literally rendered into Latin in Professor
Margoliouth's *Analecta Orientalia* (D. Nutt, 1887),
are as yet accessible to those like myself who are
not Arabic scholars; and that even if the whole
were before us in a literal translation, it could not
safely be used by any one unfamiliar with Syriac
and Arabic save with the utmost caution and
subject to the advice of experts. Of the precise
value of this version for the criticism of the
text, no final estimate can yet be made. But it

seems clear that in several passages it carries us back to a Greek original earlier than any of our existing MSS. Two striking instances may here be noted :—

(1) i. 6–7. 1447 a 29 ff., where the Arabic confirms Ueberweg's excision of ἐποποιία and the insertion of ἀνώνυμος before τυγχάνουσα, according to the brilliant conjecture of Bernays (see Margoliouth, *Analecta Orientalia*, p. 47).

(2) xxi. 1. 1457 a 36, where for μεγαλιωτῶν of the MSS. Diels has, by the aid of the Arabic, restored the word Μασσαλιωτῶν, and added a most ingenious and convincing explanation of ʽΕρμοκαϊκόξανθος (see Critical Notes). This emendation is introduced for the first time into the present edition. Professor Margoliouth tells me that Diels' restoration of ἐπευξάμενος in this passage is confirmed by the fact that the same word is employed in the Arabic of Aristotle's *Rhetoric* to render εὔχεσθαι.

Another result of great importance has been established. In some fifty instances where the Arabic points to a Greek original diverging from the text of A°, it confirms the reading found in one or other of the 'apographa,' or conjectures made either at the time of the Renaissance or in a more recent period. It would be too long to enumerate the passages here ; they will be found noted as they occur. In most of these examples

the reading attested by the Arabic commands our
undoubting assent. It is, therefore, no longer
possible to concede to A^c the unique authority
claimed for it by Vahlen.

I have consulted by the side of Professor
Margoliouth's book various criticisms of it, e.g. by
Susemihl in *Berl. Phil. Wochenschr.* 1891, p. 1546,
and by Diels in *Sitzungsber. der Berl. Akad.*
1888, p. 49. But I have also enjoyed the special
benefit of private communication with Professor
Margoliouth himself upon a number of difficulties
not dealt with in his *Analecta Orientalia.* He has
most generously put his learning at my disposal,
and furnished me, where it was possible to do so,
with a literal translation. In some instances the
Arabic is itself obscure and throws no light on
the difficulty; frequently, however, I have been
enabled to indicate in the notes whether the existing text is supported by the Arabic or not.

In the following passages I have in this edition
adopted emendations which are suggested or confirmed by the Arabic, but which did not find a
place in the first edition :—

ii. 3. 1448 a 15, ὥσπερ οἱ τοὺς [1]
vi. 7. 1450 a 17, <ὁ δὲ βίος>, omitting καὶ εὐδαιμονίας
   καὶ ἡ εὐδαιμονία of the MSS.
xi. 6. 1452 b 10, [τούτων δὲ . . . εἴρηται]
xviii. 6. 1456 a 24, <καὶ> εἰκὸς [2]

[1] In ed. 3 I simply give the MSS. reading in the text, ὥσπερ † γᾶς †.
[2] In ed. 3 the word here added is omitted in the text.

xx. 5. 1456 b 35, <οὐκ> ἄνευ¹

xxi. 1. 1457 a 34, [καὶ ἀσήμου]. The literal translation of the Arabic is 'and of this some is compounded of significant and insignificant, only not in so far as it is significant in the noun'

xxi. 1. 1457 a 36, Μασσαλιωτῶν (see above, p. xv.)

xxv. 17. 1461 b 12, <καὶ ἴσως ἀδύνατον>

I hesitate to add to this list of corroborated conjectures that of Dacier, now admitted into the text of xxiii. 1. 1459 a 21, καὶ μὴ ὁμοίας ἱστορίαις τὰς συνθέσεις, for καὶ μὴ ὁμοίας ἱστορίας τὰς συνήθεις of the MSS. (In defence of the correction see note, p. 165.) The Arabic, as I learn from Professor Margoliouth, is literally 'and in so far as he does not introduce (or, there do not enter) into these compositions stories which resemble.' This version appears to deviate both from our text and from Dacier's conjecture. There is nothing here to correspond to συνήθεις of the MSS. ; on the other hand, though συνθέσεις may in some form have appeared in the Greek original, it is not easy to reconstruct the text which the translation implies. Another conjecture, communicated privately to me by Mr. T. M'Vey, well deserves mention. It involves the simpler change of ὁμοίας to οἵας. The sense then is, 'and must not be like the ordinary histories'; the demonstr. τοιούτους being sunk in

¹ In ed. 3 the word here added is omitted in the text.

οἴας, so that οἶαι ἱστορίαι αἱ συνήθεις becomes by attraction, οἴας ἱστορίας τὰς συνήθεις.

I subjoin a few other notes derived from correspondence with Professor Margoliouth :—

(a) Passages where the Arabic confirms the reading of the MSS. as against proposed emendation :—

> iv. 14. 1449 a 27, ἐκβαίνοντες τῆς λεκτικῆς ἁρμονίας : Arabic, 'when we depart from dialectic composition.' (The meaning, however, is obviously misunderstood.)
>
> vi. 18. 1450 b 13, τῶν μὲν λόγων : Arabic, 'of the speech.' The μέν is not represented, but, owing to the Syriac form of that particle being identical with the Syriac for the preposition 'of,' it was likely to be omitted here by the translator or copyist.
>
> xviii. 1. 1455 b 25. The Arabic agrees with the MSS. as to the position of πολλάκις, 'as for things which are from without and certain things from within sometimes.'
>
> xviii. 5. 1456 a 19, καὶ ἐν τοῖς ἁπλοῖς πράγμασι: Arabic, 'and in the simple matters.'
>
> xix. 2. 1456 a 38, τὰ πάθη παρασκευάζειν : Arabic, 'to prepare the sufferings.'

More doubtful is xvii. 2. 1455 a 30, ἀπὸ τῆς αὐτῆς φύσεως : Arabic, 'in one and the same nature.' The Arabic mode of translation is not decisive as between the MSS. reading and the conjecture ἀπ' αὐτῆς τῆς φύσεως, but rather favours the former.

(b) Passages where the conjectural omission of words is apparently supported by the Arabic :—

ix. 9. 1451 b 31, οἷα ἂν εἰκὸς γενέσθαι καὶ δυνατὰ γενέσθαι : Arabic, 'there is nothing to prevent the condition of some things being therein like those which are supposed to be.' But we can hardly say with certainty which of the two phrases the Arabic represents.

xvi. 4. 1454 b 31, οἷον 'Ορέστης ἐν τῇ 'Ιφιγενείᾳ ἀνεγνώρισεν ὅτι 'Ορέστης : Arabic, 'as in that which is called Iphigenia, and that is whereby Iphigenia argued that it was Orestes.' This seems to point to the omission of the first Ορέστης.[1]

In neither of these passages, however, have I altered the MSS. reading.

(c) Passages on which the Arabic throws no light :—

i. 9. 1447 b 22. The only point of interest that emerges is that in the Arabic rendering ('of all the metres we ought to call him poet') there is no trace of καί, which is found alike in A^c and the 'apographa.'

x. 3. 1452 a 20. The words γίγνεσθαι ταῦτα are simply omitted in the Arabic.

xxv. 18. 1461 b 18, ὥστε καὶ αὐτὸν MSS. The line containing these words is not represented in the Arabic.

xxv. 19. 1461 b 19, ὅταν μὴ ἀνάγκης οὔσης μηδὲν . . . The words in the Arabic are partly obliterated, partly corrupt.

---

[1] Vahlen (*Hermeneutische Bemerkungen zu Aristoteles' Poetik* ii. 1898, pp. 3–4) maintains that the inference drawn from the Arabic is doubtful, and he adds strong objections on other grounds to Diels' excision of the first 'Ορέστης.

Apart from the revision of the Text, the Translation has, I hope, been improved in many passages, and the improvements are largely due to the invaluable aid I have received from my friend and colleague, Professor W. R. Hardie. To him I would return my warmest thanks; and also to another friend, Professor Tyrrell, who has read through the proof-sheets of the earlier portion of the volume, and has greatly assisted me by his literary and critical skill.

The Essays are substantially unchanged, though they have undergone revision in detail and some expansion. In the notes to the Essays some new matter will be found, e.g. pp. 142–4 (on ch. i. 6–9), pp. 376–9 (on ch. ix. 4–5), pp. 259–260 (on ch. xiii. 2).

In conclusion, I desire to acknowledge my obligations to friends, such as Mr. B. Bosanquet (whose *History of Aesthetic* ought to be in the hands of all students of the subject), Dr. A. W. Verrall, Mr. W. J. Courthope, Mr. A. O. Prickard, and Rev. Dr. Lock, who have written me notes on particular points, and to many reviewers by whose criticism I have profited. In a special sense I am indebted to Professor Susemihl for his review of my first edition in the *Berl. Phil. Wochenschr.*, 28th September 1895, as well as for the instruction derived from his numerous articles on the *Poetics*, extending over many years in Bursian's *Jahresbericht* and elsewhere. Among other reviewers to whom I feel grateful, I would mention Mr. Herbert Richards in the *Classical Review*, May 1895 ; Mr. R. P. Hardie in *Mind*, vol. iv. No. 15 ; and the authors of the unsigned articles in the *Saturday Review*, 2nd March 1895, and the *Oxford Magazine*, 12th June 1895.

To Messrs. R. & R. Clark's Reader I would once again express no merely formal thanks.

EDINBURGH, *November* 1897.

PREFACE TO THE THIRD EDITION

In preparing this third edition for the press I have expanded the critical notes and introduced some fresh material here and there into the Essays. The whole has been subjected to minute revision, and nothing of importance, I hope, has escaped me either in the criticisms of reviewers or in recent contributions made to the study of the text or to the general literature of the subject. Certain topics, indeed, might well have invited fuller treatment, but I have been reluctant to allow the volume to grow to an unwieldy size.

In the revision of the text I have had the advantage of consulting two new editions, based on very different principles, those of Professor Bywater and Professor Tucker, from both of which I have derived assistance. In Professor Bywater's edition I have noted the following passages in which manuscript authority (Parisinus 2038) is cited for readings which hitherto have been given as conjectural:—i. 4. 1447 a 21 ; xi. 5. 1452 b 3

and 4; xv. 1. 1454 a 19; xviii. 1. 1455 b 32;
xxii. 7. 1458 b 20 and 29; xxiv. 8. 1460 a 13;
xxv. 4. 1460 b 19; xxv. 16. 1461 b 3 and 17.
1461 b 13; xxvi. 3. 1462 a 5; xxvi. 6. 1462 b 6.
I am also indebted to Professor Bywater's text
for several improvements in punctuation. Most
of his important emendations had appeared before
the publication of my earlier editions, and had
already found a place in the text or in the notes.

I now append the chief passages in which the
text of this edition differs from that of the last :—

> vii. 6. 1451 a 9. Here I keep the reading of the
> MSS., ὥσπερ ποτὲ καὶ ἄλλοτέ φασιν. Schmidt's
> correction εἰώθασιν for φασίν seemed at first
> sight to be confirmed by the Arabic, but, as
> Vahlen argues (*Hermeneutische Bemerkungen zu
> Aristoteles' Poetik*, 1897), this is doubtful, and
> —a more fundamental objection—the question
> arises whether the correction can, after all, con-
> vey the sense intended. Can the words as
> emended refer to a known practice in *present*
> time, 'as is the custom on certain other occasions
> also,' i.e. in certain other contests, the ἀγῶνες of
> the law-courts being thus suggested? As to
> this I have always had misgivings. Further
> observation has convinced me that ποτὲ καὶ ἄλλοτε
> can only mean 'at some other time also,'
> in an indefinite past or future. With φασίν
> (sc. ἀγωνίσασθαι) the reference must be to the
> past. This lands us in a serious difficulty, for
> the use of the κλεψύδρα in regulating dramatic
> representations is otherwise unheard of. Still
> it is conceivable that a report of some such

old local custom had reached the ears of Aristotle, and that he introduces it in a parenthesis with the φασίν of mere hearsay.

ix. 7. 1451 b 21. I accept Welcker's 'Ανθεῖ for ἄνθει. Professor Bywater is, I think, the first editor who has admitted this conjecture into the text.

xvii. 5. 1455 b 22. I restore the MSS. reading ἀναγνωρίσας τινάς, which has been given up by almost all editors, even the most conservative. Hitherto a parallel was wanting for the required meaning, 'having made certain persons acquainted with him,' 'having caused them to recognise him.' But Vahlen (Herm. Bemerk. 1898) has, if I am not mistaken, established beyond question this rare and idiomatic use of the verb by a reference to Diodorus Siculus iv. 59. 6, and by the corresponding use of γνωρίζω in Plut. Vit. Thes. ch. xii.

xix. 3. 1456 b 8. For ἡδέα of the MSS. I now read ἡ διάνοια. (Previously I had accepted Tyrwhitt's correction ἤδη ἃ δεῖ.) This conjecture was first made by Spengel, and strong arguments in its favour have recently been urged by V. Wróbel in a pamphlet in which this passage is discussed (Leopoli, 1900).

xxv. 6. 1458 b 12. For μέτρον I now read μέτριον with Spengel. (So also Bywater.) Is it possible that in xxvi. 6. 1462 b 7 we should similarly read τῷ τοῦ μετρίου (μέτρου codd.) μήκει, 'a fair s⁀ⁿdard of length'?

In xiv. 8–9. 1454 a 2–4 a much vexed question is, I am disposed to think, cleared up by a simple alteration proposed by Neidhardt, who in a 2 reads

c

κράτιστον for δεύτερον, and in a 4 δεύτερον for
κράτιστον. This change, however, I have not introduced into the text.

The Arabic version once more throws interesting
light on a disputed reading. In xvii. 2 ἐκστατικοί
instead of ἐξεταστικοί is a conjecture supported by
one manuscript. In confirmation of this reading,
which has always seemed to me correct, I extract
the following note by Professor Margoliouth (*Class.
Rev.* 1901, vol. xv. 54):—'Professor Butcher . . .
informed me that a continental scholar had asserted
that the Arabic read ἐκστατικοί for ἐξεταστικοί in
this passage. I had been unable to satisfy myself
about the Arabic word intended by the writer of
the Paris MS., and therefore could not confirm
this; but I must regret my want of perspicacity,
for I have now no doubt that the word intended is
ajabiyyīna, which is vulgar Arabic for "buffoons,"
literally "men of wonder." The Syriac translated
by this word will almost certainly have been
mathh'rānē, a literal translation of ἐκστατικοί,
which the Syriac translator probably thought
meant "men who produce ecstasies." The verb
ἐξίστασθαι is not unfrequently rendered by the
Syriac verb whence this word is derived.'

In a few other passages the Critical Notes or
Translation contain new matter; e.g. ix. 8. 1451
b 23; xvi. 7. 1455 a 14; xxiv. 10. 1460 b 1;
xxvi. 6. 1462 b 7.

Turning now from the text to the subject-matter of the treatise, I must mention a valuable book, *Platon und die Aristotelische Poetik*, by G. Finsler (Leipzig, 1900). Aristotle's debt to Plato is here set forth in fuller detail than has ever been done before; and though in some instances it may be doubted whether the obligation is not exaggerated and the ideas of these two thinkers brought into rather forced relation, yet there is much to be learned from the volume. In the notes to the Essays I have added many fresh illustrations from Plato, which have been suggested by reading Finsler.

Mr. W. J. Courthope's *Oxford Lectures* form another noteworthy volume, concerned chiefly with modern poetry, but embodying Aristotelian principles. The estimate of the *Poetics* in the lecture on 'Aristotle as a Critic' is marked by rare insight and sureness of judgment.

The learned and interesting *History of Criticism*, by Professor Saintsbury, ought also to be consulted by all students of the *Poetics*. The first five chapters of vol. i. give an instructive survey of Greek criticism, chapter iii. being devoted to Aristotle. I would direct attention, moreover, to the *History of Literary Criticism in the Renaissance* (New York, 1899), by J. E. Spingarn, to which frequent reference is made in the notes.

I owe to the kindness of Professor Sonnenschein

the information as to the significant names in
Roman comedy contained in the note pp. 376 ff.
In rewriting this whole note, as also that on p. 259,
I have slightly modified my former view. Another
note, pp. 344–5, gives in a compressed form the
result of a conversation with Mr. A. C. Bradley,
whom I desire to thank, not for the first time.
The remarks added on pp. 225–6 are designed
further to elucidate the relation between Art and
Morality as I believe it to have been conceived by
Aristotle. A few observations on Ibsen's drama
will be found on pp. 270–1. It is needless to
specify other minor additions of a like kind.

I cannot in concluding omit a word of cordial
thanks to Messrs. R. & R. Clark's accomplished
Reader.

EDINBURGH, *October* 1902.

PREFACE TO THE FOURTH EDITION

THIS edition differs but little from the last, the only two changes of any importance being in the interpretation of ζῷον (ch. vii. 4–5, xxiii. 1) p. 188, and of περιπέτεια pp. 329–331. On particular points, including bibliographical matter, I have received kind assistance from Dr. J. E. Sandys. I desire also to express once more my obligations to Messrs. R. & R. Clark's Reader.

LONDON, *January* 1907.

PREFACE TO REPRINT OF 1911

IN a set of sheets of this book found among my brother's papers after his death, he had introduced a few corrections both in the textual notes and in the translation as far as p. 110. These have been embodied in the present reprint, which is otherwise an exact reproduction of the edition of 1907, when the book was for the first time printed from electrotype plates. The additions to the textual notes consist mainly of references to two MSS., Parisinus 2038 and Riccardianus 46. The slight verbal changes in the English version are in every case aimed at conveying the sense more closely, and are interesting illustrations of the author's scrupulous care in such matters.

J. G. BUTCHER.

CONTENTS

ARISTOTLE'S THEORY OF POETRY AND THE FINE ARTS

CHAPTER I
ART AND NATURE

CHAPTER II
'IMITATION' AS AN AESTHETIC TERM

xxxi

CHAPTER III

POETIC TRUTH

CHAPTER IV

THE END OF FINE ART

CHAPTER V

ART AND MORALITY

CHAPTER VI

THE FUNCTION OF TRAGEDY

CHAPTER VII

THE DRAMATIC UNITIES

CHAPTER VIII

The Ideal Tragic Hero

CHAPTER IX

Plot and Character in Tragedy

CHAPTER X

THE GENERALISING POWER OF COMEDY

CHAPTER XI

POETIC UNIVERSALITY IN GREEK LITERATURE

ARISTOTELIAN LITERARY
CRITICISM

By
John Gassner

HALF a century earlier, an introduction to a combined edition of Aristotle's POETICS and S. H.
Butcher's notable commentary would have been unnecessary. Today, however, Aristotle's thoughts on
art are apt to seem remote to the general reader and
disputable to critics. The values of a moral and
philosophical nature that interpenetrate Aristotle's
esthetics have been challenged in our time, and it is
yet to be determined by events beyond the control
of both artists and philosophers whether such values
will have much hold upon the century's turbulent
generations. The arts, moreover, have been subject
to such upheavals, both separately and collectively,
that a classical theory may at first glance seem about
as useful in sustaining art as a sieve is in retaining
water.

What is it, then, that nevertheless still keeps mind and spirit fastened on a twenty-four century old document? For the POETICS still concerns us to a greater degree than a cursory glance at Western culture would suggest—this even in America, where the classical tradition is virtually extinct. We are attracted, I would suggest, by a way of looking equally at art and humanity as objects of rational inquiry and ideal expectations.

Call the POETICS, if you will, a mere manual on poetry in general and on epic and dramatic literature in particular. And a fragmentary manual at that! Yet implicated in it is virtually everything that makes esthetics truly and deeply practical rather than an airy exercise for life's and society's ineffectuals. No typical Greek thinker, and Aristotle least of all, was apt to exercise himself in a partial vacuum filled only with private sensibilities. A cool lucidity in the POETICS involves the total experience that is life.

I

In Aristotle's fragment we find an urbane, open-minded man of the fourth century B.C. observing the specific literary products of Greek civilization and drawing generalizations from them concerning the craft of writing. We find him inquiring into the nature of each literary medium and into its potentialities. Even more remarkably, we see him continually mingling with his judgments on art a sense of how man, the public at whom every artist aims his effects, is apt to respond by nature, moral bent, and emotional involvement. ("Audience psychology" is the popular American term for this last-mentioned inquiry.) Here, then, is an eminently empirical approach that observes and appraises works of art in terms of their forms, possibilities, and effects.

The POETICS is the first extant essay on art that is honestly exploratory. Such criticism was unusual in Aristotle's time, and it continued to be rare long after his death when he was considered the supreme arbiter in esthetic judgment. It is, indeed, one of the ironies of history that Aristotle's admirers from the sixteenth to the eighteenth centuries should have tried to convert the explorer into an absolute law-maker. It was their chief ambition, next to that of establishing themselves as legislators, too, by standing under the ample shadow of the great man's reputation. (Did Aristotle say undogmatically that the action of a tragedy—that is, of Greek tragedies—*tended* to be restricted, "as far as possible," to "a single revolution of the sun"? That was not enough for the new arbiters; they made it imperative for tragic action to transpire within twenty-four or even within twelve hours. Did Aristotle take note of a tendency toward concentration in tragedy? Instantly, although he never so much as mentioned "unity of place," they ordered playwrights to keep all their action in a single place.) Nor has dogmatic criticism been so rare in a century full of manifestoes from almost every conceivable school of art and politics that the POETICS can no longer set us a good example of empirical criticism today.

Still, it is one of the marks of the comprehensive Greek mind that the practical involves the ideal. By viewing art in terms of its effect, Aristotle places humanity squarely in the center of his esthetics. He makes humanistic values paramount from the beginning by asking the right—or, at least, the current, modern—question of how the artist can please men. Since, moreover, man is a creature endowed with reason, art is viewed by Aristotle under the category of rational procedure, and this involves a sense of appropriateness, measure, and organization in artistry. And in this respect, art is seen only as another aspect of an ideal of man first developed in Greece and left as a legacy to civilization.

It is true that in stressing the pleasure-giving feature of art, this dispassionate thinker broke with the moralistic attitudes of Plato and asserted the freedom of the arts from moral censorship. Yet he also mediated between the artists and the philosophers of Greece; and in doing so, he found a perfect solution equally satisfactory to free men in fourth century Greek and twentieth century Western civilization. The mediating concept is *ideality* or *universality*. The ideal, to Aristotle, is that which is free from idiosyncrasy or specialness, and art is an abstract—although not an unliving symbol—of what all men are in their humanity. For realism of detail such a view substitutes the ideality of significant outline. It is not, as Butcher rightly notes, the opposite of the real, but rather its fulfillment and perfection—in the sense that reality stands in clear relief and becomes meaningful.

Without actually crossing boundaries and employing the methods of discursive reason, true art is akin to philosophy in arriving at general truth and coordinating the data of existence. It is actually, says Aristotle, more philosophic than history. Art creates an idea of order where, to the inartistic or unphilosophical observer, life is only a whirl of action and a chaos of emotion. In literature, and especially in its highest form, which for Aristotle is tragedy, the writer creates a logical sequence and causal connection of events. The crude matter of life assumes significance from the shaping hand of the artist.

We also see the same connection between practicality and ideality in Aristotle's discussion of characterization and style. It is only plain sense for Aristotle to maintain that comedy revolves around men whose defects can provoke ridicule and that tragedy concentrates on characters that we can take seriously, for which reason they must possess some degree of importance in our eyes and be neither unregenerately villainous nor flawless. Other conclusions are inevitable from this premise, and it is little wonder, for example, that the Aristotelian principle of *hamartia,* or the "tragic flaw," should recur so frequently in our thinking about tragedy. Underlying Aristotle's thought, here as elsewhere, is his acute awareness of "final ends" or ultimate objectives. The tragedian's objective is to move us with the meaningful experience of human beings with whom we can identify ourselves to the extent of suffering with them—from which, in turn, other conclusions follow. All the reasoning is pragmatic, and Aristotle is disconcertingly bland by comparison with seventeenth or twentieth century authors who speak glowingly of the grandeur of tragedy. Aristotle, indeed, sounds flat and business-like. But we may never forget that the business in hand is that of stirring us with a presentation of human destiny, and there is no higher subject available to our experience. The *ends* of tragedy are implicit in Aristotle's discussion of the *means*.

The stress on the efficiency or, as Aristotle would have said, "the efficient causes," in art cannot, then, be our sole and final impression of the POETICS. The essay assumes standards by its very concern with the problem of affecting an audience. Success in this respect is measured by high humanistic standards, and Aristotle's frame of reference when he discusses tragedy is an "ideal" spectator—which does not, of course, mean a superhuman one. The writer of tragedies, unlike a Hollywood showman, is not expected to titillate everybody by resorting to sensational effects and to cater to the sentimentalism of the immature. The tragic effect must reside in the matter and mode of the written drama rather than in the "spectacle" on the stage; the tragedian works on the heart and the mind. Nor are we to be melted with "pity," as sentimentalists suggested, but stirred by the more exacting experience of "pity *and* fear." And so tragedy involves our capacity to feel for others and fear for ourselves, too, by knowing that we share in their humanity and that they share in ours, which rules out the possibility of our ever dismissing humane considerations concerning other members of the species.

Tragic art is for those who are not merely mature but humanely mature. It does not address itself to the storm-trooper any more than to the sentimentalist. We can imagine men who would be pleased to see villainous and degraded individuals succeed and innocent and noble people destroyed. What can we *not* imagine concerning the taste and appetites, the delusions and frenzies, of the species? Nor do we have to conjure up these possibilities out of thin air when history—including, unfortunately, recent history—provides so many examples. Aristotle measures the effects of art with reference to reasonable men rather than lunatics, grown-up men rather than infants, and men capable of sympathy rather than inveterate sadists. He also makes assumptions inherent in the Greek worldly, though not necessarily anti-spiritual, view. We can imagine, for instance, a convocation of saints exulting in the trials of the flesh as a preparation for the heavenly life or an assembly of yogis completely unmoved by tragic events because suffering is only "Maya" or illusion. It is more than possible, too, that a completely collectivistic society, as envisioned by Aldous Huxley or George Orwell, would consider individual misfortune inconsequential. But none of the anti-humanist approaches to the human situation are entertained by Aristotle, and his standards have been potent for so long a time precisely because they have been those of Western humanistic society until now.

II

In reading the POETICS, nevertheless, we dare not be easily satisfied that we know what we are reading. There is the Aristotle of the bald text, now at last painstakingly established, and also the Aristotle of all the extant treatises correctly ascribed to him. The one without the other is obscure and incomplete. To know what the POETICS means at every point we must know what certain concepts meant to Aristotle in his other works. For example, what do the terms "imitation" and "action" mean to him? Only by determining this can we understand why he calls art an "imitation" and why he places "action" at the head of all the elements that constitute a play. Also, what particular process did he have in mind when he wrote that tragedy effects a *katharsis* or purgation of "pity and fear" by exciting "pity and fear" in the spectator? There is trouble, besides, with the very language he employs, since many Greek nouns lack distinct single equivalents in modern languages, and since Aristotle, the great synthesizer, is apt to subsume several ideas under a single term.

There is, moreover, a third Aristotle—the Aristotle of his many interpreters, who encrusted the POETICS with their own artistic and social attitudes. It is always a problem to determine how far we are to accept critics' adumbrations as consonant with Aristotelian thought. One might word the question simply as "whom are we following, Aristotle or his interpreters?" We can try to determine this, and we can succeed up to a point. But there is the Aristotle who is significant precisely because so many attitudes and ideas have accreted around his words. This Aristotle cannot be ignored either, without depriving ourselves of important stimulations and gratifications. Besides, it is almost impossible for most of us to read the POETICS now with pristine innocence.

It was in order to correct misconceptions and prevent further perversions of Aristotle's book that late nineteenth century English scholars undertook the exacting labor of preparing definitive editions and commentaries. The present book, a product of many decades of modern scholarship and revised continually between 1895 and 1911, is, along with Ingram Bywater's ARISTOTLE ON THE ART OF POETRY, the most reliable introduction to the POETICS available in English. Although it is still possible to disagree on particular readings of the text and on details of translation, the reader can turn to Butcher's memorable book with confidence. As the notes show us, Butcher substantiated disputable points with a painstaking scholarship that belongs to the grand tradition of English learning. Moreover, Butcher's commentary, "Aristotle's Theory of Poetry and the Fine Arts," appended to the Greek text and the translation, leaves nothing to be desired; nothing that Butcher could have supplied without venturing into unresolved discussions of modern drama. At all points the scholar appears to be as thoroughly in accord with Aristotle's mode of thinking as anyone can be over the wide chasm of the centuries. A mere smattering of Greek enables us to realize this, and no Greek is necessary for the reader to sense that this must be so.

We can avoid disappointment, however, only by resigning ourselves to the limitations of the text that has come down to us. It was written around 330 B.C., but the oldest surviving Greek text is dated about the year 1000 A.D., and a section on comedy was apparently lost by then. We have, besides a general introduction to the nature and types of literature, only that part of the treatise which deals with epic poetry and tragedy. And even this part is incomplete and apparently unrevised, as if it had been intended solely for the author's use in delivering lectures on the subject. It is frustrating not to be able to follow some of the illustrations cited by Aristotle from the literature known to him and lost to us, and it is disconcerting to be forced to resort to speculations on how he expected tragedy to purge us by means of pity and fear. Are we to assume that, according to Aristotle, many men are troubled by too much inclination toward pity and fear, and that in experiencing these emotions in the theatre we discharge them successfully by means of empathy? Are we to include other emotions too under the terms? Are we to content ourselves with the probability that, in accordance with the views of Greek medicine, Aristotle thought of the process of *katharsis* as a sort of homeopathic practice, whereby we are cured by taking a hair of the dog that bit us? Or are we to assume that the complex of pity and fear in us is transformed into an ennobling experience by being directed outwardly toward characters dis-

tanced by the stage and, at the same time, exalted
by the tragic poet to such a degree that they sum up
the human situation and universalize it? Are we,
as Butcher maintains, "lifted above the special case
and brought face to face with universal law and the
divine plan of the world?" And, finally, is there no
katharsis in comedy as well—no purgation, different
in quality, by means of which our dislikes, our re-
belliousness at social restraints, and our own tendencies to self-depreciation or self-criticism are discharged on the deserving object of a comically drawn
character? On these and other matters Aristotle is
by no means as explicit as we should have liked him
to be. His students in Greece were probably better
served than his readers have been since his spare
essay was recovered for us.

Only when we know, indeed, what not to expect,
can we make the most of the extant portions of the
Poetics and pursue the lines of inquiry they open
up to us. And we may be sure it will not be a
fruitless inquiry when we reflect that it was under-
taken with variable results by Ben Jonson, Milton,
Corneille, Dryden, Lessing, and Goethe among other
luminaries of the literary world. To this very day,
in far from classically minded America, statements
in the Poetics have engaged the interest of influential critics such as Joseph Wood Krutch and
John Mason Brown and successful playwrights such
as Maxwell Anderson and Arthur Miller. It is
surely significant that a playwright so closely bound
to the contemporary social scene as Miller should
have attempted to reconcile his practice in *Death of*

a *Salesman* with the Aristotelian criterion that a
tragic hero should possess stature. Although Aristotle's knowledge of epic and dramatic literature was
confined to writings in the Greek language before the
end of the fourth century B.C., his essay has been
found relevant to the literary production of later
ages. Ever since the POETICS was translated into
Latin by the Italian humanist Valla in 1498, we have
tended to employ Aristotle's terms and standards
even in our judgment of literary productions unin-
fluenced by the book: to oriental epics and plays, to
medieval epics and romances, and to the work of
Shakespeare, Lope de Vega, and other writers for
the popular stage who were either ignorant of Aristotle's essay or indifferent to it. Nor have we hesi-
tated to apply his ideas to the experiments of modern
dramatists such as Ibsen, Strindberg, Chekhov, and
Shaw, who struck out in their several new directions
with scant respect, if any, for tradition. Whether or
not we think we apply or should apply Aristotelian
criteria, the fact is that we do apply them.

The problem is merely one of accommodation to
the civilization and art of the latest transitional
period the generations of Western man have experienced since the nineteenth century. Aristotelian
esthetic theory is bound to be viewed in our time
with the perspectives laid down by modern Romanti-
cism and Realism, terms under which we may include the creative and critical approaches of Symbolism, Expressionism, Surrealism, and modern psychological and social literature. Although at least
one of Aristotle's ideas—the spiritual significance of

tragedy—actually looms larger than ever in critical thought, many of his observations now require reconsideration. Whether we can mediate between them and our own observations is an important question to writers, critics, and teachers. I believe that, on the whole, we can. I am convinced, in fact, that Aristotle's thinking is still a useful corrective to whatever views we maintain on the subject of narrative and dramatic art, since he is free from our habits of excessive romanticization of ideas and ideals, including those we promulgate in his name.

III

Aristotle looks into the craft of writing with a lively interest, concerning himself with language, diction, style, the forms of literature, the characteristic qualities of the medium, the nature of effects, and how they are achieved. He sets later criticism a lesson in intelligent, systematic, and inductive procedure. But it is true that we shall not find in his work certain refinements of the modern critical approach, such as "levels of meaning," symbolization, and chains of association. He treats broad and generally direct or objective effects. He is no more concerned with the poet's unique personality or special creative processes than he is with the state of his own soul, for which he claims no notable uniqueness. Art is not a divine madness or a manifestation of subjective intimations. Nor is criticism a purely personal adventure among masterpieces.

The reason becomes apparent in the second paragraph of the treatise. Romanticists have stressed the element of self-expression in art, whereas Aristotle defines art as an "imitation," a term that Butcher's scholarship will clarify and broaden for us. An entire field of critical inquiry is opened up by the difference between the Aristotelian and the romantic view. For example, are the two views entirely irreconcilable? Does "imitation" necessarily exclude self-expression or, for that matter, even symbolization? Is there no possibility of self-expression *through* imitation, since we view reality through a temperament and we comment on it through the very acts of perceiving and representing objects and experience. Also, is not all communication and, indeed, the very apprehension of reality an act of symbolization on our part? Suzanne Langer's PHILOSOPHY IN A NEW KEY points out that even the eye and the ear make abstractions, so that these organs present our mental faculties with already symbolized data. At what point, too, does "self-expression" lead to private or coterie art as incommunicable to the average intelligent man as, let us say, FINNEGAN'S WAKE? To what degree this is artistically and socially defensible became, in fact, the main issue in the arts of the twentieth century, a controversy as keen as was the "battle between the ancients and the moderns" in the eighteenth century. If Aristotle was aware of any such problem, and it is extremely doubtful that he could have been in his time, he gives no attention to it, and many centuries were to pass before even the literal sense of his theory of "imitation" would be challenged. Aristotle fastens our attention on everything that is directly communicable and socially digestible in artistic endeavor.

Next we may note that Aristotle stirs up a veritable beehive by maintaining that tragedy is "an imitation, not of men, but of action and of life, and life consists in action, and its end is a mode of action, not a quality," for which reason he gives preeminence to plot. Modern writers tend to bristle at this statement, overlooking the fact that he has earlier declared that the "action implies distinctive qualities both of character and thought; for it is by these that we qualify actions themselves, and these— thought and character—are the two natural causes from which actions spring." And Butcher, indeed, helps us to understand that by the term "action" he must have meant more than simply external events. Nevertheless, the phrase "not of men, but of an action" gives rise to the question of the relative importance of character and action; and, in extreme cases of modern theory and practice, even to the question whether external action or plot is needed at all. What could O'Neill, for example, have considered more important, action or inner stress, in *Strange Interlude?* He continually stopped stage activity in order that his characters might express their hidden feelings, and yet large audiences found the story of Nina and her lovers absorbing and dramatic. Did not Zola and other champions of modern drama, besides, make the subordination of "plot" to representations of human nature and environment the prime requisite for dramaturgy? Did not Shaw in the eighteen-nineties also proclaim the superiority of the "discussion play," as written by Ibsen and himself? And did not Galsworthy, actually a moderate iconoclast, declare that "character is the best plot there is?" The fact is that modern drama, as well as fiction, for we also have the "plotless" short story and novel, has conformed to prescriptions of priority for characterization, "psychology" and psychological analysis, environment, discussion, and mood—the latter, often by "symbolist" suggestion and subconscious association. Some playwrights—most conspicuously, Maeterlinck and Andreyev—even went so far as to condemn action as barbaric and to call for the representation of a "stasis" on the stage. In modern times, as Andreyev wrote in 1914, "life has gone within."

We can try to mediate, of course, between Aristotle and the latter-day writers by maintaining that the difference between the Aristotelian and the modern emphasis is only a matter of degree. It would seem, too, that the argument over the priority of characterization reduces itself to the absurd question of which comes first, the chicken or the egg. We may ask, besides, how character or psychological reality can manifest itself effectively, especially in the theatre, without a sequence of revelatory responses, decisions taken or evaded, and externalized feelings and thoughts. Does not this sequence, too, constitute "action" and "plot"? To what extent is the mental action of discussion, especially when Shaw presents it, *not* action? Or is the self-revelation of characters not action when Shakespeare writes a

soliloquy in *Hamlet* or Strindberg a dramatic monologue in *The Stronger?* Is not even a succession of
moods, as in Maeterlinck's *The Intruder,* "action,"
and is not the organization of the mood—with a
"beginning, middle, and end," with a rising intensity
and a final discharge of tension—"plot."?

It may have to be conceded, nevertheless, that a
complete reconciliation cannot be effected between
the introspective moderns and Aristotle. It is precisely matters of degree that are decisive in art, and
a strong inclination in one direction or another determines the singular quality of an author's writing.
We are forced back, as is Butcher, to the position
that for Aristotle, too, action could not be consonant
solely with external activity. Aristotle, moreover,
does not think of action without characters—characters so fully realized, indeed, that he pays special
attention to their ethical disposition, or *ethos,* and
their intellectual content, or *dianoia.* It is because
Aristotle kept his mind on the nature of the drama
as the medium in which things are represented rather
than narrated, and surely not because he was less
interested in man than we are, that he gave priority
to action. If he refrained from painting a nimbus
around characterization as an element in drama, we
may be certain that he took it for granted that
tragedy's sole consideration was man and his destiny.
Nor was there, indeed, any want of characterization
or even "psychological interest" in the classical
works he knew and admired. They are actually less
plotty than many later tragedies. If character development is less marked in the Greek tragedies than

in Shakespearian and some modern dramas, the main reason is structural: a Greek tragedy is shorter and starts closer to the crisis of the story.

Can we be so certain, finally, that the trend in modern literature has been in all respects contrary to the Aristotelian emphasis on action or that we may not actually come full circle round to it? Two nineteenth century ideas in criticism have proved seminal in our time. One is Hegel's dialectical view that a conflict of opposites is the driving force in tragedy, and the other is Brunetière's stress on the volitional factor in drama—specifically, that "drama is the representation of the will of man in conflict." Both concepts are more honored in the teaching and practice of playwriting today than is the romanticist Schlegel's preference for subjective experience and sensation; this in spite of later symbolist theory in literature and in spite of Gordon Craig's emphasis on nuance and suggestion in the art of theatrical production. Both ideas, "tragic conflict" and "the will of man in conflict," have found a specially active realization in social, especially "class-struggle," drama in our century; and this, in spite of theories of social determinism in human behavior. Today, in fact, the tide may often be seen running counter to introspective writing, which has been subjected to denunciation from both the political right and the political left. Activism in art has been propounded by Malraux during both his communist and De Gaullist phases. "Epic drama," as preached and practiced by the German poet-playwright Brecht, regards action as the very end of dramatic demonstration. So much so, indeed, that Brecht deprecates a *katharsis* or purgation of the emotions, lest the emotional involvement of the spectator blind him to courses of action and drain him of the will and ability to be effective in life! In Sartre's existentialism, too, action is considered the exclusive test of character. Propagandist "class-struggle" literature never fails, of course, to represent action and to clamor for it, and "Socialist Realism," entrenched in a large segment of the world, rules out subjectivity in the arts as a symptom of middle-class decadence. It is, indeed, a question whether, were Aristotle alive today, he would not be more disconcerted by those who could agree than by those who would disagree with him on the primacy of action.

IV

The largest area of discussion is opened up by Aristotle's special enthusiasm for tragedy as a literary form, although the subject might not have loomed as large as it does in his book if the POETICS contained the treatment of comedy promised by him. With the examples of the ODYSSEY and ILIAD before him, Aristotle, it is true, esteems epic poetry highly. Yet after noting the attributes epic poetry has in common with tragedy, he gives his accolade to the latter as the more unified and concentrated art. It is possible to contend, as it has indeed been contended, that the novel, which is the present equivalent of the epic, is the superior form of modern literature. Weighty evidence can be collected in

favor of this view if we confine ourselves only to THE
RED AND THE BLACK, WAR AND PEACE, THE BROTH-
ERS KARAMAZOV, Proust's novelistic cycle, THE
MAGIC MOUNTAIN, and, perhaps, ULYSSES, in which
Joyce paralleled the epic events and structure of the
ODYSSEY. Those who, like T. S. Eliot, set a higher
valuation on THE DIVINE COMEDY than on Shake-
speare's work, can also throw Dante's epic into the
scales. And it might also be contended that had
Aristotle known *Hamlet, King Lear*, and *Antony and
Cleopatra*, he might not have been able to draw the
line between epic and dramatic form quite so sharply.
Today, indeed, we find the school of "epic drama,"
led by Piscator and Brecht, maintaining that drama
needs epic scope if it is to express modern life. But
Aristotle's ideal tragic form does have a valid claim
to esthetic superiority in so far as, other qualities
being equal, a work that exerts a single concentrated
effect is superior to a work that does not. As a
logician, too, Aristotle could hardly resist favoring
the tightly closed system of Greek tragedy, and we
may also remember that he was the spiritual heir of
the fifth century Athenian civilization in which the
classic drama attained its perfection after epic writing had lost vitality.

We are primarily concerned, then, with tragedy
when we read the POETICS, and it is a subject full of
pitfalls and miasmas largely of our own making since
the sixteenth century. Involved in this subject are
such matters as the character of the tragic hero, the
manner in which tragic purification is effected, the
matter with which tragedy can treat, and the va-

rieties of tragic effect. The accepted view is that tragedy must concern itself with a character well above the common level, that we must be emotionally shattered and yet somehow purified by his experience, and that there is only one kind of drama—a character's downfall—that can effect all this. These ideas dominate most thinking about tragedy, judgments on plays, and prescriptions for the stage. We may wonder, however, whether these have not been employed too narrowly and without reference to correctives supplied by Aristotle himself. We shall not perhaps feel entirely reconciled to modern drama until we realize how broadly operative his thinking is by comparison with the tendency to seize upon one of his ideas and erect it into a taboo or a prescription.

When we talk of the uncommon nature of the hero, for example, as well as when we tend to think of tragedy occurring only in a rarified atmosphere of conflict uncontaminated by ordinary life, it is useful to recall that for Aristotle the gratification of art comes first of all from "recognition." In harmony with his theory of art as an "imitation," he declares that our pleasure comes from "seeing a likeness," although he is not so dogmatic as to assert that gratification may not also have other sources, such as artistic execution. And surely, if this is so, is there not a place in tragedy for an ordinary man? Not merely for a man of low station, which is now granted by modern critics, but for a man whose *mentality* is common and whose spiritual endowment is not notably above the ordinary. Many effectively realized characters of serious modern drama fall into this category. Are modern plays that revolve around them, such as *Ghosts, Drayman Henschel,* and *The Lower Depths,* automatically ruled out as tragedies, as many a critic has maintained, or is there a type of "naturalistic tragedy" to which we owe respect as a high form of dramatic art even if it does not satisfy the standardized requirements for so-called high tragedy?

May we not wonder in the case of such a powerful example of intermediate drama as Arthur Miller's *Death of a Salesman* whether the audiences have not been more strongly moved and, indeed, uplifted by the superannuated salesman's close likeness to themselves and people they know than by anything extraordinary in the character? Here the critic for whom tragic experience is the prime requisite, if he does not rule the play out of the argument as pathetic rather than tragic, has only one recourse. He can maintain that Miller's drama scales the tragic heights because the character Willy Loman is extraordinary in the persistent efforts he makes to hold on to high evaluations of himself and his son Biff, in the passionateness of his nature, and in his exceptional capacity for suffering. Yet even if this contention is correct in every particular (and not everyone will grant this in America while few have granted it in England), it is undeniable that the element of "recognition" is dominant and decisive in *Death of a Salesman.* Audiences would have dismissed Willy as simply an untragic, merely pathetic, dolt if he had not been so much like themselves and their relatives and acquaintances whose defects are neither heroic like Macbeth's nor ludicrous like Malvolio's. If his struggles and sufferings provided them with tragic exultation, it was less because Willy was eminent than because he epitomized their own lack of eminence. If they did not consider him ignoble, it was because they do not consider themselves ignoble. If he made large claims upon their sympathy, it was because, along with Arthur Miller, they attributed his failure, as well as their own, to entrapment in social delusions and circumstances. If they considered him heroic at all, they did so essentially in terms of their awareness of how much fortitude the soul must bring to common everyday situations, his and theirs. If our aristocratic sensibilities shudder at the thought of this democratization of tragedy, and if Aristotle himself, living in a society founded on slave labor, was actually unlikely to conceive of tragedies devoted to the Willy Lomans of the world, the trend in this direction has been nonetheless strong. And Aristotle's own plain words are less of a prohibition of tragic gratification on Willy Loman's democratic level than his interpreters assume when they rhapsodize, as he definitely did not, over the spiritual elevation of tragic heroes.

As for Aristotle's principle of *katharsis* through "pity and fear," continually stressed after him, should we not also limit the degree of emotional involvement required for purgation by tragedy? "Objects," Aristotle writes, "which in themselves we view with pain, we delight to contemplate when reproduced with minute fidelity." Implicit here is the doctrine of "esthetic distance"—to wit, that we derive gratification in art from being able to stand at some remove from the object. The death of a character simulated on the stage or described in the pages of a book can be artistically gratifying whereas, in normal cases, the actual death of a person in our presence is only painful. If Aristotle does cite the arousing of "pity and fear" as the specific characteristic of tragedy, he does not insist that it is the *only* element that makes the pain of tragedy "pleasurable." *Katharsis* in tragedy is more dependent than has been generally realized upon this esthetic distance and upon the perspectives it affords. Otherwise it would be impossible to explain how we are to be liberated from the pity and fear we are supposed to experience in witnessing a tragedy. And to what end would Aristotle have made *dianoia* or the thought (or intellect) of characters an important dramatic element and described it as containing the subdivisions of "proof and refutation" and the "suggestion of importance and its opposite" if he had considered nothing but emotion important in tragedy?*

*In "Catharsis and the Modern Theatre" (EUROPEAN THEORIES OF DRAMA, ed. by Barrett H. Clark, Crown Publishers, 1947), I have maintained that there can be no complete purgation for the spectator or reader without "enlightenment" ensuing upon the "pity and fear" he has experienced; and there can surely be no enlightenment concerning an experience that we cannot view from some emotional distance. Maxwell Anderson, in THE ESSENCE OF TRAGEDY, postulated that the tragic hero must make some decisive discovery about himself and about the world that will alter his course of action. This, of course, affords realizations to the audience as well, and neither the tragic hero nor his audience can of course arrive at such realizations while engaged in purely emotional reactions.

Merely being enabled by the artist to stand at some distance from a painful experience, to observe and understand it, can in itself afford some release from our tensions. And if it is our own tension or plight that we are able to discover and evaluate in others, our release from it is all the greater. In a sense, we master what we manage to observe objectively. In harping continually on the idea of "pity and fear," critics and writers, ever since the great critic Lessing hammered away at it in his HAMBURG DRAMATURGY, in order to discredit feeble neoclassic French tragedy, have virtually given the impression that tragedy is an emotional orgy. Unquestionably an orgy can exhaust us to such a degree that we are no longer capable of feeling our own and our fellow-creature's pain. But is this the most desirable way to be "released," and is it consonant with the dignity of tragic art, which is expected to sharpen our sensibilities instead of dulling or numbing them? Emotional involvement *and* detachment, "pity and fear" *and* objectivity, are present in tragedy, and to varying degrees in different plays, as well as in different effective productions of the same play.

Aristotle's thinking, indeed, allows for far greater latitude than is usually assumed in the major qualifying statement of the POETICS which reads: "Whether Tragedy has yet perfected its proper types or not, and whether it is to be judged in itself or in relation also to the audience—this raises another question." This single sentence, which gives us freedom to reconsider tragic art since his time, should certainly give pause to critics who maintain that

playwrights since Ibsen have not written true tragedies because the plays fail to conform to the postulated absolutes for tragic art.

Cannot a problem play, for example, be a tragedy?
Aristotle never had to consider this question in our
particular terms because the problems he found in
such Greek tragedies as *Antigone* and *The Trojan
Women*—the rival claims of private conscience and
obedience to the state or the inhumanity of war—
were surely inherent in the traditional material upon
which they were based. Is there not, besides, a
genuine tragedy of *attrition*, best exemplified by
The Three Sisters and *The Cherry Orchard*, as more
or less distinct from the classic tragedy of a re-
sounding fall from a great height? And have we not
overstressed the "fall" as a tragic element even in
the older drama? Is not attrition, or the "breaking
down" process, actually an element in such plays as
Oedipus the King, King Lear, and *Macbeth*. I may
not be alone in reporting that I have been more
deeply stirred by the manner in which Oedipus is
deprived of his certainties and Lear is worn out as a
human being than by a precipitate fall from greatness.* It is not that they are hurled down like

*J. Dover Wilson's description is to the point: "Lear is a king
'more sinned against than sinning.' Hell, in the person of his two
daughters and in the symbol of the storm, seems to rise up in full
panoply, first to crush the old man's pride, then to overthrow his
intellect, and last of all to break his heart." This suffering does not,
of course, deprive Lear of sublimity but actually enables his greatness to shine forth, just as fate brings out the greatness in that other,
even more ensnared, king Oedipus. "The Lear that dies," writes
Wilson, "is not a Lear defiant, but a Lear redeemed" in his late-won
humility, presenting to God "the oblation of a broken heart." (THE
ESSENTIAL SHAKESPEARE, pp. 124–27)

Lucifer from heaven but that they crumble in some
fundamental respect, as many men do, that moves
me most. And I should have been so moved, I suspect, even if Oedipus had not gouged out his eyes
at the end and Lear had not died. To be ground
down is the most universal—the only truly universal
—destiny. It can also be made just as pitiful and
fear-inspiring as physical destruction. Even Macbeth, who falls like a tower, is most profoundly
tragic in the gradual deterioration of his character,
and the most plangent notes in the play come after
his way of life is "fall'n into the sear, the yellow
leaf" in the great "Tomorrow, and tomorrow, and
tomorrow" soliloquy of universal disenchantment.
The only difference between his end and that of such
modern characters as "the three sisters" and the
"cherry orchard" family is that he rallies his spirits
to wage a final battle in which he is slain whereas they
rally their spirits to endure the continuance of their
misfortunes; and we may wonder which is the more
trying experience requiring the greater fortitude.

It is pertinent, indeed, to observe that Aristotle,
like the Greek playwrights and the play-contest
judges of the Theatre of Dionysus, does not insist
that all the plays the Greeks called tragedies must
end in disaster; he prefers a catastrophic ending as
the best or "perfect" for tragedy, but refers to two
possible sequences of events—"a change from bad
fortune to good, or from good fortune to bad." We
may be certain, for example, that Aristotle would
have accepted *Anna Christie* as a tragedy in spite of
the resolution in which Anna and her suitor are

reconciled. The Greeks had no separate category for "tragicomedy." And does it really matter whether we insist upon a sharp distinction, as we have tended to do? There is more high seriousness in Sophocles' *Philoctetes*, which has a "happy ending," than in gory *Gorboduc* or *Titus Andronicus*. If we put a low estimation on, let us say, some of Fletcher's tragicomedies and *Cymbeline*, not to mention Hollywood drama, our criticism is surely founded on other considerations than "the change from bad fortune to good;" we object to the unconvincing manner in which the happy ending is effected and to the organization and quality of the work as a whole. Normally, as Aristotle noted, the disastrous conclusion is more tragic, but the tendency of modern drama to omit the last rites and come to rest on what Aristotle indefinitely calls "the scene of the suffering" is not inconsonant with tragic effect? Shaw actually regarded the fatal endings in Ibsen's plays as a defect. In taking exception to the suicide of Hedda Gabler, he held that the real tragedy of the futile Heddas of the world is not that they die but that they have to live on. To have to live on is also, in a sense, the ultimate tragedy of Oedipus at the end of *Oedipus the King*.

V

For all the qualifications we may or must, indeed, make concerning any narrow interpretation of tragedy that places most modern drama beyond the pale, it is, nevertheless, true that there is an irreducible minimum below which no play can fall without losing tragic distinction. The "letter" of prescriptions for tragedy is immaterial; the spirit is all important. Even those who put altogether too narrow constructions upon the concept of tragedy may be forgiven, because their eyes are fixed on the profoundly spiritual essence of the tragic experience.

This essence is sometimes referred to as tragedy's "universality" but with questionable applications. The term has been used, for example, as a weapon in the hands of critics of modern "problem plays." It is true enough that writers of such plays should be aware of the commonplaceness and impermanence they risk when they present sociological matter. But it is not at all certain that the genius of a writer cannot under any circumstances transmute a present subject into a universal one. It was the problem Maxwell Anderson set himself in *Winterset*, even if he ultimately flew away from it on pseudo-Shakespearian wings. And, in any case, the fear of impermanence and "untragic" drama has not, and need not, deter an able playwright from taking advantage of the communion that is theatre and from having his say in it. Greatness, like lightning, strikes infrequently. While we wait for it, it is well at least to have a vital theatre that has interest and meaning for its own time. Nor is it certain that the worship of universality is not hedged about with its own dangers. The cult can encourage writing in a vacuum. It can divert the writer from his own times, about which he knows something by observation, into a world he knows only through literature. He may also become a mere echo of the great writers of the past and intoxicate himself (as, for example, George Chapman, Schiller, and occasionally Maxwell Anderson did) with his own high-sounding generalizations to the detriment of significant action and characterization. Concerning "universality," as concerning other matters, Aristotle's own words are, in fact, deflatingly modest. "By the universal," he writes, "I mean how a person of a certain type will on occasion speak or act, according to the law of probability or necessity." He does not impregnate the term with philosophical or spiritual content. We must not lay at his door the sententious magniloquence of some genuine and many pinchbeck tragedians.

Universality, if not romantically misconstrued, is a quality of tragedy. But the most distinctive value of tragic art consists of the high valuation it places upon man as a species and upon the individual as its representative. Tragic art predicates the *special* universality of man's capacity for greatness of soul and mind in spite of his *hamartia* or the flaw in his nature. Man is endowed with an acceptable or a deplorably perverse yet somehow admirable nobility (rather than eminence) in so far as his tragic representatives belong, in Edith Hamilton's apt words, "to the only true aristocracy, that of all passionate souls."* The French critic Saint-Évremond declared that tragedy induced "admiration," and it does, if

---

*Aristotle's own spare words are that tragedy is "an imitation of persons who are above the common level" and should "preserve the type and yet ennoble it," which may mean simply that the character's traits should be carried to some pitch of intensity or be given more than inconsequential dimensions.

not necessarily in the old-fashioned heroic sense of the term. Tragedy is a poetry of man. The individual is exemplified by the highest reaches of his humanity in erring and bearing the consequences, willing and suffering, groping and arriving at decisions, collaborating in his destiny (becoming its dupe when necessary but never its puppet), and affirming his personality even in defeat and dissolution.

Twentieth century critics and playwrights have fixed their expectations for the drama almost exclusively upon this view of tragedy and have subordinated virtually every Aristotelian principle to it. Romantic Aristotelianism has been the keynote of our criticism.* The latter-day Aristotelians, have

*Even practitioners of the "New Criticism," who pay more attention to the "texture" of literature than to its explicit ideas, do not provide an exception. Their talented leader John Crowe Ransom arrives at the concept of ennoblement *via* his own close consideration of writing. In the stimulating essay "The Literary Criticism of Aristotle" (LECTURES IN CRITICISM, Pantheon Books 1949), called to my attention by Dr. Dorothy Richardson of Queens College, Ransom holds that the poetry in tragedy diverts us from obsessive horror. We recover presence of mind when the mind resumes its "gallant and extravagant activities." And identification makes it possible for us to experience the tragic *katharsis* because the heroes of Greek tragedy "themselves were not terrified out of their wits but continued in the easy exercise of the most liberal powers of mind." With the tragic characters, we experience a suspension of mere animal suffering. Tragedy, then, enables our sensibility to triumph over "vile occasions."

For Ransom, "the heroic style is the thing." This is a poet's view of tragedy, and I am not certain that it is strictly applicable to plays where the characters are incapable of deathless poetry. But Ransom's view, too, gives primacy to the concept of tragedy as an exaltation of man's status in the animal world, and Ransom concludes that the tragic hero ends "in full character . . . perfect in his fidelity to the human career."

turned compulsively to tragedy as a way—as the only way—of asserting the stature or dignity of the human being in the face of the indignities of a world of real and fancied slurs on man. Whether or not they have been entirely correct in attributing the whittling down of the individual to the literature and plays, the psychopathology and psychoanalysis, and the science and philosophy, as well as the social pressures, of our time is a large question. The fact is that the critics express an unease and uncertainty characteristic of Western society in our century, and their romantic vocabulary betrays a sense of dismay, if not actually, of defeat. They speak of the "reconciliations" and "consolations" of tragedy in the accents of Schopenhauer, and even their strenuousness in affirming the strong spirit of man sounds compensatory in a familiar, Nietzschean vein. Be that as it may, their disenchantments combine with their protest against a petty world and against petty views of man to crystallize an attitude that later and perhaps happier times may set down as unduly romantic. Only theological thinking, on the one hand, and collectivist thinking, on the other, actually challenge this emphasis at present—the former by warning us that neither man nor art should be exalted without reservations, the latter by deprecating the stress on "individualism."

If Aristotle's book had not provided the fabric of this view of tragedy, it would have been spun out of the tragic literature of the past, as well as out of the needs of present-day critics and writers themselves. But it so happens that the fabric can be assembled from various elements in the POETICS—from Aristotle's references to the uncommon character of the tragic hero, the high style of tragic writing, and the distinctive function of tragedy in effecting a purgation of the soul. Aristotle's view that the spectator is to be cleansed specifically of "pity and fear" has been made to signify a general cleansing—a view that a classicist such as Aristotle would perhaps have disclaimed as fuzzy thinking. According to contemporary critics and dramatists—among whom Joseph Wood Krutch, Edith Hamilton, Philo Buck, John Mason Brown, and Maxwell Anderson have been representative—the tragic hero wins a final victory for mankind over pettiness and pain. His personality exalts the human race, his struggle exhilarates men, and even his death is an affirmation.

For Joseph Wood Krutch, in his chapter on "The Tragic Fallacy,"* tragedy was predicated upon the ability of men to believe "in the greatness and importance of men." The writer may "not believe in God, but he must believe in man." Tragedy is, then, a "profession of faith," although Mr. Krutch reflected that it could suffer the "fate of all faiths" and be "ultimately lost as a reality," as, indeed, he thought it had already been "in those distressing modern works sometimes called by its name." (And in this connection we may reflect that there have already been periods of world history in which the humanistic basis for tragedy was absent and no tragic literature was created.) Almost at the same time, in THE GREEK WAY TO WESTERN CIVILIZA-

*THE MODERN TEMPER (1929).

TION (1929), Edith Hamilton maintained a similar view. For her, tragedy is "pain transmuted into exaltation by the alchemy of poetry," and the "dignity and significance of human life" is attested by the tragic hero's rich capacity for "the high estate of pain." For Maxwell Anderson, in THE ESSENCE OF TRAGEDY (1938), a tragedy had to proceed toward a "spiritual awakening, or rejuvenation" of the hero. The tragedian must "so arrange his story that it will prove to the audience that men pass through suffering purified, that, animal though we are in many ways, there is in us all some divine, incalculable fire that urges us to be better than we are." Somewhat more ecstatically, John Mason Brown voiced the same faith in his BROADWAY IN REVIEW (1940), declaring that tragedy leaves us "spiritually cross-ventilated;" and even the less eloquent author of the present Introduction referred to the final tragic experience, in "Catharsis and the Modern Theatre" (1937, 1946), as "a state of grace . . . an Apollonian attitude . . . a clarity of mind and spirit, a resilience and cheerfulness even."

If such statements as these seem curiously rhapsodic by comparison with Aristotle's matter-of-fact notations, if they appear to be time-dictated intensifications of his bland analysis, they are, nevertheless, allied to the man-centered point of view in the POETICS. Provided we do not really turn tragic art or any form of art into an *ersatz* religion and believe that the substitute can actually take the place of the genuine article; provided, too, that we refrain from slighting the plain but serviceable humanism of good untragic drama, we serve Aristotelian humanism well with this stress on tragic ennoblement. And so it appears that the reverberations of Aristotle's book continue to be as strong as ever, and more clearly perhaps than ever before they ring out words that penetrate the heart of man. This has been a curious destiny for an incomplete first manual on literature, but it is surely the best evidence of its power of survival. Its survival can, indeed, be truly jeopardized only by the triumph of a philosophy that would abolish concepts of right and wrong and of individual responsibility, deny the possibility of free will, and reduce life to pure mechanism or to nihilistic meaninglessness. In such an event, the POETICS would be a mere relic from a vanished age. Because this possibility, indeed, seems no longer speculatively remote, there is all the more reason for interest in Aristotle's essay as a document in the history of civilization and as an affirmation.

The POETICS is, nonetheless, I repeat, a book through which a reader should move warily. We must avoid coming out of our reading with impressions either too strict or too loose. A "little knowledge" in the case of this book has proved "a dangerous thing" for many centuries and to many men, including even scholars. Butcher's ARISTOTLE'S THEORY OF POETRY AND FINE ART, therefore, still makes large claims upon our attention.

EDITIONS, TRANSLATIONS, ETC.

THE following is a list of the chief editions and translations of the *Poetics*, and of other writings relating to this treatise, arranged in chronological order :—

Valla (G.), Latin translation. Venice, 1498.

Aldine text, in *Rhetores Graeci*. Venice, Aldus, 1508.

Latin translation, with the summary of Averroes (ob. 1198). Venice, Arrivabene, 1515.

Pazzi (A.) [Paccius], *Aristotelis Poetica, per Alexandrum Paccium, patritium Florentinum, in Latinum conversa.* Venice, Aldus, 1536.

Trincaveli, Greek text. Venice, 1536.

Robortelli (Fr.), *In librum Aristotelis de Arte Poetica explicationes.* Florence, 1548.

Segni (B.), *Rettorica e Poetica d' Aristotele tradotte di Greco in lingua vulgare.* Florence, 1549.

Maggi (V.) [Madius], *In Aristotelis librum de Poetica explanationes.* Venice, 1550.

Vettori (P.) [Victorius], *Commentationes in primum librum Aristotelis de Arte Poetarum.* Florence, 1560.

Castelvetro (L.), *Poetica d' Aristotele vulgarizzata.* Vienna, 1570 ; Basle, 1576.

Piccolomini (A.), *Annotationi nel libro della Poetica d' Aristotele, con la traduttione del medesimo libro in lingua volgare.* Venice, 1575.

Casaubon (I.), edition of Aristotle. Leyden, 1590.

Heinsius (D.) recensuit. Leyden, 1610.

Goulston (T.), Latin translation. London, 1623, and Cambridge, 1696.

Dacier, *La Poétique traduite en Français, avec des remarques critiques.* Paris, 1692.

Batteux, *Les quatres Poétiques d'Aristote, d'Horace, de Vida, de Despréaux, avec les traductions et des remarques par l'Abbé Batteux.* Paris, 1771.

lxxiii

Winstanley (T.), commentary on *Poetics*. Oxford, 1780.

Reiz, *De Poetica Liber*. Leipzig, 1786.

Metastasio (P.), *Estratto dell' Arte Poetica d' Aristotele e considerazioni su la medesima*. Paris, 1782.

Twining (T.), *Aristotle's Treatise on Poetry, Translated : with notes on the Translation, and on the original ; and two Dissertations on Poetical and Musical Imitation*. London, 1789.

Pye (H. J.), *A Commentary illustrating the Poetic of Aristotle by examples taken chiefly from the modern poets. To which is prefixed a new and corrected edition of the translation of the Poetic*. London, 1792.

Tyrwhitt (T.), *De Poetica Liber. Textum recensuit, versionem refinxit, et animadversionibus illustravit Thomas Tyrwhitt*. (Posthumously published.) Oxford, 1794.

Buhle (J. T.), *De Poetica Liber*. Göttingen, 1794.

Hermann (Godfrey), *Ars Poetica cum commentariis*. Leipzig, 1802.

Gräfenham (E. A. W.), *De Arte Poetica librum denuo recensuit, commentariis illustravit, etc.* Leipzig, 1821.

Raumer (Fr. v.), *Ueber die Poetik des Aristotles und sein Verhältniss zu den neuern Dramatikern*. Berlin, 1829.

Spengel (L.), *Ueber Aristoteles' Poetik* in *Abhandlungen der Münchener Akad. philos.-philol. Cl. II*. Munich, 1837.

Ritter (Fr.), *Ad codices antiquos recognitam, latine conversam, commentario illustratam edidit Franciscus Ritter*. Cologne, 1839.

Weil (H.), *Ueber die Wirkung der Tragoedie nach Aristoteles, Verhandlungen deutscher Philologen* x. p. 131. Basel, 1848.

Egger (M. E.), *Essai sur l'histoire de la Critique chez les Grecs, suivi de la Poétique d'Aristote et d'extraits de ses Problèmes, avec traduction française et commentaire*. Paris, 1849.

Bernays (Jacob), *Grundzüge der verlorenen Abhandlung des Aristoteles über Wirkung der Tragödie*. Breslau, 1857.

Saint-Hilaire (J. B.), *Poétique traduite en francais et accompagnée de notes perpétuelles*. Paris, 1858.

Stahr (Adolf), *Aristoteles und die Wirkung der Tragödie*. Berlin, 1859.

Stahr (Adolf), German translation, with Introduction and notes. Stuttgart, 1860.

Liepert (J.), *Aristoteles über den Zweck der Kunst*. Passau, 1862.

Susemihl (F.), *Aristoteles Ueber die Dichtkunst, Griechisch und Deutsch und mit sacherklärenden Anmerkungen*. Leipzig, 1865 and 1874.

Vahlen (J.), *Beiträge zu Aristoteles' Poetik*. Vienna, 1865.

Spengel (L.), *Aristotelische Studien IV*. Munich, 1866.

Vahlen (J.), *Aristotelis de Arte Poetica Liber : recensuit*. Berlin, 1867.

Teichmüller (G.), *Aristotelische Forschungen.* I. *Beiträge zur Erklärung der Poetik des Aristoteles.* II. *Aristoteles' Philosophie der Kunst.* Halle, 1869.

Ueberweg (F.), German translation and notes. Berlin, 1869.

Reinkens (J. H.), *Aristoteles über Kunst, besonders über Tragödie.* Vienna, 1870.

Döring (A.), *Die Kunstlehre des Aristoteles.* Jena, 1870.

Ueberweg (F.), *Aristotelis Ars Poetica ad fidem potissimum codicis antiquissimi A^c (Parisiensis 1741).* Berlin, 1870.

Bywater (I.), *Aristotelia* in *Journal of Philology,* v. 117 ff. and xiv. 40 ff. London and Cambridge, 1873 and 1885.

Vahlen (J.), *Aristotelis de Arte Poetica Liber: iterum recensuit et adnotatione critica auxit.* Berlin, 1874.

Moore (E.), Vahlen's text with notes. Oxford, 1875.

Christ (W.) recensuit. Leipzig, 1878 and 1893.

Bernays (Jacob), *Zwei Abhandlungen über die Aristotelische Theorie des Drama.* Berlin, 1880.

Brandscheid (F.), Text, German translation, critical notes and commentary. Wiesbaden, 1882.

Wharton (E. R.), Vahlen's text with English translation. Oxford, 1883.

Vahlen (J.), *Aristotelis de Arte Poetica Liber: tertiis curis recognovit et adnotatione critica auxit.* Leipzig, 1885.

Margoliouth (D.), *Analecta Orientalia ad Poeticam Aristoteleam.* London, 1887.

Bénard (C.), *L'Esthétique d'Aristote.* Paris, 1887.

Gomperz (T.), *Zu Aristoteles' Poetik,* I. (c. i.–vi.). Vienna, 1888.

Heidenhain (F.), *Averrois Paraphrasis in librum Poeticae Aristotelis Jacob Mantino interprete.* Leipzig, 1889.

Prickard (A. O.), *Aristotle on the Art of Poetry. A Lecture with two Appendices.* London, 1891.

La Poétique d'Aristote, Manuscrit 1741 Fonds Grec de la Bibliothèque Nationale. Préface de M. Henri Omont. Photolithographie de MM. Lumière. Paris, 1891.

Carroll (M.), *Aristotle's Poetics c. xxv. in the Light of the Homeric Scholia.* Baltimore, 1895.

Gomperz (T.), *Aristoteles' Poetik. Uebersetzt und eingeleitet.* Leipzig, 1895.

Gomperz (T.), *Zu Aristoteles' Poetik,* II., III. Vienna, 1896.

Bywater (I.), *Aristotelis de Arte Poetica Liber.* Oxford, 1897.

Vahlen (J.), *Hermeneutische Bemerkungen zu Aristoteles' Poetik: Sitzungsberichte der K. preussischen Akademie der Wissenschaften zu Berlin,* 1897 xxix, 1898 xxi.

Spingarn (J. E.), *A History of Literary Criticism in the Renaissance.* New York, 1899.

Tucker (T. G.), *Aristotelis Poetica.* London, 1899.

Saintsbury (G.), *A History of Criticism*, Vol. I. Edinburgh and London, 1900.

Finsler (G.), *Platon und die Aristotelische Poetik.* Leipzig, 1900.

Courthope (W. J.), *Life in Poetry: Law in Taste.* London, 1901.

Bywater (I.), *On certain technical terms in Aristotle's Poetics*, *Festschrift Theodor Gomperz dargebracht zum siebzigsten Geburtstage.* Wien, 1902, pp. 164 ff.

Tkač (J.), *Ueber den arabischer Kommentar des Averroes zur Poetik des Aristoteles*, *Wiener Studien*, xxiv. p. 70, 1902.

Carroll (Mitchell), *Aristotle's Aesthetics of Painting and Sculpture.* Geo. Washington University, 1905.

Knoke (F.), *Begriff der Tragödie nach Aristoteles.* Berlin, 1906.

NOTE

PROFESSOR BUTCHER's preceding bibliography ends in 1906. Noteworthy editions of Aristotle's text appeared after that date. These are: Ingram Bywater's edition, published in 1909; D. S. Margouliouth's, in 1911; A. Rostagni's, in 1927; and Alfred Gudeman's, in 1934.

Concerning these texts, however, critics are likely to agree with the opinion of Professor W. K. Wimsatt, Jr. (in the *New Scholasticism*, Vol. XXVI, No. 4) that the revisions of the text, derived from the Arabic version and MS Riccardianus, 48, "are not as a matter of fact important enough to have worked any substantial damage to the theoretical part of Butcher's labor."

Among English translations after 1906, the most notable were:

Cooper (Lane), *Aristotle on the Art of Poetry*, subtitled "An Amplified Version with Supplementary Illustrations for Students of English." First edition, Boston, 1913; revised edition, Ithaca, N.Y., 1947.

Bywater (Ingram), *Aristotle on the Art of Poetry.* Oxford, Clarendon Press, 1920. Professor Gilbert Murray has supplied an illuminating preface to this translation, which is a terser version than Butcher's.

Nahm (Milton C.), *Aristotle on the Art of Poetry with a Supplement: Aristotle on Music.* New York, The Liberal Arts Press, 1948. This is a slightly corrected text of Butcher's classic translation prepared by Professor Nahm of Bryn Mawr College for the "Little Library of Liberal Arts" series.

Aristotle's *Poetics*, along with his other works, continued to occupy the minds of scholars and critics to such a degree that additions to Butcher's bibliography would have to be forbiddingly extensive.

J. G.

ARISTOTLE'S POETICS

ANALYSIS OF CONTENTS

I. 'Imitation' (μίμησις) the common principle of the Arts of Poetry, Music, Dancing, Painting, and Sculpture. These Arts distinguished according to the Medium or material Vehicle, the Objects, and the Manner of Imitation. The Medium of Imitation is Rhythm, Language, and 'Harmony' (or Melody), taken singly or combined.

II. The Objects of Imitation.
Higher or lower types are represented in all the Imitative Arts. In Poetry this is the basis of the distinction between Tragedy and Comedy.

III. The Manner of Imitation.
Poetry may be in form either dramatic narrative, pure narrative (including lyric poetry), or pure drama. A digression follows on the name and original home of the Drama.

IV. The Origin and Development of Poetry.
Psychologically, Poetry may be traced to two causes, the instinct of Imitation, and the instinct of 'Harmony' and Rhythm.
Historically viewed, Poetry diverged early in two directions: traces of this twofold tendency are found in the Homeric poems: Tragedy and Comedy exhibit the distinction in a developed form.
The successive steps in the history of Tragedy are enumerated.

V. Definition of the Ludicrous (τὸ γελοῖον), and a brief sketch of the rise of Comedy. Points of comparison between Epic Poetry and Tragedy. (The chapter is fragmentary.)

Ε   1

VI. Definition of Tragedy. Six elements in Tragedy : three external, —namely, Spectacular Presentment (ὁ τῆς ὄψεως κόσμος or ὄψις), Lyrical Song (μελοποιία), Diction (λέξις) ; three internal,— namely, Plot (μῦθος), Character (ἦθος), and Thought (διάνοια). Plot, or the representation of the action, is of primary importance ; Character and Thought come next in order.

VII. The Plot must be a Whole, complete in itself, and of adequate magnitude.

VIII. The Plot must be a Unity. Unity of Plot consists not in Unity of Hero, but in Unity of Action.
The parts must be organically connected.

IX. (Plot continued.) Dramatic Unity can be attained only by the observance of Poetic as distinct from Historic Truth ; for Poetry is an expression of the Universal, History of the Particular. The rule of probable or necessary sequence as applied to the incidents. Certain plots condemned for want of Unity.
The best Tragic effects depend on the combination of the Inevitable and the Unexpected.

X. (Plot continued.) Definitions of Simple (ἁπλοῖ) and Complex (πεπλεγμένοι) Plots.

XI. (Plot continued.) Reversal of the Situation (περιπέτεια), Recognition (ἀναγνώρισις), and Tragic or disastrous Incident (πάθος) defined and explained.

XII. The 'quantitative parts' (μέρη κατὰ τὸ ποσόν) of Tragedy defined :—Prologue, Episode, etc. (Probably an interpolation.)

XIII. (Plot continued.) What constitutes Tragic Action. The change of fortune and the character of the hero as requisite to an ideal Tragedy. The unhappy ending more truly tragic than the 'poetic justice' which is in favour with a popular audience, and belongs rather to Comedy.

XIV. (Plot continued.) The tragic emotions of pity and fear should spring out of the Plot itself. To produce them by Scenery or Spectacular effect is entirely against the spirit of Tragedy. Examples of Tragic Incidents designed to heighten the emotional effect.

XV. The element of Character (as the manifestation of moral purpose) in Tragedy. Requisites of ethical portraiture. The rule of necessity or probability applicable to Character as to Plot. The 'Deus ex Machina' (a passage out of place here). How Character is idealised.

XVI. (Plot continued.) Recognition : its various kinds, with examples.

XVII. Practical rules for the Tragic Poet :
(1) To place the scene before his eyes, and to act the

parts himself in order to enter into vivid sympathy with the *dramatis personae*.

(2) To sketch the bare outline of the action before proceeding to fill in the episodes.

The Episodes of Tragedy are here incidentally contrasted with those of Epic Poetry.

XVIII. Further rules for the Tragic Poet :

(1) To be careful about the Complication (δέσις) and Dénouement (λύσις) of the Plot, especially the *Dénouement*.

(2) To unite, if possible, varied forms of poetic excellence.

(3) Not to overcharge a Tragedy with details appropriate to Epic Poetry.

(4) To make the Choral Odes—like the Dialogue—an organic part of the whole.

XIX. Thought (διάνοια), or the Intellectual element, and Diction in Tragedy.

Thought is revealed in the dramatic speeches composed according to the rules of Rhetoric.

Diction falls largely within the domain of the Art of Delivery, rather than of Poetry.

XX. Diction, or Language in general. An analysis of the parts of speech, and other grammatical details. (Probably interpolated.)

XXI. Poetic Diction. The words and modes of speech admissible in Poetry : including Metaphor, in particular.

A passage—probably interpolated—on the Gender of Nouns.

XXII. (Poetic Diction continued.) How Poetry combines elevation of language with perspicuity.

XXIII. Epic Poetry. It agrees with Tragedy in Unity of Action : herein contrasted with History.

XXIV. (Epic Poetry continued.) Further points of agreement with Tragedy. The points of difference are enumerated and illustrated,—namely, (1) the length of the poem ; (2) the metre ; (3) the art of imparting a plausible air to incredible fiction.

XXV. Critical Objections brought against Poetry, and the principles on which they are to be answered. In particular, an elucidation of the meaning of Poetic Truth, and its difference from common reality.

XXVI. A general estimate of the comparative worth of Epic Poetry and Tragedy. The alleged defects of Tragedy are not essential to it. Its positive merits entitle it to the higher rank of the two.

ABBREVIATIONS IN THE CRITICAL NOTES

$A^c =$ the Parisian manuscript (1741) of the 11th century : generally, but perhaps too confidently, supposed to be the archetype from which all other extant MSS. directly or indirectly are derived.

apogr. =   one or more of the MSS. other than A^c.

Arabs =   the Arabic version of the *Poetics* (Paris 882 A), of the middle of the 10th century, a version independent of our extant MSS. It is not directly taken from the Greek, but is a translation of a Syriac version of the *Poetics* by an unknown author, now lost. (The quotations in the critical notes are from the literal Latin translation of the Arabic, as given in Margoliouth's *Analecta Orientalia*.)

$\Sigma =$ the Greek manuscript, far older than A^c and no longer extant, which was used by the Syriac translator. (This symbol already employed by Susemihl I have taken for the sake of brevity.) It must be remembered, therefore, that the readings ascribed to Σ are those which we *infer* to have existed in the Greek exemplar, from which the Syriac translation was made.

Ald. =   the Aldine edition of *Rhetores Graeci*, published in 1508.

Vahlen =   Vahlen's text of the *Poetics* Ed. 3.

Vahlen coni. =   a conjecture of Vahlen, not admitted by him into the text.

[ ] =   words with manuscript authority (including A^c), which should be deleted from the text.

< > =   a conjectural supplement to the text.

* * =   a lacuna in the text.

† =   words which are corrupt and have not been satisfactorily restored.

4

ΑΡΙΣΤΟΤΕΛΟΥΣ
ΠΕΡΙ ΠΟΙΗΤΙΚΗΣ

ΑΡΙΣΤΟΤΕΛΟΥΣ ΠΕΡΙ ΠΟΙΗΤΙΚΗΣ

I
1447 a
10

Περὶ ποιητικῆς αὐτῆς τε καὶ τῶν εἰδῶν αὐτῆς ἥν τινα δύναμιν ἕκαστον ἔχει, καὶ πῶς δεῖ συνίστασθαι τοὺς μύθους εἰ μέλλει καλῶς ἕξειν ἡ ποίησις, ἔτι δὲ ἐκ πόσων καὶ ποίων ἐστὶ μορίων, ὁμοίως δὲ καὶ περὶ τῶν ἄλλων ὅσα τῆς αὐτῆς ἐστι μεθόδου, λέγωμεν ἀρξάμενοι κατὰ φύσιν πρῶτον ἀπὸ τῶν πρώτων. ἐποποιία δὴ καὶ ἡ τῆς τραγῳδίας 2 ποίησις ἔτι δὲ κωμῳδία καὶ ἡ διθυραμβοποιητικὴ καὶ τῆς 15 αὐλητικῆς ἡ πλείστη καὶ κιθαριστικῆς πᾶσαι τυγχάνουσιν οὖσαι μιμήσεις τὸ σύνολον, διαφέρουσι δὲ ἀλλήλων τρισίν, 3 ἢ γὰρ τῷ ἐν ἑτέροις μιμεῖσθαι ἢ τῷ ἕτερα ἢ τῷ ἑτέρως καὶ μὴ τὸν αὐτὸν τρόπον. ὥσπερ γὰρ καὶ χρώμασι 4 καὶ σχήμασι πολλὰ μιμοῦνταί τινες ἀπεικάζοντες (οἱ μὲν 20 διὰ τέχνης οἱ δὲ διὰ συνηθείας), ἕτεροι δὲ διὰ τῆς φωνῆς, οὕτω κἀν ταῖς εἰρημέναις τέχναις· ἅπασαι μὲν ποιοῦνται τὴν μίμησιν ἐν ῥυθμῷ καὶ λόγῳ καὶ ἁρμονίᾳ, τούτοις δ' ἢ χωρὶς ἢ μεμιγμένοις· οἷον ἁρμονίᾳ μὲν καὶ ῥυθμῷ χρώ-

---

12. λέγωμεν apogr. : λέγομεν Aᶜ: (habuit iam Σ var. lect., 'et dicamus et dicimus' Arabs)　　17. ἐν Forchhammer ('imitatur rebus diversis' Arabs): γένει Aᶜ　　20. τῆς φωνῆς codd. ('per sonos' Arabs): τῆς φύσεως Maggi: αὐτῆς τῆς φύσεως Spengel　　21. κἄν Parisinus 2038, Ald. : καὶ ἐν apogr. alia : καὶ Aᶜ

6

ARISTOTLE'S POETICS

I   I propose to treat of Poetry in itself and of its various
1447 a kinds, noting the essential quality of each; to inquire into
the structure of the plot as requisite to a good poem;
into the number and nature of the parts of which a
poem is composed; and similarly into whatever else falls
within the same inquiry. Following, then, the order of
nature, let us begin with the principles which come
first.

Epic poetry and Tragedy, Comedy also and Dithyrambic 2
poetry, and the music of the flute and of the lyre in
most of their forms, are all in their general conception
modes of imitation. They differ, however, from one 3
another in three respects,—the medium, the objects, the
manner or mode of imitation, being in each case
distinct.

For as there are persons who, by conscious art or 4
mere habit, imitate and represent various objects through
the medium of colour and form, or again by the voice;
so in the arts above mentioned, taken as a whole, the
imitation is produced by rhythm, language, or 'harmony,'
either singly or combined.

7

μεναι μόνον ἥ τε αὐλητικὴ καὶ ἡ κιθαριστικὴ κἂν εἴ τινες
25 ἕτεραι τυγχάνουσιν οὖσαι τοιαῦται τὴν δύναμιν, οἷον ἡ τῶν
συρίγγων· αὐτῷ δὲ τῷ ῥυθμῷ [μιμοῦνται] χωρὶς ἁρμονίας 5
ἡ τῶν ὀρχηστῶν, καὶ γὰρ οὗτοι διὰ τῶν σχηματιζομένων
ῥυθμῶν μιμοῦνται καὶ ἤθη καὶ πάθη καὶ πράξεις· ἡ δὲ 6
[ἐποποιία] μόνον τοῖς λόγοις ψιλοῖς ἢ τοῖς μέτροις καὶ τού-
1447b τοις εἴτε μιγνῦσα μετ᾽ ἀλλήλων εἴθ᾽ ἑνί τινι γένει χρωμένη
τῶν μέτρων, <ἀνώνυμος> τυγχάνει οὖσα μέχρι τοῦ νῦν· οὐδὲν 7
10 γὰρ ἂν ἔχοιμεν ὀνομάσαι κοινὸν τοὺς Σώφρονος καὶ Ξενάρχου
μίμους καὶ τοὺς Σωκρατικοὺς λόγους, οὐδὲ εἴ τις διὰ τριμέ-
τρων ἢ ἐλεγείων ἢ τῶν ἄλλων τινῶν τῶν τοιούτων ποιοῖτο τὴν
μίμησιν· πλὴν οἱ ἄνθρωποί γε συνάπτοντες τῷ μέτρῳ τὸ
ποιεῖν ἐλεγειοποιούς, τοὺς δὲ ἐποποιοὺς ὀνομάζουσιν, οὐχ ὡς
15 κατὰ τὴν μίμησιν ποιητὰς ἀλλὰ κοινῇ κατὰ τὸ μέτρον προσ-
αγορεύοντες. καὶ γὰρ ἂν ἰατρικὸν ἢ φυσικόν τι διὰ τῶν 8
μέτρων ἐκφέρωσιν, οὕτω καλεῖν εἰώθασιν· οὐδὲν δὲ κοινόν
ἐστιν Ὁμήρῳ καὶ Ἐμπεδοκλεῖ πλὴν τὸ μέτρον· διὸ τὸν μὲν
ποιητὴν δίκαιον καλεῖν, τὸν δὲ φυσιολόγον μᾶλλον ἢ ποιη-
20 τήν. ὁμοίως δὲ κἂν εἴ τις ἅπαντα τὰ μέτρα μιγνύων 9
ποιοῖτο τὴν μίμησιν καθάπερ Χαιρήμων ἐποίησε Κένταυ-
ρον μικτὴν ῥαψῳδίαν ἐξ ἁπάντων τῶν μέτρων, καὶ τοῦτον

25. τυγχάνουσιν apogr. : τυγχάνωσιν A^c   τοιαῦται add. apogr. ('aliae
artes similes vi' Arabs) : om. A^c   26. τῷ αὐτῷ δὲ Σ male (Margoliouth)
μιμοῦνται del. Spengel (confirm. Arabs)   27. ἡ apogr. ('ars instrumenti
saltationis' Arabs) : οἱ A^c : οἱ <χαριέστεροι> Gomperz : οἱ <χαριέντες>
Zeller : αἱ Reiz   ὀρχηστρῶν Σ male (Margoliouth)   29. ἐποποιία secl.
Ueberweg : om. Σ   ψιλοῖς ἢ τοῖς ψιλοῖς ἢ τοῖς ψιλοῖς sive ἢ ψιλοῖς τοῖς coni.
Vahlen   1447 b 9. ἀνώνυμος add. Bernays (confirmante Arabe 'quae
sine nomine est adhuc')   τυγχάνει οὖσα Suckow : τυγχάνουσα A^c   15.
κατὰ τὴν Guelferbytanus : τὴν κατὰ A^c   κοινῇ A^c   16. φυσικόν
Heinsius ('re physica' Arabs : confirm. Averroes) : μουσικόν codd.   22.
μικτὴν om. Σ   μικτὴν ῥαψῳδίαν del. Tyrwhitt   καὶ τοῦτον apogr. :
καὶ A^c (om. Σ) : καίτοι Rassow : οὐκ ἤδη καὶ Ald.   verba 20—22 ὁμοίως δὲ
. . . τῶν μέτρων post 12 τοιούτων transtulit Susemihl, commate post τοιούτων
posito, deletis 12 ποιοῖτο τὴν μίμησιν et 22 καὶ ποιητήν : sic efficitur ut

Thus in the music of the flute and of the lyre, 'harmony' and rhythm alone are employed; also in other arts, such as that of the shepherd's pipe, which are essentially similar to these. In dancing, rhythm 5 alone is used without 'harmony'; for even dancing imitates character, emotion, and action, by rhythmical movement.

There is another art which imitates by means of 6 language alone, and that either in prose or verse—which 1447 b verse, again, may either combine different metres or consist of but one kind—but this has hitherto been without a name. For there is no common term we could apply to 7 the mimes of Sophron and Xenarchus and the Socratic dialogues on the one hand; and, on the other, to poetic imitations in iambic, elegiac, or any similar metre. People do, indeed, add the word 'maker' or 'poet' to the name of the metre, and speak of elegiac poets, or epic (that is, hexameter) poets, as if it were not the imitation that makes the poet, but the verse that entitles them all indiscriminately to the name. Even 8 when a treatise on medicine or natural science is brought out in verse, the name of poet is by custom given to the author; and yet Homer and Empedocles have nothing in common but the metre, so that it would be right to call the one poet, the other physicist rather than poet. On the same principle, even if a writer in his poetic 9 imitation were to combine all metres, as Chaeremon did in his Centaur, which is a medley composed of metres

ποιητὴν προσαγορευτέον.   περὶ μὲν οὖν τούτων διωρίσθω
τοῦτον τὸν τρόπον· εἰσὶ δέ τινες αἳ πᾶσι χρῶνται τοῖς εἰρη- 10
25 μένοις, λέγω δὲ οἷον ῥυθμῷ καὶ μέλει καὶ μέτρῳ, ὥσπερ
ἥ τε τῶν διθυραμβικῶν ποίησις καὶ ἡ τῶν νόμων καὶ ἥ
τε τραγῳδία καὶ ἡ κωμῳδία· διαφέρουσι δὲ ὅτι αἱ μὲν
ἅμα πᾶσιν αἱ δὲ κατὰ μέρος.   ταύτας μὲν οὖν λέγω τὰς
διαφορὰς τῶν τεχνῶν, ἐν οἷς ποιοῦνται τὴν μίμησιν.

II   Ἐπεὶ δὲ μιμοῦνται οἱ μιμούμενοι πράττοντας, ἀνάγκη δὲ
1448 a
τούτους ἢ σπουδαίους ἢ φαύλους εἶναι (τὰ γὰρ ἤθη σχεδὸν
ἀεὶ τούτοις ἀκολουθεῖ μόνοις, κακίᾳ γὰρ καὶ ἀρετῇ τὰ ἤθη
διαφέρουσι πάντες), ἤτοι βελτίονας ἢ καθ᾽ ἡμᾶς ἢ χείρονας
5 ἢ καὶ τοιούτους, ὥσπερ οἱ γραφεῖς· Πολύγνωτος μὲν γὰρ
κρείττους, Παύσων δὲ χείρους, Διονύσιος δὲ ὁμοίους εἴκαζεν·
δῆλον δὲ ὅτι καὶ τῶν λεχθεισῶν ἑκάστη μιμήσεων ἕξει 2
ταύτας τὰς διαφορὰς καὶ ἔσται ἑτέρα τῷ ἕτερα μιμεῖσθαι
τοῦτον τὸν τρόπον.   καὶ γὰρ ἐν ὀρχήσει καὶ αὐλήσει καὶ 3
10 κιθαρίσει ἔστι γενέσθαι ταύτας τὰς ἀνομοιότητας· καὶ [τὸ]
περὶ τοὺς λόγους δὲ καὶ τὴν ψιλομετρίαν, οἷον Ὅμηρος
μὲν βελτίους, Κλεοφῶν δὲ ὁμοίους, Ἡγήμων δὲ ὁ Θάσιος ὁ
τὰς παρῳδίας ποιήσας πρῶτος καὶ Νικοχάρης ὁ τὴν Δειλιάδα χείρους· ὁμοίως δὲ καὶ περὶ τοὺς διθυράμβους καὶ περὶ 4
15 τοὺς νόμους, ὥσπερ †γᾶς† Κύκλωπας Τιμόθεος καὶ Φιλό-

---

verbis φυσιολόγον μᾶλλον ἢ ποιητὴν προσαγορευτέον concludatur locus
24. αἳ Ald. 1536: αἱ Riccardianus 16 : οἱ A°   26. διθυράμβων apogr.
23. πᾶσαι apogr.   οὖν apogr. : οὐ A°   29. οἷς Vettori : αἷς codd.
1448 a 3. κακίᾳ . . . ἀρετῇ apogr. Σ : κακία . . . ἀρετὴ A°   7. δὴ Morel
8. τῷ apogr. : τὸ A°   10. τὸ om. Parisinus 2038 : τῷ Bywater   12.
ὁ ante τὰς add. Parisinus 2038   13. τραγῳδίας ut videtur Σ ('qui primus
faciebat tragoediam' Arabs)   Δειλιάδα A° pr. m. (recte, ut in Iliadis
parodia, Tyrrell : cf. Castelvetro) : Δηλιάδα apogr. A° corr. (η supr. ει m. rec.)
15. ὥσπερ γᾶς codd. : ὥσπερ <Ἀργᾶς> Castelvetro : ὡς Πέρσας <καὶ>
F. Medici : ὥσπερ γὰρ coni. Vahlen : ὥσπερ οὕτως fort. Σ ('sicut imitatur
quis, sic Cyclopas etc.' Arabs) : ὥσπερ οἱ τοὺς coni. Margoliouth
Κύκλωπας] κυκλωπᾶς A°

of all kinds, we should bring him too under the general
term poet. So much then for these distinctions.

There are, again, some arts which employ all the 10
means above mentioned,—namely, rhythm, tune, and
metre. Such are Dithyrambic and Nomic poetry, and
also Tragedy and Comedy; but between them the
difference is, that in the first two cases these means
are all employed in combination, in the latter, now one
means is employed, now another.

Such, then, are the differences of the arts with respect
to the medium of imitation.

II   Since the objects of imitation are men in action, and
1448 a these men must be either of a higher or a lower type
(for moral character mainly answers to these divisions,
goodness and badness being the distinguishing marks
of moral differences), it follows that we must represent
men either as better than in real life, or as worse, or
as they are. It is the same in painting. Polygnotus
depicted men as nobler than they are, Pauson as less
noble, Dionysius drew them true to life.

Now it is evident that each of the modes of imitation 2
above mentioned will exhibit these differences, and become a distinct kind in imitating objects that are thus
distinct. Such diversities may be found even in dancing, 3
flute-playing, and lyre-playing. So again in language,
whether prose or verse unaccompanied by music. Homer,
for example, makes men better than they are; Cleophon
as they are; Hegemon the Thasian, the inventor of
parodies, and Nicochares, the author of the Deiliad, worse
than they are. The same thing holds good of Dithyrambs 4
and Nomes; here too one may portray different types, as

ξένος [μιμήσαιτο ἄν τις]· ἐν τῇ αὐτῇ δὲ διαφορᾷ καὶ ἡ
τραγῳδία πρὸς τὴν κωμῳδίαν διέστηκεν· ἡ μὲν γὰρ χείρους ἡ δὲ βελτίους μιμεῖσθαι βούλεται τῶν νῦν.

III   Ἔτι δὲ τούτων τρίτη διαφορὰ τὸ ὡς ἕκαστα τούτων μιμή-
20 σαιτο ἄν τις. καὶ γὰρ ἐν τοῖς αὐτοῖς καὶ τὰ αὐτὰ μιμεῖσθαι ἔστιν ὁτὲ μὲν ἀπαγγέλλοντα (ἢ ἕτερόν τι γιγνόμενον, ὥσπερ Ὅμηρος ποιεῖ, ἢ ὡς τὸν αὐτὸν καὶ μὴ μετα-
βάλλοντα), ἢ πάντας ὡς πράττοντας καὶ ἐνεργοῦντας [τοὺς
μιμουμένους]. ἐν τρισὶ δὴ ταύταις διαφοραῖς ἡ μίμησίς ἐστιν, 2
25 ὡς εἴπομεν κατ' ἀρχάς, ἐν οἷς τε καὶ ἃ καὶ ὥς. ὥστε τῇ
μὲν ὁ αὐτὸς ἂν εἴη μιμητὴς Ὁμήρῳ Σοφοκλῆς, μιμοῦνται
γὰρ ἄμφω σπουδαίους, τῇ δὲ Ἀριστοφάνει, πράττοντας γὰρ
μιμοῦνται καὶ δρῶντας ἄμφω. ὅθεν καὶ δράματα καλεῖ- 3
σθαί τινες αὐτά φασιν, ὅτι μιμοῦνται δρῶντας. διὸ καὶ
30 ἀντιποιοῦνται τῆς τε τραγῳδίας καὶ τῆς κωμῳδίας οἱ Δω-
ριεῖς (τῆς μὲν γὰρ κωμῳδίας οἱ Μεγαρεῖς οἵ τε ἐνταῦθα
ὡς ἐπὶ τῆς παρ' αὐτοῖς δημοκρατίας γενομένης, καὶ οἱ ἐκ
Σικελίας, ἐκεῖθεν γὰρ ἦν Ἐπίχαρμος ὁ ποιητὴς πολλῷ
πρότερος ὢν Χιωνίδου καὶ Μάγνητος· καὶ τῆς τραγῳδίας
35 ἔνιοι τῶν ἐν Πελοποννήσῳ) ποιούμενοι τὰ ὀνόματα σημεῖον·
αὐτοὶ μὲν γὰρ κώμας τὰς περιοικίδας καλεῖν φασιν, Ἀθηναίους δὲ δήμους, ὡς κωμῳδοὺς οὐκ ἀπὸ τοῦ κωμάζειν λε-

16. [μιμήσαιτο ἄν τις] secludendum coni. Vahlen   τῇ αὐτῇ δὲ Vettori
('in eadem discrepantia' Arabs): ταύτῃ δὲ τῇ M. Casaubon: αὐτῇ δὲ τῇ codd.
18. τῶν νῦν om. ut videtur Σ   21. ὁτὲ μὲν . . . γιγνόμενον] <ἢ> ὁτὲ
μὲν ἀπαγγέλλοντα <ὁτὲ δ'> ἕτερόν τι γιγνόμενον Zeller, recte, ut opinor:
eodem fere pervenit Arabem secutus Margoliouth   τι secl. Zeller, Spengel
22. τὸν secl. Bywater   23. πάντας] πάντα I. Casaubon   τοὺς μιμου-
μένους seclusi (olim secl. Vahlen): tuetur Σ: [τοὺς] μιμούμενον Friedrichs,
Schmidt   25. καὶ ἃ καὶ ὥς] ἀναγκαίως ut videtur Σ   καὶ ἃ om. Aᶜ:
add. apogr. (confirm. Arabs)   32. δημοκρατείας Aᶜ   34. Χιωνίδου
Robortello (confirm. Arabs): χωνίδου Aᶜ   35. fort. <δ'> ἔνιοι Bywater
36. αὐτοὶ Spengel: οὗτοι codd.   Ἀθηναίους edit. Oxon. 1760 et Spengel:
ἀθηναῖοι codd. (cf. 1460 b 35), tuetur Wilamowitz

Timotheus and Philoxenus differed in representing their Cyclopes. The same distinction marks off Tragedy from Comedy; for Comedy aims at representing men as worse, Tragedy as better than in actual life.

III   There is still a third difference—the manner in which each of these objects may be imitated. For the medium being the same, and the objects the same, the poet may imitate by narration—in which case he can either take another personality as Homer does, or speak in his own person, unchanged—or he may present all his characters as living and moving before us.

These, then, as we said at the beginning, are the 2 three differences which distinguish artistic imitation,—the medium, the objects, and the manner. So that from one point of view, Sophocles is an imitator of the same kind as Homer—for both imitate higher types of character; from another point of view, of the same kind as Aristophanes—for both imitate persons acting and doing. Hence, some say, the name of 'drama' is given 3 to such poems, as representing action. For the same reason the Dorians claim the invention both of Tragedy and Comedy. The claim to Comedy is put forward by the Megarians,—not only by those of Greece proper, who allege that it originated under their democracy, but also by the Megarians of Sicily, for the poet Epicharmus, who is much earlier than Chionides and Magnes, belonged to that country. Tragedy too is claimed by certain Dorians of the Peloponnese. In each case they appeal to the evidence of language. The outlying villages, they say, are by them called κῶμαι, by the Athenians δῆμοι: and they assume that Comedians were so named not from κωμάζειν, ' to

χθέντας ἀλλὰ τῇ κατὰ κώμας πλάνῃ ἀτιμαζομένους ἐκ τοῦ
1448 b ἄστεως. καὶ τὸ ποιεῖν αὐτοὶ μὲν δρᾶν, Ἀθηναίους δὲ
πράττειν προσαγορεύειν. περὶ μὲν οὖν τῶν διαφορῶν 4
καὶ πόσαι καὶ τίνες τῆς μιμήσεως εἰρήσθω ταῦτα.

IV   Ἐοίκασι δὲ γεννῆσαι μὲν ὅλως τὴν ποιητικὴν αἰτίαι δύο
5 τινὲς καὶ αὗται φυσικαί. τό τε γὰρ μιμεῖσθαι σύμφυτον 2
τοῖς ἀνθρώποις ἐκ παίδων ἐστί, καὶ τούτῳ διαφέρουσι
τῶν ἄλλων ζῴων ὅτι μιμητικώτατόν ἐστι καὶ τὰς μαθή-
σεις ποιεῖται διὰ μιμήσεως τὰς πρώτας, καὶ τὸ χαίρειν
τοῖς μιμήμασι πάντας. σημεῖον δὲ τούτου τὸ συμβαῖνον 3
10 ἐπὶ τῶν ἔργων· ἃ γὰρ αὐτὰ λυπηρῶς ὁρῶμεν, τούτων τὰς
εἰκόνας τὰς μάλιστα ἠκριβωμένας χαίρομεν θεωροῦντες, οἷον
θηρίων τε μορφὰς τῶν ἀτιμοτάτων καὶ νεκρῶν. αἴτιον δὲ 4
καὶ τούτου, ὅτι μανθάνειν οὐ μόνον τοῖς φιλοσόφοις ἥδιστον
ἀλλὰ καὶ τοῖς ἄλλοις ὁμοίως, ἀλλ᾽ ἐπὶ βραχὺ κοινωνοῦ-
15 σιν αὐτοῦ. διὰ γὰρ τοῦτο χαίρουσι τὰς εἰκόνας ὁρῶντες, ὅτι 5
συμβαίνει θεωροῦντας μανθάνειν καὶ συλλογίζεσθαι τί ἕκαστον, οἷον ὅτι οὗτος ἐκεῖνος· ἐπεὶ ἐὰν μὴ τύχῃ προεωρακώς,
οὐχ ᾗ μίμημα ποιήσει τὴν ἡδονὴν ἀλλὰ διὰ τὴν ἀπεργασίαν ἢ τὴν χροιὰν ἢ διὰ τοιαύτην τινὰ ἄλλην αἰτίαν.
20 κατὰ φύσιν δὴ ὄντος ἡμῖν τοῦ μιμεῖσθαι καὶ τῆς ἁρμονίας 6
καὶ τοῦ ῥυθμοῦ (τὰ γὰρ μέτρα ὅτι μόρια τῶν ῥυθμῶν ἐστι
φανερόν) ἐξ ἀρχῆς πεφυκότες καὶ αὐτὰ μάλιστα κατὰ
μικρὸν προάγοντες ἐγέννησαν τὴν ποίησιν ἐκ τῶν αὐτοσχε-

1448 b 1. καὶ τὸ ποιεῖν . . . προσαγορεύειν om. Arabs   4. ὅλως om.
Arabs   5. αὗται Parisinus 2038 : αὐταὶ A^c   13. καὶ τούτου apogr.
(confirm. Arabs): καὶ τοῦτο A^c: [καὶ τούτου] Zeller : καὶ [τούτου] Spengel :
καὶ <λόγος> τούτου Bonitz   18. οὐχ ᾗ Hermann, et Σ, ut videtur :
οὐχὶ codd.   τὴν ἡδονὴν om. Arabs   20. δὴ coni. Vahlen : δὲ codd.
22. καὶ αὐτὰ] πρὸς αὐτὰ Ald. : <εἰς> αὐτὰ καὶ Gomperz : καὶ αὐτὰ post
μάλιστα traiciendum esse coni. Susemihl

revel,' but because they wandered from village to village
(κατὰ κώμας), being excluded contemptuously from the
1448 b city.   They add also that the Dorian word for 'doing'
is δρᾶν, and the Athenian, πράττειν.

This may suffice as to the number and nature of the 4
various modes of imitation.

IV   Poetry in general seems to have sprung from two
causes, each of them lying deep in our nature.   First, the 2
instinct of imitation is implanted in man from childhood,
one difference between him and other animals being
that he is the most imitative of living creatures, and
through imitation learns his earliest lessons; and no less
universal is the pleasure felt in things imitated.   We 3
have evidence of this in the facts of experience.
Objects which in themselves we view with pain, we
delight to contemplate when reproduced with minute
fidelity : such as the forms of the most ignoble animals
and of dead bodies.   The cause of this again is, that to 4
learn gives the liveliest pleasure, not only to philosophers
but to men in general; whose capacity, however, of
learning is more limited.   Thus the reason why men 5
enjoy seeing a likeness is, that in contemplating it they
find themselves learning or inferring, and saying perhaps,
' Ah, that is he.'   For if you happen not to have seen
the original, the pleasure will be due not to the imitation
as such, but to the execution, the colouring, or some such
other cause.

Imitation, then, is one instinct of our nature.   Next, 6
there is the instinct for ' harmony' and rhythm, metres
being manifestly sections of rhythm.   Persons, therefore,
starting with this natural gift developed by degrees their

διασματων. διεσπάσθη δὲ κατὰ τὰ οἰκεῖα ἤθη ἡ ποίησις· 7
25 οἱ μὲν γὰρ σεμνότεροι τὰς καλὰς ἐμιμοῦντο πράξεις καὶ
τὰς τῶν τοιούτων, οἱ δὲ εὐτελέστεροι τὰς τῶν φαύλων,
πρῶτον ψόγους ποιοῦντες, ὥσπερ ἅτεροι ὕμνους καὶ ἐγκώμια.
τῶν μὲν οὖν πρὸ Ὁμήρου οὐδενὸς ἔχομεν εἰπεῖν τοιοῦτον 8
ποίημα, εἰκὸς δὲ εἶναι πολλούς, ἀπὸ δὲ Ὁμήρου ἀρξαμένοις
30 ἔστιν, οἷον ἐκείνου ὁ Μαργίτης καὶ τὰ τοιαῦτα. ἐν οἷς καὶ
τὸ ἁρμόττον [ἰαμβεῖον] ἦλθε μέτρον, διὸ καὶ ἰαμβεῖον καλεῖται νῦν, ὅτι ἐν τῷ μέτρῳ τούτῳ ἰάμβιζον ἀλλήλους. καὶ 9
ἐγένοντο τῶν παλαιῶν οἱ μὲν ἡρωικῶν οἱ δὲ ἰάμβων ποιηταί. ὥσπερ δὲ καὶ τὰ σπουδαῖα μάλιστα ποιητὴς Ὅμηρος
35 ἦν (μόνος γὰρ οὐχ ὅτι εὖ ἀλλ<ὰ> [ὅτι] καὶ μιμήσεις δραματικὰς ἐποίησεν), οὕτως καὶ τὰ τῆς κωμῳδίας σχήματα
πρῶτος ὑπέδειξεν, οὐ ψόγον ἀλλὰ τὸ γελοῖον δραματο-
ποιήσας· ὁ γὰρ Μαργίτης ἀνάλογον ἔχει, ὥσπερ Ἰλιὰς
1449 a καὶ ἡ Ὀδύσσεια πρὸς τὰς τραγῳδίας, οὕτω καὶ οὗτος πρὸς
τὰς κωμῳδίας. παραφανείσης δὲ τῆς τραγῳδίας καὶ κω- 10
μῳδίας οἱ ἐφ᾽ ἑκατέραν τὴν ποίησιν ὁρμῶντες κατὰ τὴν
οἰκείαν φύσιν οἱ μὲν ἀντὶ τῶν ἰάμβων κωμῳδοποιοὶ ἐγέ-
5 νοντο, οἱ δὲ ἀντὶ τῶν ἐπῶν τραγῳδοδιδάσκαλοι, διὰ τὸ
μείζονα καὶ ἐντιμότερα τὰ σχήματα εἶναι ταῦτα ἐκείνων.
τὸ μὲν οὖν ἐπισκοπεῖν εἰ ἄρ᾽ ἔχει ἤδη ἡ τραγῳδία τοῖς 11

---

27. ἅτεροι Spengel: ἕτεροι codd.   30. καὶ (post οἷς) Ald.: κατὰ Aᶜ
31. ιαμβίον (bis) Aᶜ   ιαμβεῖον ante ἦλθε secl. Stahr   35. ἀλλὰ Bonitz
(confirm. Arabs): ἀλλ᾽ ὅτι codd.: ἀλλ᾽ ἔτι Tucker   δραματικὰς Aᶜ et Σ:
δραματικῶς apogr.   38. ὁ apogr.: τὸ Aᶜ   1449 a 6. μείζονα apogr.:
μεῖζον Aᶜ   7. εἰ ἄρα ἔχει Parisinus 2038: παρέχει Aᶜ: ἄρ᾽ ἔχει Vahlen

special aptitudes, till their rude improvisations gave birth
to Poetry.

Poetry now diverged in two directions, according to 7
the individual character of the writers. The graver
spirits imitated noble actions, and the actions of
good men. The more trivial sort imitated the actions
of meaner persons, at first composing satires, as
the former did hymns to the gods and the praises of
famous men. A poem of the satirical kind cannot 8
indeed be put down to any author earlier than Homer;
though many such writers probably there were. But
from Homer onward, instances can be cited,—his own
Margites, for example, and other similar compositions.
The appropriate metre was also here introduced; hence
the measure is still called the iambic or lampooning
measure, being that in which people lampooned one
another. Thus the older poets were distinguished as 9
writers of heroic or of lampooning verse.

As, in the serious style, Homer is pre-eminent among
poets, for he alone combined dramatic form with
excellence of imitation, so he too first laid down the
main lines of Comedy, by dramatising the ludicrous
instead of writing personal satire. His Margites bears
1449 a the same relation to Comedy that the Iliad and Odyssey
do to Tragedy. But when Tragedy and Comedy came 10
to light, the two classes of poets still followed their
natural bent: the lampooners became writers of Comedy,
and the Epic poets were succeeded by Tragedians,
since the drama was a larger and higher form of
art.

Whether Tragedy has as yet perfected its proper 11

εἴδεσιν ἱκανῶς ἢ οὔ, αὐτό τε καθ' αὑτὸ †κρίνεται ἢ ναὶ†
καὶ πρὸς τὰ θέατρα, ἄλλος λόγος. γενομένη <δ'> οὖν ἀπ' ἀρχῆς 12
10 αὐτοσχεδιαστική, καὶ αὐτὴ καὶ ἡ κωμῳδία, καὶ ἡ μὲν ἀπὸ
τῶν ἐξαρχόντων τὸν διθύραμβον, ἡ δὲ ἀπὸ τῶν τὰ φαλλικὰ ἃ ἔτι καὶ νῦν ἐν πολλαῖς τῶν πόλεων διαμένει νο-
μιζόμενα, κατὰ μικρὸν ηὐξήθη προαγόντων ὅσον ἐγίγνετο
φανερὸν αὐτῆς, καὶ πολλὰς μεταβολὰς μεταβαλοῦσα ἡ
15 τραγῳδία ἐπαύσατο, ἐπεὶ ἔσχε τὴν αὑτῆς φύσιν. καὶ τό 13
τε τῶν ὑποκριτῶν πλῆθος ἐξ ἑνὸς εἰς δύο πρῶτος Αἰσχύλος ἤγαγε καὶ τὰ τοῦ χοροῦ ἠλάττωσε καὶ τὸν λόγον
πρωταγωνιστὴν παρεσκεύασεν, τρεῖς δὲ καὶ σκηνογραφίαν
Σοφοκλῆς. ἔτι δὲ τὸ μέγεθος ἐκ μικρῶν μύθων καὶ λέ- 14
20 ξεως γελοίας διὰ τὸ ἐκ σατυρικοῦ μεταβαλεῖν ὀψὲ ἀπε-
σεμνύνθη. τό τε μέτρον ἐκ τετραμέτρου ἰαμβεῖον ἐγένετο·
τὸ μὲν γὰρ πρῶτον τετραμέτρῳ ἐχρῶντο διὰ τὸ σατυρικὴν
καὶ ὀρχηστικωτέραν εἶναι τὴν ποίησιν, λέξεως δὲ γενομένης
αὐτὴ ἡ φύσις τὸ οἰκεῖον μέτρον εὗρε· μάλιστα γὰρ λεκτι-
25 κὸν τῶν μέτρων τὸ ἰαμβεῖόν ἐστιν· σημεῖον δὲ τούτου·
πλεῖστα γὰρ ἰαμβεῖα λέγομεν ἐν τῇ διαλέκτῳ τῇ πρὸς
ἀλλήλους, ἑξάμετρα δὲ ὀλιγάκις καὶ ἐκβαίνοντες τῆς λε-
κτικῆς ἁρμονίας. ἔτι δὲ ἐπεισοδίων πλήθη καὶ τὰ ἄλλ' 15

8. κρίνεται ἢ ναί· καὶ Aᶜ: ναί secl. Bursian: κρίνεται εἶναι καὶ apogr.: κρῖναι
καὶ Forchhammer: fort. κρίνεται εἶναι ἢ καί: αὐτώ τε κατ' αὐτό εἶναι
κρεῖττον ἢ πρὸς θάτερα Σ ut videtur (Margoliouth)   9. γενομένη δ' οὖν
Riccardianus 46 : γενομένη οὖν apogr.: γενομένης οὖν Aᶜ   10. αὐτοσχεδια-
στικὴ apogr.: αὐτοσχεδιαστικῆς Aᶜ   11. φαλλικὰ apogr.: φαϋλλικὰ Aᶜ:
φαυλικὰ vel φαῦλα Σ   12. διαμένει apogr.: διαμένειν Aᶜ   15. αὐτῆς
Bekker: ἑαυτῆς apogr.: αὑτῆς Aᶜ   19. λέξεως] λέξεις Σ ('orationes'
Arabs): <ἡ λέξις ἐκ> λέξεως Christ. Omissum vocabulum collato Arabe id
esse Margoliouth suspicatur cuius vice Graeculi ὑψηγορία usurpant   20.
σατυριακοῦ Aᶜ   21 et 25. ἰαμβίον Aᶜ   26. ἰαμβία Aᶜ   27. ἑξάμετρα]
τετράμετρα Winstanley   εἰς λεκτικὴν ἁρμονίαν Wecklein (cf. Rhet. iii. 8.
1408 b 32): codicum lect. tutatur Arabs   verba 25 σημεῖον—28 ἁρμονίας
suadente Usener secl. Susemihl   28. post πλήθη punctum del. Gomperz
ἄλλα ὡς apogr. (confirm. Arabs): ἄλλως Aᶜ: ἄλλα οἷς Hermann

types or not; and whether it is to be judged in itself, or
in relation also to the audience,—this raises another
question.   Be that as it may, Tragedy—as also Comedy 12
—was at first mere improvisation.   The one originated
with the authors of the Dithyramb, the other with those
of the phallic songs, which are still in use in many of
our cities.   Tragedy advanced by slow degrees; each
new element that showed itself was in turn developed.
Having passed through many changes, it found its natural
form, and there it stopped.

Aeschylus first introduced a second actor; he dimin- 13
ished the importance of the Chorus, and assigned the
leading part to the dialogue.   Sophocles raised the number
of actors to three, and added scene-painting.   Moreover, 14
it was not till late that the short plot was discarded for
one of greater compass, and the grotesque diction of the
earlier satyric form for the stately manner of Tragedy.
The iambic measure then replaced the trochaic tetrameter,
which was originally employed when the poetry was of
the satyric order, and had greater affinities with dancing.
Once dialogue had come in, Nature herself discovered the
appropriate measure.   For the iambic is, of all measures,
the most colloquial: we see it in the fact that con-
versational speech runs into iambic lines more frequently
than into any other kind of verse; rarely into hexa-
meters, and only when we drop the colloquial in-
tonation.   The additions to the number of 'episodes' 15
or acts, and the other accessories of which tradition

ὡς ἕκαστα κοσμηθῆναι λέγεται ἔστω ἡμῖν εἰρημένα· πο-
30 λὺ γὰρ ἂν ἴσως ἔργον εἴη διεξιέναι καθ᾽ ἕκαστον.

V   Ἡ δὲ κωμῳδία ἐστὶν ὥσπερ εἴπομεν μίμησις φαυλοτέρων
μέν, οὐ μέντοι κατὰ πᾶσαν κακίαν, ἀλλὰ τοῦ αἰσχροῦ
ἐστι τὸ γελοῖον μόριον. τὸ γὰρ γελοῖόν ἐστιν ἁμάρτημά τι καὶ αἶσχος ἀνώδυνον καὶ οὐ φθαρτικόν, οἷον εὐ-
35 θὺς τὸ γελοῖον πρόσωπον αἰσχρόν τι καὶ διεστραμμένον
ἄνευ ὀδύνης. αἱ μὲν οὖν τῆς τραγῳδίας μεταβάσεις καὶ 2
δι᾽ ὧν ἐγένοντο οὐ λελήθασιν, ἡ δὲ κωμῳδία διὰ τὸ μὴ
1449 b σπουδάζεσθαι ἐξ ἀρχῆς ἔλαθεν· καὶ γὰρ χορὸν κωμῳδῶν
ὀψέ ποτε ὁ ἄρχων ἔδωκεν, ἀλλ᾽ ἐθελονταὶ ἦσαν. ἤδη δὲ
σχήματά τινα αὐτῆς ἐχούσης οἱ λεγόμενοι αὐτῆς ποιηταὶ
μνημονεύονται. τίς δὲ πρόσωπα ἀπέδωκεν ἢ προλόγους ἢ 3
5 πλήθη ὑποκριτῶν καὶ ὅσα τοιαῦτα, ἠγνόηται. τὸ δὲ μύθους ποιεῖν [Ἐπίχαρμος καὶ Φόρμις] τὸ μὲν ἐξ ἀρχῆς
ἐκ Σικελίας ἦλθε, τῶν δὲ Ἀθήνησιν Κράτης πρῶτος ἦρξεν
ἀφέμενος τῆς ἰαμβικῆς ἰδέας καθόλου ποιεῖν λόγους καὶ
μύθους. ἡ μὲν οὖν ἐποποιία τῇ τραγῳδίᾳ μέχρι μὲν τοῦ μετὰ 4
10 μέτρου [μεγάλου] μίμησις εἶναι σπουδαίων ἠκολούθησεν· τῷ
δὲ τὸ μέτρον ἁπλοῦν ἔχειν καὶ ἀπαγγελίαν εἶναι, ταύτῃ

29. περὶ μὲν οὖν τούτων τοσαῦτα add. Ald. ante ἔστω   32. ἀλλ᾽ ῇ τοῦ
αἰσχροῦ Friedreich : ἀλλὰ <κατὰ τὸ γελοῖον,> τοῦ <δ᾽> αἰσχροῦ Christ : 'sed
tantum res ridicula est de genere foedi quae est portio et ridicula Arabs, i.e.
ἀλλὰ μόνον τὸ γελοῖόν ἐστι τοῦ αἰσχροῦ ὃ μόριόν ἐστι καὶ τὸ γελοῖον Σ, quod ex
duabus lectionibus conflatum esse censet Susemihl (1) ἀλλὰ μόριον μόνον τὸ
γελοῖόν ἐστι τοῦ αἰσχροῦ, (2) ἀλλὰ τοῦ αἰσχροῦ μόριόν ἐστι καὶ τὸ γελοῖον
33. γελοιον (bis) Aᶜ   1449 b 3. οἱ λεγόμενοι] ὀλίγοι μὲν οἱ Castelvetro :
ὀλίγοι μὲν [οἱ] Usener   4. προλόγους Aᶜ : πρόλογον Christ : λόγους Hermann   6. Ἐπίχαρμος καὶ Φόρμις secl. Susemihl : <ἐκεῖθεν γὰρ ἧστην>
Ἐπίχαρμος καὶ Φόρμις post ἦλθε Bywater, collato Themistio, Or. xxvii. p. 337 A,
recte, ut opinor   8. εἰδέας Aᶜ   9—10. μέχρι μὲν τοῦ μετὰ μέτρου Thurot
(cf. Arab.) : μέχρι μόνου μέτρου μεγάλου codd. : μέχρι μὲν τοῦ μέτρῳ <ἐν μήκει>
μεγάλῳ coni. Susemihl : μέχρι μὲν τοῦ μέτρῳ Tyrwhitt : μέχρι μόνου <τοῦ διὰ
λόγου ἐμ>μέτρου μεγάλου Ueberweg   10. μεγάλου codd.: secl. Bursian:
μετὰ λόγου Ald. et, ut videtur, Σ   τῷ Ald.: τὸ Aᶜ   11. ταύτῃ Aᶜ

tells, must be taken as already described; for to discuss them in detail would, doubtless, be a large undertaking.

V   Comedy is, as we have said, an imitation of characters of a lower type,—not, however, in the full sense of the word bad, the Ludicrous being merely a subdivision of the ugly. It consists in some defect or ugliness which is not painful or destructive. To take an obvious example, the comic mask is ugly and distorted, but does not imply pain.

The successive changes through which Tragedy passed, 2 and the authors of these changes, are well known, whereas Comedy has had no history, because it was not at first 1449 b treated seriously. It was late before the Archon granted a comic chorus to a poet; the performers were till then voluntary. Comedy had already taken definite shape when comic poets, distinctively so called, are heard of. Who furnished it with masks, or prologues, or increased 3 the number of actors,—these and other similar details remain unknown. As for the plot, it came originally from Sicily; but of Athenian writers Crates was the first who, abandoning the 'iambic' or lampooning form, generalised his themes and plots.

Epic poetry agrees with Tragedy in so far as it is an 4 imitation in verse of characters of a higher type. They differ, in that Epic poetry admits but one kind of metre, and is narrative in form. They differ, again,

διαφέρουσιν· ἔτι δὲ τῷ μήκει, <ἐπεὶ> ἡ μὲν ὅτι μάλιστα
πειρᾶται ὑπὸ μίαν περίοδον ἡλίου εἶναι ἢ μικρὸν ἐξαλλάττειν,
ἡ δὲ ἐποποιία ἀόριστος τῷ χρόνῳ, καὶ τούτῳ διαφέρει· καίτοι
15 τὸ πρῶτον ὁμοίως ἐν ταῖς τραγῳδίαις τοῦτο ἐποίουν καὶ ἐν
τοῖς ἔπεσιν. μέρη δ᾽ ἐστὶ τὰ μὲν ταὐτά, τὰ δὲ ἴδια τῆς 5
τραγῳδίας· διόπερ ὅστις περὶ τραγῳδίας οἶδε σπουδαίας
καὶ φαύλης, οἶδε καὶ περὶ ἐπῶν· ἃ μὲν γὰρ ἐποποιία
ἔχει, ὑπάρχει τῇ τραγῳδίᾳ, ἃ δὲ αὐτῇ, οὐ πάντα ἐν τῇ
20 ἐποποιίᾳ.

VI   Περὶ μὲν οὖν τῆς ἐν ἑξαμέτροις μιμητικῆς καὶ περὶ κωμῳδίας ὕστερον ἐροῦμεν, περὶ δὲ τραγῳδίας λέγωμεν ἀναλαβόντες αὐτῆς ἐκ τῶν εἰρημένων τὸν γινόμενον ὅρον τῆς
οὐσίας.   ἔστιν οὖν τραγῳδία μίμησις πράξεως σπουδαίας 2
25 καὶ τελείας μέγεθος ἐχούσης, ἡδυσμένῳ λόγῳ χωρὶς ἑκάστῳ τῶν εἰδῶν ἐν τοῖς μορίοις, δρώντων καὶ οὐ δι᾽ ἀπαγγελίας, δι᾽ ἐλέου καὶ φόβου περαίνουσα τὴν τῶν τοιούτων
παθημάτων κάθαρσιν.   λέγω δὲ ἡδυσμένον μὲν λόγον τὸν 3
ἔχοντα ῥυθμὸν καὶ ἁρμονίαν καὶ μέλος, τὸ δὲ χωρὶς τοῖς
30 εἴδεσι τὸ διὰ μέτρων ἔνια μόνον περαίνεσθαι καὶ πάλιν ἕτερα
διὰ μέλους.   ἐπεὶ δὲ πράττοντες ποιοῦνται τὴν μίμησιν, 4
πρῶτον μὲν ἐξ ἀνάγκης ἂν εἴη τι μόριον τραγῳδίας ὁ
τῆς ὄψεως κόσμος, εἶτα μελοποιία καὶ λέξις· ἐν τούτοις γὰρ
ποιοῦνται τὴν μίμησιν.   λέγω δὲ λέξιν μὲν αὐτὴν τὴν τῶν

---

12. διαφέρει Hermann (confirm. Arabs)   <ἐπεὶ> ἡ μὲν Gomperz : <ᾗ>
ἡ μὲν coni. Vahlen : <εἰ> ἡ μὲν Tucker : ἡ μὲν γὰρ apogr.   14. τούτῳ
(? τοῦτο pr. m.) Aᶜ   διαφέρουσιν Christ   16. ἔπεσιν et ἅπασι var. lect.
Σ (Diels), 'in omnibus epesi' Arabs   ταὐτὰ apogr. : ταῦτα Aᶜ   19.
αὐτῆι Aᶜ : αὐτῇ apogr. : αὕτη Reiz : ἐν αὐτῇ Richards   21. μὲν add. apogr. :
om. Aᶜ   22. ἀναλαβόντες Bernays : ἀπολαβόντες codd.   25. ἑκάστῳ
Reiz : ἑκάστου codd.   28. παθημάτων corr. apogr., Σ : μαθημάτων
Aᶜ   29. καὶ μέλος] καὶ μέτρον Vettori : secl. Tyrwhitt   30. μόνον]
μόρια Σ ('partes' Arabs)   34. αὐτὴν] ταύτην Bywater

in their length: for Tragedy endeavours, as far as possible, to confine itself to a single revolution of the sun, or but slightly to exceed this limit; whereas the Epic action has no limits of time. This, then, is a second point of difference; though at first the same freedom was admitted in Tragedy as in Epic poetry.

Of their constituent parts some are common to both, 5 some peculiar to Tragedy: whoever, therefore, knows what is good or bad Tragedy, knows also about Epic poetry. All the elements of an Epic poem are found in Tragedy, but the elements of a Tragedy are not all found in the Epic poem.

VI   Of the poetry which imitates in hexameter verse, and of Comedy, we will speak hereafter. Let us now discuss Tragedy, resuming its formal definition, as resulting from what has been already said.

Tragedy, then, is an imitation of an action that is 2 serious, complete, and of a certain magnitude; in language embellished with each kind of artistic ornament, the several kinds being found in separate parts of the play; in the form of action, not of narrative; through pity and fear effecting the proper purgation of these emotions. By 3 'language embellished,' I mean language into which rhythm, 'harmony,' and song enter. By 'the several kinds in separate parts,' I mean, that some parts are rendered through the medium of verse alone, others again with the aid of song.

Now as tragic imitation implies persons acting, it neces- 4 sarily follows, in the first place, that Spectacular equipment will be a part of Tragedy. Next, Song and Diction, for these are the medium of imitation. By 'Diction'

35 μέτρων σύνθεσιν, μελοποιίαν δὲ ὃ τὴν δύναμιν φανερὰν
ἔχει πᾶσιν. ἐπεὶ δὲ πράξεώς ἐστι μίμησις, πράττεται δὲ 5
ὑπὸ τινῶν πραττόντων, οὓς ἀνάγκη ποιούς τινας εἶναι κατά
τε τὸ ἦθος καὶ τὴν διάνοιαν (διὰ γὰρ τούτων καὶ τὰς
1450 a πράξεις εἶναί φαμεν ποιάς τινας, πέφυκεν δὲ αἴτια δύο τῶν
πράξεων εἶναι, διάνοιαν καὶ ἦθος, καὶ κατὰ ταύτας καὶ
τυγχάνουσι καὶ ἀποτυγχάνουσι πάντες), ἔστιν δὴ τῆς μὲν 6
πράξεως ὁ μῦθος ἡ μίμησις· λέγω γὰρ μῦθον τοῦτον, τὴν
5 σύνθεσιν τῶν πραγμάτων, τὰ δὲ ἤθη, καθ' ὃ ποιούς τινας
εἶναί φαμεν τοὺς πράττοντας, διάνοιαν δέ, ἐν ὅσοις λέγοντες ἀποδεικνύασίν τι ἢ καὶ ἀποφαίνονται γνώμην. ἀνάγκη 7
οὖν πάσης τραγῳδίας μέρη εἶναι ἕξ, καθ' ἃ ποιά τις ἐστὶν
ἡ τραγῳδία· ταῦτα δ' ἐστὶ μῦθος καὶ ἤθη καὶ λέξις καὶ
10 διάνοια καὶ ὄψις καὶ μελοποιία. οἷς μὲν γὰρ μιμοῦνται,
δύο μέρη ἐστίν, ὡς δὲ μιμοῦνται, ἕν, ἃ δὲ μιμοῦνται, τρία,
καὶ παρὰ ταῦτα οὐδέν. τούτοις μὲν οὖν <πάντες> [οὐκ ὀλίγοι 8
αὐτῶν]ὣς εἰπεῖν κέχρηνται τοῖς εἴδεσιν· καὶ γὰρ ὄψεις ἔχει πᾶν
καὶ ἦθος καὶ μῦθον καὶ λέξιν καὶ μέλος καὶ διάνοιαν ὡσαύ-
15 τως.   μέγιστον δὲ τούτων ἐστὶν ἡ τῶν πραγμάτων σύστασις· 9

35. μέτρων] ὀνομάτων Hermann, collato 1450 b 15   36. πᾶσιν Maggi:
πᾶσαν codd.   38. διὰ δὲ Zeller   διὰ γὰρ τούτων . . . πάντες in
parenthesi Thurot   1450 a 1. πέφυκεν δὲ apogr.: πέφυκεν Aᶜ   αἴτια
codd.: αἰτίας Christ   3. δὴ Eucken: δὲ codd.   4. τοῦτον] τοῦτο
Maggi: secl. Christ (cf. Arab.)   5. καθὸ Aᶜ: καθ' ἃ apogr.]   8.
καθ' ἃ ποιά apogr.: καθοποιά Aᶜ   12. οὐκ ὀλίγοι αὐτῶν ὡς εἰπεῖν codd.:
ὀλίγου αὐτῶν <ἅπαντες> ὡς εἰπεῖν coni. Bywater: οὐκ ὀλίγοι αὐτῶν <ἀλλὰ
πάντες> ὡς εἰπεῖν Bursian: οὐκ ὀλίγοι αὐτῶν om. Σ, sed πάντως (?=πάντες)
add. (vid. Margoliouth).   Secluso igitur tanquam glossemate οὐκ ὀλίγοι
αὐτῶν, scripsi <πάντες> ὡς εἰπεῖν: cf. Rhet. i. 1. 1354 a 12, ὀλίγον codd.:
οὐδὲν ὡς εἰπεῖν Aᶜ marg., ubi ὀλίγον glossema esse suspicor, veram lect. οὐδὲν
ὡς εἰπεῖν: Dem. or. xxxviii. 6 πάντων τῶν πλείστων ὡς εἰπεῖν, ubi τῶν
πλείστων secluserim.   Viam monstravit Diels, qui tamen πάντες quoque
omisso, τούτοις μὲν οὖν ὡς εἰπεῖν scripsit: οὐκ ὀλίγοι αὐτῶν <ἀλλ' ἐν πᾶσι
πάντες> Gomperz: οὐκ ὀλίγοι αὐτῶν <ἀλλὰ πάντες πᾶσι> Zeller: <πάντες
ἐν πᾶσιν αὐτῆς> Susemihl   13. ὄψεις vel ὄψιν apogr.: ὄψις Aᶜ   πᾶ·
iure suspexeris

I mean the mere metrical arrangement of the words : as for ' Song,' it is a term whose sense every one understands.

Again, Tragedy is the imitation of an action ; and an 5 action implies personal agents, who necessarily possess certain distinctive qualities both of character and thought; 1450 a for it is by these that we qualify actions themselves, and these—thought and character--are the two natural causes from which actions spring, and on actions again all success or failure depends.   Hence, the Plot is the 6 imitation of the action :—for by plot I here mean the arrangement of the incidents.   By Character I mean that in virtue of which we ascribe certain qualities to the agents.   Thought is required wherever a statement is proved, or, it may be, a general truth enunciated. Every Tragedy, therefore, must have six parts, which 7 parts determine its quality—namely, Plot, Character, Diction, Thought, Spectacle, Song.   Two of the parts constitute the medium of imitation, one the manner, and three the objects of imitation.   And these complete the list. These elements have been employed, we may say, by the 8 poets to a man ; in fact, every play contains Spectacular elements as well as Character, Plot, Diction, Song, and Thought.

But most important of all is the structure of the 9

ἡ γὰρ τραγῳδία μίμησίς ἐστιν οὐκ ἀνθρώπων ἀλλὰ πράξεως καὶ βίου· <ὁ δὲ βίος> ἐν πράξει ἐστὶν καὶ τὸ τέλος
πρᾶξίς τις ἐστίν, οὐ ποιότης· εἰσὶν δὲ κατὰ μὲν τὰ ἤθη ποιοί 10
τινες, κατὰ δὲ τὰς πράξεις εὐδαίμονες ἢ τοὐναντίον. οὔκουν
20 ὅπως τὰ ἤθη μιμήσωνται πράττουσιν, ἀλλὰ τὰ ἤθη συμπαραλαμβάνουσιν διὰ τὰς πράξεις· ὥστε τὰ πράγματα καὶ
ὁ μῦθος τέλος τῆς τραγῳδίας, τὸ δὲ τέλος μέγιστον ἁπάντων.
ἔτι ἄνευ μὲν πράξεως οὐκ ἂν γένοιτο τραγῳδία, ἄνευ δὲ 11
ἠθῶν γένοιτ᾽ ἄν. αἱ γὰρ τῶν νέων τῶν πλείστων ἀήθεις
25 τραγῳδίαι εἰσὶν καὶ ὅλως ποιηταὶ πολλοὶ τοιοῦτοι, οἷον καὶ
τῶν γραφέων Ζεῦξις πρὸς Πολύγνωτον πέπονθεν· ὁ μὲν γὰρ
Πολύγνωτος ἀγαθὸς ἠθογράφος, ἡ δὲ Ζεύξιδος γραφὴ οὐδὲν
ἔχει ἦθος. ἔτι ἐάν τις ἐφεξῆς θῇ ῥήσεις ἠθικὰς καὶ λέξει 12
καὶ διανοίᾳ εὖ πεποιημένας, οὐ ποιήσει ὃ ἦν τῆς τραγῳ-
30 δίας ἔργον, ἀλλὰ πολὺ μᾶλλον ἡ καταδεεστέροις τούτοις
κεχρημένη τραγῳδία, ἔχουσα δὲ μῦθον καὶ σύστασιν πραγμάτων. πρὸς δὲ τούτοις τὰ μέγιστα οἷς ψυχαγωγεῖ ἡ 13
τραγῳδία, τοῦ μύθου μέρη ἐστίν, αἵ τε περιπέτειαι καὶ ἀναγνωρίσεις. ἔτι σημεῖον ὅτι καὶ οἱ ἐγχειροῦντες ποιεῖν πρό- 14
35 τερον δύνανται τῇ λέξει καὶ τοῖς ἤθεσιν ἀκριβοῦν ἢ τὰ
πράγματα συνίστασθαι, οἷον καὶ οἱ πρῶτοι ποιηταὶ σχεδὸν
ἅπαντες. ἀρχὴ μὲν οὖν καὶ οἷον ψυχὴ ὁ μῦθος τῆς τρα-

---

16. ἀλλὰ πράξεως καὶ βίου καὶ εὐδαιμονίας καὶ ἡ κακοδαιμονία ἐν πράξει codd.,
sed alio spectat Arabs ('sed in operibus et vita. Et <vita> est in opere');
unde Margoliouth ἀλλὰ πράξεως καὶ βίου, <ὁ δὲ βίος> ἐν πράξει, quod pro-
bant Diels, Zeller, Susemihl. Codicum lectionem ita supplet Vahlen, καὶ
εὐδαιμονίας <καὶ κακοδαιμονίας, ἡ δὲ εὐδαιμονία> καὶ ἡ κακοδαιμονία
20. πράττουσιν] πράττοντας ποιοῦσιν coni. Vahlen   συμπαραλαμβάνουσι
Guelferbytanus pr. m., Spengel: συμπεριλαμβάνουσιν Aᶜ   26 et 27.
Πολύγνωστον et Πολύγνωστος Aᶜ   28. λέξει καὶ διανοίᾳ Vahlen (confirm.
Arabs): λέξεις καὶ διανοίας codd.   29. οὐ add. apogr. ('nequaquam'
Arabs): om. Aᶜ: fort. οὐδαμῶς Margoliouth   20. ἡ apogr.: ἢ Aᶜ   36.
συνίστασθαι codd.: συνιστάναι Thurot

incidents. For Tragedy is an imitation, not of men, but of an action and of life, and life consists in action, and its end is a mode of action, not a quality. Now 10 character determines men's qualities, but it is by their actions that they are happy or the reverse. Dramatic action, therefore, is not with a view to the representation of character: character comes in as subsidiary to the actions. Hence the incidents and the plot are the end of a tragedy; and the end is the chief thing of all. Again, 11 without action there cannot be a tragedy; there may be without character. The tragedies of most of our modern poets fail in the rendering of character; and of poets in general this is often true. It is the same in painting; and here lies the difference between Zeuxis and Polygnotus. Polygnotus delineates character well: the style of Zeuxis is devoid of ethical quality. Again, if you string 12 together a set of speeches expressive of character, and well finished in point of diction and thought, you will not produce the essential tragic effect nearly so well as with a play which, however deficient in these respects, yet has a plot and artistically constructed incidents. Besides which, the most powerful elements of emotional 13 interest in Tragedy—Peripeteia or Reversal of the Situation, and Recognition scenes—are parts of the plot. A further proof is, that novices in the art attain to finish 14 of diction and precision of portraiture before they can construct the plot. It is the same with almost all the early poets.

The Plot, then, is the first principle, and, as it were,

γῳδίας, δεύτερον δὲ τὰ ἤθη· παραπλήσιον γάρ ἐστιν καὶ 15
1450 b ἐπὶ τῆς γραφικῆς· εἰ γάρ τις ἐναλείψειε τοῖς καλλίστοις
φαρμάκοις χύδην, οὐκ ἂν ὁμοίως εὐφράνειεν καὶ λευκογραφήσας εἰκόνα· ἔστιν τε μίμησις πράξεως καὶ διὰ ταύτην
μάλιστα τῶν πραττόντων. τρίτον δὲ ἡ διάνοια· τοῦτο δέ 16
5 ἐστιν τὸ λέγειν δύνασθαι τὰ ἐνόντα καὶ τὰ ἁρμόττοντα,
ὅπερ ἐπὶ τῶν λόγων τῆς πολιτικῆς καὶ ῥητορικῆς ἔργον
ἐστίν· οἱ μὲν γὰρ ἀρχαῖοι πολιτικῶς ἐποίουν λέγοντας, οἱ
δὲ νῦν ῥητορικῶς. ἔστιν δὲ ἦθος μὲν τὸ τοιοῦτον ὃ δηλοῖ τὴν 17
προαίρεσιν ὁποῖά τις προαιρεῖται ἢ φεύγει· διόπερ οὐκ
10 ἔχουσιν ἦθος τῶν λόγων ἐν οἷς οὐκ ἔστι δῆλον ἢ ἐν
οἷς μηδ' ὅλως ἔστιν ὅ τι προαιρεῖται ἢ φεύγει ὁ λέγων·
διάνοια δέ, ἐν οἷς ἀποδεικνύουσί τι ὡς ἔστιν ἢ ὡς οὐκ ἔστιν
ἢ καθόλου τι ἀποφαίνονται. τέταρτον δὲ τῶν λεγομένων ἡ 18
λέξις· λέγω δέ, ὥσπερ πρότερον εἴρηται, λέξιν εἶναι τὴν
15 διὰ τῆς ὀνομασίας ἑρμηνείαν, ὃ καὶ ἐπὶ τῶν ἐμμέτρων καὶ
ἐπὶ τῶν λόγων ἔχει τὴν αὐτὴν δύναμιν. τῶν δὲ λοιπῶν 19
[πέντε] ἡ μελοποιία μέγιστον τῶν ἡδυσμάτων, ἡ δὲ ὄψις
ψυχαγωγικὸν μέν, ἀτεχνότατον δὲ καὶ ἥκιστα οἰκεῖον τῆς ποιη-
τικῆς· <ἴσ>ως γὰρ τῆς τραγῳδίας δύναμις καὶ ἄνευ ἀγῶνος

---

38. παραπλήσιον . . . εἰκόνα supra post πραγμάτων v. 31 collocavit Castelvetro.   1450 b l. ἕνα λείψειε A°   3. τε codd.: γὰρ Hermann   6.
ἐπὶ τῶν λόγων secl. M. Schmidt   9—11. ὁποῖά τις . . . φεύγει ὁ λέγων
Gomperz, alios secutus: ὁποῖά τις (ὁ ποῖα τίς) ἐν οἷς οὐκ ἔστι δῆλον ἢ
προαιρεῖται ἢ φεύγει· διόπερ οὐκ ἔχουσιν ἦθος τῶν λόγων ἐν οἷς μηδ' ὅλως ἔστιν
ὅ τις (ὅ τι apogr.) προαιρεῖται ἢ φεύγει ὁ λέγων A°: ὁποία τις· διόπερ οὐκ
ἔχουσιν . . . φεύγει ὁ λέγων (verbis ἐν οἷς οὐκ ἔστι δῆλον ἢ προαιρεῖται ἢ
φεύγει omissis cum Arabe) Margoliouth. Suspicatur Susemihl ἐν οἷς οὐκ
ἔστι . . . ἢ φεύγει et ἐν οἷς μηδ' ὅλως ἔστιν . . . ἢ φεύγει duplicem lectionem
fuisse   11. τι apogr.: τις A°   13. λεγομένων Gomperz: μὲν λόγων
codd.: ἐν λόγῳ Bywater   17. πέντε A°: secl. Spengel (confirm. Arabs):
πέμπτον apogr.   18. ἀπεχνώτατον A°   19. ἴσως Meiser: ὡς A°: ἡ
apogr. : ὅλως Gomperz

the soul of a tragedy : Character holds the second place.
1450 b A similar fact is seen in painting. The most beautiful 15
colours, laid on confusedly, will not give as much pleasure
as the chalk outline of a portrait. Thus Tragedy is the
imitation of an action, and of the agents mainly with a
view to the action.

Third in order is Thought,—that is, the faculty of 16
saying what is possible and pertinent in given circumstances. In the case of oratory, this is the function of
the political art and of the art of rhetoric : and so indeed
the older poets make their characters speak the language
of civic life; the poets of our time, the language of the
rhetoricians. Character is that which reveals moral 17
purpose, showing what kind of things a man chooses or
avoids. Speeches, therefore, which do not make this
manifest, or in which the speaker does not choose or
avoid anything whatever, are not expressive of character.
Thought, on the other hand, is found where something is
proved to be or not to be, or a general maxim is
enunciated.

Fourth among the elements enumerated comes 18
Diction ; by which I mean, as has been already said, the
expression of the meaning in words; and its essence is
the same both in verse and prose.

Of the remaining elements Song holds the chief place 19
among the embellishments.

The Spectacle has, indeed, an emotional attraction of
its own, but, of all the parts, it is the least artistic, and
connected least with the art of poetry. For the power
of Tragedy, we may be sure, is felt even apart from
representation and actors. Besides, the production of

20 καὶ ὑποκριτῶν ἔστιν, ἔτι δὲ κυριωτέρα περὶ τὴν ἀπεργασίαν
τῶν ὄψεων ἡ τοῦ σκευοποιοῦ τέχνη τῆς τῶν ποιητῶν ἐστιν.

VII   Διωρισμένων δὲ τούτων, λέγωμεν μετὰ ταῦτα ποίαν
τινὰ δεῖ τὴν σύστασιν εἶναι τῶν πραγμάτων, ἐπειδὴ τοῦτο
καὶ πρῶτον καὶ μέγιστον τῆς τραγῳδίας ἐστίν. κεῖται δὴ 2
25 ἡμῖν τὴν τραγῳδίαν τελείας καὶ ὅλης πράξεως εἶναι μίμησιν ἐχούσης τι μέγεθος· ἔστιν γὰρ ὅλον καὶ μηδὲν ἔχον
μέγεθος. ὅλον δέ ἐστιν τὸ ἔχον ἀρχὴν καὶ μέσον καὶ τε- 3
λευτήν. ἀρχὴ δέ ἐστιν ὃ αὐτὸ μὲν μὴ ἐξ ἀνάγκης μετ'
ἄλλο ἐστίν, μετ' ἐκεῖνο δ' ἕτερον πέφυκεν εἶναι ἢ γίνεσθαι·
30 τελευτὴ δὲ τοὐναντίον ὃ αὐτὸ μετ' ἄλλο πέφυκεν εἶναι ἢ
ἐξ ἀνάγκης ἢ ὡς ἐπὶ τὸ πολύ, μετὰ δὲ τοῦτο ἄλλο οὐδέν·
μέσον δὲ ὃ καὶ αὐτὸ μετ' ἄλλο καὶ μετ' ἐκεῖνο ἕτερον.
δεῖ ἄρα τοὺς συνεστῶτας εὖ μύθους μήθ' ὁπόθεν ἔτυχεν
ἄρχεσθαι μήθ' ὅπου ἔτυχε τελευτᾶν, ἀλλὰ κεχρῆσθαι ταῖς
35 εἰρημέναις ἰδέαις. ἔτι δ' ἐπεὶ τὸ καλὸν καὶ ζῷον καὶ ἅπαν 4
πρᾶγμα ὃ συνέστηκεν ἐκ τινῶν οὐ μόνον ταῦτα τεταγμένα
δεῖ ἔχειν ἀλλὰ καὶ μέγεθος ὑπάρχειν μὴ τὸ τυχόν· τὸ
γὰρ καλὸν ἐν μεγέθει καὶ τάξει ἐστίν, διὸ οὔτε πάμμικρον
ἄν τι γένοιτο καλὸν ζῷον (συγχεῖται γὰρ ἡ θεωρία ἐγγὺς
40 τοῦ ἀναισθήτου χρόνου γινομένη), οὔτε παμμέγεθες (οὐ γὰρ
1451 a ἅμα ἡ θεωρία γίνεται ἀλλ' οἴχεται τοῖς θεωροῦσι τὸ ἓν
καὶ τὸ ὅλον ἐκ τῆς θεωρίας), οἷον εἰ μυρίων σταδίων εἴη
ζῷον· ὥστε δεῖ καθάπερ ἐπὶ τῶν σωμάτων καὶ ἐπὶ τῶν 5
ζῴων ἔχειν μὲν μέγεθος, τοῦτο δὲ εὐσύνοπτον εἶναι, οὕτω

---

24. δὴ Bywater : δ' Aᶜ   28. μὴ ἐξ ἀνάγκης codd. : ἐξ ἀνάγκης μὴ Pazzi
35. ἰδέαις apogr. : εἰδέαις Aᶜ   38. πάμμικρον Riccardianus 16 : πᾶν μικρὸν
Aᶜ : πάνυ μικρὸν Laurentianus lx. 16   40. χρόνου secl. Bonitz : tutatur
Arabs   παμμέγεθες Riccardianus 16 : πᾶν μέγεθος Aᶜ : πάνυ μέγα Laurentianus lx. 16   **1451 a 3.** σωμάτων] συστημάτων Bywater

spectacular effects depends more on the art of the stage machinist than on that of the poet.

VII   These principles being established, let us now discuss the proper structure of the Plot, since this is the first and most important thing in Tragedy.

Now, according to our definition, Tragedy is an 2 imitation of an action that is complete, and whole, and of a certain magnitude; for there may be a whole that is wanting in magnitude. A whole is that which has 3 a beginning, a middle, and an end. A beginning is that which does not itself follow anything by causal necessity, but after which something naturally is or comes to be. An end, on the contrary, is that which itself naturally follows some other thing, either by necessity, or as a rule, but has nothing following it. A middle is that which follows something as some other thing follows it. A well constructed plot, therefore, must neither begin nor end at haphazard, but conform to these principles.

Again, a beautiful object, whether it be a living 4 organism or any whole composed of parts, must not only have an orderly arrangement of parts, but must also be of a certain magnitude; for beauty depends on magnitude and order. Hence a very small animal organism cannot be beautiful; for the view of it is confused, the object being seen in an almost imperceptible moment of time. Nor, again, can one of vast size be 1451 a beautiful; for as the eye cannot take it all in at once, the unity and sense of the whole is lost for the spectator; as for instance if there were one a thousand miles long. As, therefore, in the case of animate bodies and 5 organisms a certain magnitude is necessary, and a magni-

5 καὶ ἐπὶ τῶν μύθων ἔχειν μὲν μῆκος, τοῦτο δὲ εὐμνημόνευτον εἶναι. τοῦ μήκους ὅρος <ὁ> μὲν πρὸς τοὺς ἀγῶνας καὶ 6
τὴν αἴσθησιν οὐ τῆς τέχνης ἐστίν· εἰ γὰρ ἔδει ἑκατὸν
τραγῳδίας ἀγωνίζεσθαι, πρὸς κλεψύδρας ἂν ἠγωνίζοντο,
ὥσπερ ποτὲ καὶ ἄλλοτέ φασιν. ὁ δὲ κατ᾽ αὐτὴν τὴν φύσιν 7
10 τοῦ πράγματος ὅρος, ἀεὶ μὲν ὁ μείζων μέχρι τοῦ σύνδηλος εἶναι καλλίων ἐστὶ κατὰ τὸ μέγεθος· ὡς δὲ ἁ-
πλῶς διορίσαντας εἰπεῖν, ἐν ὅσῳ μεγέθει κατὰ τὸ εἰκὸς ἢ
τὸ ἀναγκαῖον ἐφεξῆς γιγνομένων συμβαίνει εἰς εὐτυχίαν
14 ἐκ δυστυχίας ἢ ἐξ εὐτυχίας εἰς δυστυχίαν μεταβάλλειν,
VIII ἱκανὸς ὅρος ἐστὶν τοῦ μεγέθους. Μῦθος δ᾽ ἐστὶν εἷς
οὐχ ὥσπερ τινὲς οἴονται ἐὰν περὶ ἕνα ᾖ· πολλὰ γὰρ
καὶ ἄπειρα τῷ ἑνὶ συμβαίνει, ἐξ ὧν [ἐνίων] οὐδέν ἐστιν
ἕν· οὕτως δὲ καὶ πράξεις ἑνὸς πολλαί εἰσιν, ἐξ ὧν
μία οὐδεμία γίνεται πρᾶξις. διὸ πάντες ἐοίκασιν ἁμαρ- 2
20 τάνειν ὅσοι τῶν ποιητῶν Ἡρακληίδα Θησηίδα καὶ τὰ
τοιαῦτα ποιήματα πεποιήκασιν· οἴονται γάρ, ἐπεὶ εἷς ἦν
ὁ Ἡρακλῆς, ἕνα καὶ τὸν μῦθον εἶναι προσήκειν. ὁ δ᾽ Ὅ- 3
μηρος ὥσπερ καὶ τὰ ἄλλα διαφέρει καὶ τοῦτ᾽ ἔοικεν καλῶς ἰδεῖν ἤτοι διὰ τέχνην ἢ διὰ φύσιν· Ὀδύσσειαν γὰρ
25 ποιῶν οὐκ ἐποίησεν ἅπαντα ὅσα αὐτῷ συνέβη, οἷον πλη-
γῆναι μὲν ἐν τῷ Παρνασῷ, μανῆναι δὲ προσποιήσασθαι ἐν

---

6. ὁ add. Bursian   μὲν πρὸς Aᶜ: πρὸς μὲν apogr.   8. κλεψύδραν
apogr.   9. ἄλλοτε φασίν codd.: ἄλλοτ᾽ εἰώθασιν M. Schmidt; quod olim
recepi, sed ποτὲ καὶ ἄλλοτε vix aliud significare potest quam 'olim
aliquando.' Quae in Arabe leguntur ('sicut solemus dicere etiam aliquo
tempore et aliquando'), alterutri lectioni subsidio esse possunt   17.
ἐνὶ Guelferbytanus: γένει Aᶜ (cf. 1447 a 17): τῷ γ᾽ ἐνὶ Vettori   ἐνίων
secl. Spengel   18. αἱ ante πολλαί add. apogr.

tude which may be easily embraced in one view; so in the plot, a certain length is necessary, and a length which can be easily embraced by the memory. The 6 limit of length in relation to dramatic competition and sensuous presentment, is no part of artistic theory. For had it been the rule for a hundred tragedies to compete together, the performance would have been regulated by the water-clock,—as indeed we are told was formerly done. But the limit as fixed by the nature of the 7 drama itself is this:—the greater the length, the more beautiful will the piece be by reason of its size, provided that the whole be perspicuous. And to define the matter roughly, we may say that the proper magnitude is comprised within such limits, that the sequence of events, according to the law of probability or necessity, will admit of a change from bad fortune to good, or from good fortune to bad.

VIII   Unity of plot does not, as some persons think, consist in the unity of the hero. For infinitely various are the incidents in one man's life which cannot be reduced to unity; and so, too, there are many actions of one man out of which we cannot make one action. Hence the 2 error, as it appears, of all poets who have composed a Heracleid, a Theseid, or other poems of the kind. They imagine that as Heracles was one man, the story of Heracles must also be a unity. But Homer, as in all 3 else he is of surpassing merit, here too—whether from art or natural genius—seems to have happily discerned the truth. In composing the Odyssey he did not include all the adventures of Odysseus—such as his wound on Parnassus, or his feigned madness at the mustering of

τῷ ἀγερμῷ, ὧν οὐδὲν θατέρου γενομένου ἀναγκαῖον ἦν
ἢ εἰκὸς θάτερον γενέσθαι, ἀλλὰ περὶ μίαν πρᾶξιν οἴαν
λέγομεν τὴν Ὀδύσσειαν συνέστησεν, ὁμοίως δὲ καὶ τὴν
30 Ἰλιάδα. χρὴ οὖν καθάπερ καὶ ἐν ταῖς ἄλλαις μιμητικαῖς ἡ μία 4
μίμησις ἑνός ἐστιν οὕτω καὶ τὸν μῦθον, ἐπεὶ πράξεως μίμησίς
ἐστι, μιᾶς τε εἶναι καὶ ταύτης ὅλης καὶ τὰ μέρη συνεστάναι τῶν πραγμάτων οὕτως ὥστε μετατιθεμένου τινὸς μέρους
ἢ ἀφαιρουμένου διαφέρεσθαι καὶ κινεῖσθαι τὸ ὅλον· ὃ γὰρ
35 προσὸν ἢ μὴ προσὸν μηδὲν ποιεῖ ἐπίδηλον, οὐδὲν μόριον τοῦ
ὅλου ἐστίν.

IX   Φανερὸν δὲ ἐκ τῶν εἰρημένων καὶ ὅτι οὐ τὸ τὰ
γενόμενα λέγειν, τοῦτο ποιητοῦ ἔργον ἐστίν, ἀλλ᾽ οἷα ἂν
γένοιτο καὶ τὰ δυνατὰ κατὰ τὸ εἰκὸς ἢ τὸ ἀναγκαῖον. ὁ γὰρ 2
1451 b ἱστορικὸς καὶ ὁ ποιητὴς οὐ τῷ ἢ ἔμμετρα λέγειν ἢ ἄμετρα
διαφέρουσιν (εἴη γὰρ ἂν τὰ Ἡροδότου εἰς μέτρα τεθῆναι,
καὶ οὐδὲν ἧττον ἂν εἴη ἱστορία τις μετὰ μέτρου ἢ ἄνευ μέτρων)·
ἀλλὰ τούτῳ διαφέρει, τῷ τὸν μὲν τὰ γενόμενα λέγειν,
5 τὸν δὲ οἷα ἂν γένοιτο. διὸ καὶ φιλοσοφώτερον καὶ 3
σπουδαιότερον ποίησις ἱστορίας ἐστίν· ἡ μὲν γὰρ ποίησις
μᾶλλον τὰ καθόλου, ἡ δ᾽ ἱστορία τὰ καθ᾽ ἕκαστον λέγει.
ἔστιν δὲ καθόλου μέν, τῷ ποίῳ τὰ ποῖα ἄττα συμβαίνει 4
λέγειν ἢ πράττειν κατὰ τὸ εἰκὸς ἢ τὸ ἀναγκαῖον, οὗ στο-
10 χάζεται ἡ ποίησις ὀνόματα ἐπιτιθεμένη· τὸ δὲ καθ᾽ ἕκαστον, τί Ἀλκιβιάδης ἔπραξεν ἢ τί ἔπαθεν. ἐπὶ μὲν οὖν τῆς 5
κωμῳδίας ἤδη τοῦτο δῆλον γέγονεν· συστήσαντες γὰρ τὸν

28. ἢ add. apogr.   29. λέγομεν apogr. : λέγοιμεν Aᶜ : ἂν λέγοιμεν Vahlen
32. καὶ ταύτης] ταύτης καὶ Susemihl   34. διαφέρεσθαι] διαφθείρεσθαι
Twining ('corrumpatur et confundatur' Arabs): habuit fort. utramque
lect. Σ (Margoliouth): fort. διαφορεῖσθαι (cf. de Div. 2. 464 b 13)   35.
ποιεῖ, ἐπίδηλον ὡς apogr.   37. οὐ τὸ apogr. (confirm. Arabs): οὕτω Aᶜ
38. γενόμενα Riccardianus 16 : γινόμενα cett.   39. καὶ τὰ δυνατὰ secl.
Maggi   1451 b 4. τούτῳ . . . τῷ apogr. : τοῦτο . . . τῷ Aᶜ: τοῦτο . . . τὸ
Spengel   10. τὸ apogr. : τὸν Aᶜ

the host—incidents between which there was no necessary
or probable connexion : but he made the Odyssey, and
likewise the Iliad, to centre round an action that in our
sense of the word is one. As therefore, in the other 4
imitative arts, the imitation is one when the object imitated
is one, so the plot, being an imitation of an action, must
imitate one action and that a whole, the structural union
of the parts being such that, if any one of them is
displaced or removed, the whole will be disjointed and
disturbed. For a thing whose presence or absence makes
no visible difference, is not an organic part of the
whole.

IX   It is, moreover, evident from what has been said,
that it is not the function of the poet to relate what
has happened, but what may happen,—what is possible
according to the law of probability or necessity. The 2
1451 b poet and the historian differ not by writing in verse or
in prose. The work of Herodotus might be put into
verse, and it would still be a species of history, with
metre no less than without it. The true difference is
that one relates what has happened, the other what may
happen. Poetry, therefore, is a more philosophical and 3
a higher thing than history : for poetry tends to express
the universal, history the particular. By the universal 4
I mean how a person of a certain type will on occasion
speak or act, according to the law of probability or
necessity; and it is this universality at which poetry
aims in the names she attaches to the personages. The
particular is—for example—what Alcibiades did or
suffered. In Comedy this is already apparent : for here 5
the poet first constructs the plot on the lines of prob-

μῦθον διὰ τῶν εἰκότων οὐ τὰ τυχόντα ὀνόματα ὑποτιθέασιν, καὶ οὐχ ὥσπερ οἱ ἰαμβοποιοὶ περὶ τὸν καθ' ἕκαστον
15 ποιοῦσιν. ἐπὶ δὲ τῆς τραγῳδίας τῶν γενομένων ὀνομάτων 6
ἀντέχονται. αἴτιον δ' ὅτι πιθανόν ἐστι τὸ δυνατόν. τὰ μὲν
οὖν μὴ γενόμενα οὔπω πιστεύομεν εἶναι δυνατά, τὰ δὲ γενόμενα φανερὸν ὅτι δυνατά, οὐ γὰρ ἂν ἐγένετο, εἰ ἦν ἀδύνατα. οὐ μὴν ἀλλὰ καὶ ἐν ταῖς τραγῳδίαις ἐνίαις μὲν ἓν 7
20 ἢ δύο τῶν γνωρίμων ἐστὶν ὀνομάτων, τὰ δὲ ἄλλα πεποιημένα, ἐν ἐνίαις δὲ οὐδ' ἕν, οἷον ἐν τῷ Ἀγάθωνος Ἀνθεῖ· ὁμοίως
γὰρ ἐν τούτῳ τά τε πράγματα καὶ τὰ ὀνόματα πεποίηται, καὶ
οὐδὲν ἧττον εὐφραίνει. ὥστ' οὐ πάντως εἶναι ζητητέον τῶν 8
παραδεδομένων μύθων, περὶ οὓς αἱ τραγῳδίαι εἰσίν, ἀντ-
25 έχεσθαι. καὶ γὰρ γελοῖον τοῦτο ζητεῖν, ἐπεὶ καὶ τὰ γνώ-
ριμα ὀλίγοις γνώριμά ἐστιν ἀλλ' ὅμως εὐφραίνει πάντας.
δῆλον οὖν ἐκ τούτων ὅτι τὸν ποιητὴν μᾶλλον τῶν μύθων 9
εἶναι δεῖ ποιητὴν ἢ τῶν μέτρων, ὅσῳ ποιητὴς κατὰ τὴν μί-
μησίν ἐστιν, μιμεῖται δὲ τὰς πράξεις. κἂν ἄρα συμβῇ γενό-
30 μενα ποιεῖν, οὐθὲν ἧττον ποιητής ἐστι· τῶν γὰρ γενομένων
ἔνια οὐδὲν κωλύει τοιαῦτα εἶναι οἷα ἂν εἰκὸς γενέσθαι καὶ
δυνατὰ γενέσθαι, καθ' ὃ ἐκεῖνος αὐτῶν ποιητής ἐστιν.
    τῶν δὲ ἄλλων μύθων καὶ πράξεων αἱ ἐπεισοδιώδεις 10

13. οὐ scripsi ('nequaquam' Arabs): οὕτω codd. (cf. 1451 a 37)   ἐπι-
τιθέασι apogr.   14. τὸν Aᶜ: τῶν apogr.   16. πειθανόν Aᶜ   19. ἐν
ante ἐνίαις add. ₑpogr. (ceterum cf. Dem. or. iii. 11, xviii. 12)   21. οὐδ' ἕν]
οὐθ' ἕν Aᶜ: οὐθέν apogr.   οἷον ... Ἀνθεῖ] 'quemadmodum si quis unum esse
bonum statuit' Arabs; male Syrus legisse videtur ἐν τὸ ἀγαθὸν ὃς ἂν θῇ
(Margoliouth)   Ἀνθεῖ Welcker: ἄνθει codd.   23. ὥστ' οὐ] ὡς τοῦ
Aᶜ   οὐ πάντως εἶναι, si sana sunt, arte cohaerent (cf. οὐχ ἐκὼν εἶναι,
κατὰ δύναμιν εἶναι, κατὰ τοῦτο εἶναι)   εἶναι secl. Spengel : ἂν εἴη M. Schmidt·
24. αἱ <εὐδοκιμοῦσαι> τραγῳδίαι coni. Vahlen   31. καὶ δυνατὰ γενέσθαι
secl. Vorländer : om. Arabs   33. τῶν δὲ ἄλλων Tyrwhitt : τῶν δὲ ἁπλῶν
codd. : ἁπλῶς δὲ τῶν Castelvetro

ability, and then inserts characteristic names ;—unlike
the lampooners who write about particular individuals.
But tragedians still keep to real names, the reason being 6
that what is possible is credible : what has not happened
we do not at once feel sure to be possible : but what has
happened is manifestly possible : otherwise it would not
have happened.   Still there are even some tragedies in 7
which there are only one or two well known names, the rest
being fictitious.   In others, none are well known,—as
in Agathon's Antheus, where incidents and names alike
are fictitious, and yet they give none the less pleasure.
We must not, therefore, at all costs keep to the received 8
legends, which are the usual subjects of Tragedy.   Indeed,
it would be absurd to attempt it ; for even subjects that
are known are known only to a few, and yet give pleasure
to all.   It clearly follows that the poet or 'maker' 9
should be the maker of plots rather than of verses ;
since he is a poet because he imitates, and what he
imitates are actions.   And even if he chances to take
an historical subject, he is none the less a poet ; for
there is no reason why some events that have actually
happened should not conform to the law of the probable
and possible, and in virtue of that quality in them he is
their poet or maker.

Of all plots and actions the epeisodic are the worst. 10

εἰσὶν χείρισται· λέγω δ᾽ ἐπεισοδιώδη μῦθον ἐν ᾧ τὰ ἐπεισ-
35 όδια μετ᾽ ἄλληλα οὔτ᾽ εἰκὸς οὔτ᾽ ἀνάγκη εἶναι. τοιαῦται
δὲ ποιοῦνται ὑπὸ μὲν τῶν φαύλων ποιητῶν δι᾽ αὐτούς, ὑπὸ
δὲ τῶν ἀγαθῶν διὰ τοὺς ὑποκριτάς· ἀγωνίσματα γὰρ
ποιοῦντες καὶ παρὰ τὴν δύναμιν παρατείνοντες μῦθον πολ-
1452 a λάκις διαστρέφειν ἀναγκάζονται τὸ ἐφεξῆς. ἐπεὶ δὲ οὐ 11
μόνον τελείας ἐστὶ πράξεως ἡ μίμησις ἀλλὰ καὶ φοβερῶν
καὶ ἐλεεινῶν, ταῦτα δὲ γίνεται [καὶ] μάλιστα ὅταν γένηται
παρὰ τὴν δόξαν, καὶ μᾶλλον <ὅταν> δι᾽ ἄλληλα· τὸ γὰρ θαυ- 12
5 μαστὸν οὕτως ἕξει μᾶλλον ἢ εἰ ἀπὸ τοῦ αὐτομάτου καὶ
τῆς τύχης, ἐπεὶ καὶ τῶν ἀπὸ τύχης ταῦτα θαυμασιώτατα
δοκεῖ ὅσα ὥσπερ ἐπίτηδες φαίνεται γεγονέναι, οἷον ὡς ὁ
ἀνδριὰς ὁ τοῦ Μίτυος ἐν Ἄργει ἀπέκτεινεν τὸν αἴτιον τοῦ
θανάτου τῷ Μίτυι, θεωροῦντι ἐμπεσών· ἔοικε γὰρ τὰ τοιαῦτα
10 οὐκ εἰκῇ γενέσθαι· ὥστε ἀνάγκη τοὺς τοιούτους εἶναι καλλίους μύθους.

X   Εἰσὶ δὲ τῶν μύθων οἱ μὲν ἁπλοῖ οἱ δὲ πεπλεγμένοι,
καὶ γὰρ αἱ πράξεις ὧν μιμήσεις οἱ μῦθοί εἰσιν ὑπάρχου-
σιν εὐθὺς οὖσαι τοιαῦται. λέγω δὲ ἁπλῆν μὲν πρᾶξιν ἧς 2
15 γινομένης ὥσπερ ὥρισται συνεχοῦς καὶ μιᾶς ἄνευ περιπετείας ἢ ἀναγνωρισμοῦ ἡ μετάβασις γίνεται, πεπλεγμένη
δ᾽ ἐστὶν ἧς μετὰ ἀναγνωρισμοῦ ἢ περιπετείας ἢ ἀμφοῖν ἡ
μετάβασίς ἐστιν. ταῦτα δὲ δεῖ γίνεσθαι ἐξ αὐτῆς τῆς συ- 3
στάσεως τοῦ μύθου, ὥστε ἐκ τῶν προγεγενημένων συμβαίνειν

37. ὑποκριτὰς Aᶜ (cf. Rhet. iii. 11. 1403 b 33): κριτὰς apogr.   38. παρατείνοντες apogr.: παρατείναντες Aᶜ   1452 a 2. ἡ secl. Gomperz   3.
καὶ secl. Susemihl   4. καὶ μᾶλλον post καὶ μάλιστα codd.: post δόξαν
Reiz (cf. Rhet. iii. 9. 1410 a 21): καὶ κάλλιον Tucker: καὶ μᾶλλον sive καὶ
μάλιστα secl. Spengel: καὶ μᾶλλον ante καὶ μάλιστα Richards   ὅταν
add. Reiz   9. μήτυϊ Aᶜ   17. δ᾽ ἐστὶν ἧς Susemihl: δὲ λέξις Aᶜ: δὲ ἐξ
ἧς Riccardianus 16: δὲ πρᾶξις apogr.: δέ ἐστιν ἐξ ἧς (h. e. δέ ´Λ´ εξης) Vahlen

I call a plot 'epeisodic' in which the episodes or acts succeed one another without probable or necessary sequence. Bad poets compose such pieces by their own fault, good poets, to please the players; for, as they write show pieces for competition, they stretch the plot beyond its 1452 a capacity, and are often forced to break the natural continuity.

But again, Tragedy is an imitation not only of a 11 complete action, but of events inspiring fear or pity. Such an effect is best produced when the events come on us by surprise; and the effect is heightened when, at the same time, they follow as cause and effect. The tragic 12 wonder will then be greater than if they happened of themselves or by accident; for even coincidences are most striking when they have an air of design. We may instance the statue of Mitys at Argos, which fell upon his murderer while he was a spectator at a festival, and killed him. Such events seem not to be due to mere chance. Plots, therefore, constructed on these principles are necessarily the best.

X   Plots are either Simple or Complex, for the actions in real life, of which the plots are an imitation, obviously show a similar distinction. An action which is one and 2 continuous in the sense above defined, I call Simple, when the change of fortune takes place without Reversal of the Situation and without Recognition.

A Complex action is one in which the change is accompanied by such Reversal, or by Recognition, or by both. These last should arise from the internal 3 structure of the plot, so that what follows should be the

20 ἢ ἐξ ἀνάγκης ἢ κατὰ τὸ εἰκὸς γίγνεσθαι ταῦτα· διαφέρει
γὰρ πολὺ τὸ γίγνεσθαι τάδε διὰ τάδε ἢ μετὰ τάδε.

XI   Ἔστι δὲ περιπέτεια μὲν ἡ εἰς τὸ ἐναντίον τῶν πραττομένων μεταβολή, [καθάπερ εἴρηται,] καὶ τοῦτο δὲ ὥσπερ
λέγομεν κατὰ τὸ εἰκὸς ἢ ἀναγκαῖον· ὥσπερ ἐν τῷ Οἰδίποδι
25 ἐλθὼν ὡς εὐφρανῶν τὸν Οἰδίπουν καὶ ἀπαλλάξων τοῦ πρὸς
τὴν μητέρα φόβου, δηλώσας ὃς ἦν, τοὐναντίον ἐποίησεν·
καὶ ἐν τῷ Λυγκεῖ ὁ μὲν ἀγόμενος ὡς ἀποθανούμενος, ὁ δὲ
Δαναὸς ἀκολουθῶν ὡς ἀποκτενῶν, τὸν μὲν συνέβη ἐκ τῶν
πεπραγμένων ἀποθανεῖν, τὸν δὲ σωθῆναι.   ἀναγνώρισις 2
30 δέ, ὥσπερ καὶ τοὔνομα σημαίνει, ἐξ ἀγνοίας εἰς γνῶσιν
μεταβολὴ ἢ εἰς φιλίαν ἢ εἰς ἔχθραν τῶν πρὸς εὐτυχίαν ἢ
δυστυχίαν ὡρισμένων· καλλίστη δὲ ἀναγνώρισις, ὅταν ἅμα
περιπέτειαι γίνωνται, οἷον ἔχει ἡ ἐν τῷ Οἰδίποδι.   εἰσὶν μὲν 3
οὖν καὶ ἄλλαι ἀναγνωρίσεις· καὶ γὰρ πρὸς ἄψυχα καὶ τὰ
35 τυχόντα ἔστιν ὡς <ὅ>περ εἴρηται συμβαίνει, καὶ εἰ πέ-
πραγέ τις ἢ μὴ πέπραγεν ἔστιν ἀναγνωρίσαι.   ἀλλ᾽ ἡ μάλιστα τοῦ μύθου καὶ ἡ μάλιστα τῆς πράξεως ἡ εἰρημένη
ἐστίν· ἡ γὰρ τοιαύτη ἀναγνώρισις καὶ περιπέτεια ἢ ἔλεον 4
1452 b ἕξει ἢ φόβον, οἵων πράξεων ἡ τραγῳδία μίμησις ὑπόκειται·
ἔτι δὲ καὶ τὸ ἀτυχεῖν καὶ τὸ εὐτυχεῖν ἐπὶ τῶν τοιούτων

---

20. ταῦτα] τάναντία Bonitz : τὰ ὕστερα Gomperz   23. καθάπερ εἴρηται secl.
Zeller : <ἢ> καθ᾽ ἃ προήρηται (deleto commate post μεταβολή) Essen
31. Post ἔχθραν add. ἢ ἄλλο τι Gomperz   32. ἅμα περιπετείᾳ Gomperz
33. γίνονται Aᶜ   οἵαν Bywater   35. ὡς ὅπερ Spengel : ὥσπερ Aᶜ :
ὅθ᾽ <ὅ>περ Gomperz   συμβαίνει Aᶜ : συμβαίνειν apogr.   36. ἢ
apogr. : εἰ Aᶜ   38. καὶ περιπέτεια secl. Susemihl   καὶ <μάλιστ᾽ ἐὰν
καὶ> περιπέτεια ἢ ἔλεον coni. Vahlen   1452 b 1. οἵων apogr.: οἷον Aᶜ
2. ἔτι δὲ] ἐπειδὴ Susemihl (commate post ὑπόκειται posito)

necessary or probable result of the preceding action. It makes all the difference whether any given event is a case of *propter hoc* or *post hoc*.

XI   Reversal of the Situation is a change by which the action veers round to its opposite, subject always to our rule of probability or necessity. Thus in the Oedipus, the messenger comes to cheer Oedipus and free him from his alarms about his mother, but by revealing who he is, he produces the opposite effect. Again in the Lynceus, Lynceus is being led away to his death, and Danaus goes with him, meaning to slay him; but the outcome of the preceding incidents is that Danaus is killed and Lynceus saved.

Recognition, as the name indicates, is a change from 2 ignorance to knowledge, producing love or hate between the persons destined by the poet for good or bad fortune. The best form of recognition is coincident with a Reversal of the Situation, as in the Oedipus. There are indeed other 3 forms. Even inanimate things of the most trivial kind may in a sense be objects of recognition. Again, we may recognise or discover whether a person has done a thing or not. But the recognition which is most intimately connected with the plot and action is, as we have said, the recognition of persons. This recognition, combined 4 1452 b with Reversal, will produce either pity or fear; and actions producing these effects are those which, by our definition, Tragedy represents. Moreover, it is upon such situations that the issues of good or bad fortune will depend.

συμβήσεται. ἐπεὶ δὴ ἡ ἀναγνώρισις τινῶν ἐστιν ἀναγνώρισις, 5
αἱ μὲν θατέρου πρὸς τὸν ἕτερον μόνον, ὅταν ᾖ δῆλος ἅτερος
5 τίς ἐστιν, ὁτὲ δὲ ἀμφοτέρους δεῖ ἀναγνωρίσαι, οἷον ἡ
μὲν Ἰφιγένεια τῷ Ὀρέστῃ ἀνεγνωρίσθη ἐκ τῆς πέμψεως
τῆς ἐπιστολῆς, ἐκείνου δὲ πρὸς τὴν Ἰφιγένειαν ἄλλης ἔδει
ἀναγνωρίσεως.

Δύο μὲν οὖν τοῦ μύθου μέρη περὶ ταῦτ᾽ ἐστί, περιπέτεια 6
10 καὶ ἀναγνώρισις, τρίτον δὲ πάθος.   [τούτων δὲ περιπέτεια μὲν
καὶ ἀναγνώρισις εἴρηται,] πάθος δέ ἐστι πρᾶξις φθαρτικὴ ἢ
ὀδυνηρά, οἷον οἵ τε ἐν τῷ φανερῷ θάνατοι καὶ αἱ περι-
ωδυνίαι καὶ τρώσεις καὶ ὅσα τοιαῦτα.

XII   [Μέρη δὲ τραγῳδίας οἷς μὲν ὡς εἴδεσι δεῖ χρῆσθαι
15 πρότερον εἴπομεν, κατὰ δὲ τὸ ποσὸν καὶ εἰς ἃ διαιρεῖται
κεχωρισμένα τάδε ἐστίν, πρόλογος ἐπεισόδιον ἔξοδος χο-
ρικόν, καὶ τούτου τὸ μὲν πάροδος τὸ δὲ στάσιμον· κοινὰ μὲν
ἁπάντων ταῦτα, ἴδια δὲ τὰ ἀπὸ τῆς σκηνῆς καὶ κόμμοι.
ἔστιν δὲ πρόλογος μὲν μέρος ὅλον τραγῳδίας τὸ πρὸ χοροῦ 2
20 παρόδου, ἐπεισόδιον δὲ μέρος ὅλον τραγῳδίας τὸ μεταξὺ
ὅλων χορικῶν μελῶν, ἔξοδος δὲ μέρος ὅλον τραγῳδίας
μεθ᾽ ὃ οὐκ ἔστι χοροῦ μέλος· χορικοῦ δὲ πάροδος μὲν ἡ
πρώτη λέξις ὅλη χοροῦ, στάσιμον δὲ μέλος χοροῦ τὸ ἄνευ
ἀναπαίστου καὶ τροχαίου, κόμμος δὲ θρῆνος κοινὸς χοροῦ καὶ
25 <τῶν> ἀπὸ σκηνῆς.   μέρη δὲ τραγῳδίας οἷς μὲν ὡς εἴδεσι δεῖ 3

---

3. ἐπεὶ δὴ Parisinus 2038 : ἐπειδὴ codd. cett.   4. ἕτερον] ἑταῖρον Σ, ut
videtur   ἅτερος Parisinus 2038, coni. Bernays : ἕτερος codd. cett.
7. ἐκείνου Bywater : ἐκείνω Aᶜ : ἐκείνῳ apogr.   9. περὶ om. Riccardianus 46
et, ut videtur, Σ   ταῦτ᾽] ταὐτὰ Twining   10. τούτων δὲ . . . εἴρηται
secl. Susemihl: om. Arabs   12. οἵ τε apogr. : ὅτε Aᵒ   14. totum
hoc cap. secl. Ritter, recte, ut opinor   17. κοινὰ μὲν . . . κόμμοι del.
Susemihl   19. προχωροῦ Aᶜ   23. ὅλη Westphal: ὅλου Aᵒ   25.
τῶν add. Christ praeeunte Ritter   ὡς εἴδεσι add. apogr.

Recognition, then, being between persons, it may happen 5
that one person only is recognised by the other—when
the latter is already known—or it may be necessary that
the recognition should be on both sides. Thus Iphigenia
is revealed to Orestes by the sending of the letter; but
another act of recognition is required to make Orestes
known to Iphigenia.

Two parts, then, of the Plot—Reversal of the Situation 6
and Recognition—turn upon surprises. A third part is
the Scene of Suffering. The Scene of Suffering is a
destructive or painful action, such as death on the stage,
bodily agony, wounds and the like.

XII   [The parts of Tragedy which must be treated as
elements of the whole have been already mentioned.
We now come to the quantitative parts—the separate
parts into which Tragedy is divided—namely, Prologue,
Episode, Exode, Choric song; this last being divided
into Parode and Stasimon. These are common to all
plays: peculiar to some are the songs of actors from the
stage and the Commoi.

The Prologue is that entire part of a tragedy which 2
precedes the Parode of the Chorus. The Episode is
that entire part of a tragedy which is between complete
choric songs. The Exode is that entire part of a tragedy
which has no choric song after it. Of the Choric part
the Parode is the first undivided utterance of the
Chorus: the Stasimon is a Choric ode without anapaests
or trochaic tetrameters: the Commos is a joint lamenta-
tion of Chorus and actors. The parts of Tragedy which 3
must be treated as elements of the whole have been

χρῆσθαι πρότερον εἴπαμεν, κατὰ δὲ τὸ ποσὸν καὶ εἰς ἃ
διαιρεῖται κεχωρισμένα ταῦτ᾽ ἐστίν.]

XIII   Ὧν δὲ δεῖ στοχάζεσθαι καὶ ἃ δεῖ εὐλαβεῖσθαι συν-
ιστάντας τοὺς μύθους καὶ πόθεν ἔσται τὸ τῆς τραγῳδίας ἔρ-
30 γον, ἐφεξῆς ἂν εἴη λεκτέον τοῖς νῦν εἰρημένοις. ἐπειδὴ οὖν 2
δεῖ τὴν σύνθεσιν εἶναι τῆς καλλίστης τραγῳδίας μὴ ἁπλῆν
ἀλλὰ πεπλεγμένην καὶ ταύτην φοβερῶν καὶ ἐλεεινῶν εἶναι
μιμητικήν (τοῦτο γὰρ ἴδιον τῆς τοιαύτης μιμήσεως ἐστίν),
πρῶτον μὲν δῆλον ὅτι οὔτε τοὺς ἐπιεικεῖς ἄνδρας δεῖ μετα-
35 βάλλοντας φαίνεσθαι ἐξ εὐτυχίας εἰς δυστυχίαν, οὐ γὰρ
φοβερὸν οὐδὲ ἐλεεινὸν τοῦτο ἀλλὰ μιαρόν ἐστιν· οὔτε τοὺς
μοχθηροὺς ἐξ ἀτυχίας εἰς εὐτυχίαν, ἀτραγῳδότατον γὰρ
τοῦτ᾽ ἐστὶ πάντων, οὐδὲν γὰρ ἔχει ὧν δεῖ, οὔτε γὰρ φιλάνθρω-
1453 a πον οὔτε ἐλεεινὸν οὔτε φοβερόν ἐστιν· οὐδ᾽ αὖ τὸν σφόδρα
πονηρὸν ἐξ εὐτυχίας εἰς δυστυχίαν μεταπίπτειν· τὸ μὲν γὰρ
φιλάνθρωπον ἔχοι ἂν ἡ τοιαύτη σύστασις ἀλλ᾽ οὔτε ἔλεον
οὔτε φόβον, ὁ μὲν γὰρ περὶ τὸν ἀνάξιόν ἐστιν δυστυχοῦντα,
5 ὁ δὲ περὶ τὸν ὅμοιον, ἔλεος μὲν περὶ τὸν ἀνάξιον, φόβος δὲ
περὶ τὸν ὅμοιον, ὥστε οὔτε ἐλεεινὸν οὔτε φοβερὸν ἔσται τὸ
συμβαῖνον. ὁ μεταξὺ ἄρα τούτων λοιπός. ἔστι δὲ τοιοῦτος 3
ὁ μήτε ἀρετῇ διαφέρων καὶ δικαιοσύνῃ, μήτε διὰ κακίαν
καὶ μοχθηρίαν μεταβάλλων εἰς τὴν δυστυχίαν ἀλλὰ δι᾽
10 ἁμαρτίαν τινά, τῶν ἐν μεγάλῃ δόξῃ ὄντων καὶ εὐτυχίᾳ,

---

28. ὧν Parisinus 2038 : ὡς Aᶜ   1453 a 1. αὖ τὸν Parisinus 2038 : αὐτὸ Aᶜ
5. ἔλεος μὲν . . . τὸν ὅμοιον secl. Ritter (non confirm. Arabs)

already mentioned.   The quantitative parts—the separate parts into which it is divided—are here enumerated.]

XIII   As the sequel to what has already been said, we must proceed to consider what the poet should aim at, and what he should avoid, in constructing his plots; and by what means the specific effect of Tragedy will be produced.

A perfect tragedy should, as we have seen, be arranged 2 not on the simple but on the complex plan.   It should, moreover, imitate actions which excite pity and fear, this being the distinctive mark of tragic imitation.   It follows plainly, in the first place, that the change of fortune presented must not be the spectacle of a virtuous man brought from prosperity to adversity: for this moves neither pity nor fear; it merely shocks us.   Nor, again, that of a bad man passing from adversity to prosperity : for nothing can be more alien to the spirit of Tragedy; it 1453 a possesses no single tragic quality; it neither satisfies the moral sense nor calls forth pity or fear.   Nor, again, should the downfall of the utter villain be exhibited.   A plot of this kind would, doubtless, satisfy the moral sense, but it would inspire neither pity nor fear; for pity is aroused by unmerited misfortune, fear by the misfortune of a man like ourselves.   Such an event, therefore, will be neither pitiful nor terrible. There remains, then, the character between these two 3 extremes,—that of a man who is not eminently good and just, yet whose misfortune is brought about not by vice or depravity, but by some error or frailty.   He must be one who is highly renowned and prosperous,—a

οἷον Οἰδίπους καὶ Θυέστης καὶ οἱ ἐκ τῶν τοιούτων γενῶν
ἐπιφανεῖς ἄνδρες. ἀνάγκη ἄρα τὸν καλῶς ἔχοντα μῦθον 4
ἁπλοῦν εἶναι μᾶλλον ἢ διπλοῦν, ὥσπερ τινές φασι, καὶ μεταβάλλειν οὐκ εἰς εὐτυχίαν ἐκ δυστυχίας ἀλλὰ τοὐναντίον
15 ἐξ εὐτυχίας εἰς δυστυχίαν, μὴ διὰ μοχθηρίαν ἀλλὰ δι'
ἁμαρτίαν μεγάλην ἢ οἵου εἴρηται ἢ βελτίονος μᾶλλον ἢ
χείρονος. σημεῖον δὲ καὶ τὸ γιγνόμενον· πρῶτον μὲν γὰρ 5
οἱ ποιηταὶ τοὺς τυχόντας μύθους ἀπηρίθμουν, νῦν δὲ περὶ
ὀλίγας οἰκίας αἱ κάλλισται τραγῳδίαι συντίθενται, οἷον
20 περὶ Ἀλκμέωνα καὶ Οἰδίπουν καὶ Ὀρέστην καὶ Μελέαγρον
καὶ Θυέστην καὶ Τήλεφον καὶ ὅσοις ἄλλοις συμβέβηκεν
ἢ παθεῖν δεινὰ ἢ ποιῆσαι. ἡ μὲν οὖν κατὰ τὴν τέχνην
καλλίστη τραγῳδία ἐκ ταύτης τῆς συστάσεώς ἐστι. διὸ καὶ 6
οἱ Εὐριπίδῃ ἐγκαλοῦντες τοῦτ' αὐτὸ ἁμαρτάνουσιν, ὅτι τοῦτο
25 δρᾷ ἐν ταῖς τραγῳδίαις καὶ πολλαὶ αὐτοῦ εἰς δυστυχίαν
τελευτῶσιν. τοῦτο γάρ ἐστιν ὥσπερ εἴρηται ὀρθόν· σημεῖον
δὲ μέγιστον· ἐπὶ γὰρ τῶν σκηνῶν καὶ τῶν ἀγώνων τραγικώταται αἱ τοιαῦται φαίνονται, ἂν κατορθωθῶσιν, καὶ ὁ
Εὐριπίδης εἰ καὶ τὰ ἄλλα μὴ εὖ οἰκονομεῖ ἀλλὰ τρα-
30 γικώτατός γε τῶν ποιητῶν φαίνεται. δευτέρα δ' ἡ πρώτη 7
λεγομένη ὑπὸ τινῶν ἐστιν [σύστασις] ἡ διπλῆν τε τὴν σύστασιν ἔχουσα, καθάπερ ἡ Ὀδύσσεια, καὶ τελευτῶσα ἐξ ἐναντίας τοῖς βελτίοσι καὶ χείροσιν. δοκεῖ δὲ εἶναι πρώτη διὰ
τὴν τῶν θεάτρων ἀσθένειαν· ἀκολουθοῦσι γὰρ οἱ ποιηταὶ
35 κατ' εὐχὴν ποιοῦντες τοῖς θεαταῖς. ἔστιν δὲ οὐχ αὕτη 8

11. Οἰδίπους apogr.: δίπους A^c   16. ἡ βελτίονος A^c   19. κάλλισται
secl. Christ: om. Arabs   20. Ἀλκμέωνα Bywater (cf. Meisterhans Gramm.
Att. Inschr. p. 35): Ἀλκμαίωνα codd.   24. τοῦτ' αὐτὸ Thurot: τὸ αὐτὸ
codd. : αὐτὸ Bywater: αὐτοὶ Reiz: secl. Margoliouth collato Arabe   25.
<αἱ> πολλαὶ Knebel: fort. πολλαὶ <αἱ> Tyrrell   31. σύστασις secl.
Twining   ἡ] ἢ A^c   33. βελτίωσι A^c   34. θεάτρων A^c et Σ, ut
videtur (cf. 1449 a 9, Herod. vi. 21 ἐς δάκρυα ἔπεσε τὸ θέητρον, Aristoph.
Eq. 233 τὸ γὰρ θέατρον δεξιόν): θεατῶν Riccardianus 16

personage like Oedipus, Thyestes, or other illustrious
men of such families.

A well constructed plot should, therefore, be single 4
in its issue, rather than double as some maintain. The
change of fortune should be not from bad to good, but,
reversely, from good to bad. It should come about as
the result not of vice, but of some great error or frailty,
in a character either such as we have described, or better
rather than worse. The practice of the stage bears out 5
our view. At first the poets recounted any legend that
came in their way. Now, the best tragedies are founded
on the story of a few houses,—on the fortunes of Alcmaeon,
Oedipus, Orestes, Meleager, Thyestes, Telephus, and those
others who have done or suffered something terrible. A
tragedy, then, to be perfect according to the rules of art
should be of this construction. Hence they are in error 6
who censure Euripides just because he follows this
principle in his plays, many of which end unhappily.
It is, as we have said, the right ending. The best proof
is that on the stage and in dramatic competition, such
plays, if well worked out, are the most tragic in effect ;
and Euripides, faulty though he may be in the general
management of his subject, yet is felt to be the most
tragic of the poets.

In the second rank comes the kind of tragedy which 7
some place first. Like the Odyssey, it has a double
thread of plot, and also an opposite catastrophe for the
good and for the bad. It is accounted the best because
of the weakness of the spectators ; for the poet is guided
in what he writes by the wishes of his audience. The 8
pleasure, however, thence derived is not the true tragic

48   XIII. 8—XIV. 4.   1453 a 36—1453 b 19

<ἤ> ἀπὸ τραγῳδίας ἡδονὴ ἀλλὰ μᾶλλον τῆς κωμῳδίας οἰκεία·
ἐκεῖ γὰρ οἳ ἂν ἔχθιστοι ὦσιν ἐν τῷ μύθῳ, οἷον Ὀρέστης
καὶ Αἴγισθος, φίλοι γενόμενοι ἐπὶ τελευτῆς ἐξέρχονται
καὶ ἀποθνῄσκει οὐδεὶς ὑπ᾽ οὐδενός.

XIV   Ἔστιν μὲν οὖν τὸ φοβερὸν καὶ ἐλεεινὸν ἐκ τῆς ὄψεως γί-
1453 b
γνεσθαι, ἔστιν δὲ καὶ ἐξ αὐτῆς τῆς συστάσεως τῶν πραγμάτων,
ὅπερ ἐστὶ πρότερον καὶ ποιητοῦ ἀμείνονος. δεῖ γὰρ καὶ ἄνευ
τοῦ ὁρᾶν οὕτω συνεστάναι τὸν μῦθον, ὥστε τὸν ἀκούοντα τὰ
5 πράγματα γινόμενα καὶ φρίττειν καὶ ἐλεεῖν ἐκ τῶν συμβαινόν-
των· ἅπερ ἂν πάθοι τις ἀκούων τὸν τοῦ Οἰδίπου μῦθον.
τὸ δὲ διὰ τῆς ὄψεως τοῦτο παρασκευάζειν ἀτεχνό- 2
τερον καὶ χορηγίας δεόμενόν ἐστιν. οἱ δὲ μὴ τὸ φοβερὸν διὰ τῆς ὄψεως ἀλλὰ τὸ τερατῶδες μόνον παρασκευά-
10 ζοντες οὐδὲν τραγῳδίᾳ κοινωνοῦσιν· οὐ γὰρ πᾶσαν δεῖ
ζητεῖν ἡδονὴν ἀπὸ τραγῳδίας ἀλλὰ τὴν οἰκείαν. ἐπεὶ δὲ 3
τὴν ἀπὸ ἐλέου καὶ φόβου διὰ μιμήσεως δεῖ ἡδονὴν παρασκευάζειν τὸν ποιητήν, φανερὸν ὡς τοῦτο ἐν τοῖς πράγμασιν ἐμποιητέον. ποῖα οὖν δεινὰ ἢ ποῖα οἰκτρὰ φαίνεται
15 τῶν συμπιπτόντων, λάβωμεν. ἀνάγκη δὴ ἢ φίλων εἶναι 4
πρὸς ἀλλήλους τὰς τοιαύτας πράξεις ἢ ἐχθρῶν ἢ μηδε-
τέρων. ἂν μὲν οὖν ἐχθρὸς ἐχθρόν, οὐδὲν ἐλεεινὸν οὔτε
ποιῶν οὔτε μέλλων, πλὴν κατ᾽ αὐτὸ τὸ πάθος· οὐδ᾽ ἂν
μηδετέρως ἔχοντες· ὅταν δ᾽ ἐν ταῖς φιλίαις ἐγγένηται τὰ

---

36. <ἤ> coni. Vahlen   37. οἳ ἂν Bonitz : ἂν οἱ codd. : κἂν οἱ Spengel
1453 b 4. συνεστάναι Aᶜ   7. ἀτεχνότερον apogr. : ἀτεχνώτερον Aᶜ   15.
δὴ Spengel : δὲ codd.   17. ἐχθρὸν <ἀποκτείνῃ> Pazzi   <φοβερὸν>
οὐδ᾽ ἐλεεινὸν Ueberweg

pleasure. It is proper rather to Comedy, where those who, in the piece, are the deadliest enemies—like Orestes and Aegisthus—quit the stage as friends at the close, and no one slays or is slain.

XIV   Fear and pity may be aroused by spectacular means;
1453 b but they may also result from the inner structure of the piece, which is the better way, and indicates a superior poet. For the plot ought to be so constructed that, even without the aid of the eye, he who hears the tale told will thrill with horror and melt to pity at what takes place. This is the impression we should receive from hearing the story of the Oedipus. But to produce this 2 effect by the mere spectacle is a less artistic method, and dependent on extraneous aids. Those who employ spectacular means to create a sense not of the terrible but only of the monstrous, are strangers to the purpose of Tragedy; for we must not demand of Tragedy any and every kind of pleasure, but only that which is proper to it. And since the pleasure which the poet should 3 afford is that which comes from pity and fear through imitation, it is evident that this quality must be impressed upon the incidents.

Let us then determine what are the circumstances which strike us as terrible or pitiful.

Actions capable of this effect must happen between 4 persons who are either friends or enemies or indifferent to one another. If an enemy kills an enemy, there is nothing to excite pity either in the act or the intention, —except so far as the suffering in itself is pitiful. So again with indifferent persons. But when the tragic incident occurs between those who are near or dear to

E

20 πάθη, οἷον εἰ ἀδελφὸς ἀδελφὸν ἢ υἱὸς πατέρα ἢ μήτηρ
υἱὸν ἢ υἱὸς μητέρα ἀποκτείνει ἢ μέλλει ἤ τι ἄλλο τοιοῦτον
δρᾷ, ταῦτα ζητητέον. τοὺς μὲν οὖν παρειλημμένους μύθους 5
λύειν οὐκ ἔστιν, λέγω δὲ οἷον τὴν Κλυταιμήστραν ἀποθα-
νοῦσαν ὑπὸ τοῦ Ὀρέστου καὶ τὴν Ἐριφύλην ὑπὸ τοῦ Ἀλκμέ-
25 ωνος, αὐτὸν δὲ εὑρίσκειν δεῖ καὶ τοῖς παραδεδομένοις χρῆσθαι καλῶς. τὸ δὲ καλῶς τί λέγομεν, εἴπωμεν σαφέστερον.
ἔστι μὲν γὰρ οὕτω γίνεσθαι τὴν πρᾶξιν, ὥσπερ οἱ παλαιοὶ 6
ἐποίουν εἰδότας καὶ γιγνώσκοντας, καθάπερ καὶ Εὐριπίδης
ἐποίησεν ἀποκτείνουσαν τοὺς παῖδας τὴν Μήδειαν· ἔστιν δὲ
30 πρᾶξαι μέν, ἀγνοοῦντας δὲ πρᾶξαι τὸ δεινόν, εἶθ' ὕστερον
ἀναγνωρίσαι τὴν φιλίαν, ὥσπερ ὁ Σοφοκλέους Οἰδίπους· τοῦτο μὲν οὖν ἔξω τοῦ δράματος, ἐν δ' αὐτῇ τῇ τραγῳδίᾳ οἷον
ὁ Ἀλκμέων ὁ Ἀστυδάμαντος ἢ ὁ Τηλέγονος ὁ ἐν τῷ τραυ-
ματίᾳ Ὀδυσσεῖ. ἔτι δὲ τρίτον παρὰ ταῦτα * * τὸ μέλλον- 7
35 τα ποιεῖν τι τῶν ἀνηκέστων δι' ἄγνοιαν ἀναγνωρίσαι πρὶν
ποιῆσαι. καὶ παρὰ ταῦτα οὐκ ἔστιν ἄλλως. ἢ γὰρ πρᾶξαι
ἀνάγκη ἢ μὴ καὶ εἰδότας ἢ μὴ εἰδότας. τούτων δὲ τὸ μὲν
γινώσκοντα μελλῆσαι καὶ μὴ πρᾶξαι χείριστον· τό τε γὰρ
μιαρὸν ἔχει, καὶ οὐ τραγικόν· ἀπαθὲς γάρ. διόπερ οὐδεὶς
1454 a ποιεῖ ὁμοίως, εἰ μὴ ὀλιγάκις, οἷον ἐν Ἀντιγόνῃ τὸν Κρέοντα
ὁ Αἵμων. τὸ δὲ πρᾶξαι δεύτερον. βέλτιον δὲ τὸ ἀγνοοῦντα 8

20. οἷον εἰ Sylburg : οἷον ἢ codd.   22. δρᾷ apogr. : δρᾶν A⁰   23.
Κλυταιμήστραν Σ : Κλυταιμνήστραν codd.   24. Ἀλκμαίωνος codd.   26.
εἴπωμεν apogr. : εἴπομεν A⁰   33. Ἀλκμαίων ὁ Gryphius : Ἀλκμαίωνος codd.
34. παρὰ ταῦτα, <τὸ μελλῆσαι γινώσκοντα καὶ μὴ ποιῆσαι, καὶ τέταρτον> coni.
Vahlen   τὸ Bonitz : τὸν codd.   1454 a 2. δεύτερον] κράτιστον Neidhardt, recte, ut opinor

one another—if, for example, a brother kills, or intends to kill, a brother, a son his father, a mother her son, a son his mother, or any other deed of the kind is done—these are the situations to be looked for by the poet. He may not indeed destroy the framework of the received legends—the 5 fact, for instance, that Clytemnestra was slain by Orestes and Eriphyle by Alcmaeon—but he ought to show invention of his own, and skilfully handle the traditional material. Let us explain more clearly what is meant by skilful handling.

The action may be done consciously and with know- 6 ledge of the persons, in the manner of the older poets. It is thus too that Euripides makes Medea slay her children. Or, again, the deed of horror may be done, but done in ignorance, and the tie of kinship or friend- ship be discovered afterwards. The Oedipus of Sophocles is an example. Here, indeed, the incident is outside the drama proper ; but cases occur where it falls within the action of the play : one may cite the Alcmaeon of Astydamas, or Telegonus in the Wounded Odysseus. Again, 7 there is a third case,—< to be about to act with knowledge of the persons and then not to act. The fourth case is> when some one is about to do an irreparable deed through ignorance, and makes the discovery before it is done. These are the only possible ways. For the deed must either be done or not done,—and that wittingly or unwittingly. But of all these ways, to be about to act knowing the persons, and then not to act, is the worst. It is shocking without being tragic, for no disaster follows. It is, there- 1454 a fore, never, or very rarely, found in poetry. One instance, however, is in the Antigone, where Haemon threatens to kill Creon. The next and better way is that the deed 8

μὲν πρᾶξαι, πράξαντα δὲ ἀναγνωρίσαι· τό τε γὰρ μιαρὸν
οὐ πρόσεστιν καὶ ἡ ἀναγνώρισις ἐκπληκτικόν.   κράτιστον δὲ 9
5 τὸ τελευταῖον, λέγω δὲ οἷον ἐν τῷ Κρεσφόντῃ ἡ Μερόπη
μέλλει τὸν υἱὸν ἀποκτείνειν, ἀποκτείνει δὲ οὔ, ἀλλ᾽ ἀν-
εγνώρισε, καὶ ἐν τῇ Ἰφιγενείᾳ ἡ ἀδελφὴ τὸν ἀδελφόν, καὶ
ἐν τῇ Ἕλλῃ ὁ υἱὸς τὴν μητέρα ἐκδιδόναι μέλλων ἀνεγνώρισεν.   διὰ γὰρ τοῦτο, ὅπερ πάλαι εἴρηται, οὐ περὶ πολλὰ
10 γένη αἱ τραγῳδίαι εἰσίν.   ζητοῦντες γὰρ οὐκ ἀπὸ τέχνης
ἀλλ᾽ ἀπὸ τύχης εὗρον τὸ τοιοῦτον παρασκευάζειν ἐν τοῖς
μύθοις· ἀναγκάζονται οὖν ἐπὶ ταύτας τὰς οἰκίας ἀπαντᾶν
ὅσαις τὰ τοιαῦτα συμβέβηκε πάθη.   περὶ μὲν οὖν τῆς
τῶν πραγμάτων συστάσεως καὶ ποίους τινὰς εἶναι δεῖ τοὺς
15 μύθους εἴρηται ἱκανῶς.

XV   Περὶ δὲ τὰ ἤθη τέτταρά ἐστιν ὧν δεῖ στοχάζεσθαι, ἓν
μὲν καὶ πρῶτον ὅπως χρηστὰ ᾖ.   ἕξει δὲ ἦθος μὲν ἐὰν
ὥσπερ ἐλέχθη ποιῇ φανερὸν ὁ λόγος ἢ ἡ πρᾶξις προαίρεσίν
τινα, χρηστὸν δὲ ἐὰν χρηστήν.   ἔστιν δὲ ἐν ἑκάστῳ
20 γένει· καὶ γὰρ γυνή ἐστιν χρηστὴ καὶ δοῦλος, καίτοι
γε ἴσως τούτων τὸ μὲν χεῖρον, τὸ δὲ ὅλως φαῦλόν
ἐστιν.   δεύτερον δὲ τὸ ἁρμόττοντα· ἔστιν γὰρ ἀνδρεῖον 2
μέν τι ἦθος, ἀλλ᾽ οὐχ ἁρμόττον γυναικὶ τὸ ἀνδρείαν ἢ
δεινὴν εἶναι.   τρίτον δὲ τὸ ὅμοιον.   τοῦτο γὰρ ἕτερον τοῦ 3

4. κράτιστον] δεύτερον Neidhardt, recte, ut opinor   8. Ἕλλῃ] Ἀντιόπῃ
Valckenaer   18. φανερὰν Ald., Bekker   19. τινα Parisinus 2038 :
τινὰ ᾖ Aᶜ : τινα <ἢ τις ἂν> ᾖ coni. Vahlen (? cf. Arab.): <ἤν>τινα <δ>ἢ
Bywater: τινα ἢ <φυγήν> Düntzer : τινα <ἔχοντα, ὁποία τις ἂν> ᾖ
Gomperz: τινα, φαῦλον μὲν ἐὰν φαύλῃ ᾖ apogr.   22. τὸ Vahlen (ed. 1):
τὰ codd.   23. τι ἦθος Hermann : τὸ ἦθος codd.   τὸ apogr.: * * τῷ
Aᶜ: οὕτως Vahlen collato Pol. iii. 4. 1277 b 20. Desunt in Arabe verba
τῷ ἀνδρείαν . . . εἶναι, quorum vicem supplet haec clausula, 'ne ut appareat
quidem in ea omnino' (Margoliouth); unde Diels τῷ ἀνδρείαν . . . εἶναι
glossema esse arbitratus quod veram lectionem eiecerit. scribendum esse coni.

should be perpetrated. Still better, that it should be
perpetrated in ignorance, and the discovery made afterwards. There is then nothing to shock us, while the
discovery produces a startling effect. The last case is the 9
best, as when in the Cresphontes Merope is about to slay
her son, but, recognising who he is, spares his life. So
in the Iphigenia, the sister recognises the brother just in
time. Again in the Helle, the son recognises the mother
when on the point of giving her up. This, then, is why
a few families only, as has been already observed, furnish
the subjects of tragedy. It was not art, but happy
chance, that led the poets in search of subjects to
impress the tragic quality upon their plots. They are
compelled, therefore, to have recourse to those houses
whose history contains moving incidents like these.

Enough has now been said concerning the structure
of the incidents, and the right kind of plot.

XV   In respect of Character there are four things to be
aimed at. First, and most important, it must be good.
Now any speech or action that manifests moral purpose
of any kind will be expressive of character : the character
will be good if the purpose is good. This rule is relative
to each class. Even a woman may be good, and also a
slave ; though the woman may be said to be an inferior
being, and the slave quite worthless. The second thing 2
to aim at is propriety. There is a type of manly valour ;
but valour in a woman, or unscrupulous cleverness, is inappropriate. Thirdly, character must be true to life : for 3

5 χρηστὸν τὸ ἦθος καὶ ἁρμόττον ποιῆσαι ὥσπερ εἴρηται.
τέταρτον δὲ τὸ ὁμαλόν. κἂν γὰρ ἀνώμαλός τις ᾖ ὁ τὴν 4
μίμησιν παρέχων καὶ τοιοῦτον ἦθος ὑποτιθείς, ὅμως ὁμα-
λῶς ἀνώμαλον δεῖ εἶναι. ἔστιν δὲ παράδειγμα πονηρίας μὲν 5
ἤθους μὴ ἀναγκαίου οἷον ὁ Μενέλαος ὁ ἐν τῷ Ὀρέστῃ, τοῦ
30 δὲ ἀπρεποῦς καὶ μὴ ἁρμόττοντος ὅ τε θρῆνος Ὀδυσσέως ἐν
τῇ Σκύλλῃ καὶ ἡ τῆς Μελανίππης ῥῆσις, τοῦ δὲ ἀνωμάλου
ἡ ἐν Αὐλίδι Ἰφιγένεια· οὐδὲν γὰρ ἔοικεν ἡ ἱκετεύουσα τῇ
ὑστέρᾳ.   χρὴ δὲ καὶ ἐν τοῖς ἤθεσιν ὥσπερ καὶ ἐν τῇ τῶν 6
πραγμάτων συστάσει ἀεὶ ζητεῖν ἢ τὸ ἀναγκαῖον ἢ τὸ εἰκός,
35 ὥστε τὸν τοιοῦτον τὰ τοιαῦτα λέγειν ἢ πράττειν ᾖ ἀναγκαῖον
ἢ εἰκός, καὶ τοῦτο μετὰ τοῦτο γίνεσθαι ᾖ ἀναγκαῖον ἢ εἰκός.

φανερὸν οὖν ὅτι καὶ τὰς λύσεις τῶν μύθων ἐξ αὐτοῦ δεῖ τοῦ 7
1454 b μύθου συμβαίνειν, καὶ μὴ ὥσπερ ἐν τῇ Μηδείᾳ ἀπὸ μη-
χανῆς καὶ ἐν τῇ Ἰλιάδι τὰ περὶ τὸν ἀπόπλουν· ἀλλὰ μη-
χανῇ χρηστέον ἐπὶ τὰ ἔξω τοῦ δράματος, ἢ ὅσα πρὸ τοῦ
γέγονεν ἃ οὐχ οἷόν τε ἄνθρωπον εἰδέναι, ἢ ὅσα ὕστερον, ἃ
5 δεῖται προαγορεύσεως καὶ ἀγγελίας· ἅπαντα γὰρ ἀποδί-

ὥστε μηδὲ φαίνεσθαι καθόλου: 'The manly character is indeed sometimes
found even in a woman (ἔστιν γὰρ ἀνδρεῖον μὲν τὸ ἦθος), but it is not
appropriate to her, so that it never appears as a general characteristic
of the sex.' Sed hoc aliter dicendum fuisse suspicari licet ; itaque Susemihl
huiusmodi aliquid tentavit, ὥστε μηδὲ φαίνεσθαι ἐν αὐτῇ ὡς ἐπίπαν, vel ὡς
ἐπίπαν εἰπεῖν : 'There is indeed a character (τι ἦθος) of manly courage, but it
is not appropriate to a woman, and as a rule is not found in her at all'
25. lacunam ante ὥσπερ statuit Spengel   ὥσπερ εἴρηται fort. secludendum : ἅπερ εἴρηται Hermann   29. ἀναγκαίου Marcianus 215, Bywater :
ἀναγκαῖον A^c : ἀναγκαίας Thurot   οἷον secl. E. Müller   30. <ὁ>
Ὀδυσσέως Tucker : <ὁ τοῦ> Ὀδυσσέως Bywater   31. Σκύλλῃ τῇ θαλαττίᾳ
Σ, ut videtur   post ῥῆσις exemplum τοῦ ἀνομοίου intercidisse coni.
Vettori   35 et 36. ᾖ Hermann : ἢ codd.   36. <ὡς> καὶ τοῦτο
olim Bywater   37. τῶν μύθων] τῶν ἠθῶν Σ, ut videtur   1454
b 2. ἀπόπλουν Riccardianus 16 : ἀνάπλουν Parisinus 2038, Σ, ut videtur :
ἀπλοῦν A^c   3. ἐπὶ τὰ apogr.: ἔπειτα A^c   4. οἷόν τε apogr.:
οἴονται A^c   post ὕστερον distinguit W. R. Hardie, qui ἀγγελίας ad ὅσα
πρὸ τοῦ refert, προαγορεύσεως ad ὅσα ὕστερον

this is a distinct thing from goodness and propriety, as here described. The fourth point is consistency: for though 4 the subject of the imitation, who suggested the type, be inconsistent, still he must be consistently inconsistent. As an example of motiveless degradation of character, we 5 have Menelaus in the Orestes: of character indecorous and inappropriate, the lament of Odysseus in the Scylla, and the speech of Melanippe: of inconsistency, the Iphigenia at Aulis,—for Iphigenia the suppliant in no way resembles her later self.

As in the structure of the plot, so too in the por- 6 traiture of character, the poet should always aim either at the necessary or the probable. Thus a person of a given character should speak or act in a given way, by the rule either of necessity or of probability; just as this event should follow that by necessary or probable sequence. It is therefore evident that the unravelling 7 of the plot, no less than the complication, must arise out 1454 b of the plot itself, it must not be brought about by the *Deus ex Machina*—as in the Medea, or in the Return of the Greeks in the Iliad. The *Deus ex Machina* should be employed only for events external to the drama,— for antecedent or subsequent events, which lie beyond the range of human knowledge, and which require to be

δομεν τοῖς θεοῖς ὁρᾶν.   ἄλογον δὲ μηδὲν εἶναι ἐν τοῖς πράγμασιν, εἰ δὲ μή, ἔξω τῆς τραγῳδίας, οἷον τὸ ἐν τῷ
Οἰδίποδι τῷ Σοφοκλέους.   ἐπεὶ δὲ μίμησίς ἐστιν ἡ τραγῳ- 8
δία βελτιόνων <ἢ καθ'> ἡμᾶς, δεῖ μιμεῖσθαι τοὺς ἀγαθοὺς
10 εἰκονογράφους· καὶ γὰρ ἐκεῖνοι ἀποδιδόντες τὴν ἰδίαν μορφὴν
ὁμοίους ποιοῦντες καλλίους γράφουσιν· οὕτω καὶ τὸν ποιητὴν
μιμούμενον καὶ ὀργίλους καὶ ῥαθύμους καὶ τἆλλα τὰ τοιαῦτα
ἔχοντας ἐπὶ τῶν ἠθῶν, τοιούτους ὄντας ἐπιεικεῖς ποιεῖν
[παράδειγμα σκληρότητος], οἷον τὸν Ἀχιλλέα Ἀγάθων καὶ
15 Ὅμηρος.   ταῦτα δὴ <δεῖ> διατηρεῖν καὶ πρὸς τούτοις τὰς 9
παρὰ τὰ ἐξ ἀνάγκης ἀκολουθούσας αἰσθήσεις τῇ ποιητικῇ·
καὶ γὰρ κατ' αὐτὰς ἔστιν ἁμαρτάνειν πολλάκις· εἴρηται
δὲ περὶ αὐτῶν ἐν τοῖς ἐκδεδομένοις λόγοις ἱκανῶς.

XVI   Ἀναγνώρισις δὲ τί μέν ἐστιν, εἴρηται πρότερον· εἴδη
20 δὲ ἀναγνωρίσεως, πρώτη μὲν ἡ ἀτεχνοτάτη καὶ ᾗ πλείστῃ
χρῶνται δι' ἀπορίαν, ἡ διὰ τῶν σημείων.   τούτων δὲ τὰ μὲν 2
σύμφυτα, οἷον "λόγχην ἣν φοροῦσι Γηγενεῖς" ἢ ἀστέρας
οἵους ἐν τῷ Θυέστῃ Καρκίνος, τὰ δὲ ἐπίκτητα, καὶ τούτων
τὰ μὲν ἐν τῷ σώματι, οἷον οὐλαί, τὰ δὲ ἐκτός, τὰ περι-
25 δέραια καὶ οἷον ἐν τῇ Τυροῖ διὰ τῆς σκάφης.   ἔστιν δὲ καὶ
τούτοις χρῆσθαι ἢ βέλτιον ἢ χεῖρον, οἷον Ὀδυσσεὺς διὰ 3
τῆς οὐλῆς ἄλλως ἀνεγνωρίσθη ὑπὸ τῆς τροφοῦ καὶ ἄλλως

---

7. τὸ Aᶜ (? τω pr. Aᶜ) : τὸ vel τῷ apogr. : τὰ Ald.   9. ἢ καθ' add. Stahr
(confirm. Arabs)   14. παράδειγμα σκληρότητος secl. Bywater : οἷον ante
παράδειγμα ponit Tucker   ἀγάθων apogr. : ἀγαθῶν Aᶜ   15. δὴ δεῖ Ald. :
δὴ Aᶜ : δεῖ apogr.   τὰς παρὰ τὰ vel τὰ παρὰ τὰς apogr. : τὰς παρὰ τὰς
Aᶜ   20. ᾗ πλείστῃ apogr. : ἡ πλείστη Aᶜ   21. ἡ apogr. : ἢ Aᶜ   22.
ἀστέρες Richards   24. περιδέραια apogr. pauca : περιδέρρεα Aᶜ   25. οἷον
apogr. : οἱ Aᶜ   σκάφης] σπάθης Σ, ut videtur, 'ensis' Arabs : (R. Ellis)
26. <ὁ> Ὀδυσσεὺς Bywater

reported or foretold ; for to the gods we ascribe the power of seeing all things. Within the action there must be nothing irrational. If the irrational cannot be excluded, it should be outside the scope of the tragedy. Such is the irrational element in the Oedipus of Sophocles.

Again, since Tragedy is an imitation of persons who 8 are above the common level, the example of good portrait-painters should be followed. They, while reproducing the distinctive form of the original, make a likeness which is true to life and yet more beautiful. So too the poet, in representing men who are irascible or indolent, or have other defects of character, should preserve the type and yet ennoble it. In this way Achilles is portrayed by Agathon and Homer.

These then are rules the poet should observe. Nor 9 should he neglect those appeals to the senses, which, though not among the essentials, are the concomitants of poetry ; for here too there is much room for error. But of this enough has been said in our published treatises.

XVI   What Recognition is has been already explained. We will now enumerate its kinds.

First, the least artistic form, which, from poverty of wit, is most commonly employed—recognition by signs. Of these some are congenital,—such as 'the spear which 2 the earth-born race bear on their bodies,' or the stars introduced by Carcinus in his Thyestes. Others are acquired after birth ; and of these some are bodily marks, as scars ; some external tokens, as necklaces, or the little ark in the Tyro by which the discovery is effected. Even 3 these admit of more or less skilful treatment. Thus in the recognition of Odysseus by his scar, the discovery is

ὑπὸ τῶν συβοτῶν· εἰσὶ γὰρ αἱ μὲν πίστεως ἕνεκα ἀτεχνό-
τεραι, καὶ αἱ τοιαῦται πᾶσαι, αἱ δὲ ἐκ περιπετείας, ὥσ-
30 περ ἡ ἐν τοῖς Νίπτροις, βελτίους. δεύτεραι δὲ αἱ πεποιη- 4
μέναι ὑπὸ τοῦ ποιητοῦ, διὸ ἄτεχνοι. οἷον Ὀρέστης ἐν τῇ
Ἰφιγενείᾳ ἀνεγνώρισεν ὅτι Ὀρέστης· ἐκείνη μὲν γὰρ διὰ τῆς
ἐπιστολῆς, ἐκεῖνος δὲ αὐτὸς λέγει ἃ βούλεται ὁ ποιητὴς ἀλλ᾽
οὐχ ὁ μῦθος· διὸ ἐγγύς τι τῆς εἰρημένης ἁμαρτίας ἐστίν, ἐξῆν
35 γὰρ ἂν ἔνια καὶ ἐνεγκεῖν. καὶ ἐν τῷ Σοφοκλέους Τηρεῖ ἡ
τῆς κερκίδος φωνή. ἡ τρίτη διὰ μνήμης, τῷ αἰσθέσθαι 5
1455 a τι ἰδόντα, ὥσπερ ἡ ἐν Κυπρίοις τοῖς Δικαιογένους· ἰδὼν γὰρ
τὴν γραφὴν ἔκλαυσεν· καὶ ἡ ἐν Ἀλκίνου ἀπολόγῳ· ἀκούων
γὰρ τοῦ κιθαριστοῦ καὶ μνησθεὶς ἐδάκρυσεν, ὅθεν ἀνεγνω-
ρίσθησαν. τετάρτη δὲ ἡ ἐκ συλλογισμοῦ, οἷον ἐν Χοηφόροις, 6
5 ὅτι ὅμοιός τις ἐλήλυθεν, ὅμοιος δὲ οὐθεὶς ἀλλ᾽ ἢ ὁ Ὀρέστης,
οὗτος ἄρα ἐλήλυθεν. καὶ ἡ Πολυΐδου τοῦ σοφιστοῦ περὶ τῆς
Ἰφιγενείας· εἰκὸς γὰρ τὸν Ὀρέστην συλλογίσασθαι ὅτι ἥ τ᾽
ἀδελφὴ ἐτύθη καὶ αὐτῷ συμβαίνει θύεσθαι. καὶ ἐν τῷ
Θεοδέκτου Τυδεῖ, ὅτι ἐλθὼν ὡς εὑρήσων υἱὸν αὐτὸς ἀπόλ-
10 λυται. καὶ ἡ ἐν τοῖς Φινείδαις. ἰδοῦσαι γὰρ τὸν τόπον συν-
ελογίσαντο τὴν εἱμαρμένην ὅτι ἐν τούτῳ εἵμαρτο ἀποθανεῖν

31. οἷον <ὁ> Bywater   Ὀρέστης secl. Diels (confirmante fort. Arabe)
32. ἀνεγνωρίσθη Spengel   34. διὸ ἐγγύς τι Vahlen : δι᾽ ὅτι ἐγγὺς Aᶜ :
διό τι ἐγγὺς Bywater   35. alia Σ legisse videtur, 'haec sunt in eo
quod dixit Sophocles se audiisse vocem radii contempti' (Arabs) ; unde
W. R. Hardie coni. τοιαύτη δ᾽ ἡ ἐν τῷ [Σοφοκλέους ?] Τηρεῖ "τῆς ἀναύδου,"
φησί, "κερκίδος φωνὴν κλύω"   36. ἡ τρίτη Spengel : ἤτοι τηι Aᶜ : τρίτη ἡ
apogr.   αἰσθεσθαί Aᶜ   1455 a 1. τοῖς apogr. : τῆς Aᶜ   2. ἀπολόγῳ
Parisinus 2038 : ἀπὸ λόγων Aᶜ   4. Χοηφόροις Vettori : χλοηφόροις Aᶜ
6. Πολυΐδου Tyrwhitt : πολυείδου apogr. : πολυείδους Aᶜ   10. Φινείδαις
Reiz : φινίδαις codd.

made in one way by the nurse, in another by the swine-
herds. The use of tokens for the express purpose of proof
—and, indeed, any formal proof with or without tokens
—is a less artistic mode of recognition. A better kind
is that which comes about by a turn of incident, as in
the Bath Scene in the Odyssey.

Next come the recognitions invented at will by the 4
poet, and on that account wanting in art. For example,
Orestes in the Iphigenia reveals the fact that he is
Orestes. She, indeed, makes herself known by the letter;
but he, by speaking himself, and saying what the poet,
not what the plot requires. This, therefore, is nearly
allied to the fault above mentioned:—for Orestes might
as well have brought tokens with him. Another similar
instance is the 'voice of the shuttle' in the Tereus of
Sophocles.

1455 a   The third kind depends on memory when the sight of 5
some object awakens a feeling: as in the Cyprians of
Dicaeogenes, where the hero breaks into tears on seeing
the picture; or again in the 'Lay of Alcinous,' where
Odysseus, hearing the minstrel play the lyre, recalls the
past and weeps ; and hence the recognition.

The fourth kind is by process of reasoning. Thus in 6
the Choëphori :—'Some one resembling me has come :
no one resembles me but Orestes : therefore Orestes has
come.' Such too is the discovery made by Iphigenia
in the play of Polyidus the Sophist. It was a natural
reflexion for Orestes to make, 'So I too must die at the
altar like my sister.' So, again, in the Tydeus of
Theodectes, the father says, 'I came to find my son, and
I lose my own life.' So too in the Phineidae: the
women, on seeing the place, inferred their fate :—' Here

αὐταῖς, καὶ γὰρ ἐξετέθησαν ἐνταῦθα. ἔστιν δέ τις καὶ συν- 7
θετὴ ἐκ παραλογισμοῦ τοῦ θατέρου, οἷον ἐν τῷ 'Οδυσσεῖ τῷ
ψευδαγγέλῳ· ὁ μὲν γὰρ τὸ τόξον ἔφη * * * γνώσεσθαι ὃ
15 οὐχ ἑωράκει, τὸ δὲ ὡς δὴ ἐκείνου ἀναγνωριοῦντος διὰ τούτου
ποιῆσαι, παραλογισμός. πασῶν δὲ βελτίστη ἀναγνώρισις ἡ ἐξ 8
αὐτῶν τῶν πραγμάτων τῆς ἐκπλήξεως γιγνομένης δι' εἰκότων, οἷον [ὁ] ἐν τῷ Σοφοκλέους Οἰδίποδι καὶ τῇ 'Ιφιγενείᾳ·
εἰκὸς γὰρ βούλεσθαι ἐπιθεῖναι γράμματα. αἱ γὰρ τοιαῦται
20 μόναι ἄνευ τῶν πεποιημένων σημείων καὶ δερσίων. δεύτεραι δὲ αἱ ἐκ συλλογισμοῦ.

XVII   Δεῖ δὲ τοὺς μύθους συνιστάναι καὶ τῇ λέξει συναπ-
εργάζεσθαι ὅτι μάλιστα πρὸ ὀμμάτων τιθέμενον· οὕτω γὰρ
ἂν ἐναργέστατα [ὁ] ὁρῶν ὥσπερ παρ' αὐτοῖς γιγνόμενος τοῖς
25 πραττομένοις εὑρίσκοι τὸ πρέπον καὶ ἥκιστα ἂν λανθάνοι
τὰ ὑπεναντία. σημεῖον δὲ τούτου ὃ ἐπετιμᾶτο Καρκίνῳ·
ὁ γὰρ 'Αμφιάραος ἐξ ἱεροῦ ἀνήει, ὃ μὴ ὁρῶντα [τὸν
θεατὴν] ἐλάνθανεν, ἐπὶ δὲ τῆς σκηνῆς ἐξέπεσεν δυσχερα-
νάντων τοῦτο τῶν θεατῶν. ὅσα δὲ δυνατὸν καὶ τοῖς σχή-
30 μασιν συναπεργαζόμενον. πιθανώτατοι γὰρ ἀπὸ τῆς αὐτῆς 2

13. θατέρου Bursian, praeeunte Hermann : θεάτρου codd.   14–16. ὁ μὲν
γάρ . . . παραλογισμός] multo plura hic legisse videtur Arabs (Margoliouth) ;
post ἔφη lacunam indicavi ; vide quae supra in versione addidi, Arabem
quoad potui secutus   14. ὁ μὲν apogr.: τὸ μὲν A° το ante τόξον om.
apogr.   15. δὴ Tyrwhitt: δι' codd.   16. ποιῆσαι codd.: ἐποίησε Ald.
παραλογισμός Riccardianus 46, Vahlen (confirm. Arabs): παραλογισμόν
codd.   17. ἐκπλήξεως apogr.: πλήξεως A° τῆς ἐκπλήξεως . . . εἰκότων
om. Arabs   εἰκόντων A°   18. ὁ secl. Vahlen: τὸ Bywater: ὃ Tucker:
ἡ apogr. pauca   19–20. αἱ γὰρ τοιαῦται . . . περιδεραίων secl. Gomperz
20. δεραίων apogr. corr.: δέρεων A°: περιδεραίων apogr. pauca   σημείων
καὶ δεραίων secl. Tucker, fort. recte   24. ἐναργέστατα apogr.: ἐνεργέστατα
A°   ὁ om. Parisinus 2038   25. λανθάνοι τὸ A°: λανθάνοιτο apogr.
plura (το deletum est in nonnullis)   ἐπετιμᾶτο marg. Riccardiani 16 :
ἐπιτιμᾶ τῶι A° (cf. 1462 a 10)   27. ἀνήει Guelferbytanus (confirm. Arabs) :
ἂν εἴη A°   ὁρῶντα codd.: ὁρῶντ' ἂν Vahlen   27–28. τὸν θεατὴν seclusi
(cf. Rhet. i. 2. 1358 a 8 τοὺς ἀκροατὰς in textum irrepsit): τὸν ποιητὴν Dacier
μὴ ὁρῶντ' αὐτὸν [θεατὴν] Gomperz, emendationis meae, credo, inscius
30. ἀπὸ τῆς αὐτῆς codd. (confirmare videtur Arabs): ἀπ' αὐτῆς τῆς Tyrwhitt

we are doomed to die, for here we were cast forth.'
Again, there is a composite kind of recognition involving 7
false inference on the part of one of the characters, as in
the Odysseus Disguised as a Messenger.   A said <that
no one else was able to bend the bow; . . . hence B
(the disguised Odysseus) imagined that A would>
recognise the bow which, in fact, he had not seen; and
to bring about a recognition by this means—the expectation that A would recognise the bow—is false inference.

But, of all recognitions, the best is that which arises 8
from the incidents themselves, where the startling discovery is made by natural means.   Such is that in the
Oedipus of Sophocles, and in the Iphigenia; for it was
natural that Iphigenia should wish to dispatch a letter.
These recognitions alone dispense with the artificial aid
of tokens or amulets.   Next come the recognitions by
process of reasoning.

XVII   In constructing the plot and working it out with
the proper diction, the poet should place the scene,
as far as possible, before his eyes.   In this way, seeing
everything with the utmost vividness, as if he were a
spectator of the action, he will discover what is in keeping
with it, and be most unlikely to overlook inconsistencies.
The need of such a rule is shown by the fault found in
Carcinus.   Amphiaraus was on his way from the temple.
This fact escaped the observation of one who did not see
the situation.   On the stage, however, the piece failed,
the audience being offended at the oversight.

Again, the poet should work out his play, to the
best of his power, with appropriate gestures; for 2

φύσεως οἱ ἐν τοῖς πάθεσίν εἰσιν καὶ χειμαίνει ὁ χειμαζόμενος
καὶ χαλεπαίνει ὁ ὀργιζόμενος ἀληθινώτατα. διὸ εὐφυοῦς ἡ
ποιητική ἐστιν ἢ μανικοῦ· τούτων γὰρ οἱ μὲν εὔπλαστοι οἱ δὲ
ἐκστατικοί εἰσιν. τούς τε λόγους καὶ τοὺς πεποιημένους 3
1455 b δεῖ καὶ αὐτὸν ποιοῦντα ἐκτίθεσθαι καθόλου, εἶθ' οὕτως ἐπεισοδιοῦν καὶ παρατείνειν. λέγω δὲ οὕτως ἂν θεωρεῖσθαι τὸ καθόλου, οἷον τῆς Ἰφιγενείας· τυθείσης τινὸς κόρης καὶ ἀφα-
νισθείσης· ἀδήλως τοῖς θύσασιν, ἱδρυνθείσης δὲ εἰς ἄλλην
5 χώραν, ἐν ᾗ νόμος ἦν τοὺς ξένους θύειν τῇ θεῷ ταύτην ἔσχε
τὴν ἱερωσύνην· χρόνῳ δὲ ὕστερον τῷ ἀδελφῷ συνέβη ἐλθεῖν
τῆς ἱερείας (τὸ δὲ ὅτι ἀνεῖλεν ὁ θεὸς διά τινα αἰτίαν, ἔξω τοῦ
καθόλου [ἐλθεῖν ἐκεῖ], καὶ ἐφ' ὅ τι δέ, ἔξω τοῦ μύθου). ἐλθὼν
δὲ καὶ ληφθεὶς θύεσθαι μέλλων ἀνεγνώρισεν, εἴθ' ὡς Εὐρι-
10 πίδης εἴθ' ὡς Πολύιδος ἐποίησεν, κατὰ τὸ εἰκὸς εἰπὼν ὅτι
οὐκ ἄρα μόνον τὴν ἀδελφὴν ἀλλὰ καὶ αὐτὸν ἔδει τυθῆναι,
καὶ ἐντεῦθεν ἡ σωτηρία. μετὰ ταῦτα δὲ ἤδη ὑποθέντα τὰ 4
ὀνόματα ἐπεισοδιοῦν· ὅπως δὲ ἔσται οἰκεῖα τὰ ἐπεισόδια,
οἷον ἐν τῷ Ὀρέστῃ ἡ μανία δι' ἧς ἐλήφθη καὶ ἡ σω-
15 τηρία διὰ τῆς καθάρσεως. ἐν μὲν οὖν τοῖς δράμασιν τὰ 5
ἐπεισόδια σύντομα, ἡ δ' ἐποποιία τούτοις μηκύνεται. τῆς

---

33. duplicem lect. εὔπλαστοι et ἄπλαστοι habuisse videtur Σ (Diels) 34.
ἐκστατικοί Riccardianus 46 (confirm. Arabs, vid. Margoliouth, Class. Rev.
xv. 54): ἐξεταστικοί codd. cett. τούς τε vel τούτους τε τοὺς apogr. :
τούτους τε Aᶜ, sed ne Graece quidem dicitur παρειλημμένους coni. Vahlen
1455 b 2. ἐπεισοδίου Aᶜ παρατείνειν Riccardianus 46, Vettori : περιτείνειν
codd. 7-8. secludendum videtur aut ἐλθεῖν ἐκεῖ (Bekker ed. 3) aut ἔξω
τοῦ καθόλου (Düntzer) 8. καθόλου] fort. μύθου Vahlen μύθου] fort.
καθόλου Vahlen 9. ἀνεγνωρίσθη M. Schmidt 10. Πολύειδος codd.
(cf. 1455 a 6) 15. δράμασι (vel ἄσμασι) apogr. : ἄρμασιν Aᶜ

those who feel emotion are most convincing through natural sympathy with the characters they represent; and one who is agitated storms, one who is angry rages, with the most life-like reality. Hence poetry implies either a happy gift of nature or a strain of madness. In the one case a man can take the mould of any character; in the other, he is lifted out of his proper self.

As for the story, whether the poet takes it ready 3 1455 b made or constructs it for himself, he should first sketch its general outline, and then fill in the episodes and amplify in detail. The general plan may be illustrated by the Iphigenia. A young girl is sacrificed; she disappears mysteriously from the eyes of those who sacrificed her; she is transported to another country, where the custom is to offer up all strangers to the goddess. To this ministry she is appointed. Some time later her own brother chances to arrive. The fact that the oracle for some reason ordered him to go there, is outside the general plan of the play. The purpose, again, of his coming is outside the action proper. However, he comes, he is seized, and, when on the point of being sacrificed, reveals who he is. The mode of recognition may be either that of Euripides or of Polyidus, in whose play he exclaims very naturally :— ' So it was not my sister only, but I too, who was doomed to be sacrificed'; and by that remark he is saved.

After this, the names being once given, it remains 4 to fill in the episodes. We must see that they are relevant to the action. In the case of Orestes, for example, there is the madness which led to his capture, and his deliverance by means of the purificatory rite. In the drama, the episodes are short, but it is these that 5

γὰρ Ὀδυσσείας <οὐ> μακρὸς ὁ λόγος ἐστίν· ἀποδημοῦντός
τινος ἔτη πολλὰ καὶ παραφυλαττομένου ὑπὸ τοῦ Ποσειδῶνος
καὶ μόνου ὄντος, ἔτι δὲ τῶν οἴκοι οὕτως ἐχόντων ὥστε τὰ χρή-
20 ματα ὑπὸ μνηστήρων ἀναλίσκεσθαι καὶ τὸν υἱὸν ἐπιβου-
λεύεσθαι, αὐτὸς δὲ ἀφικνεῖται χειμασθεὶς καὶ ἀναγνωρίσας
τινὰς αὐτὸς ἐπιθέμενος αὐτὸς μὲν ἐσώθη τοὺς δ' ἐχθροὺς
διέφθειρε. τὸ μὲν οὖν ἴδιον τοῦτο, τὰ δ' ἄλλα ἐπεισόδια.

XVIII   Ἔστι δὲ πάσης τραγῳδίας τὸ μὲν δέσις τὸ δὲ λύσις, τὰ
25 μὲν ἔξωθεν καὶ ἔνια τῶν ἔσωθεν πολλάκις ἡ δέσις, τὸ
δὲ λοιπὸν ἡ λύσις. λέγω δὲ δέσιν μὲν εἶναι τὴν ἀπ' ἀρχῆς μέχρι τούτου τοῦ μέρους ὃ ἔσχατόν ἐστιν ἐξ οὗ μεταβαί-
νειν εἰς εὐτυχίαν ἢ εἰς ἀτυχίαν <συμβαίνει>, λύσιν δὲ τὴν
ἀπὸ τῆς ἀρχῆς τῆς μεταβάσεως μέχρι τέλους· ὥσπερ ἐν
30 τῷ Λυγκεῖ τῷ Θεοδέκτου δέσις μὲν τά τε προπεπραγμένα
καὶ ἡ τοῦ παιδίου λῆψις καὶ πάλιν †ἡ αὐτῶν δὴ * *†
λύσις δ' ἡ ἀπὸ τῆς αἰτιάσεως τοῦ θανάτου μέχρι τοῦ
τέλους. * * τραγῳδίας δὲ εἴδη εἰσὶ τέσσαρα, [τοσαῦτα γὰρ 2
καὶ τὰ μέρη ἐλέχθη,] ἡ μὲν πεπλεγμένη, ἧς τὸ ὅλον ἐστὶν

---

17. οὐ add. Vulcanius (confirm. Arabs)   μακρὸς A^c: μικρὸς apogr.   19.
ἔτι Riccardianus 16, Σ: ἐπεὶ A^c   21. δὲ codd.: δὴ coni. Vahlen   22.
τινὰς αὐτὸς codd.: ὅτι αὐτὸς coni. Bywater: τινὰς αὐτὸς olim seclusi: αὐτὸς
secl. Spengel.   Codicum lectionem stabilivit Vahlen (1898) citato Diodoro
Siculo iv. 59. 6 τὸν Αἰγέα διὰ τῶν συμβόλων ἀνεγνώρισεν: simili fortasse sensu
Plutarch. Vit. Thes. ch. xii συναγαγὼν τοὺς πολίτας ἐγνώριζεν   25. πολλάκις post ἔξωθεν collocavit Ueberweg: codd. lect. confirm. Arabs   28. εἰς
εὐτυχίαν ἢ εἰς ἀτυχίαν O^b: εἰς εὐτυχίαν codd. cett.: εἰς εὐτυχίαν <ἐκ δυστυχίας
συμβαίνει ἢ ἐξ εὐτυχίας εἰς δυστυχίαν> coni. Vahlen: <εἰς δυστυχίαν συμβαίνει
ἢ> εἰς εὐτυχίαν Gomperz   30. λυγκεῖ apogr.: λυκεῖ A^c   31. δὴ A^c:
δὴ <ἀπαγωγή,> coni. Vahlen: δή<λωσις,> Christ ('et ea quae patefecit'
Arabs)   32. λύσις δὲ ἡ Parisinus 2038, coni. Vahlen: om. cett. ('solutio
autem est quod fiebat' Arabs)   τοῦ θανάτου] fort. τοῦ Δαναοῦ (Vahlen
et Spengel)   τοῦ τέλους] huc transferenda quae leguntur 1456 a
7–10 δίκαιον—κρατεῖσθαι (Susemihl)   33. τοσαῦτα γὰρ—ἐλέχθη secl. Susemihl
ed. 1   34. καὶ τὰ μέρη A^c: κατὰ μέρη Heine: καὶ τὰ μύθων Tyrwhitt:
καὶ τὰ μύθου Susemihl   ἡ μὲν <ἁπλῆ ἡ δὲ> Zeller (Vahlen post
ἀναγνώρισις 35 <ἡ δὲ ἁπλῆ> cum definitione deesse suspicatur)

give extension to Epic poetry. Thus the story of the Odyssey can be stated briefly. A certain man is absent from home for many years; he is jealously watched by Poseidon, and left desolate. Meanwhile his home is in a wretched plight—suitors are wasting his substance and plotting against his son. At length, tempest-tost, he himself arrives; he makes certain persons acquainted with him; he attacks the suitors with his own hand, and is himself preserved while he destroys them. This is the essence of the plot; the rest is episode.

XVIII   Every tragedy falls into two parts,—Complication and Unravelling or *Dénouement*. Incidents extraneous to the action are frequently combined with a portion of the action proper, to form the Complication; the rest is the Unravelling. By the Complication I mean all that extends from the beginning of the action to the part which marks the turning-point to good or bad fortune. The Unravelling is that which extends from the beginning of the change to the end. Thus, in the Lynceus of Theodectes, the Complication consists of the incidents presupposed in the drama, the seizure of the child, and then again * * <The Unravelling> extends from the accusation of murder to the end.

There are four kinds of Tragedy, the Complex, depend- 2 ing entirely on Reversal of the Situation and Recognition ;

35 περιπέτεια καὶ ἀναγνώρισις, ἡ δὲ παθητική, οἷον οἵ τε Αἴαν-
1456 a τες καὶ οἱ Ἰξίονες, ἡ δὲ ἠθική, οἷον αἱ Φθιώτιδες καὶ ὁ
Πηλεύς. τὸ δὲ τέταρτον <ἡ ἁπλῆ> * * † ὄης † οἷον αἵ τε
Φορκίδες καὶ Προμηθεὺς καὶ ὅσα ἐν ᾅδου. μάλιστα μὲν οὖν 3
ἅπαντα δεῖ πειρᾶσθαι ἔχειν, εἰ δὲ μή, τὰ μέγιστα καὶ πλεῖ-
5 στα, ἄλλως τε καὶ ὡς νῦν συκοφαντοῦσιν τοὺς ποιητάς· γε-
γονότων γὰρ καθ᾽ ἕκαστον μέρος ἀγαθῶν ποιητῶν, ἑκάστου τοῦ
ἰδίου ἀγαθοῦ ἀξιοῦσι τὸν ἕνα ὑπερβάλλειν. δίκαιον δὲ καὶ
τραγῳδίαν ἄλλην καὶ τὴν αὐτὴν λέγειν οὐδεν<ὶ> ἴσως <ὡς>
τῷ μύθῳ· τοῦτο δέ, ὧν ἡ αὐτὴ πλοκὴ καὶ λύσις. πολλοὶ δὲ
10 πλέξαντες εὖ λύουσι κακῶς· δεῖ δὲ ἄμφω ἀεὶ κρατεῖσθαι.
χρὴ δὲ ὅπερ εἴρηται πολλάκις μεμνῆσθαι καὶ μὴ ποιεῖν ἐπο- 4
ποιικὸν σύστημα τραγῳδίαν (ἐποποιικὸν δὲ λέγω τὸ πολύμυθον), οἷον εἴ τις τὸν τῆς Ἰλιάδος ὅλον ποιοῖ μῦθον. ἐκεῖ
μὲν γὰρ διὰ τὸ μῆκος λαμβάνει τὰ μέρη τὸ πρέπον μέγεθος,
15 ἐν δὲ τοῖς δράμασι πολὺ παρὰ τὴν ὑπόληψιν ἀποβαίνει. ση- 5
μεῖον δέ, ὅσοι πέρσιν Ἰλίου ὅλην ἐποίησαν καὶ μὴ κατὰ μέρος
ὥσπερ Εὐριπίδης, <ἢ> Νιόβην καὶ μὴ ὥσπερ Αἰσχύλος,
ἢ ἐκπίπτουσιν ἢ κακῶς ἀγωνίζονται, ἐπεὶ καὶ Ἀγάθων ἐξ-

1456 a 2. ἡ ἁπλῆ add. Susemihl   post ἡ ἁπλῆ nonnulla intercidisse puto
τὸ δὲ τέταρτον ὄης Aᶜ: τὸ δὲ τέταρτον ὄψις (cf. ad 1458 a 6) Bywater, recte,
nisi fallor, quod ad ὄψις attinet, sed τὰ εἴδη in hoc loco eadem utique esse
debent quae in xxiv. 1: τὸ δὲ τέταρτον τερατῶδες Schrader: τὸ δὲ τερατῶδες
<ἀλλότριον> Wecklein   5. ἄλλως τε apogr.: ἀλλ᾽ ὥς γε Aᶜ   6.
ἑκάστου Marcianus 215, Parisinus 2038: ἕκαστον Aᶜ   7-10. δίκαιον—
κρατεῖσθαι v. ad 1455 b 33   8. οὐδενὶ ἴσως ὡς Bonitz: οὐδενὶ ὡς Tyrwhitt:
οὐδὲν ἴσως τῷ codd.   9. τοῦτο] ταὐτὸ Teichmüller: τούτῳ Bursian   10.
κρατεῖσθαι (cf. Polit. iv. (vii.) 13. 1331 b 38) Vahlen et Σ ('prensarunt
utrumque' Arabs): κροτεῖσθαι codd.   12. δὲ ante τὸ add. Aᶜ: om. apogr.
17. ἢ add. Vahlen   Νιόβην] Ἑκάβην Valla, unde Ἑκάβην [καὶ . . .
Αἰσχύλος,] Reinach   18. ἀγαθῶν pr. Aᶜ et Σ

1456 a the Pathetic (where the motive is passion),—such as the tragedies on Ajax and Ixion ; the Ethical (where the motives are ethical),—such as the Phthiotides and the Peleus. The fourth kind is the Simple. < We here exclude the purely spectacular element>, exemplified by the Phorcides, the Prometheus, and scenes laid in Hades. The poet should endeavour, if possible, to combine all 3 poetic elements ; or failing that, the greatest number and those the most important; the more so, in face of the cavilling criticism of the day. For whereas there have hitherto been good poets, each in his own branch, the critics now expect one man to surpass all others in their several lines of excellence.

In speaking of a tragedy as the same or different, the best test to take is the plot. Identity exists where the Complication and Unravelling are the same. Many poets tie the knot well, but unravel it ill. Both arts, however, should always be mastered.

Again, the poet should remember what has been often 4 said, and not make an Epic structure into a Tragedy— by an Epic structure I mean one with a multiplicity of plots—as if, for instance, you were to make a tragedy out of the entire story of the Iliad. In the Epic poem, owing to its length, each part assumes its proper magnitude. In the drama the result is far from answering to the poet's expectation. The proof is that 5 the poets who have dramatised the whole story of the Fall of Troy, instead of selecting portions, like Euripides; or who have taken the whole tale of Niobe, and not a part of her story, like Aeschylus, either fail utterly or meet with poor success on the stage. Even Agathon

ἔπεσεν ἐν τούτῳ μόνῳ· ἐν δὲ ταῖς περιπετείαις [καὶ ἐν τοῖς
20 ἁπλοῖς πράγμασι] στοχάζεται ὧν βούλονται θαυμαστῶς·
τραγικὸν γὰρ τοῦτο καὶ φιλάνθρωπον. ἔστιν δὲ τοῦτο, ὅταν 6
ὁ σοφὸς [μὲν] μετὰ πονηρίας ἐξαπατηθῇ, ὥσπερ Σίσυ-
φος, καὶ ὁ ἀνδρεῖος μὲν ἄδικος δὲ ἡττηθῇ. ἔστιν δὲ τοῦτο
εἰκὸς ὥσπερ Ἀγάθων λέγει, εἰκὸς γὰρ γίνεσθαι πολλὰ
25 καὶ παρὰ τὸ εἰκός.   καὶ τὸν χορὸν δὲ ἕνα δεῖ ὑπολα- 7
βεῖν τῶν ὑποκριτῶν, καὶ μόριον εἶναι τοῦ ὅλου καὶ συναγω-
νίζεσθαι μὴ ὥσπερ Εὐριπίδῃ ἀλλ' ὥσπερ Σοφοκλεῖ.   τοῖς
δὲ λοιποῖς τὰ ᾀδόμενα <οὐδὲν> μᾶλλον τοῦ μύθου ἢ ἄλλης
τραγῳδίας ἐστίν· διὸ ἐμβόλιμα ᾄδουσιν πρῶτου ἄρξαντος
30 Ἀγάθωνος τοῦ τοιούτου.   καίτοι τί διαφέρει ἢ ἐμβόλιμα
ᾄδειν ἢ εἰ ῥῆσιν ἐξ ἄλλου εἰς ἄλλο ἁρμόττοι ἢ ἐπεισόδιον
ὅλον ;

XIX   Περὶ μὲν οὖν τῶν ἄλλων ἤδη εἴρηται, λοιπὸν δὲ περὶ
λέξεως καὶ διανοίας εἰπεῖν.   τὰ μὲν οὖν περὶ τὴν διάνοιαν ἐν
35 τοῖς περὶ ῥητορικῆς κείσθω, τοῦτο γὰρ ἴδιον μᾶλλον ἐκείνης
τῆς μεθόδου.   ἔστι δὲ κατὰ τὴν διάνοιαν ταῦτα, ὅσα ὑπὸ
τοῦ λόγου δεῖ παρασκευασθῆναι.   μέρη δὲ τούτων τό τε ἀπο- 2
δεικνύναι καὶ τὸ λύειν καὶ τὸ πάθη παρασκευάζειν, οἷον
1456 b ἔλεον ἢ φόβον ἢ ὀργὴν καὶ ὅσα τοιαῦτα, καὶ ἔτι μέγεθος

19-20. καὶ ἐν . . . πράγμασι secl. Susemihl: tuetur Arabs   ἐν τοῖς ἁπλοῖς]
ἐν τοῖς διπλοῖς Twining: ἁπλῶς ἐν τοῖς Gomperz   20. στοχάζεται Heinsius:
στοχάζονται codd.   21. τραγικὸν—φιλάνθρωπον infra post ἡττηθῇ collocat
Susemihl   22. aut secludendum μὲν (Margoliouth cum Arabe) aut δὲ
post πονηρίας legendum (add. Riccardianus 16)   23. ἡττήθη Aᶜ   24.
καὶ εἰκὸς ὥσπερ Riccardianus 46 (confirm. Arabs)   27. ὥσπερ παρ'—ὥσπερ
παρὰ Ald., ceterum cf. Pol. 1339 b 8   28. λοιποῖς] πολλοῖς Margoliouth
cum Arabe   ᾀδόμενα Maggi ('quae canuntur' Arabs): διδόμενα Aᶜ
οὐδὲν add. Vahlen, et Σ ('nihil . . . aliud amplius' Arabs): οὐ add. Maggi
30. τοιούτου] ποιητοῦ Σ, ut videtur   33. ἤδη apogr. : ἤδ' Aᶜ: εἰδεῶν Σ,
ut videtur   34. καὶ Hermann : ἢ codd.   38. πάθη secl. Bernays,
tuetur Arabs

has been known to fail from this one defect. In his Reversals of the Situation, however, he shows a marvellous skill in the effort to hit the popular taste,—to produce a tragic effect that satisfies the moral sense. This effect is 6 produced when the clever rogue, like Sisyphus, is outwitted, or the brave villain defeated. Such an event is probable in Agathon's sense of the word : 'it is probable,' he says, 'that many things should happen contrary to probability.'

The Chorus too should be regarded as one of the 7 actors; it should be an integral part of the whole, and share in the action, in the manner not of Euripides but of Sophocles. As for the later poets, their choral songs pertain as little to the subject of the piece as to that of any other tragedy. They are, therefore, sung as mere interludes,—a practice first begun by Agathon. Yet what difference is there between introducing such choral interludes, and transferring a speech, or even a whole act, from one play to another ?

XIX   It remains to speak of Diction and Thought, the other parts of Tragedy having been already discussed. Concerning Thought, we may assume what is said in the Rhetoric, to which inquiry the subject more strictly belongs. Under Thought is included every effect which has to be produced by speech, the subdivisions being,— 2 proof and refutation; the excitation of the feelings, such 1456 b as pity, fear, anger, and the like; the suggestion of

καὶ μικρότητας.   δῆλον δὲ ὅτι καὶ [ἐν] τοῖς πράγμασιν ἀπὸ 3
τῶν αὐτῶν ἰδεῶν δεῖ χρῆσθαι, ὅταν ἢ ἐλεεινὰ ἢ δεινὰ ἢ
μεγάλα ἢ εἰκότα δέῃ παρασκευάζειν· πλὴν τοσοῦτον δια-
5 φέρει, ὅτι τὰ μὲν δεῖ φαίνεσθαι ἄνευ διδασκαλίας, τὰ δὲ
ἐν τῷ λόγῳ ὑπὸ τοῦ λέγοντος παρασκευάζεσθαι καὶ παρὰ
τὸν λόγον γίγνεσθαι.   τί γὰρ ἂν εἴη τοῦ λέγοντος ἔργον, εἰ
φαίνοιτο ἡ διάνοια καὶ μὴ διὰ τὸν λόγον ;   τῶν δὲ περὶ τὴν 4
λέξιν ἓν μέν ἐστιν εἶδος θεωρίας τὰ σχήματα τῆς λέξεως,
10 ἅ ἐστιν εἰδέναι τῆς ὑποκριτικῆς καὶ τοῦ τὴν τοιαύτην ἔχοντος ἀρχιτεκτονικήν, οἷον τί ἐντολὴ καὶ τί εὐχὴ καὶ διή-
γησις καὶ ἀπειλὴ καὶ ἐρώτησις καὶ ἀπόκρισις καὶ εἴ τι ἄλλο
τοιοῦτον.   παρὰ γὰρ τὴν τούτων γνῶσιν ἢ ἄγνοιαν οὐδὲν 5
εἰς τὴν ποιητικὴν ἐπιτίμημα φέρεται ὅ τι καὶ ἄξιον σπου-
15 δῆς.   τί γὰρ ἄν τις ὑπολάβοι ἡμαρτῆσθαι ἃ Πρωταγόρας
ἐπιτιμᾷ, ὅτι εὔχεσθαι οἰόμενος ἐπιτάττει εἰπὼν " μῆνιν ἄειδε
θεά," τὸ γὰρ κελεῦσαι φησὶν ποιεῖν τι ἢ μὴ ἐπίταξίς ἐστιν.
διὸ παρείσθω ὡς ἄλλης καὶ οὐ τῆς ποιητικῆς ὂν θεώρημα.

XX   [Τῆς δὲ λέξεως ἁπάσης τάδ᾽ ἐστὶ τὰ μέρη, στοι-
20 χεῖον συλλαβὴ σύνδεσμος ὄνομα ῥῆμα [ἄρθρον] πτῶσις
λόγος.   στοιχεῖον μὲν οὖν ἐστιν φωνὴ ἀδιαίρετος, οὐ πᾶσα 2

1456 b 2. μικρότητας A^c : σμικρότητα Parisinus 2038   ἐν secl. Ueberweg :
<τοῖς> ἐν Wrobel   3. ἰδεῶν apogr. : εἰδεῶν A^c   4. δέῃ Parisinus
2038 : δ᾽ ἢ A^c   8. φαίνοιτο scripsi : φανοῖτο codd.   ἡ διάνοια
Margoliouth, Wrobel (praeeunte Spengel) : ἡδέα codd. ('voluptates' Arabs) :
ἤδη Castelvetro : ᾖ δέοι Vahlen (ed. 2) : ἤδη ἃ δεῖ Tyrwhitt : ἤδη τῇ θέᾳ
Gomperz   20. ἄρθρον secl. Hartung (quem dubitantius secutus sum) :
post σύνδεσμος transtulit Spengel (confirm. Arabs) : σύνδεσμος <ἢ> ἄρθρον
Steinthal

importance or its opposite. Now, it is evident that 3 the dramatic incidents must be treated from the same points of view as the dramatic speeches, when the object is to evoke the sense of pity, fear, importance, or probability. The only difference is, that the incidents should speak for themselves without verbal exposition; while the effects aimed at in speech should be produced by the speaker, and as a result of the speech. For what were the business of a speaker, if the Thought were revealed quite apart from what he says?

Next, as regards Diction. One branch of the inquiry 4 treats of the Modes of Utterance. But this province of knowledge belongs to the art of Delivery and to the masters of that science. It includes, for instance, —what is a command, a prayer, a statement, a threat, a question, an answer, and so forth. To know or not 5 to know these things involves no serious censure upon the poet's art. For who can admit the fault imputed to Homer by Protagoras,—that in the words, 'Sing, goddess, of the wrath,' he gives a command under the idea that he utters a prayer? For to tell some one to do a thing or not to do it is, he says, a command. We may, therefore, pass this over as an inquiry that belongs to another art, not to poetry.

XX   [Language in general includes the following parts:— Letter, Syllable, Connecting word, Noun, Verb, Inflexion or Case, Sentence or Phrase.

A Letter is an indivisible sound, yet not every such 2 sound, but only one which can form part of a group of

72   XX. 2—6.   1456 b 22—1457 a 2

δὲ ἀλλ' ἐξ ἧς πέφυκε συνθετὴ γίγνεσθαι φωνή· καὶ γὰρ τῶν
θηρίων εἰσὶν ἀδιαίρετοι φωναί, ὧν οὐδεμίαν λέγω στοιχεῖον. ταύτης δὲ μέρη τό τε φωνῆεν καὶ τὸ ἡμίφωνον καὶ
25 ἄφωνον. ἔστιν δὲ φωνῆεν μὲν <τὸ> ἄνευ προσβολῆς ἔχον 3
φωνὴν ἀκουστήν, ἡμίφωνον δὲ τὸ μετὰ προσβολῆς ἔχον
φωνὴν ἀκουστήν, οἷον τὸ Σ καὶ τὸ Ρ, ἄφωνον δὲ τὸ μετὰ
προσβολῆς καθ' αὑτὸ μὲν οὐδεμίαν ἔχον φωνήν, μετὰ δὲ
τῶν ἐχόντων τινὰ φωνὴν γινόμενον ἀκουστόν, οἷον τὸ Γ καὶ
30 τὸ Δ. ταῦτα δὲ διαφέρει σχήμασίν τε τοῦ στόματος καὶ 4
τόποις καὶ δασύτητι καὶ ψιλότητι καὶ μήκει καὶ βραχύ-
τητι, ἔτι δὲ ὀξύτητι καὶ βαρύτητι καὶ τῷ μέσῳ· περὶ ὧν
καθ' ἕκαστον [ἐν] τοῖς μετρικοῖς προσήκει θεωρεῖν. συλλαβὴ 5
δέ ἐστιν φωνὴ ἄσημος συνθετὴ ἐξ ἀφώνου καὶ φωνὴν ἔχον-
35 τος· καὶ γὰρ τὸ ΓΡ ἄνευ τοῦ Α συλλαβὴ καὶ μετὰ τοῦ
Α, οἷον τὸ ΓΡΑ. ἀλλὰ καὶ τούτων θεωρῆσαι τὰς διαφορὰς
τῆς μετρικῆς ἐστιν. σύνδεσμος δέ ἐστιν φωνὴ ἄσημος ἢ οὔ- 6
1457 a τε κωλύει οὔτε ποιεῖ φωνὴν μίαν σημαντικὴν ἐκ πλειόνων
φωνῶν, πεφυκυῖα [συν]τίθεσθαι καὶ ἐπὶ τῶν ἄκρων καὶ ἐπὶ

---

22. συνθετὴ apogr. ('compositae voci' Arabs): συνετὴ Aᶜ   25. τὸ add.
Reiz   33. ἐν secl. Spengel   34. post φωνὴν ἔχοντος coni. Christ
<ἢ πλειόνων ἀφώνων καὶ φωνὴν ἔχοντος>   35—36. καὶ γὰρ τὸ ΓΡ ἄνευ
τοῦ Α συλλαβὴ καὶ μετὰ τοῦ Α Aᶜ: 'nam Γ et Ρ sine A non faciunt syllabam,
quoniam tantum fiunt syllaba cum A' Arabs, unde καὶ γὰρ τὸ ΓΡ <οὐκ>
ἄνευ τοῦ Ρ συλλαβή, ἀλλὰ μετὰ τοῦ Α Margoliouth (similia Susemihl ed. 1):
καὶ γὰρ τὸ ΓΑ ἄνευ τοῦ Ρ συλλαβὴ καὶ μετὰ τοῦ Ρ Tyrwhitt: καὶ γὰρ τὸ Α ἄνευ
τοῦ ΓΡ συλλαβὴ καὶ μετὰ τοῦ ΓΡ M. Schmidt   1457 a 1–8. ἢ οὔτε κωλύει
—ἤτοι, δέ. Hartung, Susemihl.   Codicum fide ita vulgo legitur: ἢ οὔτε
κωλύει οὔτε ποιεῖ φωνὴν μίαν σημαντικήν, ἐκ πλειόνων φωνῶν πεφυκυῖαν συντίθεσθαι, καὶ ἐπὶ τῶν ἄκρων καὶ ἐπὶ τοῦ μέσου, ἢν μὴ ἁρμόττει (ἢν μὴ ἁρμόττῃ
apogr.) ἐν ἀρχῇ τιθέναι καθ' αὑτόν (αὑτὴν Tyrwhitt), οἷον μέν (μεν, Aᶜ), ἤτοι
(ἤτοι, Aᶜ), δέ (δε Aᶜ). ἢ φωνὴ ἄσημος ἢ ἐκ πλειόνων μὲν φωνῶν μιᾶς σημαντικῶν
(Robortelli: σημαντικὸν Aᶜ) δὲ ποιεῖν πέφυκεν μίαν σημαντικὴν φωνήν. ἄρθρον
δ' ἐστὶ φωνὴ ἄσημος, ἢ λόγου ἀρχὴν ἢ τέλος ἢ διορισμὸν δηλοῖ, οἷον τὸ ἀμφί
(Hartung: φ. μ. ι. Aᶜ: φημί Ald., Bekker) καὶ τὸ περί (π. ε. ρ. ι. Aᶜ) καὶ τὰ ἄλλα.

sounds. For even brutes utter indivisible sounds, none
of which I call a letter. The sound I mean may be 3
either a vowel, a semi-vowel, or a mute. A vowel is
that which without impact of tongue or lip has an
audible sound. A semi-vowel, that which with such
impact has an audible sound, as S and R. A mute,
that which with such impact has by itself no sound,
but joined to a vowel sound becomes audible, as G and
D. These are distinguished according to the form 4
assumed by the mouth and the place where they are
produced; according as they are aspirated or smooth,
long or short; as they are acute, grave, or of an intermediate tone; which inquiry belongs in detail to the
writers on metre.

A Syllable is a non-significant sound, composed of a 5
mute and a vowel: for GR without A is a syllable, as
also with A,—GRA. But the investigation of these
differences belongs also to metrical science.

A Connecting word is a non-significant sound, which 6
1457 a neither causes nor hinders the union of many sounds
into one significant sound; it may be placed at either

σύνδεσμος δέ ἐστιν φωνὴ ἄσημος ἡ ἐκ πλειόνων μὲν φωνῶν, μιᾶς σημαντικῶν
δὲ ποιεῖν πέφυκεν μίαν σημαντικὴν φωνήν, ἣν μὴ ἁρμόττει ἐν ἀρχῇ λόγου
τιθέναι καθ' αὐτήν, οἷον τὸ ἀμφί καὶ τὸ περί καὶ τὰ ἄλλα. ἄρθρον δ' ἐστὶ
φωνὴ ἄσημος, ἡ οὔτε κωλύει οὔτε ποιεῖ φωνὴν μίαν σημαντικὴν ἐκ πλειόνων
φωνῶν [πεφυκυῖαν] συντίθεσθαι, <ἀλλ'> ἡ λόγου ἀρχὴν ἡ τέλος ἡ διορισμὸν
δηλοῖ, πεφυκυῖα τίθεσθαι καὶ ἐπὶ τῶν ἄκρων καὶ ἐπὶ τοῦ μέσου, οἷον μέν, ἤτοι,
δέ. Nullam tamen Arabis rationem Döring habuit, et Arabs quidem cum
nostris codicibus parum congruit. Ipse ut in re nondum satis explicata
ἐπέχειν me fateor   2. πεφυκυῖα τίθεσθαι Winstanley : πεφυκυῖαν συντίθεσθαι codd.

τοῦ μέσου· ἡ φωνὴ ἄσημος ἢ ἐκ πλειόνων μὲν φωνῶν μιᾶς, σημαντικῶν δέ, ποιεῖν πέφυκεν μίαν σημαντικὴν
5 φωνήν, οἷον τὸ ἀμφί καὶ τὸ περί καὶ τὰ ἄλλα· <ἢ> φωνὴ 7
ἄσημος ἢ λόγου ἀρχὴν ἢ τέλος ἢ διορισμὸν δηλοῖ, ἢν μὴ
ἁρμόττει ἐν ἀρχῇ λόγου τιθέναι καθ᾽ αὑτήν, οἷον μέν, ἤτοι,
δέ. [ἡ φωνὴ ἄσημος ἢ οὔτε κωλύει οὔτε ποιεῖ φωνὴν
μίαν σημαντικὴν ἐκ πλειόνων φωνῶν πεφυκυῖα τίθεσθαι καὶ
10 ἐπὶ τῶν ἄκρων καὶ ἐπὶ τοῦ μέσου.] ὄνομα δέ ἐστι φωνὴ 8
συνθετὴ σημαντικὴ ἄνευ χρόνου ἧς μέρος οὐδέν ἐστι καθ᾽
αὐτὸ σημαντικόν· ἐν γὰρ τοῖς διπλοῖς οὐ χρώμεθα ὡς καὶ
αὐτὸ καθ᾽ αὑτὸ σημαῖνον, οἷον ἐν τῷ Θεοδώρῳ τὸ δῶρον
οὐ σημαίνει. ῥῆμα δὲ φωνὴ συνθετὴ σημαντικὴ μετὰ χρό- 9
15 νου ἧς οὐδὲν μέρος σημαίνει καθ᾽ αὑτό, ὥσπερ καὶ ἐπὶ τῶν
ὀνομάτων· τὸ μὲν γὰρ ἄνθρωπος ἢ λευκόν οὐ σημαίνει τὸ
πότε, τὸ δὲ βαδίζει ἢ βεβάδικεν προσσημαίνει τὸ μὲν τὸν
παρόντα χρόνον τὸ δὲ τὸν παρεληλυθότα. πτῶσις δ᾽ ἐστὶν 10
ὀνόματος ἢ ῥήματος ἡ μὲν τὸ κατὰ τὸ τούτου ἢ τούτῳ ση-
20 μαῖνον καὶ ὅσα τοιαῦτα, ἡ δὲ κατὰ τὸ ἑνὶ ἢ πολλοῖς, οἷον
ἄνθρωποι ἢ ἄνθρωπος, ἡ δὲ κατὰ τὰ ὑποκριτικά, οἷον κατ᾽
ἐρώτησιν, ἐπίταξιν· τὸ γὰρ ἐβάδισεν; ἢ βάδιζε πτῶσις
ῥήματος κατὰ ταῦτα τὰ εἴδη ἐστίν. λόγος δὲ φωνὴ συνθετὴ 11
σημαντικὴ ἧς ἔνια μέρη καθ᾽ αὑτὰ σημαίνει τι· οὐ γὰρ
25 ἅπας λόγος ἐκ ῥημάτων καὶ ὀνομάτων σύγκειται, οἷον "ὁ
τοῦ ἀνθρώπου ὁρισμός"· ἀλλ᾽ ἐνδέχεται <καὶ> ἄνευ ῥημάτων

4. σημαντικῶν Robortelli : σημαντικὸν Aᶜ   7. ἤτοι] δή τοί Bywater
8–10. ἢ . . . μέσου seclus. Reiz   17. ποτὲ Spengel   βαδίζει apogr. :
βαδίζειν Aᶜ   προσσημαίνει Parisinus 2038 : προσημαίνει Aᶜ   19. τὸ
κατὰ τὸ Riccardianus 16 : τὸ κατὰ Aᶜ : κατὰ τὸ Reiz   22. ἐβάδισεν; (nota
interrogationis addita) Tyrwhitt : <ἆρ᾽> ἐβάδισεν ; Vahlen   βαδίζε
Riccardianus 16 : ἐβάδιζεν Aᶜ   26. καὶ add. Gomperz

end or in the middle of a sentence.   Or, a non-significant
sound, which out of several sounds, each of them significant, is capable of forming one significant sound,—as
ἀμφί, περί, and the like.   Or, a non-significant sound, 7
which marks the beginning, end, or division of a sentence;
such, however, that it cannot correctly stand by itself at
the beginning of a sentence,—as μέν, ἤτοι, δέ.

A Noun is a composite significant sound, not marking 8
time, of which no part is in itself significant: for in
double or compound words we do not employ the
separate parts as if each were in itself significant.   Thus
in Theodorus, 'god-given,' the δῶρον or 'gift' is not in
itself significant.

A Verb is a composite significant sound, marking 9
time, in which, as in the noun, no part is in itself significant.   For 'man,' or 'white' does not express the idea
of 'when'; but 'he walks,' or 'he has walked' does
connote time, present or past.

Inflexion belongs both to the noun and verb, and 10
expresses either the relation 'of,' 'to,' or the like; or
that of number, whether one or many, as 'man' or
'men'; or the modes or tones in actual delivery, e.g. a
question or a command.   'Did he go?' and 'go' are
verbal inflexions of this kind.

A Sentence or Phrase is a composite significant 11
sound, some at least of whose parts are in themselves
significant; for not every such group of words consists
of verbs and nouns—'the definition of man,' for example
—but it may dispense even with the verb.   Still it will

εἶναι λόγον. μέρος μέντοι ἀεί τι σημαῖνον ἔξει, οἷον "ἐν τῷ
βαδίζειν," "Κλέων ὁ Κλέωνος." εἷς δέ ἐστι λόγος διχῶς, ἢ γὰρ 12
ὁ ἓν σημαίνων, ἢ ὁ ἐκ πλειόνων συνδέσμῳ, οἷον ἡ Ἰλιὰς μὲν
30 συνδέσμῳ εἷς, ὁ δὲ τοῦ ἀνθρώπου τῷ ἓν σημαίνειν.]

XXI   Ὀνόματος δὲ εἴδη τὸ μὲν ἁπλοῦν, ἁπλοῦν δὲ λέγω ὃ
μὴ ἐκ σημαινόντων σύγκειται, οἷον γῆ, τὸ δὲ διπλοῦν· τούτου
δὲ τὸ μὲν ἐκ σημαίνοντος καὶ ἀσήμου (πλὴν οὐκ ἐν τῷ
ὀνόματι σημαίνοντος [καὶ ἀσήμου]), τὸ δὲ ἐκ σημαινόντων
35 σύγκειται. εἴη δ' ἂν καὶ τριπλοῦν καὶ τετραπλοῦν ὄνομα καὶ
πολλαπλοῦν, οἷον τὰ πολλὰ τῶν Μασσαλιωτῶν· Ἑρμοκαϊ-
1457 b κόξανθος <ἐπευξάμενος Διὶ πατρί>. ἅπαν δὲ ὄνομά ἐστιν 2
ἢ κύριον ἢ γλῶττα ἢ μεταφορὰ ἢ κόσμος ἢ πεποιημένον
ἢ ἐπεκτεταμένον ἢ ὑφῃρημένον ἢ ἐξηλλαγμένον. λέγω 3
δὲ κύριον μὲν ᾧ χρῶνται ἕκαστοι, γλῶτταν δὲ ᾧ
5 ἕτεροι· ὥστε φανερὸν ὅτι καὶ γλῶτταν καὶ κύριον εἶναι
δυνατὸν τὸ αὐτό, μὴ τοῖς αὐτοῖς δέ· τὸ γὰρ σίγυννον
Κυπρίοις μὲν κύριον, ἡμῖν δὲ γλῶττα. μεταφορὰ δέ 4
ἐστιν ὀνόματος ἀλλοτρίου ἐπιφορὰ ἢ ἀπὸ τοῦ γένους ἐπὶ
εἶδος ἢ ἀπὸ τοῦ εἴδους ἐπὶ τὸ γένος ἢ ἀπὸ τοῦ εἴ-

28. βαδίζειν Aᶜ: βαδίζει Parisinus 2038   Κλέων ὁ Κλέωνος M. Schmidt
(Κλέωνος habuit Σ): Κλέων ὁ Κλέων codd.   ἐν τῷ "βαδίζει Κλέων" ὁ
(τὸ Bigg) Κλέων edd. plerique   29. συνδέσμῳ Riccardianus 16: συνδέσμων
Aᶜ   30. τῷ apogr.: τὸ Aᶜ   33. ἐν τῷ ὀνόματι Vahlen, et Σ, ut
videtur: ἐν τῷ ὀνόματος codd.: ἐντὸς τοῦ ὀνόματος Tucker   34. καὶ ἀσήμου
om. Σ, ut videtur ('non tamen indicans in nomine' Arabs). Idem effecit
Ussing deleto καὶ ἀσήμου in v. 33 et mutata interpunctione, ἐκ σημαίνοντος,
πλὴν οὐκ ἐν τῷ ὀνόματι σημαίνοντος, καὶ ἀσήμου, κτλ.   36. μεγαλιωτῶν
codd.: Μασσαλιωτῶν Diels, qui collato Arabe ('sicut multa de Massiliotis
Hermocaicoxanthus qui supplicabatur dominum caelorum') totum versum
Ἑρμοκ. — πατρί tanquam epici carminis, comice scripti, ex coniectura
restituit: unde μετὰ <γέλωτος οἷον Μασσα>λιωτῶν coni. Rutherford. Ἑρμοκ.
ad Phocaeam spectat, Massiliae μητρόπολιν, urbem inter Hermum et Caïcum
sitam. Ceteras emendationes licet iam missas facere, e.g. μεγαλείων ὡς
Winstanley: μεγαλείων οἷον Bekker ed. 3: μεγαλείων ὢν Vahlen   1457 b 3.
ἀφῃρημένον Spengel (cf. 1458 a 1)   9. τὸ om. apogr.

always have some significant part, as 'in walking,' or
' Cleon son of Cleon.' A sentence or phrase may form 12
a unity in two ways,—either as signifying one thing, or
as consisting of several parts linked together. Thus the
Iliad is one by the linking together of parts, the definition
of man by the unity of the thing signified.]

XXI   Words are of two kinds, simple and double. By
simple I mean those composed of non-significant elements,
such as γῆ. By double or compound, those composed
either of a significant and non-significant element
(though within the whole word no element is significant),
or of elements that are both significant. A word may
likewise be triple, quadruple, or multiple in form, like
1457 b so many Massilian expressions, e.g. ' Hermo-caico-xanthus
‹who prayed to Father Zeus›.'

Every word is either current, or strange, or meta- 2
phorical, or ornamental, or newly-coined, or lengthened,
or contracted, or altered.

By a current or proper word I mean one which is 3
in general use among a people ; by a strange word, one
which is in use in another country. Plainly, therefore,
the same word may be at once strange and current, but
not in relation to the same people. The word σίγυνον,
' lance,' is to the Cyprians a current term but to us a
strange one.

Metaphor is the application of an alien name by 4
transference either from genus to species, or from species
to genus, or from species to species, or by analogy, that is,

10 δους ἐπὶ εἶδος ἢ κατὰ τὸ ἀνάλογον. λέγω δὲ ἀπὸ γένους μὲν 5
ἐπὶ εἶδος οἷον "νηῦς δέ μοι ἥδ' ἕστηκεν·" τὸ γὰρ ὁρμεῖν ἐστιν
ἑστάναι τι. ἀπ' εἴδους δὲ ἐπὶ γένος "ἦ δὴ μυρί' Ὀδυσσεὺς
ἐσθλὰ ἔοργεν·" τὸ γὰρ μυρίον πολύ <τί> ἐστιν, ᾧ νῦν ἀντὶ
τοῦ πολλοῦ κέχρηται. ἀπ' εἴδους δὲ ἐπὶ εἶδος οἷον "χαλκῷ
15 ἀπὸ ψυχὴν ἀρύσας" καὶ "ταμὼν ἀτειρέι χαλκῷ·" ἐνταῦθα
γὰρ τὸ μὲν ἀρύσαι ταμεῖν, τὸ δὲ ταμεῖν ἀρύσαι εἴρηκεν·
ἄμφω γὰρ ἀφελεῖν τί ἐστιν. τὸ δὲ ἀνάλογον λέγω, ὅταν 6
ὁμοίως ἔχῃ τὸ δεύτερον πρὸς τὸ πρῶτον καὶ τὸ τέταρτον
πρὸς τὸ τρίτον· ἐρεῖ γὰρ ἀντὶ τοῦ δευτέρου τὸ τέταρτον ἢ
20 ἀντὶ τοῦ τετάρτου τὸ δεύτερον, καὶ ἐνίοτε προστιθέασιν ἀνθ'
οὗ λέγει πρὸς ὅ ἐστι. λέγω δὲ οἷον ὁμοίως ἔχει φιάλη πρὸς
Διόνυσον καὶ ἀσπὶς πρὸς Ἄρη· ἐρεῖ τοίνυν τὴν φιάλην ἀσπίδα
Διονύσου καὶ τὴν ἀσπίδα φιάλην Ἄρεως. ἢ ὃ γῆρας πρὸς
βίον, καὶ ἑσπέρα πρὸς ἡμέραν· ἐρεῖ τοίνυν τὴν ἑσπέραν γῆ-
25 ρας ἡμέρας καὶ τὸ γῆρας ἑσπέραν βίου ἤ, ὥσπερ Ἐμπεδοκλῆς,
δυσμὰς βίου. ἐνίοις δ' οὐκ ἔστιν ὄνομα κείμενον τῶν ἀνά- 7
λογον, ἀλλ' οὐδὲν ἧττον ὁμοίως λεχθήσεται· οἷον τὸ τὸν
καρπὸν μὲν ἀφιέναι σπείρειν, τὸ δὲ τὴν φλόγα ἀπὸ τοῦ
ἡλίου ἀνώνυμον· ἀλλ' ὁμοίως ἔχει τοῦτο πρὸς τὸν ἥλιον καὶ
30 τὸ σπείρειν πρὸς τὸν καρπόν, διὸ εἴρηται "σπείρων θεοκτίσταν
φλόγα." ἔστι δὲ τῷ τρόπῳ τούτῳ τῆς μεταφορᾶς χρῆσθαι 8
καὶ ἄλλως, προσαγορεύσαντα τὸ ἀλλότριον ἀποφῆσαι τῶν

11. ὁρμῖν Aᶜ   12. ἑστᾶναι (ᾶ ut videtur ex ά) Aᶜ   ἢ δὴ apogr. :
ἤδη Aᶜ   13. μύριον Aᶜ   τί add. Twining   15. ἀρύσας καὶ
Tyrwhitt (ἀρύσας Leidensis, corr. Vaticanus 1400, καὶ Laurentianus lx. 21) :
ἀερύσασκε Aᶜ   ταμὼν Bekker (ed. 3) : τεμῶν Aᶜ   ατηρει Aᶜ   25—26.
ἡμέρας—δυσμὰς Riccardianus 16, Parisinus 2038 : ἡμέρας ἢ ὥσπερ Ἐμπεδοκλῆς
καὶ τὸ γῆρας ἑσπέραν βίου ἢ δυσμὰς Aᶜ   28. ἀπὸ] ἐπὶ M. Schmidt   30.
<τὸν ἀφιέντα> τὸν καρπόν Castelvetro

proportion.   Thus from genus to species, as : 'There lies 5 my ship'; for lying at anchor is a species of lying. From species to genus, as : 'Verily ten thousand noble deeds hath Odysseus wrought'; for ten thousand is a species of large number, and is here used for a large number generally.   From species to species, as : 'With blade of bronze drew away the life,' and 'Cleft the water with the vessel of unyielding bronze.'   Here ἀρύσαι, 'to draw away,' is used for ταμεῖν, 'to cleave,' and ταμεῖν again for ἀρύσαι,—each being a species of taking away. Analogy or proportion is when the second term is to the 6 first as the fourth to the third.   We may then use the fourth for the second, or the second for the fourth. Sometimes too we qualify the metaphor by adding the term to which the proper word is relative.   Thus the cup is to Dionysus as the shield to Ares.   The cup may, therefore, be called 'the shield of Dionysus,' and the shield 'the cup of Ares.'   Or, again, as old age is to life, so is evening to day.   Evening may therefore be called 'the old age of the day,' and old age, 'the evening of life,' or, in the phrase of Empedocles, 'life's setting sun.' For some of the terms of the proportion there is at times 7 no word in existence; still the metaphor may be used. For instance, to scatter seed is called sowing : but the action of the sun in scattering his rays is nameless.   Still this process bears to the sun the same relation as sowing to the seed.   Hence the expression of the poet 'sowing the god-created light.'   There is another way in which 8 this kind of metaphor may be employed.   We may apply an alien term, and then deny of that term one of its

οἰκείων τι, οἷον εἰ τὴν ἀσπίδα εἴποι φιάλην μὴ Ἄρεως ἀλλ᾽ ἄοινον. <κόσμος δὲ . . . >. πεποιημένον δ᾽ ἐστὶν ὃ ὅλως 9 35 μὴ καλούμενον ὑπὸ τινῶν αὐτὸς τίθεται ὁ ποιητής, (δοκεῖ γὰρ ἔνια εἶναι τοιαῦτα) οἷον τὰ κέρατα ἐρνύγας καὶ τὸν ἱερέα 1458 a ἀρητῆρα. ἐπεκτεταμένον δέ ἐστιν ἢ ἀφῃρημένον τὸ μὲν ἐὰν 10 φωνήεντι μακροτέρῳ κεχρημένον ἢ τοῦ οἰκείου ἢ συλλαβῇ ἐμβεβλημένῃ, τὸ δὲ ἂν ἀφῃρημένον τι ᾖ αὐτοῦ, ἐπεκτεταμένον μὲν οἷον τὸ πόλεως πόληος καὶ τὸ Πηλείδου Πηληιάδεω, 5 ἀφῃρημένον δὲ οἷον τὸ κρῖ καὶ τὸ δῶ καὶ " μία γίνεται ἀμφοτέρων ὄψ." ἐξηλλαγμένον δ᾽ ἐστὶν ὅταν τοῦ ὀνομαζομένου 11 τὸ μὲν καταλείπῃ τὸ δὲ ποιῇ, οἷον τὸ " δεξιτερὸν κατὰ μαζόν" ἀντὶ τοῦ δεξιόν.

[αὐτῶν δὲ τῶν ὀνομάτων τὰ μὲν ἄρρενα τὰ δὲ θήλεα τὰ 12 10 δὲ μεταξύ, ἄρρενα μὲν ὅσα τελευτᾷ εἰς τὸ Ν καὶ Ρ καὶ Σ καὶ ὅσα ἐκ τούτου σύγκειται (ταῦτα δ᾽ ἐστὶν δύο, Ψ καὶ Ξ), θήλεα δὲ ὅσα ἐκ τῶν φωνηέντων εἴς τε τὰ ἀεὶ μακρά, οἷον εἰς Η καὶ Ω, καὶ τῶν ἐπεκτεινομένων εἰς Α· ὥστε ἴσα συμβαίνει πλήθη εἰς ὅσα τὰ ἄρρενα καὶ τὰ θήλεα· τὸ γὰρ Ψ καὶ τὸ Ξ 15 <τῷ Σ> ταὐτά ἐστιν. εἰς δὲ ἄφωνον οὐδὲν ὄνομα τελευτᾷ, οὐδὲ εἰς φωνῆεν βραχύ. εἰς δὲ τὸ Ι τρία μόνον, μέλι κόμμι πέπερι. εἰς δὲ τὸ Υ πέντε. τὰ δὲ μεταξὺ εἰς ταῦτα καὶ Ν καὶ Σ.]

XXII   Λέξεως δὲ ἀρετὴ σαφῆ καὶ μὴ ταπεινὴν εἶναι. σαφεστάτη μὲν οὖν ἐστιν ἡ ἐκ τῶν κυρίων ὀνομάτων, ἀλλὰ 20 ταπεινή· παράδειγμα δὲ ἡ Κλεοφῶντος ποίησις καὶ ἡ

---

33. ἀλλ᾽ ἄοινον Vettori : ἀλλὰ οἴνου Aᶜ et Σ   34. <κόσμος δὲ . . .>
Maggi   1458 a 2. κεχρημένος Hermann   ᾖ] ἢ Aᶜ   συλλαβῇ ἐμβεβλημένῃ Aᶜ   3. ἀφήρη μὲν ὄντι ἢ Aᶜ   4. πόλεος Aᶜ   πηλείδου Parisinus
2038: πηλέος Aᶜ: Πηλέος <Πηλῆος καὶ τὸ Πηλείδου>M. Schmidt   6. ὄψ
Vettori ; ὄης Aᶜ (O+IC=OΨIC)   10. καὶ Σ Riccardianus 16 (confirm.
Arabs): om. Aᶜ   14. πλήθη Aᶜ: πλήθει apogr.   15. τῷ Σ add.
anon. ap. Tyrwhitt   17. post πέντε add. τὸ πῶν τὸ νᾶπυ τὸ γόνυ τὸ
δόρυ τὸ ἄστυ Riccardianus 16   ταῦτα <καὶ Α> καὶ Ν <καὶ Ρ> καὶ Σ
Morel

proper attributes; as if we were to call the shield, not 'the cup of Ares,' but 'the wineless cup.'

<An ornamental word . . .>

A newly-coined word is one which has never been 9 even in local use, but is adopted by the poet himself. Some such words there appear to be: as ἐρνύγες, 'sprouters,' for κέρατα, 'horns,' and ἀρητήρ, 'supplicator,' for ἱερεύς, 'priest.'

1453 a A word is lengthened when its own vowel is exchanged 10 for a longer one, or when a syllable is inserted. A word is contracted when some part of it is removed. Instances of lengthening are,—πόληος for πόλεως, and Πηληιάδεω for Πηλείδου: of contraction,—κρῖ, δῶ, and ὄψ, as in μία γίνεται ἀμφοτέρων ὄψ.

An altered word is one in which part of the ordinary 11 form is left unchanged, and part is re-cast; as in δεξιτερὸν κατὰ μαζόν, δεξιτερόν is for δεξιόν.

[Nouns in themselves are either masculine, feminine, 12 or neuter. Masculine are such as end in ν, ρ, ς, or in some letter compounded with ς,—these being two, ψ and ξ. Feminine, such as end in vowels that are always long, namely η and ω, and—of vowels that admit of lengthening—those in α. Thus the number of letters in which nouns masculine and feminine end is the same; for ψ and ξ are equivalent to endings in ς. No noun ends in a mute or a vowel short by nature. Three only end in ι,—μέλι, κόμμι, πέπερι: five end in υ. Neuter nouns end in these two latter vowels; also in ν and ς.]

XXII The perfection of style is to be clear without being mean. The clearest style is that which uses only current or proper words; at the same time it is mean:—witness the poetry of Cleophon and of Sthenelus. That diction,

Σθενέλου. σεμνὴ δὲ καὶ ἐξαλλάττουσα τὸ ἰδιωτικὸν ἡ τοῖς
ξενικοῖς κεχρημένη· ξενικὸν δὲ λέγω γλῶτταν καὶ μεταφορὰν καὶ ἐπέκτασιν καὶ πᾶν τὸ παρὰ τὸ κύριον. ἀλλ' ἄν 2
τις ἅμα ἅπαντα τοιαῦτα ποιήσῃ, ἢ αἴνιγμα ἔσται ἢ βαρβα-
25 ρισμός· ἂν μὲν οὖν ἐκ μεταφορῶν, αἴνιγμα, ἐὰν δὲ ἐκ
γλωττῶν, βαρβαρισμός· αἰνίγματός τε γὰρ ἰδέα αὕτη ἐστί,
τὸ λέγοντα ὑπάρχοντα ἀδύνατα συνάψαι. κατὰ μὲν οὖν τὴν
τῶν <ἄλλων> ὀνομάτων σύνθεσιν οὐχ οἷόν τε τοῦτο ποιῆσαι
κατὰ δὲ τὴν μεταφορὰν ἐνδέχεται, οἷον " ἄνδρ' εἶδον πυρὶ χαλ-
30 κὸν ἐπ' ἀνέρι κολλήσαντα," καὶ τὰ τοιαῦτα. ἐκ τῶν γλωττῶν βαρβαρισμός. δεῖ ἄρα κεκρᾶσθαί πως τούτοις· τὸ 3
μὲν γὰρ μὴ ἰδιωτικὸν ποιήσει μηδὲ ταπεινόν, οἷον ἡ γλῶττα
καὶ ἡ μεταφορὰ καὶ ὁ κόσμος καὶ τἆλλα τὰ εἰρημένα
εἴδη, τὸ δὲ κύριον τὴν σαφήνειαν. οὐκ ἐλάχιστον δὲ μέρος 4
1458 b συμβάλλεται εἰς τὸ σαφὲς τῆς λέξεως καὶ μὴ ἰδιωτικὸν
αἱ ἐπεκτάσεις καὶ ἀποκοπαὶ καὶ ἐξαλλαγαὶ τῶν ὀνομά-
των· διὰ μὲν γὰρ τὸ ἄλλως ἔχειν ἢ ὡς τὸ κύριον, παρὰ
τὸ εἰωθὸς γιγνόμενον, τὸ μὴ ἰδιωτικὸν ποιήσει, διὰ δὲ τὸ κοι-
5 νωνεῖν τοῦ εἰωθότος τὸ σαφὲς ἔσται. ὥστε οὐκ ὀρθῶς ψέγου- 5
σιν οἱ ἐπιτιμῶντες τῷ τοιούτῳ τρόπῳ τῆς διαλέκτου καὶ δια-
κωμῳδοῦντες τὸν ποιητήν, οἷον Εὐκλείδης ὁ ἀρχαῖος, ὡς
ῥᾴδιον ποιεῖν, εἴ τις δώσει ἐκτείνειν ἐφ' ὁπόσον βούλεται,
ἰαμβοποιήσας ἐν αὐτῇ τῇ λέξει " Ἐπιχάρην εἶδον Μαρα-

24. ἅμα ἅπαντα Riccardianus 16, Parisinus 2038 : ἂν ἅπαντα Aᶜ: ἅπαντα al.
ποιήσῃ apogr. : ποιῆσαι Aᶜ   28. ἄλλων add. Margoliouth, collato Arabe
'reliqua nomina': κυρίων add. Heinsius   σύνθεσιν] συνήθειαν Tucker
οὐχοίονται Aᶜ   29. fort. μεταφορῶν Bywater   ἴδον Aᶜ   πυρὶ
χαλκὸν Vettori: πυρίχαλκον codd.   30–31. ante vel post ἐκ—βαρβαρισμός lacunam statuit Gomperz   31. κεκρᾶσθαι Maggi e cod. Lampridii ('si miscentur haec' Arabs): κεκρίσθαι codd. cett.   1458 b 1.
συμβάλεται Aᶜ : συμβάλλονται apogr.   9. Ἐπιχάρην Bursian : ἤτει χάριν Aᶜ :
ἐπὶ χάριν Σ, ut videtur ('appellatum cum favore' Arabs)   εἶδον apogr. :
ἴδον Aᶜ : ἰδὼν Gomperz

on the other hand, is lofty and raised above the commonplace which employs unusual words. By unusual, I
mean strange (or rare) words, metaphorical, lengthened,—
anything, in short, that differs from the normal idiom.
Yet a style wholly composed of such words is either a 2
riddle or a jargon ; a riddle, if it consists of metaphors ;
a jargon, if it consists of strange (or rare) words. For the
essence of a riddle is to express true facts under impossible combinations. Now this cannot be done by any
arrangement of ordinary words, but by the use of metaphor it can. Such is the riddle :—' A man I saw who
on another man had glued the bronze by aid of fire,' and
others of the same kind. A diction that is made up of
strange (or rare) terms is a jargon. A certain infusion, 3
therefore, of these elements is necessary to style ; for the
strange (or rare) word, the metaphorical, the ornamental,
and the other kinds above mentioned, will raise it above
the commonplace and mean, while the use of proper
words will make it perspicuous. But nothing contributes 4
1458 b more to produce a clearness of diction that is remote
from commonness than the lengthening, contraction, and
alteration of words. For by deviating in exceptional
cases from the normal idiom, the language will gain
distinction ; while, at the same time, the partial conformity with usage will give perspicuity. The critics, 5
therefore, are in error who censure these licenses of
speech, and hold the author up to ridicule. Thus
Eucleides, the elder, declared that it would be an easy
matter to be a poet if you might lengthen syllables at
will. He caricatured the practice in the very form of
his diction, as in the verse :

10 θῶνάδε βαδίζοντα," καὶ "οὐκ ἄν γ' ἐράμενος τὸν ἐκείνου ἐλλέβορον." τὸ μὲν οὖν φαίνεσθαί πως χρώμενον τούτῳ τῷ 6
τρόπῳ γελοῖον· τὸ δὲ μέτριον κοινὸν ἁπάντων ἐστὶ τῶν με-
ρῶν· καὶ γὰρ μεταφοραῖς καὶ γλώτταις καὶ τοῖς ἄλλοις
εἴδεσι χρώμενος ἀπρεπῶς καὶ ἐπίτηδες ἐπὶ τὰ γελοῖα τὸ
15 αὐτὸ ἂν ἀπεργάσαιτο. τὸ δὲ ἁρμόττον ὅσον διαφέρει ἐπὶ 7
τῶν ἐπῶν θεωρείσθω ἐντιθεμένων τῶν <κυρίων> ὀνομάτων εἰς
τὸ μέτρον. καὶ ἐπὶ τῆς γλώττης δὲ καὶ ἐπὶ τῶν μεταφορῶν
καὶ ἐπὶ τῶν ἄλλων ἰδεῶν μετατιθεὶς ἄν τις τὰ κύρια ὀνόματα
κατίδοι ὅτι ἀληθῆ λέγομεν· οἷον τὸ αὐτὸ ποιήσαντος ἰαμ-
20 βεῖον Αἰσχύλου καὶ Εὐριπίδου, ἐν δὲ μόνον ὄνομα μεταθέντος, ἀντὶ [κυρίου] εἰωθότος γλῶτταν, τὸ μὲν φαίνεται καλὸν
τὸ δ' εὐτελές. Αἰσχύλος μὲν γὰρ ἐν τῷ Φιλοκτήτῃ ἐποίησε
　　φαγέδαινα <δ'> ἥ μου σάρκας ἐσθίει ποδός,
ὁ δὲ ἀντὶ τοῦ ἐσθίει τὸ θοινᾶται μετέθηκεν. καὶ
25 　　νῦν δέ μ' ἐὼν ὀλίγος τε καὶ οὐτιδανὸς καὶ ἀεικής,[1]
　　εἴ τις λέγοι τὰ κύρια μετατιθεὶς
　　νῦν δέ μ' ἐὼν μικρός τε καὶ ἀσθενικὸς καὶ ἀειδής·

---

[1] Odyss. ix. 515, νῦν δέ μ' ἐὼν ὀλίγος τε καὶ οὐτιδανὸς καὶ ἄκικυς.

---

10. ἄν γ' ἐράμενος apogr.: ἂν γεράμενος Aᶜ: ἂν γευσάμενος Tyrwhitt: ἂν
πριάμενος Gomperz　　11. πῶς Aᶜ: ἀπρεπῶς Twining: πάντως Hermann
12. μέτριον Spengel: μέτρον codd.　　14. ἐπὶ τὰ apogr.: ἔπειτα
Aᶜ　　ἐπὶ τὰ γελοῖα secl. Gomperz　　15. ἁρμόττον apogr.: ἁρμόττοντος Aᶜ: ἁρμοττόντως Tucker　　16. ἐπῶν] ἐπεκτάσεων Tyrwhitt
<κυρίων> coni. Vahlen　　19. ἰάμβιον Aᶜ　　20. Αἰσχύλῳ Εὐριπίδου
Essen: Εὐριπίδου καὶ Αἰσχύλου Richards　　μεταθέντος Parisinus 2038,
Ald. : μετατιθέντος Aᶜ　　21. aut κυρίου aut εἰωθότος secludendum esse
coni. Vahlen　　<καὶ> εἰωθότος Heinsius　　23. φαγέδαινα δ' ἤ Ritter:
φαγέδαινα ἤ apogr. : φαγάδενα ἤ Λᶜ: φαγέδαιναν ἤ Hermann : φαγέδαιν' ἀεὶ
Nauck　　25. δὲ μεων Aᶜ　　ἀεικής Riccardianus 46 ('ut non conveniat'
Arabs): ἀειδής Aᶜ: ἄκικυς (cum var. lect. ἀεικής) Od. ix. 515　　27. δὲ
υεων Aᶜ　　μικρὸς δὲ Aᶜ

Ἐπιχάρην εἶδον Μαραθῶνάδε βαδίζοντα,

or,

οὐκ ἄν γ' ἐράμενος τὸν ἐκείνου ἐλλέβορον.

To employ such license at all obtrusively is, no doubt, 6 grotesque; but in any mode of poetic diction there must be moderation. Even metaphors, strange (or rare) words, or any similar forms of speech, would produce the like effect if used without propriety and with the express purpose of being ludicrous. How great a differ- 7 ence is made by the appropriate use of lengthening, may be seen in Epic poetry by the insertion of ordinary forms in the verse. So, again, if we take a strange (or rare) word, a metaphor, or any similar mode of expression, and replace it by the current or proper term, the truth of our observation will be manifest. For example Aeschylus and Euripides each composed the same iambic line. But the alteration of a single word by Euripides, who employed the rarer term instead of the ordinary one, makes one verse appear beautiful and the other trivial. Aeschylus in his Philoctetes says:

φαγέδαινα < δ' > ἥ μου σάρκας ἐσθίει ποδός·

Euripides substitutes θοινᾶται 'feasts on' for ἐσθίει 'feeds on.' Again, in the line,

νῦν δέ μ' ἐὼν ὀλίγος τε καὶ οὐτιδανὸς καὶ ἀεικής,

the difference will be felt if we substitute the common words,

νῦν δέ μ' ἐὼν μικρός τε καὶ ἀσθενικὸς καὶ ἀειδής.

καὶ

δίφρον ἀεικέλιον καταθεὶς ὀλίγην τε τράπεζαν,[1]
30   δίφρον μοχθηρὸν καταθεὶς μικράν τε τράπεζαν·
καὶ τὸ "ἠιόνες βοόωσιν,"[2] ἠιόνες κράζουσιν.   ἔτι δὲ Ἀριφρά- 8
δης τοὺς τραγῳδοὺς ἐκωμῴδει, ὅτι ἃ οὐδεὶς ἂν εἴποι ἐν τῇ διαλέκτῳ τούτοις χρῶνται, οἷον τὸ δωμάτων ἄπο ἀλλὰ μὴ
ἀπὸ δωμάτων, καὶ τὸ σέθεν καὶ τὸ ἐγὼ δέ νιν καὶ τὸ
1459 a Ἀχιλλέως πέρι ἀλλὰ μὴ περὶ Ἀχιλλέως, καὶ ὅσα ἄλλα
τοιαῦτα.   διὰ γὰρ τὸ μὴ εἶναι ἐν τοῖς κυρίοις ποιεῖ τὸ μὴ
ἰδιωτικὸν ἐν τῇ λέξει ἅπαντα τὰ τοιαῦτα·   ἐκεῖνος δὲ τοῦτο
ἠγνόει.   ἔστιν δὲ μέγα μὲν τὸ ἑκάστῳ τῶν εἰρημένων πρεπόν- 9
5 τως χρῆσθαι, καὶ διπλοῖς ὀνόμασι καὶ γλώτταις, πολὺ δὲ
μέγιστον τὸ μεταφορικὸν εἶναι.   μόνον γὰρ τοῦτο οὔτε παρ᾽
ἄλλου ἔστι λαβεῖν εὐφυΐας τε σημεῖόν ἐστι· τὸ γὰρ εὖ
μεταφέρειν τὸ τὸ ὅμοιον θεωρεῖν ἐστιν.   τῶν δ᾽ ὀνομάτων τὰ 10
μὲν διπλᾶ μάλιστα ἁρμόττει τοῖς διθυράμβοις, αἱ δὲ γλῶτται
10 τοῖς ἡρωικοῖς, αἱ δὲ μεταφοραὶ τοῖς ἰαμβείοις.   καὶ ἐν
μὲν τοῖς ἡρωικοῖς ἅπαντα χρήσιμα τὰ εἰρημένα, ἐν δὲ τοῖς
ἰαμβείοις διὰ τὸ ὅτι μάλιστα λέξιν μιμεῖσθαι ταῦτα ἁρμόττει τῶν ὀνομάτων ὅσοις κἂν ἐν λόγοις τις χρή-
σαιτο· ἔστι δὲ τὰ τοιαῦτα τὸ κύριον καὶ μεταφορὰ καὶ κόσμος.
15 περὶ μὲν οὖν τραγῳδίας καὶ τῆς ἐν τῷ πράττειν μιμήσεως ἔστω ἡμῖν ἱκανὰ τὰ εἰρημένα.

---

[1] Odyss. xx. 259, δίφρον ἀεικέλιον καταθεὶς ὀλίγην τε τράπεζαν.
[2] Iliad xvii. 265.

---

29. ἀεικέλιον Parisinus 2038, coni. Susemihl: τ᾽ ἀεικέλιον A[c]: τ᾽ αἰκέλιον
Vahlen   31. τὸ ἴωνες βοῶσιν ἢ ἴωνες A[c]   32. εἴποι apogr.: εἴπηι
A[c]   1459 a 4. τὸ apogr.: τῶι A[c]   10 et 12. ἰαμβίοις A[c]   13. κἂν
Riccardianus 46 : καὶ A[c]   ὅσοις post ἐν add. A[c]: om. apogr.: τοῖς
Gomperz : ὁδοῖς Σ, ut videtur (Ellis)   τις apogr. : τί A[c]

Or, if for the line,

δίφρον ἀεικέλιον καταθεὶς ὀλίγην τε τράπεζαν,

we read,

δίφρον μοχθηρὸν καταθεὶς μικράν τε τράπεζαν.

Or, for ἠιόνες βοόωσιν, ἠιόνες κράζουσιν.

Again, Ariphrades ridiculed the tragedians for using 8 phrases which no one would employ in ordinary speech : for example, δωμάτων ἄπο instead of ἀπὸ δωμάτων, σέθεν, ἐγὼ δέ νιν, 'Αχιλλέως πέρι instead of περὶ 'Αχιλλέως, and the like. It is precisely because such phrases are not part of the current idiom that they give distinction to the style. This, however, he failed to see.

It is a great matter to observe propriety in these 9 several modes of expression, as also in compound words, strange (or rare) words, and so forth. But the greatest thing by far is to have a command of metaphor. This alone cannot be imparted by another; it is the mark of genius, for to make good metaphors implies an eye for resemblances.

Of the various kinds of words, the compound are 10 best adapted to dithyrambs, rare words to heroic poetry, metaphors to iambic. In heroic poetry, indeed, all these varieties are serviceable. But in iambic verse, which reproduces, as far as may be, familiar speech, the most appropriate words are those which are found even in prose. These are,—the current or proper, the metaphorical, the ornamental.

Concerning Tragedy and imitation by means of action this may suffice.

XXIII   Περὶ δὲ τῆς διηγηματικῆς κἂν ἐν<ὶ> μέτρῳ μιμητικῆς,
ὅτι δεῖ τοὺς μύθους καθάπερ ἐν ταῖς τραγῳδίαις συνιστάναι
δραματικοὺς καὶ περὶ μίαν πρᾶξιν ὅλην καὶ τελείαν, ἔχουσαν
20 ἀρχὴν καὶ μέσα καὶ τέλος, ἵν᾽ ὥσπερ ζῷον ἓν ὅλον ποιῇ τὴν
οἰκείαν ἡδονήν, δῆλον, καὶ μὴ ὁμοίας ἱστορίαις τὰς συνθέσεις εἶναι, ἐν αἷς ἀνάγκη οὐχὶ μιᾶς πράξεως ποιεῖσθαι
δήλωσιν ἀλλ᾽ ἑνὸς χρόνου, ὅσα ἐν τούτῳ συνέβη περὶ ἕνα
ἢ πλείους, ὧν ἕκαστον ὡς ἔτυχεν ἔχει πρὸς ἄλληλα. ὥσπερ 2
25 γὰρ κατὰ τοὺς αὐτοὺς χρόνους ἥ τ᾽ ἐν Σαλαμῖνι ἐγένετο
ναυμαχία καὶ ἡ ἐν Σικελίᾳ Καρχηδονίων μάχη οὐδὲν
πρὸς τὸ αὐτὸ συντείνουσαι τέλος, οὕτω καὶ ἐν τοῖς ἐφεξῆς
χρόνοις ἐνίοτε γίνεται θάτερον μετὰ θάτερον, ἐξ ὧν ἓν
οὐδὲν γίνεται τέλος. σχεδὸν δὲ οἱ πολλοὶ τῶν ποιητῶν τοῦτο
30 δρῶσι. διό, ὥσπερ εἴπομεν ἤδη, καὶ ταύτῃ θεσπέσιος ἂν 3
φανείη Ὅμηρος παρὰ τοὺς ἄλλους, τῷ μηδὲ τὸν πόλεμον
καίπερ ἔχοντα ἀρχὴν καὶ τέλος ἐπιχειρῆσαι ποιεῖν ὅλον·
λίαν γὰρ ἂν μέγας καὶ οὐκ εὐσύνοπτος ἔμελλεν ἔσεσθαι,
ἢ τῷ μεγέθει μετριάζοντα καταπεπλεγμένον τῇ ποικιλίᾳ.
35 νῦν δ᾽ ἓν μέρος ἀπολαβὼν ἐπεισοδίοις κέχρηται αὐτῶν
πολλοῖς, οἷον νεῶν καταλόγῳ καὶ ἄλλοις ἐπεισοδίοις, οἷς
διαλαμβάνει τὴν ποίησιν. οἱ δ᾽ ἄλλοι περὶ ἕνα ποιοῦσι
1459 b καὶ περὶ ἕνα χρόνον καὶ μίαν πρᾶξιν πολυμερῆ, οἷον ὁ

17. κἂν ἑνὶ μέτρῳ scripsi (cf. 1449 b 11, 1459 b 32): καὶ ἐν μέτρῳ codd.
18. συνιστᾶναι Aᶜ: συνεστάναι coni. Vahlen   20. ποιεῖ Aᶜ   21. ὁμοίας
ἱστορίαις τὰς συνθέσεις Dacier (confirmat aliquatenus Arabs): ὁμοίας ἱστορίαις
τὰς συνθήσεις Riccardianus 46: ὁμοίας ἱστορίας τὰς συνήθεις codd.: οἵας
ἱστορίας τὰς συνήθεις M'Vey   22. εἶναι] θεῖναι Bywater   25. Σαλαμίνη
Aᶜ   26. ναυμαχία apogr.: ναύμαχος Aᶜ   28. μετὰ θάτερον Parisinus
2038, coni. Castelvetro: μετὰ θατέρου Aᶜ   31. τῷ Riccardianus 16: τὸ
Aᶜ   33-34. μέγα (rec. corr. μέγας)—εὐσύνοπτος—μετριάζοντα Aᶜ: μέγα—
εὐσύνοπτον—μετριάζον Bursian   35. αὐτῶν secl. Christ: αὐτοῦ Heinsius
36. οἷς Riccardianus 16: δὶς pr. Aᶜ

XXIII   As to that poetic imitation which is narrative in form and employs a single metre, the plot manifestly ought, as in a tragedy, to be constructed on dramatic principles. It should have for its subject a single action, whole and complete, with a beginning, a middle, and an end. It will thus resemble a living organism in all its unity, and produce the pleasure proper to it. It will differ in structure from historical compositions, which of necessity present not a single action, but a single period, and all that happened within that period to one person or to many, little connected together as the events may be. For as the sea-fight at 2 Salamis and the battle with the Carthaginians in Sicily took place at the same time, but did not tend to any one result, so in the sequence of events, one thing sometimes follows another, and yet no single result is thereby produced. Such is the practice, we may say, of most poets. Here again, then, as has been already 3 observed, the transcendent excellence of Homer is manifest. He never attempts to make the whole war of Troy the subject of his poem, though that war had a beginning and an end. It would have been too vast a theme, and not easily embraced in a single view. If, again, he had kept it within moderate limits, it must have been over-complicated by the variety of the incidents. As it is, he detaches a single portion, and admits as episodes many events from the general story of the war—such as the Catalogue of the ships and others—thus diversifying the poem. All other poets 1459 b take a single hero, a single period, or an action single indeed, but with a multiplicity of parts. Thus did the

τὰ Κύπρια ποιήσας καὶ τὴν μικρὰν Ἰλιάδα. τοιγαροῦν ἐκ 4
μὲν Ἰλιάδος καὶ Ὀδυσσείας μία τραγῳδία ποιεῖται ἑκα-
τέρας ἢ δύο μόναι, ἐκ δὲ Κυπρίων πολλαὶ καὶ τῆς μι-
5 κρᾶς Ἰλιάδος [πλέον] ὀκτώ, οἷον ὅπλων κρίσις, Φιλοκτή-
της, Νεοπτόλεμος, Εὐρύπυλος, πτωχεία, Λάκαιναι, Ἰλίου
πέρσις καὶ ἀπόπλους [καὶ Σίνων καὶ Τρῳάδες].

XXIV   Ἔτι δὲ τὰ εἴδη ταὐτὰ δεῖ ἔχειν τὴν ἐποποιίαν τῇ τραγῳδίᾳ, ἢ γὰρ ἁπλῆν ἢ πεπλεγμένην ἢ ἠθικὴν ἢ παθητικήν·
10 καὶ τὰ μέρη ἔξω μελοποιίας καὶ ὄψεως ταὐτά· καὶ γὰρ
περιπετειῶν δεῖ καὶ ἀναγνωρίσεων καὶ παθημάτων· ἔτι
τὰς διανοίας καὶ τὴν λέξιν ἔχειν καλῶς. οἷς ἅπασιν 2
Ὅμηρος κέχρηται καὶ πρῶτος καὶ ἱκανῶς. καὶ γὰρ καὶ
τῶν ποιημάτων ἑκάτερον συνέστηκεν ἡ μὲν Ἰλιὰς ἁπλοῦν
15 καὶ παθητικόν, ἡ δὲ Ὀδύσσεια πεπλεγμένον (ἀναγνώρισις
γὰρ διόλου) καὶ ἠθική· πρὸς γὰρ τούτοις λέξει καὶ διανοίᾳ
πάντα ὑπερβέβληκεν. διαφέρει δὲ κατά τε τῆς συστάσεως 3
τὸ μῆκος ἡ ἐποποιία καὶ τὸ μέτρον. τοῦ μὲν οὖν μήκους ὅρος
ἱκανὸς ὁ εἰρημένος· δύνασθαι γὰρ δεῖ συνορᾶσθαι τὴν ἀρχὴν
20 καὶ τὸ τέλος. εἴη δ' ἂν τοῦτο, εἰ τῶν μὲν ἀρχαίων ἐλάτ-
τους αἱ συστάσεις εἶεν, πρὸς δὲ τὸ πλῆθος τραγῳδιῶν τῶν
εἰς μίαν ἀκρόασιν τιθεμένων παρήκοιεν. ἔχει δὲ πρὸς τὸ 4
ἐπεκτείνεσθαι τὸ μέγεθος πολύ τι ἡ ἐποποιία ἴδιον διὰ
τὸ ἐν μὲν τῇ τραγῳδίᾳ μὴ ἐνδέχεσθαι ἅμα πραττόμενα

1459 b 2. Κύπρια Reiz : κυπρικὰ Aᶜ   4. μόνας pr. Aᶜ   5 et 7. πλέον
et καὶ Σίνων καὶ Τρῳάδες secl. Hermann   7. πρωιάδες pr. Aᶜ (τ sup. scr.
m. rec.)   8. ἔτι δὲ bis Aᶜ   δεῖ apogr. : δὴ Aᶜ   9. ἠθικὴν om.
Σ   11. καὶ ἠθῶν post ἀναγνωρίσεων add. Susemihl   13. ἱκανῶς apogr. :
ἱκανὸς Aᶜ   14. πονημάτων Aᶜ   15. ἀναγνωρίσεις Christ   16. ἠθικὸν
corr. rec. m. Aᶜ   γὰρ Aᶜ : δὲ apogr.   17. πάντας apogr.   21. πρὸς
δὲ apogr. : πρόσθε Aᶜ   τὸ ante τραγῳδιῶν add. Tucker   22. fort.
καθιεμένων Richards

author of the Cypria and of the Little Iliad. For this 4
reason the Iliad and the Odyssey each furnish the
subject of one tragedy, or, at most, of two; while the
Cypria supplies materials for many, and the Little Iliad
for eight—the Award of the Arms, the Philoctetes, the
Neoptolemus, the Eurypylus, the Mendicant Odysseus,
the Laconian Women, the Fall of Ilium, the Departure
of the Fleet.

XXIV   Again, Epic poetry must have as many kinds as
Tragedy: it must be simple, or complex, or 'ethical,'
or 'pathetic.' The parts also, with the exception of
song and spectacle, are the same; for it requires
Reversals of the Situation, Recognitions, and Scenes of
Suffering. Moreover, the thoughts and the diction must 2
be artistic. In all these respects Homer is our earliest
and sufficient model. Indeed each of his poems has a
twofold character. The Iliad is at once simple and
'pathetic,' and the Odyssey complex (for Recognition
scenes run through it), and at the same time 'ethical.'
Moreover, in diction and thought they are supreme.

Epic poetry differs from Tragedy in the scale on 3
which it is constructed, and in its metre. As regards
scale or length, we have already laid down an adequate
limit:—the beginning and the end must be capable of
being brought within a single view. This condition
will be satisfied by poems on a smaller scale than the
old epics, and answering in length to the group of
tragedies presented at a single sitting.

Epic poetry has, however, a great—a special— 4
capacity for enlarging its dimensions, and we can see the
reason. In Tragedy we cannot imitate several lines of

25 πολλὰ μέρη μιμεῖσθαι ἀλλὰ τὸ ἐπὶ τῆς σκηνῆς καὶ τῶν
ὑποκριτῶν μέρος μόνον· ἐν δὲ τῇ ἐποποιίᾳ διὰ τὸ διήγησιν
εἶναι ἔστι πολλὰ μέρη ἅμα ποιεῖν περαινόμενα, ὑφ᾿ ὧν
οἰκείων ὄντων αὔξεται ὁ τοῦ ποιήματος ὄγκος. ὥστε τοῦτ᾿
ἔχει τὸ ἀγαθὸν εἰς μεγαλοπρέπειαν καὶ τὸ μεταβάλλειν τὸν
30 ἀκούοντα καὶ ἐπεισοδιοῦν ἀνομοίοις ἐπεισοδίοις· τὸ γὰρ
ὅμοιον ταχὺ πληροῦν ἐκπίπτειν ποιεῖ τὰς τραγῳδίας. τὸ δὲ 5
μέτρον τὸ ἡρωικὸν ἀπὸ τῆς πείρας ἥρμοκεν. εἰ γάρ τις ἐν
ἄλλῳ τινὶ μέτρῳ διηγηματικὴν μίμησιν ποιοῖτο ἢ ἐν πολλοῖς,
ἀπρεπὲς ἂν φαίνοιτο· τὸ γὰρ ἡρωικὸν στασιμώτατον καὶ
35 ὀγκωδέστατον τῶν μέτρων ἐστίν (διὸ καὶ γλώττας καὶ μετα-
φορὰς δέχεται μάλιστα· περιττὴ γὰρ καὶ <ταύτῃ> ἡ διηγη-
ματικὴ μίμησις τῶν ἄλλων). τὸ δὲ ἰαμβεῖον καὶ τετρά-
1460 a μετρον κινητικά, τὸ μὲν ὀρχηστικὸν τὸ δὲ πρακτικόν. ἔτι δὲ 6
ἀτοπώτερον, εἰ μιγνύοι τις αὐτά, ὥσπερ Χαιρήμων. διὸ
οὐδεὶς μακρὰν σύστασιν ἐν ἄλλῳ πεποίηκεν ἢ τῷ ἡρῴῳ, ἀλλ᾿
ὥσπερ εἴπομεν αὐτὴ ἡ φύσις διδάσκει τὸ ἁρμόττον [αὐτῇ]
5 [δι]αιρεῖσθαι. Ὅμηρος δὲ ἄλλα τε πολλὰ ἄξιος ἐπαινεῖσθαι 7
καὶ δὴ καὶ ὅτι μόνος τῶν ποιητῶν οὐκ ἀγνοεῖ ὃ δεῖ ποιεῖν
αὐτόν. αὐτὸν γὰρ δεῖ τὸν ποιητὴν ἐλάχιστα λέγειν· οὐ γάρ
ἐστι κατὰ ταῦτα μιμητής. οἱ μὲν οὖν ἄλλοι αὐτοὶ μὲν δι᾿ ὅλου

29. fort. [τὸ] ἀγαθὸν Bywater   33. διηγηματικὴν apogr.: διηγητικὴν Aᶜ
36. post καὶ add. ταύτῃ Twining: τῃδὶ Tucker   37. μίμησις apogr.:
κίνησις Aᶜ   ἰαμβίον Aᶜ   1460 a 1. κινητικά Ald.: κινητικαὶ Aᶜ:
κινητικὰ καὶ Riccardianus 46, Vahlen   2. μιγνύοι Parisinus 2038: μιγνύει
apogr.: μηγνύη Aᶜ (fuit μὴ, et η extremum in litura): μὴ γνοίη Σ (cf. Arab.
' si quis nesciret')   3. τῷ] τὸ Aᶜ   4. αὐτῇ apogr.: αὐτὴ Aᶜ: secl.
Gomperz   5. αἱρεῖσθαι Bonitz (confirmare videtur Arabs): διαιρεῖσθαι Aᶜ:
δεῖ αἱρεῖσθαι Tucker

actions carried on at one and the same time; we must confine ourselves to the action on the stage and the part taken by the players. But in Epic poetry, owing to the narrative form, many events simultaneously transacted can be presented; and these, if relevant to the subject, add mass and dignity to the poem. The Epic has here an advantage, and one that conduces to grandeur of effect, to diverting the mind of the hearer, and relieving the story with varying episodes. For sameness of incident soon produces satiety, and makes tragedies fail on the stage.

As for the metre, the heroic measure has proved its 5 fitness by the test of experience. If a narrative poem in any other metre or in many metres were now composed, it would be found incongruous. For of all measures the heroic is the stateliest and the most massive; and hence it most readily admits rare words and metaphors, which is another point in which the narrative form of imitation stands alone. On the other 1460 a hand, the iambic and the trochaic tetrameter are stirring measures, the latter being akin to dancing, the former expressive of action. Still more absurd would it be to 6 mix together different metres, as was done by Chaeremon. Hence no one has ever composed a poem on a great scale in any other than heroic verse. Nature herself, as we have said, teaches the choice of the proper measure.

Homer, admirable in all respects, has the special merit 7 of being the only poet who rightly appreciates the part he should take himself. The poet should speak as little as possible in his own person, for it is not this that makes him an imitator. Other poets appear themselves upon

ἀγωνίζονται, μιμοῦνται δὲ ὀλίγα καὶ ὀλιγάκις· ὁ δὲ ὀλίγα
10 φροιμιασάμενος εὐθὺς εἰσάγει ἄνδρα ἢ γυναῖκα ἢ ἄλλο τι
[ἦθος] καὶ οὐδέν' ἀήθη ἀλλ' ἔχοντα ἤθη. δεῖ μὲν οὖν ἐν ταῖς 8
τραγῳδίαις ποιεῖν τὸ θαυμαστόν, μᾶλλον δ' ἐνδέχεται ἐν
τῇ ἐποποιίᾳ τὸ ἄλογον, δι' ὃ συμβαίνει μάλιστα τὸ θαυμαστόν, διὰ τὸ μὴ ὁρᾶν εἰς τὸν πράττοντα· ἐπεὶ τὰ περὶ
15 τὴν Ἕκτορος δίωξιν ἐπὶ σκηνῆς ὄντα γελοῖα ἂν φανείη, οἱ
μὲν ἑστῶτες καὶ οὐ διώκοντες, ὁ δὲ ἀνανεύων, ἐν δὲ τοῖς
ἔπεσιν λανθάνει. τὸ δὲ θαυμαστὸν ἡδύ· σημεῖον δέ· πάντες
γὰρ προστιθέντες ἀπαγγέλλουσιν ὡς χαριζόμενοι. δεδίδαχεν 9
δὲ μάλιστα Ὅμηρος καὶ τοὺς ἄλλους ψευδῆ λέγειν ὡς δεῖ.
20 ἔστι δὲ τοῦτο παραλογισμός. οἴονται γὰρ ἄνθρωποι, ὅταν
τουδὶ ὄντος τοδὶ ᾖ ἢ γινομένου γίνηται, εἰ τὸ ὕστερον ἔστιν,
καὶ τὸ πρότερον εἶναι ἢ γίνεσθαι· τοῦτο δέ ἐστι ψεῦδος. διὸ
δή, ἂν τὸ πρῶτον ψεῦδος, ἀλλ' οὐδέ, τούτου ὄντος, ἀνάγκη
<κἀκεῖνο> εἶναι ἢ γενέσθαι [ἢ] προσθεῖναι· διὰ γὰρ τὸ τοῦτο
25 εἰδέναι ἀληθὲς ὄν, παραλογίζεται ἡμῶν ἡ ψυχὴ καὶ τὸ πρῶτον
ὡς ὄν. παράδειγμα δὲ τούτου ἐκ τῶν Νίπτρων. προαιρεῖσθαί 10
τε δεῖ ἀδύνατα εἰκότα μᾶλλον ἢ δυνατὰ ἀπίθανα· τούς τε λόγους
μὴ συνίστασθαι ἐκ μερῶν ἀλόγων, ἀλλὰ μάλιστα μὲν μη-

11. ἦθος codd., Σ: secl. Reiz: εἶδος Bursian   οὐδέν' ἀήθη Vettori: οὐδεναήθη
Urbinas 47: οὐδένα ἤθη Aᶜ   ἤθη] fort. ἦθος Christ   κἂν ταῖς
Gomperz   13. ἄλογον Vettori: ἀνάλογον codd., Σ   δι' ὃ Parisinus
2038, coni. Vettori: διὸ codd. cett.   14. ἐπεὶ apogr.: ἔπειτα Aᶜ, Σ
21. τοῦ διόντος pr. Aᶜ   τοδὶ ᾖ ἢ apogr.: τὸ δι' ἦν pr. Aᶜ (τὸ δὶ ἢ corr.
rec. m.)   23. δή] δεῖ Riccardianus 46, Bonitz   ἄλλου δὲ Aᶜ
(ἀλλ' οὐδὲ corr. rec. m.): ἄλλο δὲ codd. Robortelli: ἄλλο δ' ὃ Vahlen:
ἄλλο, ὃ Christ   23–24. cum verbis ἀλλ' οὐδὲ—ἀνάγκη—προσθεῖναι con-
tulerim Rhet. i. 2. 13. 1357 a 17, ἐὰν γὰρ ᾖ τι τούτων γνώριμον, οὐδὲ δεῖ
λέγειν· αὐτὸς γὰρ τοῦτο προστίθησιν ὁ ἀκροατής, et 18, τὸ δ' ὅτι στεφανίτης τὰ
Ὀλύμπια, οὐδὲ δεῖ προσθεῖναι   24. κἀκεῖνο add. Tucker   ἢ secl.
Bonitz: ᾖ Vahlen: ἢν Tucker   26. τούτου codex Robortelli: τοῦτο Aᶜ:
τούτων apogr.: τοῦτο <τὸ> Spengel   νίπτρω Aᶜ

the scene throughout, and imitate but little and rarely. Homer, after a few prefatory words, at once brings in a man, or woman, or other personage; none of them wanting in characteristic qualities, but each with a character of his own.

The element of the wonderful is required in Tragedy. 8 The irrational, on which the wonderful depends for its chief effects, has wider scope in Epic poetry, because there the person acting is not seen. Thus, the pursuit of Hector would be ludicrous if placed upon the stage—the Greeks standing still and not joining in the pursuit, and Achilles waving them back. But in the Epic poem the absurdity passes unnoticed. Now the wonderful is pleasing: as may be inferred from the fact that every one tells a story with some addition of his own, knowing that his hearers like it. It is Homer who 9 has chiefly taught other poets the art of telling lies skilfully. The secret of it lies in a fallacy. For, assuming that if one thing is or becomes, a second is or becomes, men imagine that, if the second is, the first likewise is or becomes. But this is a false inference. Hence, where the first thing is untrue, it is quite unnecessary, provided the second be true, to add that the first is or has become. For the mind, knowing the second to be true, falsely infers the truth of the first. There is an example of this in the Bath Scene of the Odyssey.

Accordingly, the poet should prefer probable im- 10 possibilities to improbable possibilities. The tragic plot must not be composed of irrational parts. Everything

δὲν ἔχειν ἄλογον, εἰ δὲ μή, ἔξω τοῦ μυθεύματος, ὥσπερ
30 Οἰδίπους τὸ μὴ εἰδέναι πῶς ὁ Λάιος ἀπέθανεν, ἀλλὰ μὴ ἐν
τῷ δράματι, ὥσπερ ἐν Ἠλέκτρᾳ οἱ τὰ Πύθια ἀπαγγέλλον-
τες, ἢ ἐν Μυσοῖς ὁ ἄφωνος ἐκ Τεγέας εἰς τὴν Μυσίαν ἥκων·
ὥστε τὸ λέγειν ὅτι ἀνῄρητο ἂν ὁ μῦθος γελοῖον· ἐξ ἀρχῆς
γὰρ οὐ δεῖ συνίστασθαι τοιούτους. ἂν δὲ θῇ καὶ φαίνηται
35 εὐλογωτέρως, ἐνδέχεσθαι καὶ ἄτοπον <ὄν>· ἐπεὶ καὶ τὰ ἐν
Ὀδυσσείᾳ ἄλογα τὰ περὶ τὴν ἔκθεσιν ὡς οὐκ ἂν ἦν ἀνεκτὰ
1460 b δῆλον ἂν γένοιτο, εἰ αὐτὰ φαῦλος ποιητὴς ποιήσειε· νῦν δὲ
τοῖς ἄλλοις ἀγαθοῖς ὁ ποιητὴς ἀφανίζει ἡδύνων τὸ ἄτοπον.
τῇ δὲ λέξει δεῖ διαπονεῖν ἐν τοῖς ἀργοῖς μέρεσιν καὶ μήτε 11
ἠθικοῖς μήτε διανοητικοῖς· ἀποκρύπτει γὰρ πάλιν ἡ λίαν
5 λαμπρὰ λέξις τά τε ἤθη καὶ τὰς διανοίας.
XXV   Περὶ δὲ προβλημάτων καὶ λύσεων, ἐκ πόσων τε καὶ
ποίων εἰδῶν ἐστιν, ὧδ' ἂν θεωροῦσιν γένοιτ' ἂν φανερόν.
ἐπεὶ γάρ ἐστι μιμητὴς ὁ ποιητὴς ὡσπερανεὶ ζωγράφος ἤ τις
ἄλλος εἰκονοποιός, ἀνάγκη μιμεῖσθαι τριῶν ὄντων τὸν ἀρι-
10 θμὸν ἕν τι ἀεί, ἢ γὰρ οἷα ἦν ἢ ἔστιν, ἢ οἷά φασιν καὶ δοκεῖ,
ἢ οἷα εἶναι δεῖ.   ταῦτα δ' ἐξαγγέλλεται λέξει <ἢ κυρίοις 2
ὀνόμασιν> ἢ καὶ γλώτταις καὶ μεταφοραῖς· καὶ πολλὰ πάθη

---

30. <ὁ> Οἰδίπους Bywater: Οἰδίπου Tucker   Λάιος Riccardianus 16:
ἰόλαος Aᶜ: ἰόλαος cett.   33. ἀνῄρειτο Aᶜ   35. ἀποδέχεσθαι apogr.
ἄτοπον <ὄν> scripsi: τὸ ἄτοπον Par. 2038: ἄτοπον codd. cett.   ἄτοπον
quidem pro ἄτοπόν τι nonnunquam usurpari solet, e.g. ἄτοπον ποιεῖν (Dem.
F.L. § 71, 337), ἄτοπον λέγειν (Plat. Symp. 175 A); sed in hoc loco vix
defendi potest ea locutio   1460 b 1. ποιήσειε Riccardianus 46, Heinsius:
ποιήσει codd.: ἐποίησεν Spengel   5. τά τε] τὰ δὲ Aᶜ   7. ποίων
apogr.: ποίων ἂν Aᶜ   9. τὸν ἀριθμὸν (vel τῷ ἀριθμῷ) apogr.: τῶν ἀριθμῶν
Aᶜ   11. ἢ οἷα apogr.: οἷα Aᶜ   <ἢ κυρίοις ὀνόμασιν> coni. Vahlen:
<ἢ κυρίᾳ> Gomperz   12. καὶ ὅσ' ἄλλα πάθη coni. Vahlen

irrational should, if possible, be excluded; or, at all
events, it should lie outside the action of the play (as,
in the Oedipus, the hero's ignorance as to the manner
of Laius' death); not within the drama,—as in the
Electra, the messenger's account of the Pythian games;
or, as in the Mysians, the man who has come from Tegea
to Mysia and is still speechless.   The plea that otherwise
the plot would have been ruined, is ridiculous; such a
plot should not in the first instance be constructed.
But once the irrational has been introduced and an air
of likelihood imparted to it, we must accept it in spite of
the absurdity.   Take even the irrational incidents in the
Odyssey, where Odysseus is left upon the shore of Ithaca.
How intolerable even these might have been would be
apparent if an inferior poet were to treat the subject.
1460 b As it is, the absurdity is veiled by the poetic charm
with which the poet invests it.

The diction should be elaborated in the pauses of 11
the action, where there is no expression of character
or thought.   For, conversely, character and thought are
merely obscured by a diction that is over brilliant.

XXV   With respect to critical difficulties and their solutions, the number and nature of the sources from which
they may be drawn may be thus exhibited.

The poet being an imitator, like a painter or any
other artist, must of necessity imitate one of three
objects,—things as they were or are, things as they are
said or thought to be, or things as they ought to be.
The vehicle of expression is language,—either current 2
terms or, it may be, rare words or metaphors.   There
are also many modifications of language, which we

τῆς λέξεως ἐστί, δίδομεν γὰρ ταῦτα τοῖς ποιηταῖς. πρὸς δὲ 3
τούτοις οὐχ ἡ αὐτὴ ὀρθότης ἐστὶν τῆς πολιτικῆς καὶ τῆς
15 ποιητικῆς οὐδὲ ἄλλης τέχνης καὶ ποιητικῆς. αὐτῆς δὲ τῆς
ποιητικῆς διττὴ ἁμαρτία, ἡ μὲν γὰρ καθ' αὑτήν, ἡ δὲ κατὰ
συμβεβηκός. εἰ μὲν γάρ <τι> προείλετο μιμήσασθαι, <μὴ 4
ὀρθῶς δὲ ἐμιμήσατο δι'> ἀδυναμίαν, αὐτῆς ἡ ἁμαρτία· εἰ δὲ
τῷ προελέσθαι μὴ ὀρθῶς, ἀλλὰ τὸν ἵππον <ἄμ'> ἄμφω τὰ
20 δεξιὰ προβεβληκότα, ἢ τὸ καθ' ἑκάστην τέχνην ἁμάρτημα
οἷον τὸ κατ' ἰατρικὴν ἢ ἄλλην τέχνην [ἢ ἀδύνατα πεποίηται]
ὁποιανοῦν, οὐ καθ' ἑαυτήν. ὥστε δεῖ τὰ ἐπιτιμήματα ἐν τοῖς
προβλήμασιν ἐκ τούτων ἐπισκοποῦντα λύειν. πρῶτον μὲν τὰ 5
πρὸς αὐτὴν τὴν τέχνην· εἰ ἀδύνατα πεποίηται, ἡμάρτηται·
25 ἀλλ' ὀρθῶς ἔχει, εἰ τυγχάνει τοῦ τέλους τοῦ αὑτῆς (τὸ γὰρ
τέλος εἴρηται), εἰ οὕτως ἐκπληκτικώτερον ἢ αὐτὸ ἢ ἄλλο ποιεῖ
μέρος. παράδειγμα ἡ τοῦ Ἕκτορος δίωξις. εἰ μέντοι τὸ τέλος
ἢ μᾶλλον ἢ <μὴ> ἧττον ἐνεδέχετο ὑπάρχειν καὶ κατὰ τὴν
περὶ τούτων τέχνην, [ἡμαρτῆσθαι] οὐκ ὀρθῶς· δεῖ γὰρ εἰ ἐν-
30 δέχεται ὅλως μηδαμῇ ἡμαρτῆσθαι. ἔτι ποτέρων ἐστὶ τὸ
ἁμάρτημα, τῶν κατὰ τὴν τέχνην ἢ κατ' ἄλλο συμβεβηκός; ἔλαττον γὰρ εἰ μὴ ᾔδει ὅτι ἔλαφος θήλεια κέρατα
οὐκ ἔχει ἢ εἰ ἀμιμήτως ἔγραψεν. πρὸς δὲ τούτοις ἐὰν 6
ἐπιτιμᾶται ὅτι οὐκ ἀληθῆ, ἀλλ' ἴσως <ὡς> δεῖ—οἷον καὶ

17. τι addidi　　　μὴ ὀρθῶς—δι' addidi : <ὀρθῶς, ἥμαρτε δ' ἐν τῷ μιμήσασθαι δι'> coni. Vahlen　　　18. εἰ apogr.: ἡ Aᶜ　　　19. τῷ corr. Parisinus
2038 (Bywater): τὸ Aᶜ: <διὰ> τὸ Ueberweg　　　ἄμ' add. Vahlen
21. ἢ ἀδύνατα πεποίηται secl. Düntzer: ἀδύνατα πεποίηται (deleto ἢ) post
ὁποιανοῦν traiecit Christ　　　22. ὁποίαν ὅῦν Aᶜ: ὁποιανοῦν vulg.: ὁποῖ' ἂν οὖν
Bywater: ὁποιαοῦν Winstanley　　　23. τὰ (εἰ sup. scr. m. rec.) Aᶜ　　　24. εἰ add.
Parisinus 2038: om. cett.　　　25. αὐτῆς apogr.: αὑτῆς Aᶜ　　　26. εἴρηται] εὕρηται
Heinsius: τηρεῖται M. Schmidt　　　28. ἢ <μὴ> ἧττον Ueberweg: ἧττον
Aᶜ: ἢ ἧττον corr. Aᶜ apogr.　　　29. ἡμαρτῆσθαι (μαρτῆσθαι pr. Aᶜ) secl.
Bywater, Ussing: ἡμάρτηται Ald. : <μὴ> ἡμαρτῆσθαι, Tucker, interpunctione
mutata　　　32. εἴδει (ἤ sup. scr. m. rec.) Aᶜ　　　33. ἢ] η pr. Aᶜ　　　εἰ
ἀμιμήτως] η ἀμιμήτως (corr. κάμιμήτως) Aᶜ　　　34. <ὡς> coni. Vahlen

concede to the poets. Add to this, that the standard of 3
correctness is not the same in poetry and politics, any
more than in poetry and any other art. Within the art
of poetry itself there are two kinds of faults,—those
which touch its essence, and those which are accidental.
If a poet has chosen to imitate something, <but has 4
imitated it incorrectly> through want of capacity, the
error is inherent in the poetry. But if the failure is
due to a wrong choice—if he has represented a horse
as throwing out both his off legs at once, or introduced
technical inaccuracies in medicine, for example, or in
any other art—the error is not essential to the poetry.
These are the points of view from which we should
consider and answer the objections raised by the
critics.

Firot as to matters which concern the poet's own 5
art. If he describes the impossible, he is guilty of
an error; but the error may be justified, if the end
of the art be thereby attained (the end being that
already mentioned),—if, that is, the effect of this or
any other part of the poem is thus rendered more
striking. A case in point is the pursuit of Hector.
If, however, the end might have been as well, or better,
attained without violating the special rules of the poetic
art, the error is not justified: for every kind of error
should, if possible, be avoided.

Again, does the error touch the essentials of the
poetic art, or some accident of it? For example,—not
to know that a hind has no horns is a less serious matter
than to paint it inartistically.

Further, if it be objected that the description is not 6

35 Σοφοκλῆς ἔφη αὐτὸς μὲν οἵους δεῖ ποιεῖν, Εὐριπίδην δὲ οἷοι
εἰσίν—ταύτῃ λυτέον.   εἰ δὲ μηδετέρως, ὅτι οὕτω φασίν· οἷον 7
τὰ περὶ θεῶν· ἴσως γὰρ οὔτε βέλτιον οὕτω λέγειν, οὔτ᾽ ἀληθῆ,
1461 a ἀλλ᾽ <εἰ> ἔτυχεν ὥσπερ Ξενοφάνει· ἀλλ᾽ οὖν φασι.   τὰ δὲ
ἴσως οὐ βέλτιον μέν, ἀλλ᾽ οὕτως εἶχεν, οἷον τὰ περὶ τῶν
ὅπλων, " ἔγχεα δέ σφιν ὀρθ᾽ ἐπὶ σαυρωτῆρος·"¹ οὕτω γὰρ τότ᾽
ἐνόμιζον, ὥσπερ καὶ νῦν Ἰλλυριοί.   περὶ δὲ τοῦ καλῶς ἢ μὴ 8
5 καλῶς ἢ εἴρηταί τινι ἢ πέπρακται, οὐ μόνον σκεπτέον εἰς
αὐτὸ τὸ πεπραγμένον ἢ εἰρημένον βλέποντα εἰ σπουδαῖον ἢ
φαῦλον, ἀλλὰ καὶ εἰς τὸν πράττοντα ἢ λέγοντα, πρὸς ὃν ἢ
ὅτε ἢ ὅτῳ ἢ οὗ ἕνεκεν, οἷον ἢ μείζονος ἀγαθοῦ, ἵνα γένηται, ἢ μείζονος κακοῦ, ἵνα ἀπογένηται.   τὰ δὲ πρὸς τὴν 9
10 λέξιν ὁρῶντα δεῖ διαλύειν, οἷον γλώττῃ " οὐρῆας μὲν πρῶ-
τον·"² ἴσως γὰρ οὐ τοὺς ἡμιόνους λέγει ἀλλὰ τοὺς φύ-
λακας, καὶ τὸν Δόλωνα " ὅς ῥ᾽ ἦ τοι εἶδος μὲν ἔην κακός,"³
οὐ τὸ σῶμα ἀσύμμετρον ἀλλὰ τὸ πρόσωπον αἰσχρόν, τὸ
γὰρ εὐειδὲς οἱ Κρῆτες εὐπρόσωπον καλοῦσι· καὶ τὸ " ζωρό-
15 τερον δὲ κέραιε "⁴ οὐ τὸ ἄκρατον ὡς οἰνόφλυξιν ἀλλὰ τὸ
θᾶττον.   τὰ δὲ κατὰ μεταφορὰν εἴρηται, οἷον " πάντες μέν 10

---

¹ *Iliad* x. 152.   ² *Ib.* i. 50.
³ *Ib.* x. 316.   ⁴ *Ib.* ix. 203.

---

35. Εὐριπίδην Heinsius : εὐριπίδης codd. (tuetur Gomperz, cf. 1448 a 36
ἀθηναῖοι codd.)   37. οὕτω Riccardianus 16, corr. Vaticanus 1400 : οὕτε
Aᶜ : om. Parisinus 2038   1461 a 1. <εἰ> coni. Vahlen   ξενοφάνει vel
ξενοφάνῃς apogr. : ξενοφάνη Aᶜ : παρὰ Ξενοφάνει Ritter : <οἱ περὶ> Ξενοφάνη
Tucker   οὖν Tyrwhitt : οὔ Aᶜ : οὕτω Spengel   φασί. τὰ δὲ Spengel :
φασι τάδε. Aᶜ   6. εἰ apogr. : ἢ Aᶜ   7. distinxi post λέγοντα
<ἢ> πρὸς ὃν Carroll   8. οἷον ἢ Aᶜ : οἷον εἰ apogr.   9. ἢ add.
corr. Aᶜ apogr.   12. ὅς ῥ᾽ ἦ τοι Vahlen : ὡς ῥῆτοι (corr. m. rec. ῥ᾽) Aᶜ :
ὅς ῥά τοι apogr.   ἔην apogr. : εἰ ἦν Aᶜ   15. κέραιε έου τὸ pr. Aᶜ
16. τὰ Spengel : τὸ Aᶜ   πάντες Gräfenhan : ἄλλοι Aᶜ et Homerus

true to fact, the poet may perhaps reply,—'But the objects are as they ought to be': just as Sophocles said that he drew men as they ought to be; Euripides, as they are. In this way the objection may be met. If, 7 however, the representation be of neither kind, the poet may answer,—'This is how men say the thing is.' This applies to tales about the gods. It may well be that these stories are not higher than fact nor yet true to 1461 a fact: they are, very possibly, what Xenophanes says of them. But anyhow, 'this is what is said.' Again, a description may be no better than the fact: still, it was the fact'; as in the passage about the arms: 'Upright upon their butt-ends stood the spears.' This was the custom then, as it now is among the Illyrians.

Again, in examining whether what has been said or 8 done by some one is poetically right or not, we must not look merely to the particular act or saying, and ask whether it is poetically good or bad. We must also consider by whom it is said or done, to whom, when, by what means, or for what end; whether, for instance, it be to secure a greater good, or avert a greater evil.

Other difficulties may be resolved by due regard to 9 the usage of language. We may note a rare word, as in οὐρῆας μὲν πρῶτον, where the poet perhaps employs οὐρῆας not in the sense of mules, but of sentinels. So, again, of Dolon: 'ill-favoured indeed he was to look upon.' It is not meant that his body was ill-shaped, but that his face was ugly; for the Cretans use the word εὐειδές, 'well-favoured,' to denote a fair face. Again, ζωρότερον δὲ κέραιε, 'mix the drink livelier,' does not mean 'mix it stronger' as for hard drinkers, but 'mix it quicker.'

ρα θεοί τε καὶ ἀνέρες εὗδον παννύχιοι·"[1] ἅμα δέ φησιν " ἦ
τοι ὅτ᾽ ἐς πεδίον τὸ Τρωικὸν ἀθρήσειεν, αὐλῶν συρίγγων
θ᾽ ὅμαδον·"[2] τὸ γὰρ πάντες ἀντὶ τοῦ πολλοὶ κατὰ μετα-
20 φορὰν εἴρηται, τὸ γὰρ πᾶν πολύ τι· καὶ τὸ " οἴη δ᾽ ἄμμο-
ρος"[3] κατὰ μεταφοράν, τὸ γὰρ γνωριμώτατον μόνον.   κατὰ 11
δὲ προσῳδίαν, ὥσπερ Ἱππίας ἔλυεν ὁ Θάσιος τὸ " δίδομεν
δέ οἱ"[4] καὶ " τὸ μὲν οὗ καταπύθεται ὄμβρῳ."[5]   τὰ δὲ διαιρέ- 12
σει, οἷον Ἐμπεδοκλῆς " αἶψα δὲ θνήτ᾽ ἐφύοντο, τὰ πρὶν μά-
25 θον ἀθάνατ᾽ <εἶναι>, ζωρά τε πρὶν κέκρητο."   τὰ δὲ ἀμφιβολίᾳ, 13
"παρῴχηκεν δὲ πλέω νύξ·"[6] τὸ γὰρ πλείω ἀμφίβολόν ἐστιν.
τὰ δὲ κατὰ τὸ ἔθος τῆς λέξεως· τῶν κεκραμένων <οἰονοῦν> οἶνόν 14

---

[1] *Iliad* ii. 1, ἄλλοι μέν ῥα θεοί τε καὶ ἀνέρες ἱπποκορυσταὶ
         εὗδον παννύχιοι.
  Ib. x. 1,   ἄλλοι μὲν παρὰ νηυσὶν ἀριστῆες Παναχαιῶν
         εὗδον παννύχιοι.
[2] *Ib.* x. 11,   ἦ τοι ὅτ᾽ ἐς πεδίον τὸ Τρωικὸν ἀθρήσειεν,
         θαύμαζεν πυρὰ πολλὰ τὰ καίετο Ἰλιόθι πρό,
         αὐλῶν συρίγγων τ᾽ ἐνοπὴν ὅμαδόν τ᾽ ἀνθρώπων.
[3] *Ib.* xviii. 489, οἴη δ᾽ ἄμμορός ἐστι λοετρῶν Ὠκεανοῖο.
[4] *Ib.* xxi. 297, δίδομεν δέ οἱ εὖχος ἀρέσθαι.   Sed in *Iliade* ii. 15 (de
quo hic agitur) Τρώεσσι δὲ κῆδε᾽ ἐφῆπται.
[5] *Ib.* xxiii. 328, τὸ μὲν οὐ καταπύθεται ὄμβρῳ.
[6] *Ib.* x. 251,   μάλα γὰρ νὺξ ἄνεται, ἐγγύθι δ᾽ ἠώς,
         ἄστρα δὲ δὴ προβέβηκε, παρῴχηκεν δὲ πλέων νὺξ
         τῶν δύο μοιράων, τριτάτη δ᾽ ἔτι μοῖρα λέλειπται.

---

17. ἱπποκορυσταὶ (Homerus) post ἀνέρες add. Christ, habuit iam Σ (cf. Arab.
'ceteri quidem homines et dei qui equis armati insident')   ἅπαντες
post εὗδον intercidisse suspicatur Bywater   19. θ᾽ ὅμαδον Sylburg: τε
ὁμαδόν (ὅμαδον apogr.) Aᶜ   τοῦ add. apogr.: om. Aᶜ   23. δέ οἱ
apogr. : δέοι Aᶜ   25. εἶναι Riccardianus 46, add. Vettori ex Athenaeo x.
423   ζωρά Athenaeus : ζῶα codd.   τε <ἀ> πρὶν Gomperz secutus
Bergkium   κέκρητο (ι sup. scr. m. rec.) Aᶜ: κέκριτο apogr. : ἄκρητα
Karsten (ed. Empedocles)   26. πλέω Aᶜ: πλέον apogr. : πλέων Ald.
27. τὸν κεκραμένον apogr.: τῶν κεκραμένων Aᶜ: <ὅσα> τῶν κεκραμένων
Vahlen : <ὅσα πο>τῶν κεκραμένων Ueberweg: πᾶν κεκραμένον Bursian
<οἰονοῦν> Tucker: <ἔνια> olim conieci

Sometimes an expression is metaphorical, as 'Now all 10 gods and men were sleeping through the night,'—while at the same time the poet says : 'Often indeed as he turned his gaze to the Trojan plain, he marvelled at the sound of flutes and pipes.' 'All' is here used metaphorically for 'many,' all being a species of many. So in the verse,—'alone she hath no part . . , οἴη, 'alone,' is metaphorical ; for the best known may be called the only one.

Again, the solution may depend upon accent or 11 breathing. Thus Hippias of Thasos solved the difficulties in the lines,—δίδομεν (διδόμεν) δέ οἱ, and τὸ μὲν οὖ (οὐ) καταπύθεται ὄμβρῳ.

Or again, the question may be solved by punctuation, 12 as in Empedocles,—'Of a sudden things became mortal that before had learnt to be immortal, and things un-mixed before mixed.'

Or again, by ambiguity of meaning, — as παρ- 13 ῴχηκεν δὲ πλέω νύξ, where the word πλέω is ambiguous.

Or by the usage of language. Thus any mixed 14 drink is called οἶνος, 'wine.' Hence Ganymede is said

φασιν εἶναι, [ὅθεν πεποίηται " κνημὶς νεοτεύκτου κασσιτέροιο"]¹ ὅθεν εἴρηται ὁ Γανυμήδης "Διὶ οἰνοχοεύει,"² οὐ πινόν-
30 των οἶνον, καὶ χαλκέας τοὺς τὸν σίδηρον ἐργαζομένους.   εἴη 15
δ᾽ ἂν τοῦτό γε <καὶ> κατὰ μεταφοράν.   δεῖ δὲ καὶ ὅταν ὄνομά
τι ὑπεναντίωμά τι δοκῇ σημαίνειν, ἐπισκοπεῖν ποσαχῶς ἂν
σημαίνοι τοῦτο ἐν τῷ εἰρημένῳ, οἷον τὸ "τῇ ῥ᾽ ἔσχετο χάλκεον
ἔγχος,"³ τὸ ταύτῃ κωλυθῆναι ποσαχῶς ἐνδέχεται.   ὡδὶ <δὲ> 16
35 [ἢ ὡς] μάλιστ᾽ ἄν τις ὑπολάβοι, κατὰ τὴν καταντικρὺ ἢ ὡς
1461 b Γλαύκων λέγει, ὅτι ἔνια ἀλόγως προυπολαμβάνουσιν καὶ
αὐτοὶ καταψηφισάμενοι συλλογίζονται καὶ ὡς εἰρηκότος ὅ
τι δοκεῖ ἐπιτιμῶσιν, ἂν ὑπεναντίον ᾖ τῇ αὐτῶν οἰήσει.   τοῦτο δὲ πέπονθε τὰ περὶ Ἰκάριον.   οἴονται γὰρ αὐτὸν Λάκωνα
5 εἶναι· ἄτοπον οὖν τὸ μὴ ἐντυχεῖν τὸν Τηλέμαχον αὐτῷ εἰς
Λακεδαίμονα ἐλθόντα.   τὸ δ᾽ ἴσως ἔχει ὥσπερ οἱ Κεφαλῆ-
νές φασι· παρ᾽ αὐτῶν γὰρ γῆμαι λέγουσι τὸν Ὀδυσσέα
καὶ εἶναι Ἰκάδιον ἀλλ᾽ οὐκ Ἰκάριον· δι᾽ ἁμάρτημα δὴ τὸ
πρόβλημα εἰκός ἐστιν.   ὅλως δὲ τὸ ἀδύνατον μὲν πρὸς τὴν 17
10 ποίησιν ἢ πρὸς τὸ βέλτιον ἢ πρὸς τὴν δόξαν δεῖ ἀνάγειν.

---

¹ Iliad xxi. 592.   ² Ib. xx. 234.
³ Ib. xx. 272, τῇ ῥ᾽ ἔσχετο μείλινον ἔγχος.

---

28. ὅθεν—κασσιτέροιο secl. M. Schmidt   29–30. verba ὅθεν εἴρηται—
οἶνον in codd. post ἐργαζομένους posita huc revocavit Maggi e cod. Lampridii
29. οἰνοχοεύει Aᶜ : οἰνοχοεύειν apogr.   πεινόντων pr. Aᶜ   31. καὶ add.
Heinsius   31–32. ὀνόματι ὑπεναντιώματι Aᶜ   δοκῇ apogr.: δοκεῖ Aᶜ   33.
σημαίνοι Vahlen (ed. 1): σημαίνοιε Aᶜ : σημήνειεν Parisinus 2038 : σημαίνειε
alia apographa   33–35. οἷον τὸ <ἐν τῷ> "τῇ—τὸ ταύτῃ κωλυθῆναι [ποσα-
χῶς] ἐνδέχεται διπλῶς, ἢ πῶς μάλιστ᾽ ἄν τις κ.τ.λ. M. Schmidt   34. δὲ
addidi   35. ἢ ὡς olim secl. Bywater   ὡδὶ ἢ <ὡδὶ>, ὡς Riccardianus 46
1461 b 1. ἔνιοι Vettori   2. εἰρηκότος Riccardianus 46 : εἰρηκότες ὅτι Aᶜ
3. αὐτῶν Parisinus 2038, coni. Heinsius : αὐτῶν codd.   7. αὐτῶν apogr. :
αὐτῶν Aᶜ   8. δι᾽ ἁμάρτημα Maggi : διαμάρτημα codd.   δὴ Gomperz :
δὲ codd.   9. <εἶναι> εἰκός ἐστιν Hermann (fort. recte): εἰκός ἐστι
<γενέσθαι> Gomperz   <ἢ> πρὸς Ald. fort. recte

'to pour the wine to Zeus,' though the gods do not drink wine. So too workers in iron are called χαλκέας, or workers in bronze. This, however, may also be taken as a metaphor.

Again, when a word seems to involve some incon- 15 sistency of meaning, we should consider how many senses it may bear in the particular passage. For 16 example: 'there was stayed the spear of bronze'—we should ask in how many ways we may take 'being checked there.' The true mode of interpretation is the 1461 b precise opposite of what Glaucon mentions. Critics, he says, jump at certain groundless conclusions; they pass adverse judgment and then proceed to reason on it; and, assuming that the poet has said whatever they happen to think, find fault if a thing is inconsistent with their own fancy. The question about Icarius has been treated in this fashion. The critics imagine he was a Lacedae-monian. They think it strange, therefore, that Tele-machus should not have met him when he went to Lacedaemon. But the Cephallenian story may perhaps be the true one. They allege that Odysseus took a wife from among themselves, and that her father was Icadius not Icarius. It is merely a mistake, then, that gives plausibility to the objection.

In general, the impossible must be justified by 17 reference to artistic requirements, or to the higher

πρός τε γὰρ τὴν ποίησιν αἱρετώτερον πιθανὸν ἀδύνατον ἢ
ἀπίθανον καὶ δυνατόν. <καὶ ἴσως ἀδύνατον> τοιούτους εἶναι,
οἵους Ζεῦξις ἔγραφεν· ἀλλὰ βέλτιον· τὸ γὰρ παράδειγμα δεῖ
ὑπερέχειν.   πρὸς <δ'> ἅ φασιν, τἄλογα· οὕτω τε καὶ ὅτι ποτὲ
15 οὐκ ἄλογόν ἐστιν· εἰκὸς γὰρ καὶ παρὰ τὸ εἰκὸς γίνεσθαι.   τὰ δ' 18
ὑπεναντίως εἰρημένα οὕτω σκοπεῖν, ὥσπερ οἱ ἐν τοῖς λόγοις
ἔλεγχοι, εἰ τὸ αὐτὸ καὶ πρὸς τὸ αὐτὸ καὶ ὡσαύτως, ὥστε
καὶ λυτέον ἢ πρὸς ἃ αὐτὸς λέγει ἢ ὃ ἂν φρόνιμος ὑποθῆ-
ται.   ὀρθὴ δ' ἐπιτίμησις καὶ ἀλογίᾳ καὶ μοχθηρίᾳ, ὅταν μὴ 19
20 ἀνάγκης οὔσης μηθὲν χρήσηται τῷ ἀλόγῳ, ὥσπερ Εὐριπίδης
τῷ Αἰγεῖ, ἢ τῇ πονηρίᾳ, ὥσπερ ἐν Ὀρέστῃ τοῦ Μενελάου.
τὰ μὲν οὖν ἐπιτιμήματα ἐκ πέντε εἰδῶν φέρουσιν, ἢ γὰρ ὡς 20
ἀδύνατα ἢ ὡς ἄλογα ἢ ὡς βλαβερὰ ἢ ὡς ὑπεναντία ἢ ὡς
παρὰ τὴν ὀρθότητα τὴν κατὰ τέχνην.   αἱ δὲ λύσεις ἐκ τῶν
25 εἰρημένων ἀριθμῶν σκεπτέαι, εἰσὶν δὲ δώδεκα.

XXVI   Πότερον δὲ βελτίων ἡ ἐποποιικὴ μίμησις ἢ ἡ τραγική,
διαπορήσειεν ἄν τις.   εἰ γὰρ ἡ ἧττον φορτικὴ βελτίων, τοιαύτη δ' ἡ πρὸς βελτίους θεατάς ἐστιν ἀεί, λίαν δῆλον ὅτι ἡ

---

11. πειθανὸν Aᶜ   12. ἀπείθανον Aᶜ   <καὶ ἴσως ἀδύνατον> Gomperz,
secutus Margoliouth ('fortasse enim impossibile est' Arabs): καὶ εἰ ἀδύνατον
coniecerat Vahlen   13. οἵους Parisinus 2038, Ald.: οἷον Aᶜ   14. δ' add.
Ueberweg (auctore Vahleno)   16. ὑπεναντίως Twining (cf. Arab. 'quae
dicta sunt in modum contrarii'): ὑπεναντία ὡς codd.: ὡς ὑπεναντία Heinsius
17. ὥστε καὶ λυτέον M. Schmidt: ὥστε καὶ αὐτὸν codd.   18. φρόνιμος
apogr.: φρόνημον (corr. m. rec. φρόνιμον) Aᶜ   19. ἀλογίᾳ καὶ μοχθηρίᾳ
Vahlen: ἀλογία καὶ μοχθηρία codd.   20. fort. <πρὸς> μηδὲν Gomperz
21. τῷ Αἰγεῖ ἢ τῇ margo Riccardiani 16: τῶ αἰγειήτῃ Aᶜ   <τῇ> τοῦ coni.
Vahlen   26. βελτίων apogr.: βέλτιον Aᶜ   28. δ' ἡ apogr.: δὴ Aᶜ
ἀεί, λίαν Vahlen: δειλίαν codd.

reality, or to received opinion. With respect to the requirements of art, a probable impossibility is to be preferred to a thing improbable and yet possible. Again, it may be impossible that there should be men such as Zeuxis painted. 'Yes,' we say, 'but the impossible is the higher thing; for the ideal type must surpass the reality.' To justify the irrational, we appeal to what is commonly said to be. In addition to which, we urge that the irrational sometimes does not violate reason; just as 'it is probable that a thing may happen contrary to probability.'

Things that sound contradictory should be examined 18 by the same rules as in dialectical refutation—whether the same thing is meant, in the same relation, and in the same sense. We should therefore solve the question by reference to what the poet says himself, or to what is tacitly assumed by a person of intelligence.

The element of the irrational, and, similarly, depravity 19 of character, are justly censured when there is no inner necessity for introducing them. Such is the irrational element in the introduction of Aegeus by Euripides and the badness of Menelaus in the Orestes.

Thus, there are five sources from which critical 20 objections are drawn. Things are censured either as impossible, or irrational, or morally hurtful, or contradictory, or contrary to artistic correctness. The answers should be sought under the twelve heads above mentioned.

XXVI   The question may be raised whether the Epic or Tragic mode of imitation is the higher. If the more refined art is the higher, and the more refined in every case is that which appeals to the better sort of audience,

ἄπαντα μιμουμένη φορτική· ὡς γὰρ οὐκ αἰσθανομένων ἂν
30 μὴ αὐτὸς προσθῇ, πολλὴν κίνησιν κινοῦνται, οἷον οἱ φαῦλοι
αὐληταὶ κυλιόμενοι ἂν δίσκον δέῃ μιμεῖσθαι, καὶ ἕλκοντες
τὸν κορυφαῖον ἂν Σκύλλαν αὐλῶσιν. ἡ μὲν οὖν τραγῳδία 2
τοιαύτη ἐστίν, ὡς καὶ οἱ πρότερον τοὺς ὑστέρους αὐτῶν ᾤοντο
ὑποκριτάς· ὡς λίαν γὰρ ὑπερβάλλοντα πίθηκον ὁ Μυννίσκος
35 τὸν Καλλιππίδην ἐκάλει, τοιαύτη δὲ δόξα καὶ περὶ Πιν-
1462 a δάρου ἦν· ὡς δ᾽ οὗτοι ἔχουσι πρὸς αὐτούς, ἡ ὅλη τέχνη
πρὸς τὴν ἐποποιίαν ἔχει. τὴν μὲν οὖν πρὸς θεατὰς ἐπιεικεῖς
φασιν εἶναι <οἳ> οὐδὲν δέονται τῶν σχημάτων, τὴν δὲ τραγι-
κὴν πρὸς φαύλους· εἰ οὖν φορτική, χείρων δῆλον ὅτι ἂν εἴη. 3
5 πρῶτον μὲν οὖν οὐ τῆς ποιητικῆς ἡ κατηγορία ἀλλὰ τῆς
ὑποκριτικῆς, ἐπεὶ ἔστι περιεργάζεσθαι τοῖς σημείοις καὶ ῥαψῳ-
δοῦντα, ὅπερ [ἐστὶ] Σωσίστρατος, καὶ διᾴδοντα, ὅπερ ἐποίει
Μνασίθεος ὁ Ὀπούντιος. εἶτα οὐδὲ κίνησις ἅπασα ἀποδοκι-
μαστέα, εἴπερ μηδ᾽ ὄρχησις, ἀλλ᾽ ἡ φαύλων, ὅπερ καὶ Καλλιπ-
10 πίδῃ ἐπετιμᾶτο καὶ νῦν ἄλλοις ὡς οὐκ ἐλευθέρας γυναῖκας
μιμουμένων. ἔτι ἡ τραγῳδία καὶ ἄνευ κινήσεως ποιεῖ τὸ αὑτῆς,
ὥσπερ ἡ ἐποποιία· διὰ γὰρ τοῦ ἀναγινώσκειν φανερὰ ὁποία
τίς ἐστιν· εἰ οὖν ἐστι τά γ᾽ ἄλλα κρείττων, τοῦτό γε οὐκ ἀναγκαῖον αὐτῇ ὑπάρχειν. ἔστι δ᾽ ἐπεὶ τὰ πάντ᾽ ἔχει ὅσαπερ ἡ ἐπο- 4
15 ποιία (καὶ γὰρ τῷ μέτρῳ ἔξεστι χρῆσθαι), καὶ ἔτι οὐ μικρὸν

---

30. κινοῦνται apogr.: κινοῦντα Aᶜ   1462 a 1. ἔχουσι apogr.: δ᾽ ἔχουσι
Aᶜ   αὐτοὺς Hermann: αὐτοὺς codd.   3. οἳ add. Vettori: ἐπεὶ Christ
σχημάτων τὴν apogr.: σχημά|τα αὐτὴν (τα αὐ m. rec. in litura) Aᶜ
4. εἰ apogr.: ἡ Aᶜ   5. οὖν add. Parisinus 2038, coni. Bywater, Ussing:
om. cett.   7. ἐστὶ secl. Spengel   διᾴδοντα Maggi: διάδοντα apogr.:
διάδοντα Aᶜ   8. ὁ πούντιος Aᶜ   10. ἐπιτιμᾶτο pr. Aᶜ   11. αὑτῆς
apogr.: αὐτῆς Aᶜ   12. ὁποῖα Aᶜ   14. αὐτῇ apogr.: αὐτὴ Aᶜ   ἔστι
δ᾽ ἐπεὶ Gomperz: ἔστι δ᾽, ὅτι Usener: ἔπειτα διότι codd.

the art which imitates anything and everything is manifestly most unrefined. The audience is supposed to be too dull to comprehend unless something of their own is thrown in by the performers, who therefore indulge in restless movements. Bad flute-players twist and twirl, if they have to represent ' the quoit-throw,' or hustle the coryphaeus when they perform the ' Scylla.' Tragedy, 2 it is said, has this same defect. We may compare the opinion that the older actors entertained of their successors. Mynniscus used to call Callippides 'ape' on account of the extravagance of his action, and the same 1462 a view was held of Pindarus. Tragic art, then, as a whole, stands to Epic in the same relation as the younger to the elder actors. So we are told that Epic poetry is addressed to a cultivated audience, who do not need gesture; Tragedy, to an inferior public. Being then 3 unrefined, it is evidently the lower of the two.

Now, in the first place, this censure attaches not to the poetic but to the histrionic art; for gesticulation may be equally overdone in epic recitation, as by Sosistratus, or in lyrical competition, as by Mnasitheus the Opuntian. Next, all action is not to be condemned— any more than all dancing—but only that of bad performers. Such was the fault found in Callippides, as also in others of our own day, who are censured for representing degraded women. Again, Tragedy like Epic poetry produces its effect even without action; it reveals its power by mere reading. If, then, in all other respects it is superior, this fault, we say, is not inherent in it.

And superior it is, because it has all the epic 4 elements—it may even use the epic metre—with the

μέρος τὴν μουσικὴν καὶ τὰς ὄψεις, δι᾽ ἃς αἱ ἡδοναὶ συνίσταν-
ται ἐναργέστατα· εἶτα καὶ τὸ ἐναργὲς ἔχει καὶ ἐν τῇ ἀναγνώσει καὶ ἐπὶ τῶν ἔργων· ἔτι τὸ ἐν ἐλάττονι μήκει τὸ τέλος 5
1462 b τῆς μιμήσεως εἶναι (τὸ γὰρ ἀθροώτερον ἥδιον ἢ πολλῷ κεκραμένον τῷ χρόνῳ· λέγω δ᾽ οἷον εἴ τις τὸν Οἰδίπουν θείη
τὸν Σοφοκλέους ἐν ἔπεσιν ὅσοις ἡ Ἰλιάς)· ἔτι ἧττον μία ἡ 6
μίμησις ἡ τῶν ἐποποιῶν (σημεῖον δέ· ἐκ γὰρ ὁποιασοῦν
5 [μιμήσεως] πλείους τραγῳδίαι γίνονται), ὥστε ἐὰν μὲν ἕνα
μῦθον ποιῶσιν, ἢ βραχέως δεικνύμενον μύουρον φαίνεσθαι, ἢ
ἀκολουθοῦντα τῷ συμμέτρῳ μήκει ὑδαρῆ. * * λέγω δὲ
οἷον ἐὰν ἐκ πλειόνων πράξεων ᾖ συγκειμένη, ὥσπερ ἡ Ἰλιὰς
ἔχει πολλὰ τοιαῦτα μέρη καὶ ἡ Ὀδύσσεια ἃ καὶ καθ᾽
10 ἑαυτὰ ἔχει μέγεθος· καίτοι ταῦτα τὰ ποιήματα συνέστηκεν
ὡς ἐνδέχεται ἄριστα καὶ ὅτι μάλιστα μιᾶς πράξεως μίμησις. εἰ οὖν τούτοις τε διαφέρει πᾶσιν καὶ ἔτι τῷ τῆς τέχνης 7
ἔργῳ (δεῖ γὰρ οὐ τὴν τυχοῦσαν ἡδονὴν ποιεῖν αὐτὰς ἀλλὰ
τὴν εἰρημένην), φανερὸν ὅτι κρείττων ἂν εἴη μᾶλλον τοῦ
15 τέλους τυγχάνουσα τῆς ἐποποιίας.

περὶ μὲν οὖν τραγῳδίας καὶ ἐποποιίας, καὶ αὐτῶν 8
καὶ τῶν εἰδῶν καὶ τῶν μερῶν, καὶ πόσα καὶ τί διαφέρει,
καὶ τοῦ εὖ ἢ μὴ τίνες αἰτίαι, καὶ περὶ ἐπιτιμήσεων καὶ
λύσεων, εἰρήσθω τοσαῦτα. * * *

16. καὶ τὰς ὄψεις secl. Spengel : post ἐναργέστατα collocavit Gomperz : καὶ τὴν
ὄψιν Ald.   δι᾽ ἃς (vel αἷς) coni. Vahlen : δι᾽ ἧς codd.   17. ἀναγνώσει
Maggi : ἀναγνωρίσει A^c   18. ἔτι τὸ Winstanley : ἔτι τῷ codd.
1462 b 1. ἥδιον ἢ Maggi : ἡδεῖον ἢ Riccardianus 16 : ἡδονὴ A^c   2. τὸν
δίπουν pr. A^c   θείη bis A^c   3. ἡ Ἰλιάς Riccardianus 16 : ἡ Ἰλίας (fuit
ἰδίας) A^c   μία ἡ Spengel : ἡ μία A^c : μία ὁποιασοῦν Riccardianus 16
5. μιμήσεως secl. Gomperz   6. μείουρον Parisinus 2038   7. συμμέτρῳ
Bernays : τοῦ μέτρου codd. : fort. τοῦ μετρίου (cf. 1458 b 12)   post ὑδαρῆ,
<ἐὰν δὲ πλείους> Ald. : <λέγω δὲ οἷον * * ἂν δὲ μή, οὐ μία ἡ μίμησις>
coni. Vahlen : <ἐὰν δὲ πλείους, οὐ μία ἡ μίμησις> Teichmüller : lacunam
aliter supplevi, vide versionem   9. ἃ add. apogr.   10. καίτοι ταῦτα
τὰ Riccardianus 16 : καὶ τοιαῦτ᾽ ἄττα A^c   18. ἢ apogr. : εἰ A^c

music and spectacular effects as important accessories ;
and these produce the most vivid of pleasures. Further,
it has vividness of impression in reading as well as in
representation. Moreover, the art attains its end within 5
462 b narrower limits ; for the concentrated effect is more
pleasurable than one which is spread over a long time
and so diluted. What, for example, would be the effect
of the Oedipus of Sophocles, if it were cast into a form
as long as the Iliad ? Once more, the Epic imitation 6
has less unity ; as is shown by this, that any Epic poem
will furnish subjects for several tragedies. Thus if the
story adopted by the poet has a strict unity, it must
either be concisely told and appear truncated ; or, if it
conform to the Epic canon of length, it must seem weak
and watery. <Such length implies some loss of unity,>
if, I mean, the poem is constructed out of several actions,
like the Iliad and the Odyssey, which have many such
parts, each with a certain magnitude of its own. Yet
these poems are as perfect as possible in structure ; each
is, in the highest degree attainable, an imitation of a
single action.

If, then, Tragedy is superior to Epic poetry in all these 7
respects, and, moreover, fulfils its specific function better
as an art—for each art ought to produce, not any chance
pleasure, but the pleasure proper to it, as already stated
—it plainly follows that Tragedy is the higher art, as
attaining its end more perfectly.

Thus much may suffice concerning Tragic and Epic 8
poetry in general ; their several kinds and parts, with
the number of each and their differences ; the causes
that make a poem good or bad ; the objections of the
critics and the answers to these objections. * * *

ARISTOTLE'S THEORY OF POETRY
AND THE FINE ARTS

CHAPTER I

ART AND NATURE

ARISTOTLE, it must be premised at the outset, has not dealt with fine art in any separate treatise, he has formulated no theory of it, he has not marked the organic relation of the arts to one another. While his love of logical distinctions, his tendency to rigid demarcation, is shown even in the province of literary criticism by the care with which in the *Poetics* he maps out the subordinate divisions of his subject (the different modes of recognition, the elements of the plot, etc.), yet he nowhere classifies the various kinds of poetry; still less has he given a scientific grouping of the fine arts and exhibited their specific differences. We may confidently assert that many of the aesthetic problems which have been since raised never even occurred to his mind, though precise answers to almost all such questions have been extracted from his writings

I

by the unwise zeal of his admirers. He has however left some leading principles which we shall
endeavour to follow out.

There is a special risk at the present day at-
tending any such attempt to bring together his
fragmentary remarks and present them in a connected form. His philosophy has in it the germs
of so much modern thought that we may, almost
without knowing it, find ourselves putting into his
mouth not his own language but that of Hegel.
Nor is it possible to determine by general rules
how far the thought that is implicit in a philosophical system, but which the author himself has
not drawn out, is to be reckoned as an integral
part of the system. In any case, however,
Aristotle's *Poetics* cannot be read apart from his
other writings. No author is more liable to be
misunderstood if studied piecemeal. The careless
profusion with which he throws out the suggestions
of the moment, leaving it to the intelligence or
the previous knowledge of his readers to adjust
his remarks and limit their scope, is in itself a
possible source of misapprehension. It was an
observation of Goethe that it needs some insight
into Aristotle's general philosophy to understand
what he says about the drama; that otherwise he
confuses our studies; and that modern treatises on
poetry have gone astray by seizing some accidental
side of his doctrine. If it is necessary, then, to

interpret Aristotle by himself, it will not be unfair
in dealing with so coherent a thinker to credit him
with seeing the obvious conclusions which flow
from his principles, even when he has not formally
stated them.   To bring out the lines of attachment
which subsist between the correlated parts of his
system is a very different thing from discovering
in him ideas which, even if present in the germ,
could only have ripened in another soil and under
other skies.

The distinction between fine and useful art
was first brought out fully by Aristotle.   In the
history of Greek art we are struck rather by the
union between the two forms of art than by their
independence.   It was a loss for art when the
spheres of use and beauty came in practice to be
dissevered, when the useful object ceased to be
decorative, and the things of common life no
longer gave delight to the maker and to the user.
But the theoretic distinction between fine and
useful art needed to be laid down, and to Aristotle
we owe the first clear conception of fine art as a
free and independent activity of the mind, outside
the domain both of religion and of politics, having
an end distinct from that of education or moral
improvement.   He has not indeed left us any
continuous discussion upon fine art.   The *Poetics*
furnishes no complete theory even of poetry, nor
is it probable that this is altogether due to the

imperfect form in which this treatise has come
down to us.   But Aristotle is a systematic thinker,
and numberless illustrations and analogies drawn
from one or other of the arts, and scattered through
his writings, show that he had given special
attention to the significance of art in its widest
sense ; and that as he had formed a coherent
idea of the place which art held in relation to
nature, science, and morality, so too he had in his
own mind thought out the relation in which the
two branches of art stood to one another.

'Art imitates nature' ($\dot{\eta}$ τέχνη μιμεῖται τὴν
φύσιν), says Aristotle, and the phrase has been
repeated and has passed current as a summary
of the Aristotelian doctrine of fine art.   Yet the
original saying was never intended to differentiate
between fine and useful art ; nor indeed could it
possibly bear the sense that fine art is a copy
or reproduction of natural objects.   The use of
the term 'nature' would in itself put the matter
beyond dispute ; for nature in Aristotle is not the
outward world of created things ; it is the creative
force, the productive principle of the universe.
The context in each case where the phrase occurs
determines its precise application.   In the *Physics*[1]
the point of the comparison is that alike in art and
in nature there is the union of matter (ὕλη) with
constitutive form (εἶδος), and that the knowledge

[1] *Phys.* ii. 2. 194 a 21.

of both elements is requisite for the natural philosopher as for the physician and the architect. In the *Meteorologica*[1] the reference is to cooking as an artificial mode of producing results similar to those produced by the spontaneous action of heat in the physical world; digestion (πέψις) itself (according to the medical theory of the day) being given as an instance of a process of cooking (ἕψησις) carried on by nature within the body. In the instances above quoted 'art' is limited by the context to useful art; but the analogy does not rest there. Art in its widest acceptation has, like nature, certain ends in view, and in the adaptation of means to ends catches hints from nature who is already in some sort an unconscious artist.

While art in general imitates the method of nature, the phrase has special reference to useful art, which learns from nature the precise end at which to aim. In the selection of the end she acts with infallible instinct, and her endeavour to attain it is on the whole successful. But at times she makes mistakes as indeed do the schoolmaster and

[1] *Meteor.* iv. 3. 381 b 6. The phrase 'Art imitates Nature' is also found in *de Mundo* 5. 396 b 12, which, however, cannot be reckoned among the genuine Aristotelian writings. There the order of the universe is explained to result from a union of opposites; and three illustrations, derived from painting, music, and grammar, are added of the mode in which art, in imitating nature's diversity, works out harmonious results.

the physician ;¹ failures rather than mistakes they
should be called, for the fault is not hers ; her
rational intention is liable to be frustrated by
inherent flaws in the substances with which she is
compelled to work. She is subject to limitations,
and can only make the best of her material.²

The higher we ascend in the scale of being, the
more does nature need assistance in carrying out
her designs. Man, who is her highest creation,
she brings into the world more helpless than any
other animal,—unshod, unclad, unarmed.³ But in
his seeming imperfection lies man's superiority, for
the fewer the finished appliances with which he is
provided, the greater is his need for intellectual
effort. By means of the rational faculty of art,
with which nature has endowed him richly, he is
able to come to her aid, and in ministering to his
own necessities to fulfil her uncompleted purposes.
Where from any cause nature fails, art steps in.
Nature aims at producing health ; in her restorative
processes we observe an instinctive capacity for
self-curing.⁴ But she does not always succeed, and
the art of the physician makes good the defect.

¹ *Phys.* ii. 8. 199 a 33.
² Cf. *de Part. Anim.* iv. 10. 687 a 15, ἡ δὲ φύσις ἐκ τῶν
ἐνδεχομένων ποιεῖ τὸ βέλτιστον.
³ *De Part. Anim.* iv. 10. 687 a 24.
⁴ *Phys.* ii. 8. 199 b 30, ὥστ᾽ εἰ ἐν τῇ τέχνῃ ἔνεστι τὸ ἔνεκά του,
καὶ ἐν φύσει. μάλιστα δὲ δῆλον ὅταν τις ἰατρεύῃ αὐτὸς ἑαυτόν·
τούτῳ γὰρ ἔοικεν ἡ φύσις.

He discovers one of the links of the chain which terminates in health, and uses nature's own machinery to start a series of movements which lead to the desired result.[1] Again, nature has formed man to be a 'political animal.'[2] Family and tribal life are stages on the way to a more complete existence, and the term of the process is reached when man enters into that higher order of community called the state. The state is indeed a natural institution, but needs the political art to organise it and to realise nature's full idea. The function, then, of the useful arts is in all cases 'to supply the deficiencies of nature';[3] and he who would be a master in any art must first discern

---

[1] *Metaph.* vi. 7. 1032 b 6, γίγνεται δὴ τὸ ὑγιὲς νοσήσαντος οὕτως· ἐπειδὴ τοδὶ ὑγίεια, ἀνάγκη εἰ ὑγιὲς ἔσται τοδὶ ὑπάρξαι, οἷον ὁμαλότητα, εἰ δὲ τοῦτο, θερμότητα. καὶ οὕτως ἀεὶ νοεῖ, ἕως ἂν ἀγάγῃ εἰς τοῦτο ὃ αὐτὸς δύναται ἔσχατον ποιεῖν. εἶτα ἤδη ἡ ἀπὸ τούτου κίνησις ποίησις καλεῖται, ἡ ἐπὶ τὸ ὑγιαίνειν.

[2] *Pol.* i. 2. 1253 a 2, ἄνθρωπος φύσει πολιτικὸν ζῷον.

[3] *Pol.* iv. (vii.) 17. 1337 a 1–2, πᾶσα γὰρ τέχνη καὶ παιδεία τὸ προσλεῖπον βούλεται τῆς φύσεως ἀναπληροῦν. The context here, in its reference to education, limits the scope of τέχνη to useful art. In *Phys.* ii. 8. 199 a 15, ἡ τέχνη τὰ μὲν ἐπιτελεῖ ἃ ἡ φύσις ἀδυνατεῖ ἀπεργάσασθαι, τὰ δὲ μιμεῖται it is probable that the distinction is not, as would at first sight seem, between useful and fine art, but between two aspects of useful art. The sentence is not quite logical in form, but the meaning is that useful art on the one hand satisfies those needs of man for which nature has not fully provided, on the other hand its processes are those of nature (μιμεῖται sc. τὴν φύσιν). The two clauses respectively mark the end and the method of useful art. The main argument of the chapter is in favour of this view.

the true end by a study of nature's principles, and then employ the method which she suggests for the attainment of that end.

'Nature taught Art,' says Milton; and the same Aristotelian idea was in the mind of Dante, when he makes Virgil condemn usury as a departure from nature : 'Philosophy, to him who hears it, points out not in one place alone, how Nature takes her course from the Divine Intellect, and from its art. And, if thou note well thy Physics,[1] thou wilt find, not many pages from the first, that your art as far as it can, follows her (Nature), as the scholar does his master. . . . And because the usurer takes another way, he contemns Nature in herself, and in her follower (Art), placing elsewhere his hope.'[2] The phrase on which we have been commenting is the key to this passage : useful art supplements nature, and at the same time follows her guidance.

[1] *Phys.* ii. 2.
[2] *Inferno* xi. 97–111, Carlyle's Translation.

CHAPTER II

'IMITATION' AS AN AESTHETIC TERM

THE term 'fine art' is not one that has been transmitted to us from the Greeks. Their phrase was the 'imitative arts' (μιμητικαὶ τέχναι), 'modes of imitation' (μιμήσεις),[1] or sometimes the 'liberal arts' (ἐλευθέριοι τέχναι). 'Imitation' as the common characteristic of the fine arts, including poetry, was not originated by Aristotle. In literature the phrase in this application first occurs in Plato, though, not improbably, it may have been already current in popular speech as marking the antithesis between fine art and industrial production. The idea of imitation is connected in our minds with a want of creative freedom, with a literal or servile copying: and the word, as transmitted from Plato to Aristotle, was already tinged by some such disparaging associations. The Platonic

---

[1] He applies the term μιμήσεις only to poetry and music (*Poet.* i. 2), but the constant use of the verb μιμεῖσθαι or of the adjective μιμητικός in connexion with the other arts above enumerated proves that all alike are counted arts of imitation.

121

view that the real world is a weak or imperfect
repetition of an ideal archetype led to the world
of reality being regarded in a special sense, and
on a still lower plane, as a world of mere imitation. Aristotle, as his manner was, accepted the
current phrase and interpreted it anew. True, he
may sometimes have been misled by its guidance,
and not unfrequently his meaning is obscured by
his adherence to the outworn formula. But he
deepened and enriched its signification, looking at
it from many sides in the light of the masterpieces
of Greek art and literature.

This will become apparent as we proceed.
Meanwhile—if we may so far anticipate what is to
follow—a crucial instance of the inadequacy of the
literal English equivalent 'imitation' to express
the Aristotelian idea is afforded by a passage in
ch. xxv. The artist may 'imitate things *as they
ought to be*':[1] he may place before him an
unrealised ideal. We see at once that there is no
question here of bare imitation, of a literal tran-
script of the world of reality.

It has been already mentioned that 'to imitate
nature,' in the popular acceptation of the phrase, is
not for Aristotle the function of fine art. The
actual objects of aesthetic imitation are threefold

---

[1] *Poet.* xxv. 1, ἀνάγκη μιμεῖσθαι τριῶν ὄντων τὸν ἀριθμὸν ἕν
τι ἀεί, ἢ γὰρ οἷα ἦν ἢ ἔστιν, ἢ οἷά φασι καὶ δοκεῖ, ἢ οἷα εἶναι δεῖ.
See also pp. 167 ff., 376.

—ἤθη, πάθη, πράξεις.[1] By ἤθη are meant the characteristic moral qualities, the permanent dispositions of the mind, which reveal a certain condition of the will : πάθη are the more transient emotions, the passing moods of feeling : πράξεις are actions in their proper and inward sense. An act viewed merely as an external process or result, one of a series of outward phenomena, is not the true object of aesthetic imitation. The πρᾶξις that art seeks to reproduce is mainly an inward process, a psychical energy working outwards; deeds, incidents, events, situations, being included under it so far as these spring from an inward act of will, or elicit some activity of thought or feeling.[2]

Here lies the explanation of the somewhat startling phrase used in the *Poetics*, ch. ii., that ' men in action' are the objects imitated by the fine arts :[3]—by all and not merely by dramatic or narrative poetry where action is more obviously represented. Everything that expresses the mental life, that reveals a rational personality, will fall within this larger sense of 'action.' Such actions are not necessarily processes extending over a period of time : they may realise themselves in a

[1] Cf. *Poet.* i. 5.
[2] Cf. *Eth. Nic.* i. 8. 1098 b 15, τὰς δὲ πράξεις καὶ τὰς ἐνεργείας τὰς ψυχικὰς περὶ ψυχὴν τίθεμεν. See also infra, p. 334.
[3] *Poet.* ii. 1, ἐπεὶ δὲ μιμοῦνται οἱ μιμούμενοι πράττοντας κ.τ.λ. Cf. Plat. *Rep.* x. 603 c, πράττοντας, φαμέν, ἀνθρώπους μιμεῖται ἡ μιμητικὴ βιαίους ἢ ἑκουσίας πράξεις.

single moment; they may be summed up in a
particular mood, a given situation. The phrase
is virtually an equivalent for the ἤθη, πάθη, πράξεις
above enumerated.

The common original, then, from which all the
arts draw is human life,—its mental processes, its
spiritual movements, its outward acts issuing from
deeper sources ; in a word, all that constitutes the
inward and essential activity of the soul. On this
principle landscape and animals are not ranked
among the objects of aesthetic imitation. The
whole universe is not conceived of as the raw
material of art. Aristotle's theory is in agreement
with the practice of the Greek poets and artists
of the classical period, who introduce the external
world only so far as it forms a background of
action, and enters as an emotional element into
man's life and heightens the human interest.

We may now proceed to determine more nearly
the meaning of ' imitation.'

A work of art is a likeness (ὁμοίωμα) *or reproduction of an original, and not a symbolic
representation of it;*[1] and this holds good whether
the artist draws from a model in the real world
or from an unrealised ideal in the mind. The
distinction may be shown by Aristotle's own
illustrations. A sign or symbol has no essential

[1] This point is worked out in detail by Teichmüller, *Aristotelische Forschungen,* ii. 145–154.

resemblance, no natural connexion, with the thing signified. Thus spoken words are symbols of mental states, written words are symbols of spoken words; the connexion between them is conventional.[1] On the other hand mental impressions are not signs or symbols, but copies of external reality, likenesses of the things themselves. In the act of sensuous perception objects stamp upon the mind an impress of themselves like that of a signet ring, and the picture (φάντασμα) so engraven on the memory is compared to a portrait (ζωγράφημα, εἰκών).[2] Thus the creations of art are, as it were, pictures which exist for the 'phantasy.'

Of this faculty, however, Aristotle does not give a very clear or consistent account. He defines it as ' " the movement which results upon an actual sensation " : more simply we may define it as the after-effect of a sensation, the continued presence of an impression after the object which first excited it has been withdrawn from actual experience.'[3] As such it is brought in to explain

---

[1] *De Interpret.* i. 1. 16 a 3, ἔστι μὲν οὖν τὰ ἐν τῇ φωνῇ τῶν ἐν τῇ ψυχῇ παθημάτων σύμβολα, καὶ τὰ γραφόμενα τῶν ἐν τῇ φωνῇ. In ch. 2. 16 a 27 the connexion is said to be κατὰ συνθήκην.

[2] *De Mem. et Remin.* 1. 450 a 27—451 a 17. Cf. *de Interpret.* i. 1. 16 a 7, where the παθήματα or mental impressions are said to be ὁμοιώματα of reality.

[3] E. Wallace, *Aristotle's Psychology,* Intr. p. lxxxvii.: see the whole section relating to this subject, pp. lxxxvi.-xcvii. The definition

the illusions of dreaming and other kindred
phenomena. But it is more than a receptivity
of sense,[1] it is on the border-line between sense and
thought. It is treated as an image-forming faculty,
by which we can recall at will pictures previously
presented to the mind[2] and may even accomplish
some of the processes of thought.[3] It represents
subjectively all the particular concrete objects
perceived by the external senses. From these
'phantasms' or representations of the imagination
the intellect abstracts its ideas or universal concepts. Without the imagination the intellect
cannot work through lack of matter. The idea,
therefore, which is purely intellectual, implies and
contains in itself whatever is universal, that is
intelligible, in the object of sense. When in default
of a nearer equivalent we use the term 'imagination'—that is, an image-making power—we must
remember that Aristotle's psychology does not
admit of such a faculty as a creative imagination,
which not merely reproduces objects passively
perceived, but fuses together the things of thought
and sense, and forms a new world of its own,
recombining and transmuting the materials of

is in *de Anim.* iii. 3. 429 a 1, ἡ φαντασία ἂν εἴη κίνησις ὑπὸ
τῆς αἰσθήσεως τῆς κατ᾽ ἐνέργειαν γιγνομένη. So *de Somno* 1.
459 a 17.

[1] *De Anim.* iii. 3. 428 a 5–16.
[2] *De Anim.* iii. 3. 427 b 17–20.
[3] *De Anim.* iii. 10. 433 a 10.

experience.[1] This work is for Aristotle the result
of the spontaneous and necessary union of intellect
and sense.

We have thus advanced another step in the
argument. *A work of art reproduces its original,
not as it is in itself, but as it appears to the
senses.* Art addresses itself not to the abstract
reason but to the sensibility and image-making
faculty; it is concerned with outward appearances;
it employs illusions; its world is not that which
is revealed by pure thought; it sees truth, but in
its concrete manifestations, not as an abstract idea.

Important consequences follow from the doctrine
of aesthetic semblance, first noted by Plato [2]—
though in depreciation of fine art—and firmly
apprehended by Aristotle. Art does not attempt
to embody the objective reality of things, but only
their sensible appearances. Indeed by the very

---

[1] The idea of a creative power in man which transforms the
materials supplied by the empirical world is not unknown either to
Plato or Aristotle, but it is not a separate faculty or denoted by a
distinct name.   In Philostratus (circa A.D. 210), *Vit. Apoll.* vi. 19,
φαντασία is the active imagination as opposed to the faculty of
μίμησις. φαντασία, ἔφη, ταῦτα (i.e. the sculptured forms of the
gods by a Phidias or Praxiteles) εἰργάσατο σοφωτέρα μιμήσεως
δημιουργός· μίμησις μὲν γὰρ δημιουργήσει ὃ εἶδεν, φαντασία
δὲ καὶ ὃ μὴ εἶδεν.

[2] In *Rep.* x. 598 B painting, like other imitative arts, is a
μίμησις φαντάσματος. In *Sophist* 264 C—267 A, these arts fall
under the head of φανταστική. For the importance of this contribution to aesthetic theory see Bosanquet, *History of Aesthetic*,
pp. 28-30.

principles of Aristotle's philosophy it can present
no more than a semblance; for it impresses the
artistic form upon a matter which is not proper
to that form. Thus it severs itself from material
reality and the corresponding wants. Herein lies
the secret of its emancipating power. The real
emotions, the positive needs of life, have always
in them some element of disquiet. By the union
of a form with a matter which in the world of
experience is alien to it, a magical effect is wrought.
The pressure of everyday reality is removed, and
the aesthetic emotion is released as an independent
activity. Art, then, moving in a world of images
and appearances, and creating after a pattern
existing in the mind, must be skilled in the use
of illusion. By this alone can it give coherence to
its creations and impart to its fictions an air of
reality. The doctrine of aesthetic semblance and
of τὸ πιθανόν, which depends on it, is carried so
far that the poet working by illusions 'ought
to prefer probable impossibilities to possible
improbabilities.'[1]

While all works of art are likenesses of an
original and have reference to a world independently known, the various arts reflect the image
from without by different means and with more
or less directness and vividness.

Music was held by Aristotle, as by the Greeks

[1] *Poet.* xxiv. 10, xxv. 17 : see pp. 173 ff.

generally, to be the most 'imitative' or representative of the arts. It is a direct image, a copy of
character. We generally think of it in a different
way. The emotion it suggests, the message it
conveys, corresponds but little with a reality
outside itself, with a world of feeling already
known. We cannot test its truth by its accordance
with any original. It is capable of expressing
general and elementary moods of feeling, which
will be variously interpreted by different hearers.
It cannot render the finer shades of extra-musical
emotion with any degree of certainty and precision.
Its expressive power, its capacity to reproduce independent realities, is weak in proportion as the
impression it produces is vivid and definite. But
to Aristotle, who here accepts the traditions of his
country, the very opposite seems true. Music is the
express image and reflexion of moral character.
'In rhythms and melodies we have the most realistic imitations of anger and mildness as well as of
courage, temperance and all their opposites.'[1] Not
only states of feeling but also strictly ethical
qualities and dispositions of mind are reproduced
by musical imitation, and on the close correspondence between the copy and the original depends

[1] *Pol.* v. (viii.) 5. 1340 a 18, ἔυ τι δὲ ὁμοιώματα μάλιστα παρὰ
τὰς ἀληθινὰς φύσεις ἐν τοῖς ῥυθμοῖς καὶ τοῖς μέλεσιν ὀργῆς καὶ
πραότητος ἔτι δ ἀνδρίας καὶ σωφροσύνης καὶ πάντων τῶν ἐναν-
τίων τούτοις.

K

the importance of music in the formation of character. Music in reflecting character moulds and influences it.

A partial explanation of the prevalence of such a view is to be found in the dependent position which music occupied among the Greeks. It was one of the accessories of poetry, to which it was strictly subordinate, and consisted of comparatively simple strains. Much of its meaning was derived from the associations it called up, and from the emotional atmosphere which surrounded it. It was associated with definite occasions and solemnities, it was accompanied by certain dances and attached to well-known words. 'When there are no words,' says Plato, 'it is very difficult to recognise the meaning of harmony or rhythm, or to see that any worthy object is imitated by them.'[1]

---

[1] *Laws* ii. 669 E. On the whole subject of Greek music see *The Modes of Ancient Greek Music* by D. B. Monro (Oxford, 1894). Mr. Monro after insisting on the close connexion between words and melodies thus proceeds : 'The beauty and even the persuasive effect of a voice depend, as we are more or less aware, in the first place upon the pitch or key in which it is set, and in the second place upon subtle variations of pitch, which give emphasis, or light and shade. Answering to the first of these elements, ancient music, if the main contention of this essay is right, has its system of Modes or keys. Answering to the second it has a series of scales in which the delicacy and variety of the intervals still fill us with wonder. In both these points modern music shows diminished resources. We have in the Keys the same or even a greater command of degrees of pitch ; but we seem to have lost the close relation which once obtained between a note as the result

But even apart from interpretative words it would seem that the ethical significance of music was maintained by Aristotle and his school. In the *Problems* we find it said, ' Melody even apart from words has an ethical quality.'[1] Though we may not be able entirely to comprehend the Greek point of view as to the moral import of music, we must bear in mind that the dominant element in Greek music was the rhythm ; the spirit and meaning of any given composition was felt to reside

of physical facts and the same note as an index of temper or emotion.   A change of key affects us, generally speaking, like a change of colour or of movement—not as the heightening or soothing of a state of feeling.   In respect of the second element of vocal expression, in the rise and fall of the pitch, Greek music possessed in the multiplicity of its scales a range of expression to which there is no modern parallel.   The nearest analogue may be found in the use of modulation from a major to a minor key, or the reverse.   But the changes of genus and "colour" at the disposal of an ancient musician must have been acoustically more striking, and must have come nearer to reproducing, in an idealised form, the tones and inflexions of the speaking voice.   The tendency of music that is based upon harmony is to treat the voice as one of a number of instruments, and accordingly to curtail the use of it as the great source of dramatic and emotional effect.   The consequence is two-fold.   On the one hand we lose sight of the direct influence exerted by sound of certain degrees of pitch on the human sensibility, and thus ultimately on character.   On the other hand, the music becomes an independent creation.   It may still be a vehicle of the deepest feeling ; but it no longer seeks the aid of language, or reaches its aim through the channels by which language influences the mind of man.'

[1] *Probl.* xix. 27. 919 b 26, καὶ γὰρ ἐὰν ᾖ ἄνευ λόγου μέλος, ὅμως ἔχει ἦθος.

especially here; and the doctrine which asserted
the unique imitative capacity of music had for
Aristotle its theoretic basis in this, that the external movements of rhythmical sound bear a close
resemblance to the movements of the soul. Each
single note is felt as an inward agitation. The
regular succession of musical sounds, governed by
the laws of melody and rhythm, are allied to
those πράξεις or outward activities which are the
expression of a mental state.[1]

This power which belongs in an eminent degree
to the sense of hearing is but feebly exhibited by
the other senses. Taste and touch do not directly
reflect moral qualities; sight, but little, for form
and colour are 'rather signs of moral qualities'

---

[1] In *Probl.* xix. 29. 920 a 3, the question is asked διὰ τί οἱ
ῥυθμοὶ καὶ τὰ μέλη φωνὴ οὖσα ἤθεσιν ἔοικεν; and the answer
suggested is ἢ ὅτι κινήσεις εἰσὶν ὥσπερ καὶ αἱ πράξεις; ἤδη δὲ ἡ
μὲν ἐνέργεια ἠθικὸν καὶ ποιεῖ ἦθος, οἱ δὲ χυμοὶ καὶ τὰ χρώματα
οὐ ποιοῦσιν ὁμοίως. Again in *Probl.* xix. 27. 919 b 26, the
similar question διὰ τί τὸ ἀκουστὸν μόνον ἦθος ἔχει τῶν αἰσθητῶν; is put, and again the answer is ἢ ὅτι κίνησιν ἔχει μόνον
οὐχί, ἣν ὁ ψόφος ἡμᾶς κινεῖ; . . . ἀλλὰ τῆς ἑπομένης τῷ τοιούτῳ
ψόφῳ αἰσθανόμεθα κινήσεως. It is added αἱ δὲ κινήσεις αὗται
πρακτικαί εἰσιν, αἱ δὲ πράξεις ἤθους σημασία ἐστίν. A distinction
is further drawn between the κινήσεις produced by sight and by
hearing, but the precise meaning is not beyond dispute and need
not detain us here.

The classification of melodies into ἠθικά, ἐνθουσιαστικά,
πρακτικά (*Pol.* v. (viii.) 7. 1341 b 33), corresponds, it may be
observed, with the three objects of imitative art ἤθη, πάθη,
πράξεις.

than actual imitations of them.[1] This passage of
the *Politics* would seem to imply that painting and
sculpture directly render little more than the outward and physical features of an object, and that
they convey moral and spiritual facts almost wholly
by signs or symbols. Here, it might be thought,
we are introduced to a type of art foreign to the mind
of Greece, an art in which the inner qualities are
shadowed forth in outward forms, with which they
are conventionally associated, but which suggest no
obvious and immediate resemblance.

But the phrase here used, like many of Aristotle's
obiter dicta, must be taken with considerable latitude and in conjunction with other passages. Some
emphasis, too, must be laid on the admission that
form and colour do, in however slight a degree,
reflect the moral character, and on the qualifying
'rather' prefixed to the statement that they are
'signs of moral qualities.' They are indeed less
perfect manifestations of these qualities than music,
whose rhythmical and ordered movements have a

---

[1] *Pol.* v. (viii.) 5. 1340 a 28, συμβέβηκε δὲ τῶν αἰσθητῶν ἐν
μὲν τοῖς ἄλλοις μηδὲν ὑπάρχειν ὁμοίωμα τοῖς ἤθεσιν, οἷον ἐν τοῖς
ἁπτοῖς καὶ τοῖς γευστοῖς, ἀλλ' ἐν τοῖς ὁρατοῖς ἠρέμα· σχήματα
γάρ ἐστι τοιαῦτα, ἀλλ' ἐπὶ μικρόν, . . . ἔτι δὲ οὐκ ἔστι ταῦτα
ὁμοιώματα τῶν ἠθῶν, ἀλλὰ σημεῖα μᾶλλον τὰ γινόμενα σχήματα
καὶ χρώματα τῶν ἠθῶν. The two passages just quoted from the
Problems go farther and declare that sound alone carries with it
any immediate suggestion of moral qualities ; sight, taste, and smell
are expressly excluded. This is perhaps an exaggeration of the
proper Aristotelian view.

special affinity with the nature of the soul, and reproduce with most directness the moral life, which
is itself an activity, a movement.[1] Still facial
expression, gestures, attitudes, are a dialect which
nature herself has taught, and which needs no
skilled interpreter to expound. They are in the
truest sense a natural, not an artificial medium of
expression, and convey their meaning by the force
of immediate suggestion and without a conscious
process of inference. If symbols they may be called,
they are not conventional symbols, but living signs
through which the outward frame follows and reflects
the movements of the spirit; they are a visible token
of the inner unity of body and soul.

The reading of character by gesture and facial
expression, as explained by the Aristotelian school,
rests on an assumed harmony, not in the case of
hearing only but of other organs of sense also,
between the movements within and those without.[2]
The comparisons, moreover, elsewhere made between

---

[1] *Pol.* v. (viii.) 5. 1340 b 17, καί τις ἔοικε συγγένεια ταῖς
ἁρμονίαις καὶ τοῖς ῥυθμοῖς εἶναι, where the sense, as the context
shows, is that harmonies and rhythms have a certain affinity *with
the soul*. Hence, Aristotle proceeds, some have wrongly inferred
that the soul itself is a harmony. Cf. *Probl.* xix. 38. 920 b 33,
ῥυθμῷ δὲ χαίρομεν διὰ τὸ γνώριμον καὶ τεταγμένον ἀριθμὸν ἔχειν,
καὶ κινεῖν ἡμᾶς τεταγμένως· οἰκειοτέρα γὰρ ἡ τεταγμένη κίνησις
φύσει τῆς ἀτάκτου, ὥστε καὶ κατὰ φύσιν μᾶλλον. Plato, *Tim.* 47 D, ἡ
δὲ ἁρμονία ξυγγενεῖς ἔχουσα φορὰς ταῖς ἐν ἡμῖν τῆς ψυχῆς περιόδοις.

[2] *Physiognom.* i. 2. 806 a 28, ἔκ τε γὰρ τῶν κινήσεων φυσιογνω-
μονοῦσι, καὶ ἐκ τῶν σχημάτων, καὶ ἐκ τῶν χρωμάτων, καὶ ἐκ τῶν

painting and poetry as expressive of character cease
to be relevant if we suppose that form and colour
have no natural, as distinct from a conventional,
significance in rendering the phenomena of mind.
Aristotle no doubt holds that sound is unequalled
in its power of direct expression, but he does not
deny that colour and form too have a similar capacity
though in an inferior degree. The instinctive movements of the limbs, the changes of colour produced
on the surface of the body, are something more than
arbitrary symbols; they imply that the body is of
itself responsive to the animating soul, which leaves
its trace on the visible organism.

Painting and sculpture working through an inert
material cannot indeed reproduce the life of the
soul in all its variety and successive manifestations. In their frozen and arrested movement they
fix eternally the feeling they portray. A single
typical moment is seized and becomes representative
of all that precedes or follows. Still shape and
line and colour even here retain something of
their significance, they are in their own degree a
natural image of the mind; and their meaning is
helped out by symmetry, which in the arts of repose
answers to rhythm, the chief vehicle of expression
in the arts of movement. Aristotle does not himself

ἠθῶν τῶν ἐπὶ τοῦ προσώπου ἐμφαινομένων.   806 b 28, τὰ δὲ
σχήματα καὶ τὰ παθήματα τὰ ἐπιφαινόμενα ἐπὶ τῶν προσώπων
κατὰ τὰς ὁμοιότητας λαμβάνεται τῷ πάθει.

notice the analogy between dancing and sculpture, which is brought out by later writers, but he would have perfectly apprehended the feeling which suggested the saying, 'The statues of the classic artists are the relics of ancient dancing.'[1] The correspondence lies in the common element of rhythmic form. This, which was the soul of Greek music and Greek dancing, would not on Aristotle's general principles lose all its expressive power when transferred to the material of the plastic arts, modified though it may be in the transference.

Even dancing, we read in the *Poetics*, imitates character, emotion, action.[2] The expressive power of dancing, admitted by Aristotle and by all Greek tradition, receives its most instructive commentary in Lucian's pamphlet on the subject, which, when due allowance is made for exaggeration and the playful gravity so characteristic of the writer, is still inspired by an old Greek sentiment. Rhetoricians and musicians had already written treatises on the art, and Lucian in handling the same theme imitates their semi-philosophic manner. Dancing is placed in the front rank of the fine arts, and all the

---

[1] Athen. xiv. 26 p. 629, ἔστι δὲ καὶ τὰ τῶν ἀρχαίων δημιουργῶν ἀγάλματα τῆς παλαιᾶς ὀρχήσεως λείψανα.

[2] *Poet.* i. 5, καὶ ἤθη καὶ πάθη καὶ πράξεις. Similarly (of choral dance and song) Plato, *Laws* ii. 655 D, μιμήματα τρόπων ἐστὶ τὰ περὶ τὰς χορείας, ἐν πράξεσί τε παντοδαπαῖς γιγνόμενα καὶ τύχαις καὶ ἤθεσι μιμήμασι διεξιόντων ἑκάστων, where τύχαι takes the place of πάθη.

sciences are made contributary to it. The dancer
must have a fine genius, a critical judgment of
poetry, a ready and comprehensive memory; like
Homer's Calchas he must know the past, the present,
and the future. Above all he needs to have mastered
all mythology from chaos and the origin of the
universe down to Cleopatra, queen of Egypt, and to
be able to reproduce the legends in their spirit and
their details. He must avoid the 'terrible solecisms'
of some ignorant performers. Like the orator he
should aim at being always perspicuous; he must
be understood though he is dumb and heard though
he says nothing. Dancing is not inferior to tragedy
itself in expressive capacity; it is descriptive of
every shade of character and emotion. Moreover
it harmonises the soul of the spectator, trains the
moral sympathies, and acts as a curative and
quieting influence on the passions.

Poetry unlike the other arts produces its effects
(except such as depend on metre) through symbols
alone. It cannot directly present form and colour
to the eye; it can only employ words to call up
images of the objects to be represented; nor need
these words be audible ; they may be merely written
symbols. The sign too and the thing signified are
not here so linked together by obvious suggestion
that their meaning is at once and everywhere apprehended; they vary with race and country, they
cannot claim to be a universal language. Yet poetry,

though it makes use of symbols which have to be
interpreted by the mind, is no exception to Aristotle's principle that fine art is not a body
of symbols. The image it represents is not one
which through artificial means or remote association reminds us of a reality already known.
Though signs are the medium of expression, the
representation is not purely symbolical; for the
signs are those significant words which in life are
the natural and familiar medium by which thought
and feeling are revealed. The world which poetry
creates is not explicitly stated by Aristotle to be a
likeness or ὁμοίωμα of an original, but this is implied
all through the *Poetics*. The original which it
reflects is human action and character in all their
diverse modes of manifestation; no other art has
equal range of subject-matter, or can present so
complete and satisfying an image of its original.
In the drama the poetic imitation of life attains its
perfect form; but it is here also that the idea of
imitation in its more rudimentary sense is at once
apparent; speech has its counterpart in speech, and,
if the play is put on the stage, action is rendered
by action. Indeed the term imitation, as popularly
applied to poetry, was probably suggested to the
Greeks by those dramatic forms of poetry in which
acting or recitation produced an impression allied
to that of mimicry.

Poetry, music, and dancing constitute in Aristotle a group by themselves, their common element being imitation by means of rhythm—rhythm which admits of being applied to words, sounds, and the movements of the body.[1]   The history of these arts bears out the views we find expressed in Greek writers upon the theory of music ; it is a witness to the primitive unity of music and poetry, and to the close alliance of the two with dancing. Together they form a natural triad, and illustrate a characteristic of the ancient world to retain as indivisible wholes branches of art or science which the separative spirit of modern thought has broken up into their elements.   The intimate fusion of the three arts afterwards known as the 'musical' arts —or rather, we should perhaps say, the alliance of music and dancing under the supremacy of poetry —was exhibited even in the person of the artist. The office of the poet as teacher of the chorus demanded a practical knowledge of all that passed under the term 'dancing,' including steps, gestures, attitudes, and the varied resources of rhythmical movement.   Aeschylus, we are told,[2] 'was the inventor of many orchestic attitudes,' and it is added that the ancient poets were called orchestic, not only because they trained their choruses, but also because they taught choral dances outside the

---

[1] *Poet.* i. 2–5.   On the unity of this group cf. Prickard, *Aristotle on the Art of Poetry* (Macmillan, 1891), pp. 19–21.

[2] Athenaeus i. 40.

theatre to such as wished to learn them. 'So
wise and honourable a thing,' says Athenaeus,[1]
'was dancing that Pindar calls Apollo the dancer,'
and he quotes the words : 'Ορχήστ', ἀγλαΐας ἀνάσσων,
εὐρυφάρετρ' Ἄπολλον.

Improvements in the technique of music or in
the construction of instruments are associated with
many names well known in the history of poetry.
The poet, lyric or dramatic, composed the accompaniment as well as wrote the verses; and it was
made a reproach against Euripides, who was the
first to deviate from the established usage, that he
sought the aid of Iophon, son of Sophocles, in the
musical setting of his dramas. The very word
ποιητής 'poet' in classical times often implies the
twofold character of poet and musician, and in later
writers is sometimes used, like our 'composer,' in
a strictly limited reference to music.

Aristotle does full justice to the force of rhythmic
form and movement in the arts of music and dancing.
The instinctive love of melody and rhythm is, again,
one of the two causes to which he traces the origin
of poetry,[2] but he lays little stress on this element

---

[1] xiv. 26.

[2] I take the two αἰτίαι φυσικαί (*Poet.* iv. 1) of poetry to be (1)
the instinct of μίμησις, regarded as a primitive mode of learning
(iv. 2–5), and (2) the instinct for ἁρμονία and ῥυθμός (iv. 6).
The whole passage gains much by this interpretation. The
objection to it is the abruptness with which the instinct for
harmony and rhythm is introduced in § 6, so as to suggest a

in estimating the finished products of the poetic
art. In the *Rhetoric*[1] he observes that if a sentence
has metre it will be poetry; but this is said in
a popular way. It was doubtless the received
opinion,[2] but it is one which he twice combats in
the *Poetics*, insisting that it is not metrical form
that makes a poem.[3] In one of these passages

doubt whether there is not after § 5 a lacuna in the text, in
which harmony and rhythm were mentioned as the second cause.
Mr. R. P. Hardie (in *Mind*, vol. iv. No. 15) would account for the
abruptness of § 6 in another way : 'I would suggest that the
transition to the second αἰτία is to be found in the preceding
sentence, which is to the effect that when an object imitated has
not been seen before, so that the pleasure of recognition cannot
be present, there may still be pleasure, which "will be due, not
to the imitation as such, but to the execution (ἀπεργασία), the
colouring (χροιά), or some such cause." Here plainly two kinds of
pleasure which are necessarily independent are referred to, and
there is no difficulty in supposing ἀπεργασία and χροιά to be
intended by Aristotle to correspond roughly in γραφική to ἁρμονία
and ῥυθμός in ποιητική.'

The ordinary interpretation makes the two αἰτίαι to be the
instinct of imitation, and the pleasure derived from imitation.
This interpretation is open to the objection that it gives us not two
independent αἰτίαι but two tendencies, both of which are referred
to the same αἰτία,—namely, the natural love of knowledge.

[1] *Rhet.* iii. 8. 1408 b 30, διὸ ῥυθμὸν δεῖ ἔχειν τὸν λόγον, μέτρον
δὲ μή· ποίημα γὰρ ἔσται.

[2] Cf. Plat. *Phaedr.* 258 Ε, ἐν μέτρῳ ὡς ποιητής, ἢ ἄνευ μέτρου
ὡς ἰδιώτης : and *Repub.* x. 601 Β on the κήλησις of melody and
rhythm : stripped of these adornments poetical compositions are
like faces from which the bloom of youth is gone. *Gorg.* 502 c, εἴ
τις περιέλοιτο τῆς ποιήσεως πάσης τό τε μέλος καὶ τὸν ῥυθμὸν καὶ
τὸ μέτρον, ἄλλο τι ἢ λόγοι γίγνονται τὸ λειπόμενον ;

[3] *Poet.* i. 6–9 ; ix. 2, cf. 9. See also the quotation from
Aristotle preserved in Athenaeus xi. 112 (where, however, the

(ch. i. 7–9) he goes a step farther and presents what appears to have been at the time an original view. Poetry, he explains, is a form of artistic μίμησις, and its essence lies rather in the 'imitation' of the idea than in the mere versification. Within the field of literature he recalls actual examples of such artistic 'imitation,' even in prose writings, and notes the want of a common term which would embrace every imaginative delineation of life that employs language as its medium of expression. In illustration of his point he mentions different kinds of literary composition, which have not hitherto been brought under a single distinctive designation,—(1) the mimes of Sophron and Xenarchus and the dialogues of Plato, all of them prose compositions of a dramatic or semi-dramatic character: (2) verse composition, whether written in a single metre or in heterogeneous metres. The obvious suggestion of the passage is that the

text as it stands is hardly sound), Ἀριστοτέλης δὲ ἐν τῷ περὶ ποιητῶν οὕτως γράφει " οὐκοῦν οὐδὲ ἐμμέτρους (?) τοὺς καλουμένους Σώφρονος μίμους μὴ φῶμεν εἶναι λόγους καὶ μιμήσεις ἢ τοὺς Ἀλεξαμένου τοῦ Τηίου τοὺς πρώτους (? πρότερον) γραφέντας τῶν Σωκρατικῶν διαλόγων;" 'Are we therefore to deny that the mimes of Sophron' (whose very name shows that they are imitative or mimetic), 'though in no way metrical,—or again the dialogues of Alexamenus of Teos, the first (?) Socratic dialogues that were written,—are prose and at the same time imitations (and hence, poetic compositions)?' On this passage see Bernays, Zwei Abhandlungen über die Aristotelische Theorie des Drama, p. 83. Cf. Diog. Laert. iii. 37, φησὶ δ' Ἀριστοτέλης τὴν τῶν λόγων ἰδέαν αὐτοῦ (Πλάτωνος) μεταξὺ ποιήματος εἶναι καὶ πεζοῦ λόγου.

meaning of the word 'poet' should be widened so
as to include any writer, either in prose or verse,
whose work is an 'imitation' within the aesthetic
meaning of the term.[1]

[1] The general sense of the passage (*Poet.* i. 6–9) is clear, though
the text offers difficulties in detail. In § 6 Ueberweg's deletion
of ἐποποιία and Bernays' admirable conjecture ἀνώνυμος are both
confirmed by the Arabic version and may be accepted without
hesitation. Again in § 6 μόνον τοῖς λόγοις I understand to mean
'by language alone' (i.e. without music), ψιλοῖς 'without metre'
(as e.g. *Rhet.* iii. 2. 1404 b 14 where ἐν δὲ τοῖς ψιλοῖς λόγοις is
opposed to ἐπὶ τῶν μέτρων), ψιλός as usual implying the absence
of some accompaniment or adjunct which is suggested by the
context. The order of words τοῖς λόγοις ψιλοῖς instead of τοῖς
ψιλοῖς λόγοις is due to the pause in the sense at μόνον τοῖς
λόγοις, at which point ψιλοῖς comes in with a predicative force as
if the whole phrase were to be ψιλοῖς ἢ ἐμμέτροις : τοῖς μέτροις,
however, being substituted for ἐμμέτροις.

In § 9 ὁμοίως δὲ κἂν εἴ τις κ.τ.λ. I accept the reading of the
apographa καὶ τοῦτον (καὶ Aᶜ) ποιητὴν προσαγορευτέον : 'and the
same principle will apply even if a person mixed all his metres
(and could not, therefore, be called a —ποιός of a certain metre); we
must bring him too under our general term poet ;' i.e. by shifting
the point of view, and fixing our mind on the μίμησις not on the
metrical form, we bring in another writer whom strictly we should
exclude, if we made the title to the name ποιητής to be the
construction of a certain sort of metre.

As I read the whole passage there is a transition from the
negative to the positive form of expression. In §§ 6 and 7 the
form is negative. 'The art . . . is at present without a name.
There is no common term we can apply to artistic "imitation"
in prose, in metre of a single kind—' the proper continuation of
which would have been, 'and in mixed metres.' But in the course
of §§ 7–8 the positive idea has now emerged that it is μίμησις not
verse-writing which makes the ποιητής and accordingly § 9 is cast
in a new mould, as if the whole had run thus, 'we ought to give
the comprehensive name of ποιητής to artistic imitators whether in

The general question whether metre is necessary
for poetical expression has been raised by many
modern critics and poets, and has sometimes been
answered in the negative, as by Sidney, Shelley,
Wordsworth.[1]   It is, however, worth observing
prose, or metre of a single kind, or mixed metres.'   The parenthetic
remark of § 8 διὸ τὸν μὲν ποιητὴν δίκαιον καλεῖν κ.τ.λ. may
through its positive form have had some influence in determining
the form of ὁμοίως δὲ . . . προσαγορευτέον.

If, on the other hand, we supply with Vahlen the words οὐδὲν
ἂν ἔχοιμεν ὀνομάσαι κοινόν as the apodosis to ὁμοίως δὲ κἂν εἴ τις—
ποιοῖτο, the following clause,—καὶ ποιητὴν προσαγορευτέον 'and we
must style him poet,'—tacked on to the suppressed apodosis is intolerably harsh.   The correction καίτοι ποιητὴν προσαγορευτέον
(Rassow, Zeller) obviates this objection and may be the true
reading.   But whether we read καὶ τοῦτον or καίτοι we are
relieved from the necessity of assuming, with Susemihl, a dislocation
in the general order of the clauses (see Crit. Notes) and of bracketing
certain phrases.

[1] Cf. Sir Philip Sidney, *An Apologie for Poetrie* : ' The greatest
part of the poets have apparelled their poetical inventions in that
numberous kind of writing which is called verse.   Indeed but
apparelled, verse being but an ornament and no cause to poetry,
since there have been many most excellent poets that never versified,
and now swarm many versifiers that need never answer to the name
of poets.   For Xenophon, who did imitate so excellently as to give
us *effigiem iusti imperii*—the portraiture of a just empire under the
name of Cyrus (as Cicero saith of him)—made therein an absolute
heroical poem.'

And again : ' One may be a poet without versing, and a versifier
without poetry.'

Cervantes, *Don Quixote* : ' An epic may also be as well written
in prose as in verse. '

Shelley, *A Defence of Poetry* : ' Yet it is by no means essential
that a poet should accommodate his language to this traditional form,
so that the harmony, which is its spirit, be observed.   The practice
is indeed convenient and popular, and to be preferred, especially in

that from Aristotle's point of view, which was mainly one of observation, the question to be determined was rather as to the vehicle or medium of literary μίμησις; and so far as the μίμησις doctrine is concerned, it is undeniable that some kinds of imaginative subject-matter are better expressed in prose, some in verse, and that Aristotle, who had before him experimental examples of writings poetic in spirit, but not metrical in form, had sufficient grounds for advocating an extension of meaning for the term ποιητής. But as regards the *Art* of Poetry, his reasoning does not lead us to conclude that he would have reckoned the authors of prose dialogues or romances among poets strictly so called. As Mr. Courthope truly says,[1]

such composition as includes much action : but every great poet must inevitably innovate upon the example of his predecessors in the exact structure of his peculiar versification. The distinction between poets and prose-writers is a vulgar error. . . . Plato was essentially a poet—the truth and splendour of his imagery, and the melody of his language are the most intense that it is possible to conceive. . . . Lord Bacon was a poet. His language has a sweet and majestic rhythm, which satisfies the sense, no less than the almost superhuman wisdom of his philosophy satisfies the intellect.'

Wordsworth in his *Preface* also enforces the doctrine that metre is not essential to poetry.

On the discussion in the Renaissance as to whether poetry could be written in prose see Spingarn, *Literary Criticism in the Renaissance* (New York, 1899), pp. 35 ff. The expression 'poetic prose' appears, he observes, perhaps for the first time in Minturno *L'Arte Poetica* (1564).

[1] *Life in Poetry : Law in Taste* (Macmillan, 1901), p. 70. The whole lecture (on Poetical Expression) well deserves reading.

'he does not attempt to prove that metre is
not a necessary accompaniment of the higher
conceptions of poetry,' and he, 'therefore, cannot
be ranged with those who support that extreme
opinion.'

Still there would appear to be some want of
firmness in the position he takes up as to the place
and importance of metre. In his definition of
tragedy (ch. vi. 2) ' embellished language' (ἡδυσμένος
λόγος) is included among the constituent elements
of tragedy ; and the phrase is then explained to
mean language that has the twofold charm of
metre (which is a branch of rhythm) and of
melody. But these elements are placed in a subordinate rank and are hardly treated as essentials.
They are in this respect not unlike the visible
spectacular effect (ὄψις), which, though deduced
by Aristotle from the definition, is not explicitly
mentioned in it. The essence of the poetry is the
'imitation'; the melody and the verse are the
'seasoning'[1] of the language. They hold a place,
as Teichmüller observes,[2] similar to that which

---

[1] They are ἡδύσματα: *Poet.* vi. 19, ἡ μελοποιία μέγιστον τῶν
ἡδυσμάτων. Cf. *Rhet.* iii. 3. 1406 a 18 (of Alcidamas' use of
epithets), οὐ γὰρ ἡδύσματι χρῆται ἀλλ' ὡς ἐδέσματι τοῖς ἐπιθέτοις,
—they are not the sauce but the dish itself. *Pol.* v. (viii.) 5. 1340
b 16, ἡ δὲ μουσικὴ φύσει τῶν ἡδυσμένων ἐστίν, opposed to ἀνή-
δυντον. Plato, *Rep.* x. 607 A, εἰ δὲ τὴν ἡδυσμένην Μοῦσαν παρα-
δέξει ἐν μέλεσιν ἢ ἔπεσιν. . . . Plut. *Symp. Qu.* vii. 8. 4, τὸ μέλος
καὶ ὁ ῥυθμὸς ὥσπερ ὄψον ἐπὶ τῷ λόγῳ.

[2] *Aristotelische Forschungen,* ii. 364.

'external goods' occupy in the Aristotelian definition of happiness. Without them a tragedy may
fulfil its function, but would lack its perfect charm
and fail in producing its full effect of pleasurable
emotion.

Aristotle, highly as he rates the aesthetic
capacity of the sense of hearing in his treatment
of music, says nothing to show that he values at
its proper worth the power of rhythmical sound as
a factor in poetry ; and this is the more striking in
a Greek whose enjoyment of poetry came through
the ear rather than the eye, and for whom poetry
was so largely associated with music. After all,
there can hardly be a greater difference between
two ways of saying the same thing than that one
is said in verse, the other in prose. There are some
lyrics which have lived and will always live by
their musical charm, and by a strange magic that
lies in the setting of the words. We need not
agree with a certain modern school who would
empty all poetry of poetical thought and etherealise
it till it melts into a strain of music ; who sing to
us we hardly know of what, but in such a way
that the echoes of the real world, its men and
women, its actual stir and conflict, are faint and
hardly to be discerned. The poetry, we are told,
resides not in the ideas conveyed, not in the
blending of soul and sense, but in the sound itself,
in the cadence of the verse.

Yet, false as this view may be, it is not perhaps more false than that other which wholly ignores the effect of musical sound and looks only to the thought that is conveyed. Aristotle comes perilously near this doctrine, and was saved from it, we may conjecture—if indeed he was saved—only by an instinctive reluctance to set at naught the traditional sentiment of Greece.

His omission of architecture from the list of the fine arts may also cause surprise to modern readers; for here, as in sculpture, the artistic greatness of Greece stands undisputed. In this, however, he is merely following the usage of his countrymen who reckoned architecture among the useful arts. It was linked to the practical world. It sprang out of the needs of civic and religious life, and the greatest triumphs of the art were connected with public faith and worship. To a Greek the temple, which was the culmination of architectural skill, was the house of the god, the abode of his image, a visible pledge of his protecting presence. At the same time,—and this was the decisive point—architecture had not the 'imitative' quality which was regarded as essential to fine art. Modern writers may tell us that its forms owe their origin to the direct suggestions of the physical world—of natural caverns or forest arches—and in the groined roof they may trace a marked resemblance to an avenue of interlacing

trees. Such resemblances, however, are much
fainter in Greek than in Gothic architecture ; apart
from which the argument from origin would here
be as much out of place, as it would be to maintain, in relation to music, that the reason why
people now enjoy Beethoven is, that their earliest
ancestors of arboreal habits found musical notes to
be a telling adjunct to love-making.

Be the origin of architecture what it may, it is
certain that the Greeks did not find its primitive
type and model in the outward universe. A
building as an organic whole did not call up any
image of a world outside itself, though the method
of architecture does remind Aristotle of the
structural method of nature. Even if architecture
had seemed to him to reproduce the appearances
of the physical universe, it would not have satisfied
his idea of artistic imitation ; for all the arts imitate
human life in some of its manifestations, and
imitate material objects only so far as these serve
to interpret spiritual and mental processes. The
decorative element in Greek architecture is alone
'imitative' in the Aristotelian sense, being indeed
but a form of sculpture ; but sculpture does not
constitute the building, nor is it, as in Gothic
architecture, an organic part of the whole. The
metopes in a Greek temple are, as it were, a setting
for a picture, a frame into which sculptural representations may be fitted, but the frame is not

always filled in. The temple itself, though constructed according to the laws of the beautiful,
though realising, as we might say, the idea of
the beautiful, yet is not 'imitative'; it does
not, according to Greek notions, rank as fine
art.

From the course of the foregoing argument we
gather that a work of art is an image of the
impressions or 'phantasy pictures' made by an
independent reality upon the mind of the artist,
the reality thus reflected being the facts of human
life and human nature. To this we must make
one addition, which contains the central thought of
Aristotle's doctrine. *Imitative art in its highest
form, namely poetry, is an expression of the
universal element in human life.*[1] If we may
expand Aristotle's idea in the light of his own
system,—fine art eliminates what is transient and
particular and reveals the permanent and essential
features of the original. It discovers the 'form'
(εἶδος) towards which an object tends, the result
which nature strives to attain, but rarely or never
can attain. Beneath the individual it finds the
universal. It passes beyond the bare reality given
by nature, and expresses a purified form of reality
disengaged from accident, and freed from conditions
which thwart its development. The real and the
ideal from this point of view are not opposites, as

[1] *Poet.* ix. 3.

they are sometimes conceived to be. The ideal is
the real, but rid of contradictions, unfolding itself
according to the laws of its own being, apart from
alien influences and the disturbances of chance.

We can now see the force of the phrase τὸ
βέλτιον, as applied in the *Poetics*[1] to the creations
of poetry and art. It is identical in meaning
with the οἷα εἶναι δεῖ of ch. xxv. § 1, and the
οἴους δεῖ (? εἶναι)[2] of § 6. The 'better' and the
'ought to be' are not to be taken in the moral, but
in the aesthetic sense. The expression 'the better'
is, indeed, almost a technical one in Aristotle's
general philosophy of nature, and its meaning and
associations in that connexion throw light on the
sense it bears when transferred to the sphere of Art.
Aristotle distinguishes the workings of inorganic
and organic nature. In the former case, the
governing law is the law of necessity : in the
latter, it is purpose or design; which purpose,
again, is identified with 'the better'[3] or 'the

---

[1] xxv. 17, cf. 7.   [2] See p. 370.

[3] *De Gen. Anim.* i. 4. 717 a 15, πᾶν ἡ φύσις ἡ διὰ τὸ ἀναγκαῖον
ποιεῖ ἡ διὰ τὸ βέλτιον, the distinction being that between φύσις
ἐξ ἀνάγκης ποιοῦσα, the inorganic processes of nature, and φύσις
ἕνεκά του ποιοῦσα, organic processes. So ἐξ ἀνάγκης is opposed in
de Gen. Anim. iii. 1. 731 b 21 to διὰ τὸ βέλτιον καὶ τὴν αἰτίαν
τὴν ἕνεκά τινος : *de Gen. Anim.* iii. 4. 755 a 22, to χάριν τοῦ
βελτίονος : in *de Part. Anim.* iv. 11. 692 a 3, to τοῦ βελτίονος
ἕνεκα. For τὸ βέλτιον as the aim of Nature when working
organically cf. *de Gen. et Corr.* ii. 10. 336 b 27, ἐν ἅπασιν ἀεὶ τοῦ
βελτίονος ὀρέγεσθαί φαμεν τὴν φύσιν. *Phys.* viii. 7. 260 b 22,

best.'¹ Nature, often baffled in her intentions,²
thwarted by unfavourable matter or by human
agency, yet tends towards the desirable end. She
can often enlist even the blind force of necessity
as her ally, giving a new direction to its results.³
Wherever organic processes are in operation, order
and proportion are in varying degrees apparent.
The general movement of organic life is part of a
progress to the 'better,' the several parts working
together for the good of the whole. The artist in
his mimic world carries forward this movement to a
more perfect completion. The creations of his art are
framed on those ideal lines that nature has drawn :
her intimations, her guidance are what he follows.
He too aims at something better than the actual.
He produces a new thing, not the actual thing of
experience, not a copy of reality, but a βέλτιον, or
higher reality—' for the ideal type must surpass
the actual ' ;⁴ the ideal is ' better ' than the real.

τὸ δὲ βέλτιον ἀεὶ ὑπολαμβάνομεν ἐν τῇ φύσει ὑπάρχειν, ἂν ᾖ
δυνατόν : viii. 6. 259 a 10, ἐν γὰρ τοῖς φύσει δεῖ τὸ πεπερασμένον
καὶ τὸ βέλτιον, ἂν ἐνδέχηται, ὑπάρχειν μᾶλλον.

¹ De Ingr. Anim. 8. 708 a 9, τὴν φύσιν μηθὲν ποιεῖν μάτην,
ἀλλὰ πάντα πρὸς τὸ ἄριστον ἀποβλέπουσαν ἑκάστῳ τῶν ἐνδεχομένων : 11, ἡ φύσις οὐδὲν δημιουργεῖ μάτην · . . ἀλλὰ πάντα
πρὸς τὸ βέλτιστον ἐκ τῶν ἐνδεχομένων. So passim.

² Pol. i. 6. 1255 b 2, ἡ δὲ φύσις βούλεται μὲν τοῦτο ποιεῖν,
πολλάκις μέντοι οὐ δύναται.

³ Cf. de Gen. Anim. ii. 6. 744 b 16, ὥσπερ γὰρ οἰκονόμος
ἀγαθός, καὶ ἡ φύσις οὐθὲν ἀποβάλλειν εἴωθεν ἐξ ὧν ἔστι ποιῆσαί
τι χρηστόν.

⁴ Poet. xxv. 17, ἀλλὰ βέλτιον · τὸ γὰρ παράδειγμα δεῖ ὑπερ-

Art, therefore, in imitating the universal imitates the ideal; and we can now describe *a work of art as an idealised representation of human life—of character, emotion, action—under forms manifest to sense.*

'Imitation,' in the sense in which Aristotle applies the word to poetry, is thus seen to be equivalent to 'producing' or 'creating according to a true idea,' which forms part of the definition of art in general.[1] The 'true idea' for fine art is derived from the εἶδος, the general concept which the intellect spontaneously abstracts from the details of sense. There is an ideal form which is present in each individual phenomenon but imperfectly manifested. This form impresses itself as a sensuous appearance on the mind of the artist; he seeks to give it a more complete expression, to bring to light the ideal which is only half revealed in the world of reality. His distinctive work as an artist consists in stamping the given material with the impress of the form which is universal. The process is not simply that which is described by Socrates in the conversation he is reported to have held in the studio

ἔχειν. Cf. Plat. *Rep.* v. 472 D, οἴει ἂν οὖν ἧττόν τι ἀγαθὸν ζωγράφον εἶναι, ὃς ἂν γράψας παράδειγμα, οἷον ἂν εἴη ὁ κάλλιστος ἄνθρωπος, . . . μὴ ἔχῃ ἀποδεῖξαι ὡς καὶ δυνατὸν γενέσθαι τοιοῦτον ἄνδρα; See also p. 168.

[1] *Eth. Nic.* vi. 4. 1140 a 10, ἕξις μετὰ λόγου ἀληθοῦς ποιητική.

of Parrhasius, by which the artist, who is no
servile copyist, brings together many elements
of beauty which are dispersed in nature.[1] It
is not enough to select, combine, embellish,—to
add here and to retrench there. The elements
must be harmonised into an ideal unity of
type.

'Imitation,' so understood, is a creative act.
It is the expression of the concrete thing under
an image which answers to its true idea. To
seize the universal, and to reproduce it in
simple and sensuous form is not to reflect a
reality already familiar through sense perceptions ;
rather it is a rivalry of nature, a completion
of her unfulfilled purposes, a correction of her
failures.

If, however, the 'imitation' which is the principle of fine art ultimately resolves itself into an
effort to complete in some sense the work of
nature, how, then, it may be asked, does fine art,
after all, differ from useful art ? We have seen
that the character of the useful arts is to co-
operate with nature, to complete the designs
which she has been unable to carry out. Does

---

[1] Xen. *Mem.* iii. 10. Cf. Arist. *Pol.* iii. 11. 1281 b 10, τούτῳ
διαφέρουσιν οἱ σπουδαῖοι τῶν ἀνδρῶν ἑκάστου τῶν πολλῶν, ὥσπερ
καὶ τῶν μὴ καλῶν τοὺς καλούς φασι καὶ τὰ γεγραμμένα διὰ
τέχνης τῶν ἀληθινῶν, τῷ συνῆχθαι τὰ διεσπαρμένα χωρὶς εἰς ἕν,
ἐπεὶ κεχωρισμένων γε κάλλιον ἔχειν τοῦ γεγραμμένου τουδὶ μὲν
τὸν ὀφθαλμὸν ἑτέρου δέ τινος ἕτερον μόριον.

not Aristotle's distinction, then, between the two forms of art disappear? To the question thus raised Aristotle offers no direct answer; nor perhaps did he put it to himself in this form. But if we follow out his thought, his reply would appear to be something of this kind. Nature is a living and creative energy, which by a sort of instinctive reason works in every individual object towards a specific end. In some domains the end is more clearly visible than in others; the higher we carry our observation in the scale of existence the more certainly can the end be discerned. Everywhere, however, there is a ceaseless and upward progress, an unfolding of new life in inexhaustible variety. Each individual thing has an ideal form towards which it tends, and in the realisation of this form, which is one with the essence (οὐσία) of the object, its end is attained.[1] Nature is an artist who is capable indeed of mistakes, but by slow

---

[1] The τέλος of an object is τὸ τέλος τῆς γενέσεως or κινήσεως, the term of the process of the movement. The true οὐσία or φύσις of a thing is found in the attainment of its τέλος,—that which the thing has become when the process of development is completed from the matter (ὕλη) or mere potential existence (δύναμις) to form (εἶδος) or actuality (ἐντελέχεια). *Phys.* ii. 2. 194 a 28, ἡ δὲ φύσις τέλος καὶ οὗ ἕνεκα· ὧν γὰρ συνεχοῦς τῆς κινήσεως οὔσης ἔστι τι τέλος τῆς κινήσεως, τοῦτο ἔσχατον καὶ οὗ ἕνεκα. Cf. *Pol.* i. 2. 1252 b 32. *Metaph.* iv. 4. 1015 a 10, (φύσις) . . . καὶ τὸ εἶδος καὶ ἡ οὐσία· τοῦτο δ' ἐστὶ τὸ τέλος τῆς γενέσεως. Hence (of the development of tragedy) *Poet.* iv. 12, πολλὰς μεταβολὰς μεταβαλοῦσα ἡ τραγῳδία ἐπαύσατο, ἐπεὶ ἔσχε τὴν αὑτῆς φύσιν.

advances and through many failures realises her own idea.[1] Her organising and plastic power displays itself in the manifest purpose which governs her movements. Some of the humbler members of her kingdom may appear mean if taken singly and judged by the impression they make upon the senses. Their true beauty and significance are visible to the eye of reason, which looks not to the material elements or to the isolated parts but to the structure of the whole.[2] In her structural

---

[1] *Phys.* ii. 8. 199 a 17 sqq.

[2] Cf. *de Part. Anim.* i. 5. 645 a 4 sqq., 'Having already treated of the celestial world, as far as our conjectures could reach, we proceed to treat of animals, without omitting, to the best of our ability, any member of the kingdom, however ignoble. For if some have no graces to charm the sense (πρὸς τὴν αἴσθησιν), yet even these, by disclosing to intellectual perception the artistic spirit that designed them, give immense pleasure to all who can trace links of causation and are inclined to philosophy (κατὰ τὴν θεωρίαν ὅμως ἡ δημιουργήσασα φύσις ἀμηχάνους ἡδονὰς παρέχει τοῖς δυναμένοις τὰς αἰτίας γνωρίζειν καὶ φύσει φιλοσόφοις). Indeed it would be strange if mimic representations of them were attractive because they disclose the constructive skill of the painter or sculptor, and the original realities themselves were not more interesting, to all at any rate that have eyes to discern the reason that presided over their formation' (Ogle's Trans.).

The thought of the shaping and plastic power of nature is in one form or another a persistent one in Greek philosophy and literature. In Plato (*Soph.* 265 B sqq.) God is the divine artist ; in the Stoics nature, 'artifex,' 'artificiosa,' fashions by instinct works which human skill cannot equal (Cic. *de Nat. D.* ii. 22); with them the universe is the divine poem. In Plotinus God is artist and poet. In Dion Chrysostom ('Ολυμπ. *Or.* xii. 416 R) Ζεύς is πρῶτος καὶ τελειότατος δημιουργός: in Philostratus ζωγράφος ὁ θεός.

faculty lies nature's perfection. With her the
attainment of the end 'holds the place of the
beautiful.'[1]

Now, art in its widest sense starts from a
mental conception of the ideal as thus determined.[2]
Useful art, employing nature's own machinery,
aids her in her effort to realise the ideal in the
world around us, so far as man's practical needs
are served by furthering this purpose. Fine art
sets practical needs aside; it does not seek to
affect the real world, to modify the actual. By
mere imagery it reveals the ideal form at which
nature aims in the highest sphere of organic existence,—in the region, namely, of human life, where
her intention is most manifest, though her failures
too are most numerous. Resembling nature in a
certain instinctive yet rational faculty, it does not
follow the halting course of nature's progress. The
artist ignores the intervening steps, the slow processes, by which nature attempts to bridge the
space between the potential and the actual. The
form which nature has been striving, and perhaps

---

[1] *De Part. Anim.* i. 5. 645 a 25, οὗ δ' ἔνεκα συνέστηκεν ἡ
γέγονε τέλους τὴν τοῦ καλοῦ χώραν εἴληφε.

[2] *Met.* vi. 7. 1032 a 32, ἀπὸ τέχνης δὲ γίγνεται ὅσων τὸ εἶδος
ἐν τῇ ψυχῇ. *De Part. Anim.* i. 1. 640 a 31, ἡ δὲ τέχνη λόγος τοῦ
ἔργου ὁ ἄνευ τῆς ὕλης. The mental conception of the εἶδος in a
concrete form is called νόησις, the impressing of this conception on
the matter is called ποίησις, *Met.* vi. 7. 1032 b 15. This whole
theory of art is summed up in the words ἡ γὰρ τέχνη τὸ εἶδος
(*Met.* vi. 9. 1034 a 24).

vainly striving, to attain stands forth embodied
in a creation of the mind. The ideal has taken
concrete shape, the finished product stands before
us, nor do we ask how it has come to be what it
is. The flaws and failures incident to the natural
process are removed, and in a glorified appearance
we discern nature's ideal intention. Fine art,
then, is a completion of nature in a sense not
applicable to useful art; it presents to us only an
image, but a purified image of nature's original.[1]

Such would appear to be Aristotle's position.
We may here note the difference between this
view and the attitude adopted by Plato towards
fine art, especially in the *Republic*; remembering,
however, that Plato was capable of writing also
in another strain and in a different mood.[2]   Start-

[1] In some domains nature carries out her artistic intentions
in a manner that surpasses all the efforts of art; and in one
place Aristotle actually says μᾶλλον δ' ἐστὶ τὸ οὗ ἔνεκα καὶ τὸ
καλὸν ἐν τοῖς τῆς φύσεως ἔργοις ἢ ἐν τοῖς τῆς τέχνης (de Part.
Anim. i. 1. 639 b 19).   This, however, requires to be taken with
proper qualification. Similarly the continuity of nature is contrasted with the want of continuity in a bad tragedy : Met. xiii. 3.
1090 b 19, οὐκ ἔοικε δὲ ἡ φύσις ἐπεισοδιώδης οὖσα ἐκ τῶν
φαινομένων ὥσπερ μοχθηρὰ τραγῳδία. The general position
taken up by Aristotle is not materially different from that of
Goethe when he says : 'Nature in many of her works reveals a
charm of beauty which no human art can hope to reach ; but I am
by no means of opinion that she is beautiful in all her aspects.
Her intentions are indeed always good, but not so the conditions
which are required to make her manifest herself completely.'

[2] See especially the *Phaedrus* and the *Symposium* and observe
the concessions made in the *Laws* Book ii. and Book vii. Finsler,

ing from the notion of pure Being he found
reality only in the world of ideas, sensible phenomena being but so many images which at best
remind us of the celestial archetype. To him
Becoming was the simple antithesis of Being ; it
meant the world of change, the sphere of phenomena, the region in which the individual life
appears for a moment and then vanishes away.
The poet or painter holds up a mirror to material
objects—earth, plants, animals, mankind—and
catches a reflexion of the world around him, which
is itself only the reflexion of the ideal.[1] The
actual world therefore stands nearer to the idea
than the artistic imitation, and fine art is a copy
of a copy, twice removed from truth.[2] It is con-
versant with the outward shows and semblances
of things, and produces its effects by illusions
of form and colour which dupe the senses. The
imitative artist does not need more than a surface
acquaintance with the thing he represents. He is
on a level below the skilled craftsman whose art
is intelligent and based on rational principles, and
who alone has a title to be called a 'maker' or
creator. A painter may paint a table very ad-
mirably without knowing anything of the inner
construction of a table, a knowledge which the

Platon und die Aristotelische Poetik (Leipzig, 1900), ch. vii. is worth
reading in this connexion.
[1] *Rep.* x. 596 E.   [2] *Rep.* x. 597 E.

carpenter, who would fashion it for its proper end, must possess. And poets, too, whose ideas of men are formed on a limited experience,[1] cannot pass beyond the range of that experience, they have no insight into the nature of man, into the human soul as it is in itself; this can be attained only by philosophic study.

The fundamental thought of Aristotle's philosophy, on the other hand, is Becoming not Being; and Becoming to him meant not an appearing and a vanishing away, but a process of development, an unfolding of what is already in the germ, an upward ascent ending in Being which is the highest object of knowledge. The concrete individual thing is not a shadowy appearance but the primary reality. The outward and material world, the diverse manifestations of nature's life, organic and inorganic, the processes of birth and decay, the manifold forms of sensuous beauty, all gained a new importance for his philosophy. Physical science, slighted by Plato, was passionately studied by Aristotle. Fine art was no longer twice removed from the truth of things; it was the manifestation of a higher truth, the expression of the universal which is not outside of and apart from the particular, but presupposed in each particular. The work of art was not a semblance opposed to reality, but the image of a reality which is pene-

[1] *Timaeus* 19 D.

trated by the idea, and through which the idea shows more apparent than in the actual world. Whereas Plato had laid it down that 'the greatest and fairest things are done by nature, and the lesser by art, which receives from nature all the greater and primeval creations and fashions them in detail,'[1] Aristotle saw in fine art a rational faculty which divines nature's unfulfilled intentions, and reveals her ideal to sense. The illusions which fine art employs do not cheat the mind; they image forth the immanent idea which cannot find adequate expression under the forms of material existence.

Some critics, it may be observed, have attempted to show that the fundamental principles of fine art are deduced by Aristotle from the idea of the beautiful. But this is to antedate the theory of modern aesthetics, and to read into Aristotle more than any impartial interpretation can find in him. The view cannot be supported except by forced inferences, in which many links of the argument have to be supplied, and by extracting philosophical meanings of far-reaching import out of chance expressions. Aristotle's conception of fine art, so far as it is developed, is entirely detached from any theory of the beautiful—a separation which is characteristic of all ancient aesthetic criticism down to a late period. Plotinus, working

---

[1] *Laws* x. 889 A (Jowett's Trans.).

M

out Plato's ideas with the modifications required
by his own mysticism, attempted to determine the
idea of the beautiful as a fundamental problem of
art, and with it to solve the difficult and hitherto
neglected problem as to the meaning of the ugly.
He based his theory of fine art on a particular
conception of the beautiful; but Aristotle is still
far removed from this point of view. While he
assumes almost as an obvious truth that beauty is
indispensable in a work of art and essential to the
attainment of its end, and while he throws out
hints as to the component elements of the beautiful,[1] he has nowhere analysed that idea, nor did he
perhaps regard the beautiful, in its purely aesthetic
sense, as forming a separate domain of philosophic
inquiry. It is useless, out of the fragmentary
observations Aristotle has left us, to seek to construct a theory of the beautiful. He makes beauty
a regulative principle of art, but he never says or
implies that the manifestation of the beautiful is
the end of art. The objective laws of art are
deduced not from an inquiry into the beautiful,
but from an observation of art as it is and of the
effects which it produces.

[1] *Poet.* vii. 4 ; *Met.* xii. 3. 1078 a 36 ; cf. *Probl.* xvii. 1. 915 b
36 ; Plato, *Phileb.* 64 E.

CHAPTER III

WHAT is true of fine art in general is explicitly asserted by Aristotle of poetry alone, to which in a unique manner it applies. Poetry expresses most adequately the universal element in human nature and in life. As a revelation of the universal it abstracts from human life much that is accidental. It liberates us from the tyranny of physical surroundings. It can disregard material needs and animal longings. Thought disengages itself from sense and makes itself supreme over things outward. 'It is not the function of the poet,' says Aristotle, 'to relate what has happened, but what may happen,—what is possible according to the law of probability or necessity. The poet and the historian differ not by writing in verse or in prose. The work of Herodotus might be put into verse, and it would still be a species of history, with metre no less than without it. The true difference is that one relates what has happened, the other

163

what may happen.'[1]   The first distinguishing mark, then, of poetry is that it has a higher subject-matter than history; it expresses the universal (τὰ καθόλου) not the particular (τὰ καθ' ἕκαστον), the permanent possibilities of human nature (οἷα ἂν γένοιτο); it does not merely tell the story of the individual life, 'what Alcibiades did or suffered.'[2]

Though we may be inclined to take exception to the criticism which appears to limit history to dry chronicles, and to overlook the existence of a history such as that of Thucydides,[3] yet the main thought here cannot be disputed.   History is based upon facts, and with these it is primarily concerned; poetry transforms its facts into truths. The history of Herodotus, in spite of the epic grandeur of the theme and a unity of design, which though obscured is not effaced by the numerous digressions, would still, as Aristotle says, be history and not poetry even if it were put into verse.   Next, poetry exhibits a more rigorous connexion of events; cause and event are linked together in 'probable or necessary sequence' (κατὰ τὸ εἰκὸς ἢ τὸ ἀναγκαῖον).   Historical

[1] Poet. ix. 1–2.
[2] Poet. ix. 4.   An interesting comment on this conception of poetry may be found in an article by Mr. Herbert Paul in The Nineteenth Century, Feb. 1902, on 'Art and Eccentricity.'
[3] Unless, indeed, we retain the reading συνήθεις in Poet. xxiii. 1 (see infra, p. 165), and find in it the necessary restriction.

compositions, as Aristotle observes in a later chapter, are a record of actual facts, of particular events, strung together in the order of time but without any clear causal connexion.[1] Not only in the development of the plot[2] but also in the internal working of character,[3] the drama observes a stricter and more logical order than that of actual experience. The rule of probability which Aristotle enjoins is not the narrow *vraisemblance* which it was understood to mean by many of the older French critics, which would shut the poet out from the higher regions of the imagination and confine him to the trivial round of immediate reality. The incidents of every tragedy worthy of

---

[1] *Poet.* xxiii. 1-2, καὶ (δεῖ) μὴ ὁμοίας ἱστορίαις τὰς συνθέσεις (ἱστορίας τὰς συνήθεις codd.) εἶναι, ἐν αἷς ἀνάγκη οὐχὶ μιᾶς πράξεως ποιεῖσθαι δήλωσιν ἀλλ᾽ ἑνὸς χρόνου, ὅσα ἐν τούτῳ συνέβη περὶ ἕνα ἢ πλείους, ὧν ἕκαστον ὡς ἔτυχεν ἔχει πρὸς ἄλληλα. The reading of the MSS. ἱστορίας τὰς συνήθεις makes an intolerably harsh form of inverted comparison, and Dacier's conjecture above given is possibly right : ' the structure (of the epic) should not resemble the histories. . . .' But I strongly incline to M'Vey's correction (mentioned in Preface, p. xvii.) οἵας for ὁμοίας ; no further change is then needed. The Arabic version, as I learn from Professor Margoliouth, has no equivalent for συνήθεις and seems to point, but by no means certainly, to συνθέσεις.

[2] *Poet.* ix. 1.

[3] *Poet.* xv. 6, χρὴ δὲ καὶ ἐν τοῖς ἤθεσιν ὥσπερ καὶ ἐν τῇ τῶν πραγμάτων συστάσει ἀεὶ ζητεῖν ἢ τὸ ἀναγκαῖον ἢ τὸ εἰκός, ὥστε τὸν τοιοῦτον τὰ τοιαῦτα λέγειν ἢ πράττειν ᾖ (ἢ codd.) ἀναγκαῖον ἢ εἰκός, καὶ τοῦτο μετὰ τοῦτο γίνεσθαι ᾖ (ἢ codd.) ἀναγκαῖον ἢ εἰκός.

the name are improbable if measured by the likelihood of their everyday occurrence,—improbable
in the same degree in which characters capable of
great deeds and great passions are rare. The rule
of 'probability,' as also that of 'necessity,' refers
rather to the internal structure of a poem; it is
the inner law which secures the cohesion of the
parts.

The 'probable' is not determined by a numerical
average of instances; it is not a condensed expression for what meets us in the common course of
things. The εἰκός of daily life, the empirically
usual, is derived from an observed sequence of
facts, and denotes what is normal and regular in
its occurrence, the rule, not the exception.[1] But
the rule of experience cannot be the law that
governs art. The higher creations of poetry move
in another plane. The incidents of the drama
and the epic are not those of ordinary life : the
persons, who here play their parts, are not average
men and women. The 'probable' law of their
conduct cannot be deduced from commonplace
experience, or brought under a statistical average.
The thoughts and deeds, the will and the emotions

---

[1] *Analyt. Prior.* ii. 27. 70 a 4, ὃ γὰρ ὡς ἐπὶ τὸ πολὺ ἴσασιν
οὕτω γιγνόμενον ἢ μὴ γιγνόμενον ἢ ὂν ἢ μὴ ὄν, τοῦτ' ἐστὶν εἰκός.
As an instance of the ὡς ἐπὶ τὸ πολύ (with which the εἰκός is here
identified) we have in *Analyt. Post.* ii. 12. 96 a 10 the growth of
the beard on the chin : οὐ πᾶς ἄνθρωπος ἄρρην τὸ γένειον τριχοῦται,
ἀλλ' ὡς ἐπὶ τὸ πολύ.

of a Prometheus or a Clytemnestra, a Hamlet or
an Othello, are not an epitomised rendering of the
ways of meaner mortals. The common man can
indeed enter into these characters with more or
less intelligence, just because of their full humanity.
His nature is for the moment enlarged by sympathy
with theirs : it dilates in response to the call that
is made on it. Such characters are in a sense better
known to us—γνωριμώτεροι—than our everyday
acquaintances. But we do not think of measuring
the intrinsic probability of what they say or do by
the probability of meeting their counterpart in the
actual world.

Few writers have grasped more firmly than
Aristotle the relation in which poetical truth
stands to empirical fact. He devotes a great part
of one chapter (ch. xxv.) to an inquiry into the
alleged untruths and impossibilities of poetry. He
points out the distinction between errors affecting
the essence of the poetic art, and errors of fact
relating to other arts.[1] We may here set aside the
question of minor oversights, inconsistencies, or
technical inaccuracies, holding with him that these
are not in themselves a serious flaw, provided they
leave the total impression unimpaired. But there
is a more fundamental objection which he boldly
meets and repels. The world of poetry, it is said,
presents not facts but fiction : such things have

[1] *Poet.* xxv. 3-4.

never happened, such beings have never lived.
'Untrue' (οὐκ ἀληθῆ), 'impossible' (ἀδύνατα), said
the detractors of poetry in Aristotle's day : 'these
creations are not real, not true to life.' 'Not
real,' replies Aristotle, 'but a higher reality' (ἀλλὰ
βέλτιον), 'what ought to be (ὡς δεῖ), not what is.'[1]
Poetry, he means to say, is not concerned with fact,
but with what transcends fact; it represents things
which are not, and never can be in actual experience;
it gives us the 'ought to be'; the form that answers
to the true idea.[2] The characters of Sophocles,[3]
the ideal forms of Zeuxis,[4] are unreal only in the
sense that they surpass reality. They are not
untrue to the principles of nature or to her ideal
tendencies.

It would seem that in Aristotle's day it was still
generally held that 'real events'—under which were
included the accepted legends of the people [5]—were

---

[1] *Poet.* xxv. 6 and 17. In § 17 a threefold division of τὸ ἀδύνατον is, as I take it, implicit, and a triple line of defence offered :
(i.) ἀνάγειν πρὸς τὴν ποίησιν, an appeal to the general principle of
poetic imitation, or the τέλος of the art, which prefers the πιθανόν
even if it is ἀδύνατον : (ii.) ἀνάγειν πρὸς τὸ β΄λτιον, an appeal to
the principle of ideal truth or the higher reality ; (iii.) ἀνάγειν
πρὸς τὴν δόξαν or πρὸς ἅ φασιν, an appeal to current tradition or
belief. The ἀδύνατα under (ii.) and (iii.) correspond to the οὐκ
ἀληθῆ of §§ 6–7, τὸ βέλτιον of § 17 being equivalent to the ὡς δεῖ,
οἵους δεῖ (? εἶναι) of § 6, and to the βέλτιον of § 7, while τὴν δόξαν
of § 17 answers to οὕτω φασίν of § 6 and ἀλλ᾽ οὖν φασι of § 7.
Vahlen and Susemihl take the passage otherwise.

[2] See pp. 151 ff.   [3] *Poet.* xxv. 6.   [4] *Poet.* xxv. 17.
[5] See p. 403.

alone the proper subjects for tragedy. Names and incidents were alike to be derived from this source. The traditional practice was critically defended by an argument of this kind :—'what has happened is possible: what is possible alone is πιθανόν,--likely, that is, to gain credence.'[1] In ch. ix. Aristotle pleads for an extension of the idea of the 'possible,' from τὰ γενόμενα to οἷα ἂν γένοιτο, from the δυνατά of history to those 'universal' δυνατά where the law of causation appears with more unbroken efficacy and power. He would not restrict the poet's freedom of choice. At the same time he guards himself against being supposed utterly to condemn historical or real subjects. Indeed from many passages we may infer that he regarded the consecrated legends of the past as the richest storehouse of poetic material, though few only of the traditional myths satisfied, in his opinion, the full tragic requirements. The rule of 'what may happen' does not, he observes, exclude 'what has happened.' Some real events have that internal probability or necessity which fits them for poetic treatment.[2] It is interesting to notice how guarded is his language—'some real events,' as if by a rare

---

[1] *Poet.* ix. 6.

[2] *Poet.* ix. 9, τῶν γὰρ γενομένων ἔνια οὐδὲν κωλύει τοιαῦτα εἶναι οἷα ἂν εἰκὸς γενέσθαι καὶ δυνατὰ γενέσθαι ═ τοιαῦτα οἷα ἂν κατὰ τὸ εἰκὸς γένοιτο καὶ δυνατά (ἐστι) γενέσθαι. This virtually resolves itself into the formula of ix. 1, οἷα ἂν γένοιτο καὶ τὰ δυνατὰ κατὰ τὸ εἰκὸς ἢ τὸ ἀναγκαῖον.

and happy chance.[1]   And, no doubt, in general the
poet has to extract the ore from a rude mass of
legendary or historical fact : to free it from the
accidental, the trivial, the irrelevant : to purify it,
in a word, from the dross which always mingles
with empirical reality.   Even those events which
possess an inherent poetical quality, which are, in
some sense, poetry ready-made for the dramatist,
are poetical only in certain detached parts and
incidents, not penetrated with poetry throughout.
They will need the idealisation of art before they
can be combined into the unified structure of the
drama.   The hints given in subsequent chapters
for treating the traditional legends show how all-
important in Aristotle's eyes is the shaping activity
of the artist, even when he is dealing with the
most favourable material.   Greek tragedies, though
' founded on fact '—as the phrase goes—transmute
that fact into imaginative truth.

The truth, then, of poetry is essentially different
from the truth of fact.   Things that are outside
and beyond the range of our experience, that never
have happened and never will happen, may be
more true, poetically speaking,—more profoundly
true than those daily occurrences which we can
with confidence predict.   These so-called ἀδύνατα

---

[1] Cf. the similar rule laid down in Plato for τὸ πιθανόν in
oratory : *Phaedr.* 272 E, οὐδὲ γὰρ αὖ τὰ πραχθέντα δεῖν λέγειν
ἐνίοτε, ἐὰν μὴ εἰκότως ᾖ πεπραγμένα.

are the very δυνατά of art, the stuff and substance
of which poetry is made. 'What has never
anywhere come to pass, that alone never grows
old.'[1]

There is another class of 'impossibilities' in
poetry, which Aristotle defends on a somewhat
different ground. It is the privilege, nay, the
duty, of the poet ψευδῆ λέγειν ὡς δεῖ, 'to tell lies
skilfully': he must learn the true art of fiction.[2]
The fiction here intended is, as the context shows,
not simply that fiction which is blended with
fact in every poetic narrative of real events.[3]
The reference here is rather to those tales of a
strange and marvellous character,[4] which are
admitted into epic more freely than into dramatic

---

[1] Alles wiederholt sich nur im Leben,
Ewig jung ist nur die Phantasie ;
Was sich nie und nirgends hat begeben,
Das allein veraltet nie.—SCHILLER.

[2] *Poet.* xxiv. 9. Homer, Hesiod, and the poets generally had
been accused by Plato of 'telling lies' (ψεύδεσθαι) and not even
doing so 'properly': *Rep.* ii. 377 E, ἄλλως τε καὶ ἐάν τις μὴ
καλῶς ψεύδηται. And τὸ μέγιστον καὶ περὶ τῶν μεγίστων
ψεῦδος ὁ εἰπὼν οὐ καλῶς ἐψεύσατο. Aristotle transfers the καλῶς
from the region of morality into that of art, and discovers a merit
in the point of censure. Cf. Dion Chrys. *Or.* xi. 315 R : ἀνδρειότατος
ἀνθρώπων ἦν πρὸς τὸ ψεῦδος "Ομηρος καὶ οὐδὲν ἧττον ἐθάρρει καὶ
ἐσεμνύνετο ἐπὶ τῷ ψεύδεσθαι ἢ τῷ τἀληθῆ λέγειν. Homer was in
fact 'splendide mendax.'

[3] Cf. Hor. *A. P.* 151 (of Homer),

atque ita mentitur, sic veris falsa remiscet.

[4] See Twining ii. 346 sqq.

poetry. In this art of feigning, Homer, we are told, is the supreme master ; and the secret of the art lies in a kind of παραλογισμός or fallacy. The explanation added, though given in a somewhat bald and abstract manner, renders the nature of the fallacy perfectly plain.[1] At the outset the poet must be allowed to make certain primary assumptions and create his own environment. Starting from these poetic data—the pre-suppositions of the imagination—he may go whither he will, and carry us with him, so long as he does not dash us against the prosaic ground of fact. He

---

[1] The fallacy, namely, of inferring that because a given thing is the necessary consequent of a given antecedent, the consequent necessarily implies the antecedent. Antecedent and consequent are wrongly assumed to be reciprocally convertible ; cf. de Soph. Elench. 167 b 1 sqq., an example being, 'if it rains, the ground is wet : the ground is wet : therefore it rains.' Similarly in Rhetoric the skilled speaker adopts a certain appropriate tone and manner which leads the audience to infer that the facts he states are true : Rhet. iii. 7. 1408 a 20, πιθανοῖ δὲ τὸ πρᾶγμα καὶ ἡ οἰκεία λέξις· παραλογίζεται γὰρ ἡ ψυχὴ ὡς ἀληθῶς λέγοντος, ὅτι ἐν τοῖς τοιούτοις οὕτως ἔχουσιν, ὥστ' οἴονται, εἰ καὶ μὴ οὕτως ἔχει, ὡς ὁ λέγων, τὰ πράγματα οὕτως ἔχειν. Cf. Rhet. iii. 12. 1414 a 1 sqq., iii. 16. 1416 a 36 sqq. Twining (ii. 350) compares the observation of Hobbes that 'probable fiction is similar to reasoning rightly from a false principle.'

The allusion to the Νίπτρα in Poet. xxiv. 10 is, doubtless, as Vahlen (Beitr. p. 296) shows, to Odyssey xix. 164–260. The disguised Odysseus has told Penelope that he has entertained Odysseus in Crete. The detailed description he gives of the appearance, dress, etc., of the hero is recognised by Penelope to be true. She falsely infers that, as the host would have known the appearance of the guest, the stranger who knew it had actually been the host.

feigns certain imaginary persons, strange situations, incredible adventures. By vividness of narrative and minuteness of detail, and, above all, by the natural sequence of incident and motive, things are made to happen exactly as they would have happened had the fundamental fiction been fact. The effects are so plausible, so life-like, that we yield ourselves instinctively to the illusion, and infer the existence of the supposed cause. For the time being we do not pause to dispute the πρῶτον ψεῦδος or original falsehood on which the whole fabric is reared.

Such is the essence of τὸ πιθανόν, which in various forms runs through the teaching of the *Poetics*. By artistic treatment things incredible in real life wear an air of probability. The impossible not only becomes possible, but natural and even inevitable. In the phraseology of the *Poetics*, the ἄλογα, things impossible or improbable to the reason, are so disguised that they become εὔλογα : the ἀδύνατα, things impossible in fact, become πιθανά, and hence δυνατὰ κατὰ τὸ εἰκὸς ἢ τὸ ἀναγκαῖον. Even the laws of the physical world and the material conditions of existence may conceivably be neglected, if only the inner consistency of the poetry is not sacrificed. The magic ship of the Phaeacians and the landing of Odysseus on the shores of Ithaca, which 'might have been intolerable if treated by an inferior poet,' are so skilfully managed by Homer that we forget their inherent impossibility.[1] 'Probable impossibilities are,' as Aristotle declares with twice repeated emphasis, 'to be preferred to improbable possibilities.'[2]

The ἄλογα or 'irrational elements' which the logical understanding rejects, are greater stumbling-blocks to the poetic sense than mere material impossibilities. For the impossible may cease to be thought of as such; it may become logically inevitable. But the irrational is always liable to provoke the logical faculty into a critical or hostile attitude. It seems to contradict the very law of causality to which the higher poetry is subject. It needs, therefore, a special justification, if it is to be admitted at all; and this justification Aristotle discovers in the heightened wonder and admiration, which he regards as proper, in a peculiar degree, to epic poetry.[3] The instance twice cited[4] of the

---

[1] *Poet.* xxiv. 10, *Odyss.* xiii. 93 sqq.

[2] *Poet.* xxiv. 10, προαιρεῖσθαί τε δεῖ ἀδύνατα εἰκότα μᾶλλον ἢ δυνατὰ ἀπίθανα. xxv. 17, αἱρετώτερον πιθανὸν ἀδύνατον ἢ ἀπίθανον καὶ δυνατόν.

[3] *Poet.* xxiv. 8, μᾶλλον δ' ἐνδέχεται ἐν τῇ ἐποποιίᾳ τὸ ἄλογον, δι' ὃ συμβαίνει μάλιστα τὸ θαυμαστόν.

[4] *Poet.* xxiv. 8 and xxv. 5. In the former passage the incident is pronounced to be unfit for the drama; in the latter, it is in itself a ἁμάρτημα but justified by the effect, and justified only as an epic incident. Further, in ch. xxiv. it is spoken of as an ἄλογον, in ch. xxv.—less accurately—as an ἀδύνατον. Cf. Dion Chrys. *Or.* xi. 349 R (in reference to this scene), μάλιστα γοῦν προσέοικε τοῖς ἀτόποις ἐνυπνίοις τὰ περὶ τὴν μάχην ἐκείνην. All ἄλογα are not ἀδύνατα, though all ἀδύνατα, if realised to be such, are ἄλογα. But, as above explained, the art of the poet can make the ἀδύνατα cease to be ἄλογα and become πιθανά.

pursuit of Hector in the *Iliad* illustrates the
general conditions under which he would allow
this licence. The scene here alluded to is that in
which Achilles chases Hector round the walls of
Troy : the Greek army stands motionless, Achilles
signing to them to keep still.[1] The incident, if
represented on the stage, would appear highly
improbable, and even ludicrous. The poetic
illusion would be destroyed by the scene being
placed directly before the eyes; whereas in epic
narrative, the effect produced is powerfully
imaginative. Still, even as an epic incident,
Aristotle appears—strangely enough—to think
that it is open to some censure, and justified only
by two considerations. First, the total effect is
impressive : we experience a heightened wonder, a
pleasurable astonishment, which effaces the sense
of incongruity and satisfies the aesthetic end.[2] In
the next place, a like effect could not have been
produced by other means.[3]

There is another form of 'the impossible,' and
even of 'the irrational,' which, according to Aris-

---

[1] *Iliad* xxii. 205, λαοῖσιν δ' ἀνένευε καρήατι δῖος 'Αχιλλεύς

[2] *Poet.* xxv. 5, ἡμάρτηται· ἀλλ' ὀρθῶς ἔχει, εἰ τυγχάνει τοῦ
τέλους τοῦ αὑτῆς (τὸ γὰρ τέλος εἴρηται), εἰ οὕτως ἐκπληκτικώτερον
ἢ αὐτὸ ἢ ἄλλο ποιεῖ μέρος.

[3] l.c. εἰ μέντοι τὸ τέλος ἢ μᾶλλον ἢ <μὴ> ἧττον ἐνεδέχετο
ὑπάρχειν καὶ κατὰ τὴν περὶ τούτων τέχνην, [ἡμαρτῆσθαι] οὐκ
ὀρθῶς. Cf. xxv. 19, ὀρθὴ ἐπιτίμησις ἀλογία . . . ὅταν μὴ
ἀνάγκης οὔσης μηθὲν χρήσηται τῷ ἀλόγῳ.

totle, may be admitted into poetry. Some things
there are which cannot be defended either as the
expression of a higher reality, or as constituting a
whole so coherent and connected that we acquiesce
in them without effort. They refuse to fit into
our scheme of the universe, or to blend with the
other elements of our thought. Still, it may be,
they are part of the traditional belief, and are
enshrined in popular legend or superstition. If
not true, they are believed to be true. Though
they cannot be explained rationally, it is generally
felt that there is ' something in them.' Current
beliefs like these cannot be wholly ignored or
rudely rejected by the poet. There are stories
of the gods, of which it is enough to say that,
whether true or false, above or below reality, ' yet
so runs the tale.'[1] The principle here laid down
will apply to the introduction of the marvellous
and supernatural under many forms in poetry.
But a distinction ought perhaps to be drawn.
Take a case where the imagination of a people,
such as the Greeks, has been long at work upon

---

[1] *Poet.* xxv. 7, ἀλλ' οὖν φασι. Cf. Dryden, *The Author's Apology
for Heroic Poetry and Poetic Licence* : ' Poets may be allowed the
like liberty for describing things which really exist not, if they are
founded on popular belief. Of this nature are fairies, pigmies, and
the extraordinary effects of magic ; for 't is still an imitation, tho'
of other men's fancies ; and thus are Shakespeare's *Tempest,* his
Midsummer Night's Dream, and Ben Jonson's *Masque of Witches* to
be defended.'

its own mythology, and has embodied in clear poetic form certain underlying sentiments and convictions of the race. Facts in themselves marvellous or supernatural have taken coherent shape, and been inwrought into the substance of the national belief. The results so obtained may be at variance with empirical fact, yet they are none the less proper material for the poet. The legends may be among the ἀδύνατα of experience ; they are not among the ἄλογα of poetry. It may even be within the power of the poet to efface the lines between the natural and the supernatural, and to incorporate both worlds in a single order of things, at once rational and imaginative.

Meanwhile, within the legends or traditions so clarified, there remains, we will suppose, some unassimilated material, unharmonised elements which offend the reason. A mythology which has sprung out of childlike intuitions into the truth of things, combined with a childlike ignorance of laws and facts, cannot but retain vestiges of the irrational. It is to these cruder beliefs, which come to the surface even in Hellenic poetry, that the defence to which we now allude will more especially apply :—'untrue indeed, nay irrational, but *so men say.*'

Aristotle holds that the irrational — whether under the guise of the supernatural, or under the

N

form of motiveless human activity—is less admissible in dramatic than in epic poetry.[1]   He does not assign the reason, but it is obvious. The drama is a typical representation of human action : its mainspring is motive : what is motiveless or uncaused is alien to it. Following strict rules of art Aristotle would exclude the irrational altogether: failing that, he would admit it only under protest and subject to rigid limitations. It may form part of the supposed antecedents of the plot ; it has no place within the dramatic action itself.[2] Aristotle summarily rejects the plea that if it is kept out the plot will be destroyed. 'Such a plot,' he says, 'should not in the first instance be constructed.'[3]   But he proceeds to qualify this harsh sentence by a characteristic concession to human infirmity. He will view the fault leniently, if the incidents in question are made in any degree to look plausible.[4]

From what has been said it will be evident that a material impossibility admits of artistic treatment ; hardly so, a moral improbability.   When

---

[1] *Poet.* xxiv. 8.

[2] *Poet.* xv. 7, ἄλογον δὲ μηδὲν εἶναι ἐν τοῖς πράγμασιν, εἰ δὲ μή, ἔξω τῆς τραγῳδίας.   xxiv. 10, μάλιστα μὲν μηδὲν ἔχειν ἄλογον, εἰ δὲ μή, ἔξω τοῦ μυθεύματος.

[3] *Poet.* xxiv. 10, ἐξ ἀρχῆς γὰρ οὐ δεῖ συνίστασθαι τοιούτους (sc. μύθους).

[4] l.c. ἂν δὲ θῇ καὶ φαίνηται εὐλογωτέρως, ἐνδέχεσθαι καὶ ἄτοπον <ὄν>.

once we are placed at the poet's angle of vision and see with his eyes, the material improbability presents no insuperable difficulty. The chain of cause and effect remains unbroken. Everything follows in due sequence from the acceptance of the primary fiction. But a moral improbability is an ἄλογον of a more stubborn kind. No initial act of imaginative surrender can reconcile us to a course of action that is either motiveless or based on unintelligible principles. We can sooner acquiesce in the altered facts of physical nature than in the violation of the laws which lie at the root of conduct. The instances of the irrational which Aristotle condemns are not indeed confined to moral improbabilities. But he appears to have had these mainly in his mind,—improbabilities that ultimately depend on character, and do violence either to the permanent facts of human nature, or to the feelings and motives proper to a particular situation. Such are the ignorance of Oedipus as to the manner of Laius' death : the speechless journey of Telephus from Tegea to Mysia :[1] the scene already mentioned of the pursuit of Hector. A material improbability may itself, again, often be resolved into one of the moral kind. Where the events either in themselves or in their sequence appear irrational, they are frequently the outcome of character inwardly illogical. Though Aristotle does not distinguish

[1] *Poet.* xxiv. 10.

between moral and material improbability or impossibility, it falls in with his teaching to recognise
in the first a grave artistic defect, which is not
necessarily inherent in the second. In the unbroken chain of cause and effect which he postulates
for the drama, each of the links is formed by the
contact of human will with outward surroundings.
The necessity which pervades his theory of tragedy
is a logical and moral necessity, binding together
the successive moments of a life, the parts of an
action, into a significant unity.

Since it is the office of the poet to get at the
central meaning of facts, to transform them into
truths by supplying vital connexions and causal
links, to set the seal of reason upon the outward
semblances of art, it follows that the world of
poetry rebels against the rule of chance. Now,
accident (τὸ συμβεβηκός) or chance in Aristotle,
exhibiting itself under two forms not always strictly
distinguished,[1] owes its existence to the uncertainty
and variability of matter.[2]   It is the negation

[1] Namely as τύχη, 'fortune,' and τὸ αὐτόματον, 'spontaneity.'
Cf. *Poet.* ix. 12, ἀπὸ τοῦ αὐτομάτου καὶ τῆς τύχης. The regular
distinction is that given in *Met.* ix. 8. 1065 a 25 sqq., and *Met.* xi. 3.
1070 a 6 sqq. But in *Phys.* ii. 6. 197 a 36, τὸ μὲν γὰρ ἀπὸ τύχης
πᾶν ἀπὸ ταὐτομάτου, τοῦτο δ' οὐ πᾶν ἀπὸ τύχης.   197 b 20, ἀπὸ
τύχης δέ, τούτων ὅσα ἀπὸ ταὐτομάτου γίνεται τῶν προαιρετῶν
τοῖς ἔχουσι προαίρεσιν. See Zeller, *Hist. Gr. Phil.* ii. 2. 333–6,
Stewart, *Eth. Nic.* i. 259.

[2] *Met.* v. 2. 1027 a 13, ὥστε ἡ ὕλη ἔσται αἰτία, ἡ ἐνδεχομένη
παρὰ τὸ ὡς ἐπὶ τὸ πολὺ ἄλλως, τοῦ συμβεβηκότος.

(στέρησις) of Art and Intelligence, and of Nature as an organising force.[1] Its essence is disorder (ἀταξία),[2] absence of design (τὸ ἕνεκά του),[3] want of regularity (τὸ ὡς ἐπὶ τὸ πολύ). It even borders on the non-existent.[4] Its sphere is that wide domain of human life which baffles foresight,[5] defies reason, abounds in surprises: and also those regions of Nature where we meet with abortive efforts, mistakes, strange and monstrous growths, which are 'the failures of the principle of design.'[6]

It is true that the action of Chance does not invariably defeat the purposes of Nature or Art. It may so happen that the first step in a natural

---

[1] Viewed as τύχη it is the στέρησις of τέχνη and νοῦς : viewed as τὸ αὐτόματον it is the στέρησις of φύσις.

[2] *Met.* ix. 8. 1065 a 25, λέγω δὲ τὸ κατὰ συμβεβηκός · τοῦ τοιούτου δ' ἄτακτα καὶ ἄπειρα τὰ αἴτια. *De Part. Anim.* i. 1. 641 b 22, τὸν οὐρανὸν . . . ἐν ᾧ ἀπὸ τύχης καὶ ἀταξίας οὐδ' ὁτιοῦν φαίνεται.

[3] *Anal. Post.* ii. 11. 95 a 8, ἀπὸ τύχης δ' οὐδὲν ἕνεκά του γίνεται.

[4] *Met.* v. 2. 1026 b 21, φαίνεται γὰρ τὸ συμβεβηκὸς ἐγγύς τι τοῦ μὴ ὄντος.

[5] *Met.* ix. 8. 1065 a 33 (of τύχη), διὸ ἄδηλος ἀνθρωπίνῳ λογισμῷ.

[6] *Phys.* ii. 8. 199 b 3 (just as in art there are failures in the effort to attain the end), ὁμοίως ἂν ἔχοι καὶ ἐν τοῖς φυσικοῖς, καὶ τὰ τέρατα ἁμαρτήματα ἐκείνου τοῦ ἕνεκά του. On τέρατα in Nature cf. *de Gen. Anim.* iv. 4. 770 b 9, ἔστι γὰρ τὸ τέρας τῶν παρὰ φύσιν τι, παρὰ φύσιν δ' οὐ πᾶσαν ἀλλὰ τὴν ὡς ἐπὶ τὸ πολύ. The *mere* τερατῶδες in tragedy is emphatically condemned *Poet.* xiv. 2, οἱ δὲ μὴ τὸ φοβερὸν διὰ τῆς ὄψεως ἀλλὰ τὸ τερατῶδες μόνον παρασκευάζοντες οὐδὲν τραγῳδίᾳ κοινωνοῦσιν.

or an artistic process is the result of Chance.¹ To
Chance were due some of the early experiments in
the history of poetry, which were destined to lead
to ultimate success.² But in itself Chance is the
very antithesis of Art. It is an irrational cause;
it suggests anarchy and misrule; it has no proper
place in poetry, which aims at the attainment of
an ideal unity. The law of ' the probable '—as well
as that of ' the necessary '—excludes chance;³ and
yet in a popular sense nothing is more 'probable'
than the occurrence of what is called accident.
We gather from the *Poetics* that the introduction
of anomalous and abnormal incidents in poetry was
sometimes defended by the saying of Agathon:
' It is probable that many things should happen
contrary to probability.'⁴ A similar saying appears
to have been current by way of mitigating the
appearance of monstrosities in nature : ' The un-
natural is occasionally, and in a fashion, natural.'⁵

¹ *Eth. Nic.* vi. 4. 1140 a 19, καθάπερ καὶ ᾿Αγάθων φησί·
τέχνη τύχην ἔστερξε καὶ τύχη τέχνην.
² *Poet.* xiv. 9, ζητοῦντες γὰρ οὐκ ἀπὸ τέχνης ἀλλ᾽ ἀπὸ τύχης
εὗρον τὸ τοιοῦτον παρασκευάζειν ἐν τοῖς μύθοις.
³ *De Gen. et Corr.* ii. 6. 333 b 6, τὰ δὲ παρὰ τὸ ἀεὶ καὶ ὡς
ἐπὶ τὸ πολὺ ἀπὸ ταὐτομάτου καὶ ἀπὸ τύχης. Cf. *de Caelo* i. 12.
282 a 33.
⁴ *Poet.* xviii. 6, ἔστιν δὲ τοῦτο εἰκὸς ὥσπερ ᾿Αγάθων λέγει,
εἰκὸς γὰρ γίνεσθαι πολλὰ καὶ παρὰ τὸ εἰκός. xxv. 17, οὕτω
τε καὶ ὅτι ποτὲ οὐκ ἀλογόν ἐστιν· εἰκὸς γὰρ καὶ παρὰ τὸ εἰκὸς
γίνεσθαι.
⁵ *De Gen. Anim.* iv. 4. 770 b 15, ἧττον εἶναι δοκεῖ τέρας διὰ
τὸ καὶ τὸ παρὰ φύσιν εἶναι τρόπον τινὰ κατὰ φύσιν.

But as a man of science Aristotle does not regard
the deviation from nature as in a proper sense
natural : nor, as a writer on art, does he lend his
authority to the twice quoted phrase of Agathon.
That phrase, indeed, violates the spirit, if not the
letter, of all that he has written on dramatic probability. ' Miss Edgeworth,' says Newman,[1] ' sometimes apologises for certain incidents in her tales,
by stating that they took place " by one of those
strange chances which occur in life, but seem incredible when found in writing." Such an excuse
evinces a misconception of the principle of fiction,
which being the perfection of the actual, prohibits
the introduction of any such anomalies of experience.' The 'strange chances' here spoken of,
the 'anomalies of experience,' are in fact the
'improbable possibilities'[2] which Aristotle disallows. For chance with its inherent unreason is
as far as possible banished by him from the domain
of poetry,—except indeed where the skill of the
poet can impart to it an appearance of design.[3]
Nor does this exclusion hold good only in the
more serious forms of poetry. It has been held
by some modern writers, that comedy differs from
tragedy in representing a world of chance, where
law is suspended and the will of the individual

[1] *Essays, Critical and Historical.*

[2] *Poet.* xxiv. 10, δυνατὰ ἀπίθανα.

[3] *Poet.* ix. 12, ἐπεὶ καὶ τῶν ἀπὸ τυχης ταῦτα θαυμασιώτατα
δοκεῖ ὅσα ὥσπερ ἐπίτηδες φαίνεται γεγονέναι.

reigns supreme. But this is not in accordance with the *Poetics*. The incidents of comedy—at least of such comedy as Aristotle approves—are 'framed on lines of probability.'[1] The connexion of incidents is, no doubt, looser than in tragedy ; the more rigorous rule of 'probability *or* necessity' is not prescribed : and the variation of phrase appears to be not without design. Yet the plot even of comedy is far removed from the play of accident.

To sum up in a word the results of this discussion. The whole tenor and purpose of the *Poetics* makes it abundantly clear that poetry is not a mere reproduction of empirical fact, a picture of life with all its trivialities and accidents. The world of the possible which poetry creates is more intelligible than the world of experience. The poet presents permanent and eternal facts, free from the elements of unreason which disturb our comprehension of real events and of human conduct. In fashioning his material he may transcend nature, but he may not contradict her ; he must not be disobedient to her habits and principles. He may recreate the actual, but he must avoid the lawless, the fantastic, the impossible. Poetic truth passes the bounds of reality, but it does not wantonly violate the laws which make the real world rational.

[1] *Poet.* ix. 5, συστήσαντες γὰρ τὸν μῦθον 'διὰ τῶν εἰκότων κ.τ.λ.

Thus poetry in virtue of its higher subject-matter and of the closer and more organic union of its parts acquires an ideal unity that history never possesses ; for the prose of life is never wholly eliminated from a record of actual facts. The Baconian and the Aristotelian view of poetry, instead of standing in sharp contrast as is sometimes said, will be seen to approximate closely to one another. The well-known words of Bacon run thus :—

'Therefore, because the acts or events of true history have not that magnitude which satisfieth the mind of man, Poesy feigneth acts and events greater and more heroical ; . . . because true history representeth actions and events more ordinary and less interchanged, therefore Poesy endueth them with more rareness : so as it appeareth that Poesy serveth and conferreth to magnanimity, morality, and delectation. And, therefore, it was ever thought to have some participation of divineness, because it doth raise and erect the mind, by submitting the shows of things to the desires of the mind, whereas Reason doth buckle and bow the mind unto the nature of things.'[1]

[1] Bacon, de Aug. Scient. ii. 13. The still more vigorous Latin deserves to be quoted : 'Cum res gestae et eventus, qui verae historiae subiciuntur, non sint eius amplitudinis in qua anima humana sibi satisfaciat, praesto est poesis, quae facta magis heroica confingat. . . Cum historia vera, obvia rerum satietate et simili-tudine, animae humanae fastidio sit, reficit eam poesis, inexpectata et varia et vicissitudinum plena canens. Quare et merito etiam

It may be noticed that the opposition between the poet and the historian in the *Poetics* is incidentally introduced to illustrate the sense in which a tragedy is one and a whole.[1] These two notions as understood by Aristotle are not identical. A unity is composed of a plurality of parts which cohere together and fall under a common idea, but are not necessarily combined in a definite order. The notion of a whole implies something more. The parts which constitute it must be inwardly connected, arranged in a certain order, structurally related, and combined into a system. A whole is not a mere mass or sum of external parts which may be transposed at will, any one of which may be omitted without perceptibly affecting the rest.[2] It is a unity which is unfolded and expanded according to the law of its own nature, an organism which develops from within. By the rule, again,

divinitatis cuiuspiam particeps videri possit ; quia animum erigit et in sublime rapit ; rerum simulacra ad animi desideria accommodando, non animum rebus (quod ratio facit et historia) submittendo.' In the sentence above omitted Poetry is said to correct history, setting forth 'exitus et fortunas secundum merita et ex lege Nemeseos.' This is not Aristotelian.

[1] *Poet.* ix. 1, φανερὸν δὲ ἐκ τῶν εἰρημένων κ.τ.λ.

[2] *Met.* iv. 26. 1024 a 1, ὅσων μὲν μὴ ποιεῖ ἡ θέσις διαφοραν, πᾶν λέγεται, ὅσων δὲ ποιεῖ, ὅλον. Ibid. 1023 b 26, ὅλον λέγεται οὗ τε μηδὲν ἄπεστι μέρος ἐξ ὧν λέγεται ὅλον φύσει κ.τ.λ. Cf. *Poet.* viii. 4, ὃ γὰρ προσὸν ἢ μὴ προσὸν μηδὲν ποιεῖ ἐπίδηλον, οὐδὲν μόριον τοῦ ὅλου ἐστίν. Plato, *Parm.* 137 c, οὐχὶ οὗ ἂν μέρος μηδὲν ἀπῇ, ὅλον ἂν εἴη; Aristotle is here largely indebted to Plato ; see also infra, pp. 275, 280.

of beauty, which is a first requirement of art, a poetic creation must exhibit at once unity and plurality. If it is too small the whole is perceived but not the parts; if too large the parts are perceived but not the whole.[1] The idea of an organism evidently underlies all Aristotle's rules about unity;[2] it is tacitly assumed as a first principle of art, and in one passage is expressly mentioned as that from which the rule of epic unity is deduced. 'The plot must, as in a tragedy, be dramatically constructed; it must have for its subject a single action, whole and complete, with a beginning, a middle, and an end. *It will thus resemble a*

---

[1] *Poet.* vii. 4–5 : cf. the rules laid down for the size of a city in *Pol.* iv. (vii.) 4. 1326 a 34 sqq.

[2] Cf. Stewart, *Eth. Nic.* i. 194 : 'Living organisms and works of art are σχήματα, definite after their kinds, which Nature and Man respectively form by qualifying matter. The quantity of matter used in any case is determined by the form subserved ; the size of a particular organ, or part, is determined by its form, which again is determined by the form (limiting the size) of the whole organism or work. Thus animals and plants grow to sizes determined by their separate structures, habitats, and conditions of life, and each separate organ observes the proportion of the whole to which it belongs. The painter or sculptor considers the symmetry of the whole composition in every detail of his work. The conductor of a choir is forced to exclude a voice which surpasses all the others conspicuously in beauty. *Pol.* iii. 8. 1284 b 8, οὔτε γὰρ γραφεὺς ἐάσειεν ἂν τὸν ὑπερβάλλοντα πόδα τῆς συμμετρίας ἔχειν τὸ ζῷον, οὐδ' εἰ διαφέροι τὸ κάλλος· οὔτε ναυπηγὸς πρύμναν ἢ τῶν ἄλλων τι μορίων τῶν τῆς νεώς· οὐδὲ δὴ χοροδιδάσκαλος τὸν μεῖζον καὶ κάλλιον τοῦ παντὸς χοροῦ φθεγγόμενον ἐάσει συγχορεύειν. In all cases form dominates matter, quality quantity.'

single and coherent organism, and produce the
pleasure proper to it.'[1]

[1] *Poet.* xxiii. 1, δεῖ τοὺς μύθους καθάπερ ἐν ταῖς τραγῳδίαις
συνιστάναι δραματικοὺς καὶ περὶ μίαν πρᾶξιν ὅλην καὶ τελείαν,
ἔχουσαν ἀρχὴν καὶ μέσα καὶ τέλος, ἵν᾽ ὥσπερ ζῷον ἓν ὅλον ποιῇ
τὴν οἰκείαν ἡδονήν. I now revert to my earlier opinion and
take ζῷον in the sense of 'a living organism,' not of 'a picture,'
both here (in spite of the strangeness, as it seems to us, in speaking
of an animal as giving an οἰκεία ἡδονή), and also in vii. 4–5.
The arguments in favour of ζῷον being used in its ordinary sense
in ch. vii. are, as Dr. Sandys has suggested to me, much
strengthened by the parallel passage *Pol.* iv. (vii.) 4. 1326 a 34–
1326 b 24. According to the other interpretation of vii. 4–5,
one of the conditions of τὸ καλόν, namely a certain μέγεθος, is
illustrated by an analogy between painting and poetry. This
view is advocated with much force by Mr. R. P. Hardie in *Mind*,
vol. iv. No. 15.   In the course of his argument he observes :
'The meaning of πρᾶγμα ὃ συνέστηκεν ἐκ τινῶν and τὰ σώματα
seems plain from other passages in Aristotle, for instance *de
Anima* 412 a 11, where he identifies οὐσία ὡς συνθέτη (sub-
stantia composita) with σώματα, and divides these into φυσικὰ
σώματα and the rest, the former class again being divided according as they are ἔμψυχα or ἄψυχα. Thus animated bodies
would seem to be "composite" in the fullest sense of the word.
" ζῷον " then in the present passage in the *Poetics* must be
equivalent to "picture," in which sense, however, it would naturally suggest to a Greek the picture of a ζῷον in the sense of
σῶμα ἔμψυχον.'

For other examples of ζῷον in a similar sense cf. Plat. *Laws*,
ii. 669 A, πάντες μέντ᾽ ἂν . . . τὰ καλὰ τῶν ζῴων ἐγιγνώσκομεν.
vi. 769 A, and c, ἐάν τι σφάλληται τὸ ζῷον ὑπὸ χρόνου. *Crat.*
425 A, 429 A, οὐκοῦν οἱ μὲν ἀμείνους τὰ αὐτῶν ἔργα καλλίω
παρέχονται, τὰ ζῷα, οἱ δὲ φαυλότερα; 430 D, ἐπ᾽ ἀμφοτέροις
τοῖς μιμήμασι, τοῖς τε ζῴοις καὶ τοῖς ὀνόμασιν. *Rep.* vii. 515 A,
ἀνδριάντας καὶ ἄλλα ζῷα λίθινά τε καὶ ξύλινα καὶ παντοῖα
εἰργασμένα (cf. *de Gen. Anim.* ii. 4. 740 a 15 quoted p. 190).   In
de Mundo 6. 398 b 18 ζῷον is used of a puppet worked by οἱ
νευροσπάσται.

Plato in the *Phaedrus* had insisted that every artistic composition, whether in prose or verse, should have an organic unity. ' You will allow that every discourse ought to be constructed like a living organism, having its own body and head and feet; it must have middle and extremities, drawn in a manner agreeable to one another and to the whole.' [1] Aristotle took up the hint; the passage above quoted from the *Poetics* is a remarkable echo of the words of the *Phaedrus* ; and indeed the idea may be said to be at the basis of his whole poetic criticism.

A work then of poetic art, as he conceives it, while it manifests the universal is yet a concrete and individual reality, a coherent whole, animated by a living principle—or by something which is at least the counterpart of life—and framed according to the laws of organic beauty. The artistic product is not indeed in a literal sense alive ; for life or soul is in Aristotle the result of the proper form being impressed upon the proper matter.[2] Now, in art

---

[1] *Phaedr.* 264 c, ἀλλὰ τόδε γε οἶμαί σε φάναι ἄν, δεῖν πάντα λόγον ὥσπερ ζῷον συνεστάναι σῶμά τι ἔχοντα αὐτὸν αὑτοῦ, ὥστε μήτε ἀκέφαλον εἶναι μήτε ἄπουν, ἀλλὰ μέσα τε ἔχειν καὶ ἄκρα, πρέποντ' ἀλλήλοις καὶ τῷ ὅλῳ γεγραμμένα. Cf. *Polit.* 277 c, where the discussion is compared to the sketch of a ζῷον in a painting : ἀλλ' ἀτεχνῶς ὁ λόγος ἡμῖν ὥσπερ ζῷον τὴν ἔξωθεν μὲν περιγραφὴν ἔοικεν ἱκανῶς ἔχειν, τὴν δὲ οἷον τοῖς φαρμάκοις καὶ τῇ συγκράσει τῶν χρωμάτων ἐνάργειαν οὐκ ἀπειληφέναι πω.

[2] Cf. *de Part. Anim.* i. 1. 640 b 32 sqq. A dead body has the same outward configuration as a living one, yet it is not a man ; so

the matter depends on the choice of the artist;
it has no necessary relation to the form which is
impressed on it. That form it passively receives,
but it is not thereby endowed with any active principle of life or movement. The form or essence
lives truly only in the mind of the artist who conceived the work, and it is in thought alone that it
is transferred to the dead matter with which it has
no natural affinity. The artist, or the spectator
who has entered into the artist's thought, by a
mental act lends life to the artistic creation; he
speaks, he thinks of it as a thing of life; but it has
no inherent principle of movement; it is in truth
not alive but merely the semblance of a living
reality.[1]

Returning now to the discussion about poetry
and history we shall better understand Aristotle's
general conclusion, which is contained in the words
so well known and so often misunderstood : ' Poetry
is a more philosophical and a higher thing than

too a hand of brass or of wood is a hand only in name. In *de
Gen. Anim.* ii. 4. 740 a 15 works of art are spoken of as ξυλίνων
ἢ λιθίνων ζῴων, and are contrasted with the truly living
organism.

[1] Cf. Stewart, *Eth. Nic.* ii. 42 : 'τέχνη realises its good in an
external ἔργον, and the εἶδος which it imposes on ὕλη is only a
surface form—very different from the forms penetrating to the very
heart of the ὕλη, which φύσις and ἀρετή produce (cf. *Eth. Nic.* ii.
6. 9, ἡ δ' ἀρετὴ πάσης τέχνης ἀκριβεστέρα καὶ ἀμείνων ἐστὶν
ὥσπερ καὶ ἡ φύσις : *Met.* 30. 1070 a 7, ἡ μὲν οὖν τέχνη ἀρχὴ ἐν
ἄλλῳ, ἡ δὲ φύσις ἀρχὴ ἐν αὐτῷ).'

history,'[1]—where σπουδαιότερον denotes 'higher in
the scale';[2]—not 'more serious,' for the words
apply even to comedy, nor, again, 'more moral,'
which is quite alien to the context;—and the
reason of the higher worth of poetry is that it
approaches nearer to the universal, which itself
derives its value from being a 'manifestation of
the cause'[3] or first principle of things. Poetry in
striving to give universal form to its own creations
reveals a higher truth than history, and on that
account is nearer to philosophy. But though it
has a philosophic character it is not philosophy:
'It *tends* to express the universal.' The μᾶλλον is
here a limiting and saving expression; it marks
the endeavour and direction of poetry, which
cannot however entirely coincide with philosophy.
The capacity of poetry is so far limited that it
expresses the universal not as it is in itself, but as
seen through the medium of sensuous imagery.

[1] *Poet.* ix. 3, διὸ καὶ φιλοσοφώτερον καὶ σπουδαιότερον ποίησις
ἱστορίας ἐστίν· ἡ μὲν γὰρ ποίησις μᾶλλον τὰ καθόλου, ἡ δ' ἱστορία
τὰ καθ' ἕκαστον λέγει.

[2] Teichmüller, *Aristot. Forsch.* ii. 178, who illustrates this
sense of σπουδαῖος from *Eth. Nic.* vi. 7. 1141 a 20, ἄτοπον γὰρ
εἴ τις τὴν πολιτικὴν ἢ τὴν φρόνησιν σπουδαιοτάτην ('the highest
form of knowledge') οἴεται εἶναι, εἰ μὴ τὸ ἄριστον τῶν ἐν τῷ
κόσμῳ ἄνθρωπός ἐστιν. Here σοφία is a more excellent thing
than φρόνησις because it has a higher subject-matter,—universal
principles.

[3] *Anal. Post.* i. 31. 88 a 4, τὸ δὲ καθόλου τίμιον ὅτι δηλοῖ τὸ
αἴτιον.

Plato, while condemning the poetry of his own country, had gone far towards merging an ideal poetry in philosophy. The artist who is no mere imitator, whose work is a revelation to sense of eternal ideas, being possessed by an imaginative enthusiasm which is akin to the speculative enthusiasm of the philosopher, from the things of sense ascends to that higher region where truth and beauty are one. Aristotle's phrase in this passage of the *Poetics* might, in like manner, appear almost to identify poetry with philosophy. But if we read his meaning in the light of what he says elsewhere and of the general system of his thought, we see that he does not confound the two spheres though they touch at a single point. Philosophy seeks to discover the universal in the particular ; its end is to know and to possess the truth, and in that possession it reposes. The aim of poetry is to represent the universal through the particular, to give a concrete and living embodiment of a universal truth.[1] The universal of poetry is not an abstract idea ; it is particularised to sense, it comes

---

[1] Cf. R. P. Hardie (in *Mind*, vol. iv. No. 15) : 'We must keep in mind that for poetry it is essential that this (i.e. the universal) element should be expressed in matter of some sort. It is in this respect that science differs from poetry. The whole aim of the former is to keep the εἶδος abstract, and therefore science uses not εἰκόνες but σημεῖα or σύμβολα, which never really *express* the εἶδος at all, but are of use merely to suggest the abstract εἶδος *qua* abstract.'

before the mind clothed in the form of the concrete, presented under the appearance of a living organism whose parts are in vital and structural relation to the whole.

It is the more necessary to insist on this because Aristotle's own analytical criticism may easily lead to a misconception of his meaning. In applying the method of logical abstraction to the organic parts of a poetic whole he may appear to forget that he is dealing not with a product of abstract thought but with a concrete work of art. The impression may be confirmed by a hasty reading of a later chapter,[1] where the poet is advised first to set forth his plot in its general idea (ἐκτίθεσθαι καθόλου), abstracting the accidental features of time, place, and persons, and afterwards to fill it in with detail and incident and with proper names. This order of composition is recommended whether the poet takes his plot from the traditional cycle of legends or draws upon his own invention. The example selected by Aristotle is the story of Iphigenia. As a piece of practical advice the value of the suggestion may well be questioned. But even if we pronounce the method to be faulty and unpoetical, the doctrine of the 'universal' is in no way affected. The use of the word καθόλου in two such different contexts must not mislead us. The καθόλου of ch. xvii. denotes the broad outline,

[1] *Poet.* xvii. 3–4.

O

the bare sketch of the plot, and is wholly distinct from the καθόλου of ch. ix., the general or universal truth which poetry conveys.

The process by which the poetic imagination works is illustrated by Coleridge from the following lines of Sir John Davies [1] :—

> ' Thus doth she, when from individual states
>   She doth abstract the universal kinds,
>   Which then reclothed in divers names and fates
>   Steal access thro' our senses to our minds.'

The meaning is not that a general idea is embodied in a particular example—that is the method of allegory rather than that of poetry—but that the particular case is generalised by artistic treatment. 'The young poet,' says Goethe, ' must do some sort of violence to himself to get out of the mere general idea. No doubt this is difficult ; but it is the very life of art.' ' A special case requires nothing but the treatment of a poet to become universal and poetical.' With this Aristotle would have agreed. Goethe, who tells us that with him ' every idea rapidly changed itself into an image,' was asked what idea he meant to embody in his Faust. 'As if I knew myself and could inform them. From heaven, through the world, to hell, would indeed be something ; but this is no idea, only a course of action. . . . It was, in short, not in my line, as a poet, to strive

[1] *Biog. Lit.* ch. xiv.

to embody anything abstract. I received in my mind impressions and those of a sensuous, animated, charming, varied, hundredfold kind, just as a lively imagination presented them; and I had, as a poet, nothing more to do than artistically to round them off and elaborate such views and impressions, and by means of a lively representation so to bring them forward that others might receive the same impression in hearing or reading my representation of them.'[1]

Coleridge in giving his adhesion to Aristotle's theory thinks it necessary to guard against the misconstruction to which that doctrine is exposed. 'I adopt,' he says, 'with full faith the theory of Aristotle that poetry as poetry is essentially ideal, that it avoids and excludes all accident; that its apparent individualities of rank, character, or occupation, must be representative of a class; and that the persons of poetry must be clothed with generic attributes, with the common attributes of the class; not such as one gifted individual might possibly possess, but such as from his situation it is most probable that he would possess.' And he adds in a note, 'Say not that I am recommending abstractions, for these class characteristics which constitute the instructiveness of a character are so modified and particularised in each person of the

---

[1] Eckermann's *Conversations of Goethe*, Transl. (Bohn's series), p. 258.

Shakespearian drama, that life itself does not excite more distinctly that sense of individuality which belongs to real existence. Paradoxical as it may sound, one of the essential properties of geometry is not less essential to dramatic excellence ; and Aristotle has accordingly required of the poet an involution of the universal in the individual. The chief differences are, that in geometry it is the universal truth, which is uppermost in the con-sciousness ; in poetry the individual form, in which the truth is clothed.'[1]

Some of these explanatory words themselves are, it must be owned, misleading. Such phrases as 'representative of a class,' 'generic attributes,' 'class characteristics which constitute the in-structiveness of a character,' seem to imply a false view of the 'universal' of poetry ; as though the 'individuality' were something outside the universal and of no poetic account ; yet, he says, 'the individual form' is 'uppermost.' One might think that the 'universal' was a single abstract truth instead of being *all* the truths that meet in the individual. The expression, however, 'such (attributes) as from his situation it is most probable that he would possess' is true and Aristotelian. But how can these attributes be called attributes of 'a class'?

Still it is in the main the same thought which

[1] *Biog. Lit.* ii. 41.

runs through Aristotle, Goethe, and Coleridge,—
that the poet while he seems to be concerned only
with the particular is in truth concerned with
quod semper quod ubique. He seizes and reproduces a concrete fact, but transfigures it so that
the higher truth, the idea of the universal shines
through it.

CHAPTER IV

THE END OF FINE ART

WE have seen what Aristotle means by 'imitation' as an aesthetic term. We now ask, What is the end of 'imitative' art? Here Aristotle draws a sharp distinction. The arts called 'useful' either provide the necessary means of existence and satisfy material wants, or furnish life with its full equipment of moral and intellectual resources. Their end is subordinate to another and ulterior end. The end of the fine arts is to give pleasure (πρὸς ἡδονήν) or rational enjoyment[1]

---

[1] Met. i. 1. 981 b 17 sqq., πλειόνων δ' εὑρισκομένων τεχνῶν, καὶ τῶν μὲν πρὸς τἀναγκαῖα τῶν δὲ πρὸς διαγωγὴν οὐσῶν, ἀεὶ σοφωτέρους τοὺς τοιούτους ἐκείνων ὑπολαμβάνομεν, διὰ τὸ μὴ πρὸς χρῆσιν εἶναι τὰς ἐπιστήμας αὐτῶν. The liberal arts which adorn life and minister to pleasure are here said to be πρὸς διαγωγήν, synonymous with which we find πρὸς ἡδονήν b 21. Cf. Met. i. 2. 982 b 23, πρὸς ῥᾳστώνην καὶ διαγωγήν. In all of these passages the contrasted expression is τἀναγκαῖα. διαγωγή properly means the employment of leisure, and in Aristotle fluctuates between the higher and lower kinds of pleasurable activity. In the lower sense it is combined in Eth. Nic. iv. 8. 1127 b 34 with παιδιά and is part of ἀνάπαυσις : it denotes the more playful forms of social intercourse ; in x. 6. 1176 b 12, 14 it is used of the παιδιαί of the rich and great ; in x. 6. 1177 a 9,

(πρὸς διαγωγήν). A useful art like that of cookery may happen to produce pleasure, but this is no part of its essence ; just as a fine art may incidentally produce useful results and become a moral instrument in the hands of the legislator. In neither case is the result to be confounded with the true end of the art. The pleasure, however, which is derived from an art may be of a higher or lower kind, for Aristotle recognises specific differences between pleasures. There is the harmless pleasure,[1] which is afforded by a recreation (ἀνάπαυσις) or a pastime (παιδιά): but a pastime is not an end in itself, it is the rest that fits the busy

οὐ γὰρ ἐν ταῖς τοιαύταις διαγωγαῖς ἡ εὐδαιμονία, it has a baser application to σωματικαὶ ἡδοναί. As an elevated and noble enjoyment it is associated with σχολή in *Pol.* iv. (vii.) 15. 1334 a 16. Under this aspect it admits of special application to the two spheres of art and philosophy. In *Pol.* v. (viii.) 5. 1339 a 25 it is joined with φρόνησις and stands for the higher aesthetic enjoyment which music affords. From a 30–31 it appears that the musical διαγωγή is an end in itself, and therefore distinct from a παιδιά. In *Pol.* v. (viii.) 5. 1339 b 14 sqq. three ends are mentioned which music may serve—παιδεία, παιδιά, and διαγωγή, and the last is said to combine τὸ καλόν with ἡδονή, both of which elements enter into εὐδαιμονία. Its reference is to the life of thought in *Eth. Nic.* x. 7. 1177 a 27, where it is applied to the activity of the speculative reason, and in *Met.* xi. 7. 1072 b 14, where it denotes the activity of the divine thought. Thus the higher διαγωγή, artistic or philosophic, is the delight which comes from the ideal employment of leisure (cf. τὴν ἐν τῇ σχολῇ διαγωγήν *Pol.* v. (viii.) 3. 1338 a 21); it is among the blissful moments which constitute εὐδαιμονία. Cf. *Pol.* v. (viii.) 3. 1338 a 1, τὸ δὲ σχολάζειν ἔχειν αὐτὸ δοκεῖ τὴν ἡδονὴν καὶ τὴν εὐδαιμονίαν καὶ τὸ ζῆν μακαρίως.

[1] *Pol.* v. (viii.) 5. 1339 b 25.

man for fresh exertion, and is of value as a means
to further work; it has in it no element of that
well-being or happiness which is the supreme end
of life.[1]

Though Aristotle does not assign to the different
kinds of art their respective ranks, or expressly say
that the pleasure of tragedy is superior to that of
comedy, the distinction he draws between various
forms of music may be taken as indicating the
criterion by which he would judge of other arts.
Music, apart from its other functions, may serve
as an amusement for children, it is a toy which
takes the place of the infant's rattle;[2] or, again,
it may afford a noble and rational enjoyment
and become an element of the highest happiness
to an audience that is capable of appreciating
it.[3]   Again, Aristotle asserts that the ludicrous
in general is inferior to the serious,[4] and counts
as a pastime that fits men for serious work. We
may probably infer that the same principle holds
in literature as in life; that comedy is merely
a form of sportive activity; the pleasure derived

[1] *Eth. Nic.* x. 6. 1176 b 30, ἅπαντα γὰρ ὡς εἰπεῖν ἑτέρου
ἕνεκα αἱρούμεθα πλὴν τῆς εὐδαιμονίας· τέλος γὰρ αὕτη. σπουδάζειν
δὲ καὶ πονεῖν παιδιᾶς χάριν ἠλίθιον φαίνεται καὶ λίαν παιδικόν·
παίζειν δ᾽ ὅπως σπουδάζῃ, κατ᾽ Ἀνάχαρσιν, ὀρθῶς ἔχειν δοκεῖ·
ἀναπαύσει γὰρ ἔοικεν ἡ παιδιά, ἀδυνατοῦντες δὲ συνεχῶς πονεῖν
ἀναπαύσεως δέονται. οὐ δὴ τέλος ἡ ἀνάπαυσις· γίνεται γὰρ ἕνεκα
τῆς ἐνεργείας.

[2] *Pol.* v. (viii.) 5. 1339 b 13–17 ; 6. 1340 b 30.

[3] See note 3 p. 211.   [4] *Eth. Nic.* x. 6. 1177 a 3.

from it is of corresponding quality, it ranks
with the other pleasures of sport or recreation.
But art in its highest idea is one of the serious
activities of the mind which constitute the final
well-being of man. Its end is pleasure, but the
pleasure peculiar to that state of rational enjoyment in which perfect repose is united with
perfect energy. It is not to be confounded with
the pleasure found in the rude imitations of
early art, arising from the discovery of a likeness. One passage of the *Poetics* might indeed
if it stood alone lead us to this inference.[1] The
instinct for knowledge, the pleasure of recognition, is there the chief factor in the enjoyment of
some at least of the more developed arts. But
the reference appears to be rather to the popular
appreciation of a likeness than to true aesthetic
enjoyment. This is perhaps borne out by the
explanation elsewhere given of the pleasure derived
from plastic or pictorial imitations of the lower
forms of animal life.[2] These objects do not come
within the range of artistic imitation as understood

---

[1] *Poet.* iv. 3–5. Cf. *Rhet.* i. 11. 1371 b 4, ἐπεὶ δὲ τὸ μανθάνειν
τε ἡδὺ καὶ τὸ θαυμάζειν, καὶ τὰ τοιάδε ἀνάγκη ἡδέα εἶναι οἷον τό
τε μιμούμενον, ὥσπερ γραφικὴ καὶ ἀνδριαντοποιία καὶ ποιητική,
καὶ πᾶν ὃ ἂν εὖ μεμιμημένον ᾖ, κἂν ᾖ μὴ ἡδὺ αὐτὸ τὸ μεμιμημένον.
οὐ γὰρ ἐπὶ τούτῳ χαίρει ἀλλὰ συλλογισμός ἐστιν ὅτι τοῦτο ἐκεῖνο,
ὥστε μανθάνειν τι συμβαίνει.

[2] See the passage quoted p. 156 from *de Part. Anim.* i. 5. 645 a
4 sqq., especially the words τὰς μὲν εἰκόνας αὐτῶν θεωροῦντες
χαίρομεν ὅτι τὴν δημιουργήσασαν τέχνην συνθεωροῦμεν.

by Aristotle ; they do not reproduce the human and mental life with which alone art is concerned. But they give occasion for the display of workmanlike skill; and afford a pleasure analogous to that which springs from the contemplation of nature in her adaptation of means to ends.

Aristotle was perhaps inclined unduly to accentuate the purely intellectual side of pictorial and plastic art. But in his treatment of poetry, which holds the sovereign place among the fine arts, he makes it plain that aesthetic enjoyment proper proceeds from an emotional rather than from an intellectual source. The main appeal is not to the reason but to the feelings. In a word, fine art and philosophy, while they occupy distinct territory, each find their complete fruition in a region bordering on the other. The glow of feeling which accompanies the contemplation of what is perfect in art is an elevated delight similar in quality to the glow of speculative thought. Each is a moment of joy complete in itself, and belongs to the ideal sphere of supreme happiness.[1]

[1] Cf. Introduction to Hegel's *Philosophy of Fine Art*, translated by B. Bosanquet, London, 1886, p. 12 : 'It is no doubt the case that art can be employed as a fleeting pastime, to serve the ends of pleasure and entertainment, to decorate our surroundings, to impart pleasantness to the external conditions of our life, and to emphasise other objects by means of ornament. In this mode of employment art is indeed not independent, not free, but servile. But what we mean to consider is the art which is free in its end as in its means. . . . Fine art is not real art till it is in this sense free,

Some points of difference between Plato and Aristotle are at once apparent. Pleasure to Plato was a word of base associations and a democratic pleasure was doubly ignoble. An imitative art like music is liable to become a corrupting influence, if for no other reason, because it seeks to please the masses.[1] Poetry, again, has something of the same taint; it is a kind of rhetoric,[2] a pleasant flattery addressed to mixed audiences, and falls therefore into the same group with the art of sophistry, the art of personal adornment, and the art of the pastry-cook, all of which look not to what is best or truly wholesome but to the pleasure of the moment.[3] The vulgar opinion that musical excellence is measured by pleasure seems to Plato a sort of blasphemy;[4] if pleasure is to be taken as a criterion at all, it should be that of the 'one man pre-eminent in virtue and education.'[5] Even in the *Philebus*, where the claims of pleasure, and especially of

and only achieves its highest task when it has taken its place in the same sphere with religion and philosophy.'

[1] *Laws* ii. 659 A–C.

[2] Ἁ ῥητορικὴ δημηγορία, *Gorg.* 502 D.

[3] *Gorg.* 462 E–463 B. Cf. *Rep.* ii. 373 B–C.

[4] *Laws* ii. 655 D, καίτοι λέγουσί γε οἱ πλεῖστοι μουσικῆς ὀρθότητα εἶναι τὴν ἡδονὴν ταῖς ψυχαῖς πορίζουσαν δύναμιν· ἀλλὰ τοῦτο μὲν οὔτε ἀνεκτὸν οὔτε ὅσιον τὸ παράπαν φθέγγεσθαι.

[5] *Laws* ii. 658 E, συγχωρῶ δὴ . . . δεῖν τὴν μουσικὴν ἡδονῇ κρίνεσθαι, μὴ μέντοι τῶν γε ἐπιτυχόντων, ἀλλὰ σχεδὸν ἐκείνην εἶναι Μοῦσαν καλλίστην, ἥτις τοὺς βελτίστους καὶ ἱκανῶς πεπαιδευμένους τέρπει, μάλιστα δὲ ἥτις ἕνα τὸν ἀρετῇ τε καὶ παιδείᾳ διαφέροντα.

aesthetic pleasure, are more carefully analysed and weighed than elsewhere, the highest or unmixed pleasures rank but fifth in the scale of goods. Aristotle does not share Plato's distrust of pleasure. In the *Ethics* while he admits to the full its power to mislead the judgment, and compares its gracious but dangerous influence to that of Helen among the elders of Troy;[1] while he speaks slightingly of the pleasures of the mass of men who 'can form no idea of the noble and the truly pleasant whereof they have never tasted,'[2] yet he insists on the necessity of being trained to feel pleasure and pain at the right objects; he never hints that pleasure ought to be suppressed as in itself an evil; nay, it is a normal accompaniment of the exercise of every healthy organ and faculty, it perfects that exercise as an added completeness, 'like the bloom of health on the face of the young.'[3] In the passage of the *Metaphysics* (i. 1) already referred to, the discoverers of the fine arts are said to be 'wiser' than the discoverers of the useful arts for the very reason that the former arts minister to pleasure, not to use.

Again, to Plato poetry and painting and the companion arts, as affording at the best a

---

[1] *Eth. Nic.* ii. 9. 1109 b 9.

[2] *Eth. Nic.* x. 10. 1179 b 15.

[3] *Eth. Nic.* x. 4. 1174 b 32, ὡς ἐπιγινόμενόν τι τέλος, οἷον τοῖς ἀκμαίοις ἡ ὥρα.

harmless pleasure,[1] are of the nature of a
pastime,[2]—a pastime, it may be, more 'artistic
and graceful'[3] than any other kind, but still contrasting unfavourably with medicine, husbandry,
and gymnastics, which have a serious purpose and
co-operate with nature.[4] Imitative art, in short, is
wanting in moral earnestness ; it is a jest, a sport,
child's-play upon the surface of things. Even
comedy, however, is not entirely excluded in the
Laws.[5] It may serve an educational end; for the
serious implies the ludicrous, and opposites cannot
be understood without opposites. The citizens,
therefore, may witness the representation of comedy
on the stage in order to avoid doing what is
ludicrous in life; but only under the proviso that
the characters shall not be acted except by slaves.

---

[1] *Laws* ii. 667 E, ἀβλαβῆ λέγεις ἡδονὴν μόνον. The same
phrase is used by Aristotle in reference to music as a pastime,
Pol. v. (viii.) 5. 1339 b 25, ὅσα γὰρ ἀβλαβῆ τῶν ἡδέων κ.τ.λ.
Cf. also *Laws* ii. 670 D, ἵνα . . . ᾄδοντες αὐτοί τε ἡδονὰς τὸ
παραχρῆμα ἀσινεῖς ἥδωνται κ.τ.λ.

[2] *Polit.* 288 C. Every such art may be called παίγνιόν τι,
'a plaything,' οὐ γὰρ σπουδῆς οὐδὲν αὐτῶν χάριν, ἀλλὰ παιδιᾶς
ἕνεκα πάντα δρᾶται. So *Rep.* x. 602 B (of tragic and epic poets in
particular), *Laws* vii. 816 E (of comedy), ὅσα μὲν οὖν περὶ γέλωτά
ἐστι παίγνια, ἃ δὴ κωμῳδίαν πάντες λέγομεν . . .

[3] *Soph.* 234 B, παιδιᾶς δὲ ἔχεις ἤ τι τεχνικώτερον ἢ καὶ χαριέ-
στερον εἶδος ἢ τὸ μιμητικόν ;

[4] *Laws* x. 889 D, ταύτας ὁπόσαι τῇ φύσει ἐκοίνωσαν τὴν
αὐτῶν δύναμιν.

[5] *Laws* vii. 816 D-E. Even Molière professes to hold that
'the business of comedy is to correct the vices of men' (Preface to
Tartuffe).

Aristotle distinguishes as we have seen between art as a pastime and art as a rational employment of leisure. Comedy and the lower forms of art he would probably rank as a pastime, but not so art in its higher manifestations. Tragedy is the imitation of an action that is the very opposite of a pastime, a serious action (πράξεως σπουδαίας), which is concerned with the supreme good or end of life ; and the art which reproduces this aspect of life is itself a serious art.

The end, then, of fine art, according to Aristotle's doctrine, is a certain pleasurable impression produced upon the mind of the hearer or the spectator. We must be careful here not to import the later idea that the artist works merely for his own enjoyment, that the inward satisfaction which the creative act affords is for him the end of his art. No such conception of the artist's dignity was formed in Greece, where in truth the artist was honoured less than his art. His professional skill seemed to want something of a self-sufficing and independent activity ; and though the poet stood higher in popular estimation than his fellow-artists, because he did not, like the painter and sculptor, approach to the condition of a manual labourer or as a rule make a trade of his work, he too was one who worked not for himself but for others, and so far fell short of a gentlemanly leisure. Aristotle's theory has regard to the pleasure not of the maker, but of the 'spectator' (θεατής) who contemplates the finished product. Thus while the pleasures of philosophy are for him who philosophises—for the intellectual act is an end in itself—the pleasures of art are not for the artist but for those who enjoy what he creates; or if the artist shares at all in the distinctive pleasure which belongs to his art, he does so not as an artist but as one of the public.

To those who are familiar with modern modes of thinking it may seem a serious defect in the theory of Aristotle that he makes the end of art to reside in a pleasurable emotion, not in the realisation of a certain objective character that is necessary to the perfection of the work. An artistic creation, it may be said, is complete in itself; its end is immanent not transcendental. The effect that it produces, whether that effect be immediate or remote, whether it be pleasure or moral improvement, has nothing to do with the object as it is in its essence and inmost character. The true artist concerns himself with external effects as little as does nature herself in the vital processes which are directed towards an end. It was a signal merit, we are reminded, in Aristotle's general philosophical system, that the end of an object is inherent in that object, and is reached when the object has achieved its specific excellence

and fulfils the law of its own being.¹ Why, it is
said, did not Aristotle see that a painting or a
poem, like a natural organism, attains its end not
through some external effect but in realising its
own idea? If the end of art is to be found in
a certain emotional effect, in a pleasure which
is purely subjective, the end becomes something
arbitrary and accidental, and dependent on each
individual's moods. Plato had already shown the
way to a truer conception of fine art, for greatly
as he misjudged the poetry of his own country,
yet he had in his mind the vision of a higher art
which should reveal to sense the world of ideas.
Here there was at least an objective end for fine
art. Aristotle's own definition too of art as 'a
faculty of production in accordance with a true
idea'² is quoted as showing that he was not far
from assigning to fine art an end more consistent
with his whole system. If art in general is the
faculty of realising a true idea in external form,
he might easily have arrived at a definition of fine
art not essentially different from the modern conception of it as the revelation of the beautiful in
external form.

It is probably not possible to acquit Aristotle

---

¹ *Phys.* ii. 2. 194 a 28, ἡ δὲ φύσις τέλος καὶ οὗ ἕνεκα. So
Pol. i. 2. 1252 b 32.

² *Eth. Nic.* vi. 4. 1140 a 10, ἕξις μετὰ λόγου ἀληθοῦς
ποιητική.

of some inconsistency of treatment. According to
his general theory of Aesthetics as a branch of
Art, its end ought to be the purely objective end
of realising the εἶδος in concrete form. But in
dealing with particular arts, such as poetry and
music, he assumes a subjective end consisting in
a certain pleasurable emotion. There is here a
formal contradiction from which there appears to
be no escape. It would seem that Aristotle in
generalising from the observed effects of works
of art raises the subjective side of fine art into
a prominence which is hardly in keeping with
his whole philosophical system. If we seek to
develop his line of thought, we may say that the
artist, pursuing an end which is external to his
productive activity, attains that end when the
work of art comes into existence,—that is, when
the process of change (γένεσις) is complete, when
the matter (ὕλη) has been impressed with the
artistic form (εἶδος), and the potential has been
developed into the actual.[1] How are we to know
that this end has been attained? By the hedonistic
effect produced on the mind of the percipient
subject. The work of art is in its nature an
appeal to the senses and imagination of the person
to whom it is presented; its perfection and success
depend on a subjective impression. It attains to
complete existence only within the mind, in the

[1] See p. 155, note.

P

pleasure which accompanies this mode of mental activity (ἐνέργεια). Thus the productive activity of the artist is not unnaturally subordinated to the receptive activity of the person for whom he produces.

In Aristotle the true nature of a thing can be expressed by means of that which it is ' capable of doing or suffering' (πέφυκε ποιεῖν ἢ πάσχειν). Its effect is treated as synonymous with its essential quality.[1] So it is in a work of art. If indeed we desire to characterise precisely its emotional effect we must do so by reference to the content of the activity. But the work of art and its effect being inseparable, the artistic object can loosely be spoken of in terms of the emotion it awakens.[2] This view does not, however, make the function of art to depend upon accident and individual caprice. The subjective emotion is deeply grounded in

---

[1] The δύναμις of a thing is closely allied to its οὐσία, εἶδος, λόγος, φύσις. Cf. de Gen. Anim. ii. 1. 731 b 19, τίς ἡ δύναμις καὶ ὁ λόγος τῆς οὐσίας αὐτῶν; de Sensu 3. 439 a 23, τίς ἐστι κοινὴ φύσις καὶ δύναμις; Eth. Nic. v. 4. 1130 b 1, ἄμφω γὰρ ἐν τῷ πρὸς ἕτερον ἔχουσι τὴν δύναμιν. So Poet. i. 1, ἥν τινα δύναμιν ἕκαστον ἔχει. Cf. vi. 18, ὃ καὶ ἐπὶ τῶν ἐμμέτρων καὶ ἐπὶ τῶν λόγων ἔχει τὴν αὐτὴν δύναμιν.

[2] Similarly Schiller finds the essence and end of tragedy in the effect it produces. See his Essay ' Ueber die tragische Kunst,' and a letter to Goethe of Dec. 12, 1797, ' Als dann glaube ich auch eine gewisse Berechnung auf den Zuschauer, von der sich der tragische Poet nicht dispensieren kann, der Hinblick auf einen Zweck, den äussern Eindruck, der bei dieser Dichtungsart nicht ganz verlassen wird, geniert Sie, u.s.w.'

human nature, and thence acquires a kind of objective validity. As in ethics Aristotle assumes a man of moral insight (ὁ φρόνιμος) to whose trained judgment the appreciation of ethical questions is submitted, and who, in the last resort, becomes the 'standard and the law' of right,[1] so too in fine art a man of sound aesthetic instincts (ὁ χαρίεις) is assumed, who is the standard of taste, and to him the final appeal is made. He is no mere expert, for Aristotle distrusts the verdict of specialists in the arts[2] and prefers the popular judgment,—but it must be the judgment of a cultivated public. Both in the *Politics* and in the *Poetics* he distinguishes between the lower and the higher kind of audience.[3] The 'free and educated listener' at a musical performance is opposed to one of the vulgar sort. Each class of audience enjoys a different kind of music and derives from the performance such pleasure as it is capable of. The inferior kind of enjoyment is

---

[1] *Eth. Nic.* iii. 4. 1113 a 33, the σπουδαῖος is ὥσπερ κανὼν καὶ μέτρον.

[2] Cf. *Pol.* iii. 11. 1282 a 1–21.

[3] *Pol.* v. (viii.) 7. 1342 a 18–28, ἐπεὶ δ' ὁ θεατὴς διττός, ὁ μὲν ἐλεύθερος καὶ πεπαιδευμένος, ὁ δὲ φορτικός κ.τ.λ. In *Poet.* xxvi. 1, ἡ πρὸς βελτίους θεατὰς μίμησις is ἧττον φορτική. Cf. Plat. *Laws* ii. 658 E, ἐκείνην εἶναι Μοῦσαν καλλίστην, ἥτις τοὺς βελτίστους καὶ ἱκανῶς πεπαιδευμένους τέρπει.

In *Rhet.* i. 3. 1358 a 37 the τέλος of the art of rhetoric is in relation to the ἀκροατής: σύγκειται μὲν γὰρ ἐκ τριῶν ὁ λόγος, ἔκ τε τοῦ λέγοντος καὶ περὶ οὗ λέγει καὶ πρὸς ὅν, καὶ τὸ τέλος πρὸς τοῦτόν ἐστι, λέγω δὲ τὸν ἀκροατήν.

not to be denied to those who can appreciate only
the inferior type of music—better that they should
like this music than none at all—but the lower
pleasure is not to be taken as the true end of the
musical art.[1]

In the theatre, again, it is noted that tragic
poets are tempted to gratify the weakness of their
audience by making happy endings to their
tragedies. The practice is not entirely forbidden;
only, it is insisted, such compositions do not afford
the characteristic tragic pleasure, but one that
properly belongs to comedy.[2] In fine, the end
of any art is not 'any chance pleasure,'[3] but the

[1] In *Pol.* v. (viii.) 5. 1340 a 1–2, the universal pleasure given
by music is called ἡ κοινὴ ἡδονή and is φυσική. It is distinct
from the higher kind of pleasure.

In *Probl.* xviii. 4. 916 b 36, the art of the musician and of the
actor aims only at pleasure : διὰ τί ῥήτορα μὲν καὶ στρατηγὸν καὶ
χρηματιστὴν λέγομεν δεινόν, αὐλητὴν δὲ καὶ ὑποκριτὴν οὐ λέγομεν;
ἢ ὅτι τῶν μὲν ἡ δύναμις ἄνευ πλεονεξίας (ἡδονῆς γὰρ στοχαστικὴ
ἐστι), τῶν δὲ πρὸς τὸ πλεονεκτεῖν;

[2] *Poet.* xiii. 7–8, δοκεῖ δὲ εἶναι πρώτη διὰ τὴν τῶν θεάτρων
ἀσθένειαν, . . . ἔστιν δὲ οὐχ αὕτη <ἡ> ἀπὸ τραγῳδίας ἡδονὴ
ἀλλὰ μᾶλλον τῆς κωμῳδίας οἰκεία. For the phrase τὴν τῶν
θεάτρων ἀσθένειαν cf. *Rhet.* iii. 18. 1419 a 18, οὐ γὰρ οἷόν τε πολλὰ
ἐρωτᾶν διὰ τὴν ἀσθένειαν τοῦ ἀκροατοῦ, i.e. you cannot (in debate,
etc.) put a series of questions on account of the incapacity of a
popular audience to follow a long chain of reasoning. *Rhet.* iii. 1.
1404 a 8, διὰ τὴν τοῦ ἀκροατοῦ μοχθηρίαν.

[3] *Poet.* xiv. 2, οὐ γὰρ πᾶσαν δεῖ ζητεῖν ἡδονὴν ἀπὸ τραγῳδίας
ἀλλὰ τὴν οἰκείαν. xxvi. 7, δεῖ γὰρ οὐ τὴν τυχοῦσαν ἡδονὴν
ποιεῖν αὐτάς (i.e. tragedy and epic poetry) ἀλλὰ τὴν εἰρημένην :
with which cf. *Pol.* v. (viii.) 5. 1339 b 32, ἔχει γὰρ ἴσως ἡδονήν
τινα καὶ τὸ τέλος, ἀλλ᾽ οὐ τὴν τυχοῦσαν.

pleasure which is distinctive of the art. To the
ideal spectator or listener, who is a man of educated
taste and represents an instructed public, every
fine art addresses itself; he may be called 'the
rule and standard' of that art, as the man of moral
insight is of morals; the pleasure that any given
work of art affords to him is the end of the art.
But this imaginative pleasure has a tacit reference
to man not as an isolated individual, but as existing
within the social organism.   From the Aristotelian
and Greek point of view art is an element in the
higher life of the community; the pleasure it affords
is an enduring pleasure, an aesthetic enjoyment
which is not divorced from civic ends.[1]

Though the end, then, is a state of feeling, it is
a feeling that is proper to a normally constituted
humanity.   The hedonistic effect is not alien to
the essence of the art, as has sometimes been
thought; it is the subjective aspect of a real
objective fact.   Each kind of poetry carries with
it a distinctive pleasure, which is the criterion by
which the work is judged.   A tragic action has
an inherent capacity of calling forth pity and fear;
this quality must be impressed by the poet on the
dramatic material;[2] and if it is artistically done,

---

[1] See Courthope, *Life in Poetry*, pp. 209 ff.

[2] *Poet.* xiv. 3, ἐπεὶ δὲ τὴν ἀπὸ ἐλέου καὶ φόβου διὰ μιμήσεως
δεῖ ἡδονὴν παρασκευάζειν τὸν ποιητήν, φανερὸν ὡς τοῦτο ἐν τοῖς
πράγμασιν ἐμποιητέον.

the peculiar pleasure arising out of the union of the pitiable and the terrible will be awakened in the mind of every one who possesses normal human sympathies and faculties. The test of artistic merit in a tragedy is the degree in which it fulfils this, its distinctive function. All the rules prescribed by Aristotle for the tragic poet flow from the same primary requirement,—those which determine the proper construction of the plot, the character of the ideal hero, the best form of recognition and the like. The state of pleasurable feeling is not an accidental result, but is inherently related to the object which calls it forth. Though the pleasure of the percipient is necessary to the fulfilment of the function of any art, the subjective impression has in it an enduring and universal element.

CHAPTER V

THE question as to the proper end of fine art was discussed in Greece in its special application to poetry. Two views were currently held. The traditional one, which had gained wide acceptance, was that poetry has a direct moral purpose; the primary function of a poet is that of a teacher. Even after professional teachers of the art of conduct had appeared in Greece the poets were not deposed from the educational office which time had consecrated. Homer was still thought of less as the inspired poet who charmed the imagination than as the great teacher who had laid down all the rules needed for the conduct of life, and in whom were hidden all the lessons of philosophy. The other theory, tacitly no doubt held by many, but put into definite shape first by Aristotle, was that poetry is an emotional delight, its end is to give pleasure. Strabo (circa 24 B.C.) alludes to the two conflicting opinions. Eratosthenes, he says, maintained that 'the aim of the poet always

is to charm the mind not to instruct.'[1] He himself holds with the ancients 'that poetry is a kind
of elementary philosophy, which introduces us
early to life, and gives us pleasurable instruction
in reference to character, emotion, action.'[2] The
Greek states, he argues, prescribed poetry as the
first lesson of childhood; they did so, surely, not
merely in order to please, but to afford correction
in morals.[3] In carrying the same discipline into
mature years they expressed their conviction, that
poetry as a regulative influence on morals was
adapted to every period of life.   In course of time,
he observes, philosophical and historical studies
had been introduced, but these addressed themselves only to the few, while the appeal of poetry
was to the masses.[4] Eratosthenes ought to have
modified his phrase and said that the poet writes
partly to please and partly to instruct, instead of
which he converted poetry into a privileged *racon-
teuse* of old wives' fables, with no other object
in view than to charm the mind.[5] If, however,
poetry is the art which imitates life by the medium
of speech, how can one be a poet who is senseless

[1] Strabo i. 2. 3, ποιητὴν γὰρ ἔφη πάντα στοχάζεσθαι ψυχαγωγίας οὐ διδασκαλίας.

[2] l.c. τοὐναντίον δ' οἱ παλαιοὶ φιλοσοφίαν τινὰ λέγουσι πρώτην
τὴν ποιητικὴν εἰσάγουσαν εἰς τὸν βίον ἡμᾶς ἐκ νέων καὶ διδά-
σκουσαν ἤθη καὶ πάθη καὶ πράξεις μεθ' ἡδονῆς.

[3] l.c. οὐ ψυχαγωγίας χάριν δήπουθεν ψιλῆς ἀλλὰ σωφρο-
νισμοῦ.   [4] ib. i. 2. 8.   [5] ib. i. 2. 3.

and ignorant of life? The excellence of a poet is not like that of a carpenter or a smith; it is bound up with that of the human being. No one can be a good poet who is not first a good man.[1]

This remarkable passage accurately reflects the sentiment which persisted to a late time in Greece, long after the strictly teaching functions of poetry had passed into other hands. It is to be met with everywhere in Plutarch. 'Poetry is the preparatory school of philosophy.'[2] 'It opens and awakens the youthful mind to the doctrines of philosophy.'[3] When first the young hear these doctrines they are bewildered and reject them. 'Before they pass from darkness into full sunshine they must dwell in a kind of twilight, in the soft rays of a truth that is blended with fiction, and so be prepared painlessly to face the blaze of philosophy without flinching.'[4] The novice requires wise guidance 'in order that through a schooling that

---

[1] Strabo i. 2. 5, ἡ δὲ ποιητοῦ (ἀρετή) συνέζευκται τῇ τοῦ ἀνθρώπου, καὶ οὐχ οἷόν τε ἀγαθὸν γενέσθαι ποιητὴν μὴ πρότερον γενηθέντα ἄνδρα ἀγαθόν. Compare Minturno, *De Poeta* (1559). How profoundly this view has affected modern thought is shown by the references given in Spingarn (*Lit. Crit. in Renaissance*), p. 55.

[2] Plutarch, *de Aud. Poet.* ch. 1, ἐν ποιήμασι προφιλοσοφητέον.

[3] ib. ch. 14, ἔτι δὲ προανοίγει καὶ προκινεῖ τὴν τοῦ νέου ψυχὴν τοῖς ἐν φιλοσοφίᾳ λόγοις.

[4] l.c. οὐδὲ ὑπομένοντας ἂν μὴ οἷον ἐκ σκότους πολλοῦ μέλλοντες ἥλιον ὁρᾶν ἐθισθῶσι, καθάπερ ἐν νόθῳ φωτὶ καὶ κεκραμένης μύθοις ἀληθείας αὐγὴν ἔχοντι μαλθακήν, ἀλύπως διαβλέπειν τὰ τοιαῦτα καὶ μὴ φεύγειν.

brings no estrangement he may, as a kindly and familiar friend, be conducted by poetry into the presence of philosophy.'[1]

How deeply the Greek mind was impressed with the moral office of the poet, is shown by the attitude which even Aristophanes feels constrained to take up in relation to his art. He proclaims that the comic poet not only ministers to the enjoyment of the community and educates their taste, he is also a moral teacher and political adviser.[2] 'Comedy too is acquainted with justice.'[3] It mixes earnest with its fun.[4] In the Parabasis of the *Acharnians* Aristophanes claims to be the best of poets for having had the courage to tell the Athenians what was right.[5] Good counsel he gives and will always give them; as for his satire it shall never light on what is honest and true.[6] He likens himself elsewhere to another Heracles, who attacks not ordinary

---

[1] Plutarch, de Aud. Poet. ad fin., ἵνα μὴ προδιαβληθεὶς ἀλλὰ μᾶλλον προπαιδευθεὶς εὐμενὴς καὶ φίλος καὶ οἰκεῖος ὑπὸ ποιητικῆς ἐπὶ φιλοσοφίαν προπέμπηται.

[2] *Frogs* 1009–10,   ὅτι βελτίους τε ποιοῦμεν
τοὺς ἀνθρώπους ἐν ταῖς πόλεσιν.
This claim is put into the mouth of Euripides.

[3] *Acharn.* 500, τὸ γὰρ δίκαιον οἶδε καὶ τρυγῳδία.
Frogs 686–7, τὸν ἱερὸν χορὸν δίκαιόν ἐστι χρηστὰ τῇ πόλει
ξυμπαραινεῖν καὶ διδάσκειν.

[4] *Frogs* 389–90, καὶ πολλὰ μὲν γελοῖά μ' εἰπεῖν, πολλὰ δὲ σπουδαῖα.

[5] *Acharn.* 645, ὅστις παρεκινδύνευσ' εἰπεῖν ἐν Ἀθηναίοις τὰ
δίκαια.

[6] *Acharn.* 656–8.

human beings, but Cleons and other monsters of
the earth, and who in ridding the city of such
plagues deserves the title of 'cleanser of the
land.'[1]

The censure he passes on Euripides is primarily
a moral censure. Even where the judgment may
seem to be of an aesthetic kind a moral motive
underlies it. Euripides is to him a bad citizen and
a bad poet. In him are embodied all the tendencies
of the time which the older poet most abhors. He
is the spirit of the age personified, with its restless-
ness, its scepticism, its sentimentalism, its unsparing
questioning of old traditions, of religious usages and
civic loyalty ; its frivolous disputations, which unfit
men for the practical work of life, its lowered ideal
of courage and patriotism. Every phase of the
sophistic spirit he discovers in Euripides. There
is a bewildering dialectic which perplexes the moral
sense. Duties whose appeal to the conscience is
immediate, and which are recognised as having a
binding force, are in Euripides subjected to analysis.
Again, Euripides is censured for exciting feeling by
any means that come to hand. When Dicaeopolis
in the *Acharnians* is about to plead his case with
his head on the block, he borrows from Euripides
the rags and tatters of his hero Telephus. He
carries off with him all the stage-properties of
woe, so that Euripides exclaims, 'My dear sir,

[1] *Wasps* 1029–45.

you will rob me of my tragedy.'¹ Tragic pity,
Aristophanes implies, is debased in Euripides to an
ignoble sentimentalism. Genuine misery does not
consist in a beggar's rags or in a hobbling gait.
Euripides substitutes the troubling of the senses for
genuine tragic emotion.

We are not here concerned with the fairness of
the criticism but only with the point of view of the
critic; and the coincidence of the moral and aesthetic
judgment in Aristophanes is especially noteworthy.
He puts into the mouth of Aeschylus, his ideal
tragedian, the saying that the poet is the instructor
of grown men as the teacher is of youth;² and even
the comic stage is, according to the theory if not
the practice of Aristophanes, the school of the
mature citizen.

Aristotle's treatment of poetry in the *Poetics*
stands in complete contrast to this mode of criticism. In the *Politics* he had already dealt with
the fine arts as they present themselves to the
statesman and the social reformer. He allows that
for childhood the use of poetry and music is to

¹ *Acharn.* 464 ἄνθρωπ', ἀφαιρήσει με τὴν τραγῳδίαν.
² *Frogs* 1054–5,   τοῖς μὲν γὰρ παιδαρίοισιν
ἔστι διδάσκαλος ὅστις φράζει, τοῖς ἡβῶσιν δὲ ποιηταί.
Cf. Plat. *Lys.* 213 E, ᾗ δὲ ἐτράπημεν δοκεῖ μοι χρῆναι ἰέναι,
σκοποῦντα κατὰ τοὺς ποιητάς· οὗτοι γὰρ ἡμῖν ὥσπερ πατέρες τῆς
σοφίας εἰσὶ καὶ ἡγεμόνες.
Laws ix. 858 D, τῶν . . . ποιητῶν καὶ ὅσοι ἄνευ μέτρων καὶ
μετὰ μέτρων τὴν αὐτῶν εἰς μνήμην ξυμβουλὴν περὶ βίου κατέθεντο.

convey moral instruction, and that some forms of poetry, like some kinds of plastic art, exercise a dangerous influence on youth. But the true end of an art is not to be judged by the use to which it may be put in training immature minds. He tacitly combats the position of Plato who admits poetry to his commonwealth only so far as it is subsidiary to moral and political education, and who therefore excludes every form of it except hymns and chants and praises of great and good men, or what goes under the general name of didactic poetry. He distinguishes between educational use and aesthetic enjoyment. For the grown man the poet's function is not that of a teacher, or if a teacher, he is so only by accident. The object of poetry, as of all the fine arts, is to produce an emotional delight, a pure and elevated pleasure. In the *Poetics* he writes as the literary critic and the historian of poetry. He is no longer concerned with fine art as an institution which the State recognises, and which should form part of an educational system. His inquiry is into the different forms of poetry,—their origin, their growth, the laws of their structure, their effect upon the mind. He analyses poetical compositions as he might the forms of thought. He seeks to discover what they are in themselves, and how they produce their distinctive effects. The didactic point of view is abandoned. We hear nothing of the direct ethical influence which the several kinds of poetry exert on the spectator or the reader, or of the moral intention of the poet.

In a passage of peculiar interest in ch. xxv. we read, 'The standard of correctness in poetry and politics is not the same, any more than in poetry and any other art.'[1] Aristotle had already insisted that poetical truth and scientific truth are not identical. Poetry is not a metrical version of the facts of medicine, natural science, or history;[2] he now adds that technical inaccuracies in these or other branches of knowledge do not touch the essence of the poetic art.[3] This must be judged by its own laws, its own fundamental assumptions, and not by an alien standard. The observation is extended to the relation of poetry and morality; for the comprehensive phrase 'politics' or 'political science' here, as often, has special reference to ethics. The remark is, doubtless, directed in particular against Plato,[4] whose criticisms of poetry are chiefly from the moral point of view. In the *Republic* allusion is made to the old idea that Homer knows all the arts and all the virtues; he is, therefore, the great educator of the people.

---

[1] *Poet.* xxv. 3, οὐχ ἡ αὐτὴ ὀρθότης ἐστὶν τῆς πολιτικῆς καὶ τῆς ποιητικῆς οὐδὲ ἄλλης τέχνης καὶ ποιητικῆς.

[2] *Poet.* i. 11, ix. 1–2.

[3] *Poet.* xxv. 4 (medicine), 5 (natural history).

[4] Finsler (*Platon und die Aristotelische Poetik*, pp. 163 ff.) disputes this reference; but the words of xxv. 7 and 20 are strongly reminiscent of Plato.

Plato disallows this claim; but while admitting that it would not be fair to question Homer about medicine or any of the arts to which his poems only incidentally refer,[1] he urges that in regard to war, generalship, politics, education, which are the main subjects of the poems, we have a right to ask him, what state was ever better governed by his help. Such a test of poetry Aristotle would reject as involving a confusion of standards. Again, in an earlier book of the *Republic* a still graver censure is passed on epic narrative.[2] The tales of the gods, their battles and dissensions, are condemned for the injurious influence they exercise on character; they are fictions and immoral fictions.[3] So too the cruel and evil deeds ascribed to heroes and demigods are impious and hurtful untruths. On the moral question thus raised Aristotle barely touches in this chapter; his general attitude, however, may be inferred from § 19 (and possibly also from § 8). But on the question of fact, 'true or false,' he says, 'these stories are currently told,' they are the tradition of the people; as such they have their place in poetry.[4]

[1] *Rep.* x. 599 c, τῶν μὲν τοίνυν ἄλλων πέρι μὴ ἀπαιτῶμεν λόγον Ὅμηρον κ.τ.λ.

[2] *Rep.* ii. 377 A–378 E.

[3] The βλαβερά of *Rep.* iii. 391 B is the βλαβερά of *Poet.* xxv. 20; cf. infra, p. 227, note.

[4] *Poet.* xxv. 7. The supposed objection here is "οὐκ ἀληθῆ." These are Plato's very words in *Rep.* ii. 378 B (of the wars of the

Again, personal satire had been condemned on
moral grounds by Plato.[1] Aristotle agrees in this
condemnation, but for a different reason. He ranks
it as an inferior type of art not because it encourages
low scandal or debases character, but because art
ought to represent the general not the particular.[2]
Neither in the definition of tragedy (ch. vi. 2), if
properly understood, nor in the subsequent discussion of it, is there anything to lend countenance
to the view that the office of tragedy is to work
upon men's lives, and to make them better. The
theatre is not the school. The character of the
ideal tragic hero (ch. xiii.) is deduced not from
any ethical ideal of conduct, but from the need
of calling forth the blended emotions of pity and
fear, wherein the proper tragic pleasure resides.[3]
The catastrophe by which virtue is defeated and
villainy in the end comes out triumphant is condemned by the same criterion;[4] and on a similar
principle the prosaic justice, misnamed 'poetical,'
which rewards the good man and punishes the

gods), οὐδὲ γὰρ ἀληθῆ : *Rep.* iii. 391 B (of Achilles dragging Hector
round the tomb of Patroclus), ξύμπαντα ταῦτα οὐ φήσομεν ἀληθῆ
εἰρῆσθαι, and 391 E (of other tales about the offspring of the gods),
οὔθ' ὅσια ταῦτα οὔτ' ἀληθῆ.   See also supra, p. 176.

[1] *Laws* xi. 935 E, ποιητῇ δὴ κωμῳδίας ἢ τινος ἰάμβων ἢ μουσῶν
μελῳδίας μὴ ἐξέστω μήτε λόγῳ μήτε εἰκόνι μήτε θυμῷ μήτε ἄνευ
θυμοῦ μηδαμῶς μηδένα τῶν πολιτῶν κωμῳδεῖν.

[2] *Poet.* ix. 5.

[3] See infra, ch. viii.

[4] *Poet.* xiii. 2.

wicked, is pronounced to be appropriate only to comedy.[1]

Aristotle's critical judgments on poetry rest on aesthetic and logical grounds, they take no direct account of ethical aims or tendencies. He mentions Euripides some twenty times in the *Poetics*, and in the great majority of instances with censure. He points out numerous defects, such as inartistic structure, bad character-drawing, a wrong part assigned to the chorus; but not a word is there of the immoral influence of which we hear so much in Aristophanes. In his praise as little as in his blame does Aristotle look to the moral content of a poem. Sophocles he admires not for the purity of his ethical teaching or for his deep religious intuitions, but for the unity which pervades the structure of his dramas, and the closely linked sequence of parts which work up to an inevitable end. Not that Aristotle would set aside as a matter of indifference the moral content of a poem or the moral character of the author. Nay, they are all-important factors in producing the total impression which has to be made upon the hearer. The matter of literature is life; and tragedy is in a special sense the

---

[1] *Poet.* xiii. 8. Contrast Plato, who would compel the poet to exhibit the perfect requital of vice and virtue (*Laws* ii. 660 E). So in *Rep.* iii. 392 A–B poets are forbidden to say that many wicked men are happy and good men miserable, and are commanded to sing in an opposite strain.

Q

'imitation of life,'[1] of human welfare and human misery ; it is the representation of a sustained action of a great and serious kind, in which character finds for itself outward and energetic expression. This fragment of life is typical and interpretative of the whole. The philosopher in whose theory ethics were woven into the very tissue of life, whose fabric of happiness was reared upon a moral basis, and with whom the inward and spiritual order of things dominated the outward, could not have acquiesced in any rendering of life which assigned to its various elements a perverted place and value. Aristotle does not indeed demand of the poet that he shall set before himself a didactic aim, nor does he test the merit of his performance by the moral truths that are conveyed. His test of excellence is pleasure ; but the aesthetic pleasure produced by any ideal imitation must be a sane and wholesome pleasure, which would approve itself to the better portion of the community.[2] The pleasure he contemplates could not conceivably be derived from a poem which offers low ideals of life and conduct and misinterprets human destiny.[3]

[1] *Poet.* vi. 9.   See infra, p. 336.

[2] See pp. 211–13.

[3] In my first edition I took the passage *Poet.* xxv. 8, περὶ δὲ τοῦ καλῶς ἢ μὴ καλῶς ἢ εἴρηταί τινι ἢ πέπρακται, οὐ μόνον σκεπτέον εἰς αὐτὸ τὸ πεπραγμένον ἢ εἰρημένον βλέποντα κ.τ.λ., as referring to the *morality* of the poetic representation.   But the arguments adduced by Mr. M. Carroll in his valuable Thesis *Aristotle's Poetics c. 25 in the Light of the Homeric Scholia* (Baltimore, 1895), pp.

In ch. xxv. 19 it is declared that the representation of moral depravity finds its only excuse in 'necessity.' The necessity meant is the inner necessity arising out of the structure of a piece. Vice in itself is undesirable even on the stage. But it may be subservient to the plot—one of those things ἃ βούλεται ὁ μῦθος—demanded by the cogent necessity of dramatic motive. Without it there may not be room for the proper play of contrasted character, for its effect upon the outward course of the incidents; in a word, for the due interaction of all the forces which lead to the catastrophe. Gratuitous or motiveless depravity is, however, forbidden : and as an instance of this fault, Menelaus in the *Orestes* of Euripides is cited here.[1] Nothing but the constraining needs of literary art are allowed to override the rules laid down for goodness of character in tragedy.

33–40, prove, I think, that there is an aesthetic not a moral reference here in περὶ δὲ τοῦ καλῶς ἢ μὴ καλῶς, and εἰ σπουδαῖον ἢ φαῦλον. 'Speech or action must be interpreted in the light of all the circumstances—the persons, the occasion, the end it is designed to serve ; and if, from a study of these, the speech or action shows itself to be in accordance with necessity or probability, then its artistic excellence—and this is ever supreme with Aristotle—is assured. Morality enters into consideration only as implied in the aesthetic ideal.' See the quotations given from the Scholia with explanations of Aristotle, pp. 36 ff.

[1] *Poet.* xxv. 19, ὀρθὴ δ' ἐπιτίμησις . . . μοχθηρίᾳ, ὅταν μὴ ἀνάγκης οὔσης μηθὲν χρήσηται . . . τῇ πονηρίᾳ, ὥσπερ ἐν 'Ορέστῃ τοῦ Μενελάου. Cf. xv. 5. Such a representation would be included under the βλαβερά of xxv. 20.

These rules, it must be owned, are too rigorous on their ethical side. It becomes the more necessary to call attention to them here, as we have dwelt with some emphasis on Aristotle's freedom from a narrowly moral, or moralistic, conception of poetry. This freedom, we now see, is subject to certain limitations. Traces of the older prepossession still survive, and linger around a portion of his doctrine.

In chapter ii. of the *Poetics* a broad distinction is drawn between the imitative arts, according as they represent persons morally noble (σπουδαίους opposed to φαύλους), ignoble, or of an intermediate type resembling average humanity (ὁμοίους). Some attempt has been made to empty the words σπουδαίους and φαύλους, and the synonymous expressions in the *Poetics* of any strictly moral content, and to reduce the antithesis to the aesthetic distinction between ideal and vulgar characters. It is indeed true that σπουδαῖος—serving as the adjective of ἀρετή in its widest acceptation,[1] as does φαῦλος of κακία—can denote any one that is good or excellent in his kind or in his special line. Similarly, and with like freedom, it can be applied to any object,

---

[1] *Categ.* 6. 10 b 7, οἷον ἀπὸ τῆς ἀρετῆς ὁ σπουδαῖος· τῷ γὰρ ἀρετὴν ἔχειν σπουδαῖος λέγεται, ἀλλ' οὐ παρωνύμως ἀπὸ τῆς ἀρετῆς : that is, there is no adjective formed from the noun ἀρετή : σπουδαῖος does duty for it. Cf. *Top.* v. 3. 131 b 2, where the ἴδιον ἀρετῆς is ὃ τὸν ἔχοντα ποιεῖ σπουδαῖον.

animate or inanimate.[1] In its reference to a person, the particular sphere of his excellence is expressed by a limiting phrase or adverbial addition (σπουδαῖός τι or περί τι), or by the agreement of the adjective with some noun indicating the range of its application (σπουδαῖος νομοθέτης, κιθαριστής and the like).[2] But when the word is used as the epithet of a man as such, without any qualifying reference to occupation, profession, or function, we must take it to mean morally 'good.'[3] Aristotle seems bent on making it plain, here at the outset, that the ethical sense is that which he intends. The parenthetic remark in § 1 shows that the comprehensive ideas summed up in ἀρετή and κακία as applied to morals are covered by the contrasted terms σπουδαίους and φαύλους.[4] After illustrations drawn from various forms of art, the chapter ends with the statement that 'comedy aims at representing men as worse, tragedy as better than in actual life.'[5] Consistent herewith is the observation in

[1] In Poet. v. 5, τραγῳδίας σπουδαίας καὶ φαύλης is 'good or bad tragedy' in the purely aesthetic sense.

[2] e.g. Nic. Eth. i. 6. 1098 a 11, κιθαριστοῦ μὲν γὰρ τὸ κιθαρίζειν, σπουδαίου δὲ τὸ εὖ.

[3] Nic. Eth. ix. 4. 1166 a 12, ἔοικε γὰρ . . . μέτρον ἑκάστῳ ἡ ἀρετὴ καὶ ὁ σπουδαῖος εἶναι. x. 6. 1176 b 25, καὶ τίμια καὶ ἡδέα ἐστὶ τὰ τῷ σπουδαίῳ τοιαῦτα ὄντα. So passim.

[4] Poet. ii. 1, σπουδαίους ἢ φαύλους εἶναι (τὰ γὰρ ἤθη σχεδὸν ἀεὶ τούτοις ἀκολουθεῖ μόνοις, κακίᾳ γὰρ καὶ ἀρετῇ τὰ ἤθη δια φέρουσι πάντες).

[5] Is βούλεται (Poet. ii. 4) a limiting expression, leaving room for

ch. v. 4, that epic poetry agrees with tragedy as
being a μίμησις σπουδαίων : and again the requirement of ch. xv. that the characters (ἤθη)
shall be χρηστά,[1]—once more 'good' in the ethical
sense, and barely to be distinguished from σπουδαῖα.

Aristotle, then, starts from what was, so far as
we know, the unquestioned assumption of his time,
—that the primary distinction between higher and
lower forms of art depended on the different types
of moral character represented by them. The
same view is reflected everywhere in Plato. In
the *Laws* the taste of the judges (κριταί) at the
theatrical competitions is commented on adversely.
They ought to be the instructors, they are the mere
disciples of the theatre. Their influence reacts
upon the poets. Consequently the audience ' when
they *ought to be hearing of characters morally
better than their own,* and receiving a higher
pleasure, are affected in an entirely opposite
manner.'[2] Again, the objects that music 'imitates'

the admission under certain circumstances of a vicious character in
tragedy ? Cf. πειρᾶται in v. 4.

[1] Not 'well marked'—the impossible interpretation put upon
it by Dacier, Bossu, Metastasio, and others—nor, in a merely
aesthetic sense, 'elevated.' The moral meaning is here again not
to be evaded. So in xv. 1 a χρηστὸν ἦθος depends on a χρηστὴ
προαίρεσις, which is equivalent to σπουδαία προαίρεσις of *Nic.
Eth.* vi. 2. 1139 a 25, and ἐπιεικὴς προαίρεσις of *Nic. Eth.* vii. 11.
1152 a 17. In xv. 8 ἐπιεικής is not perceptibly different from
the preceding χρηστός.

[2] *Laws* ii. 659 c, δέον γὰρ αὐτοὺς ἀεὶ βελτίω τῶν αὑτῶν ἠθῶν

are 'the characters of men better or worse,'[1]—a distinction verbally the same as in the *Poetics* ch. ii.

Yet Aristotle, while using the traditional phrases, is feeling after some more satisfactory and vital distinction. The very instances he adduces to illustrate his meaning show that the moral formula is strained to the point of breaking. The characters of Homer (§ 5) are 'better' (βελτίους) than those of ordinary reality, or than those who figure in epic parody, not solely or chiefly through superior virtue, but by powers of willing and feeling, doing and thinking, which raise them above the common herd of men. The example drawn from painting suggests a like conclusion. Three contemporary painters of an earlier date are mentioned, each typical of a certain mode of artistic treatment. 'Polygnotus depicted men as nobler (κρείττους) than they are, Pauson as less noble (χείρους), Dionysius drew them true to life (ὁμοίους).'[2] Evidently these differences do not

ἀκούοντας βελτίω τὴν ἡδονὴν ἴσχειν, νῦν αὐτοῖς δρῶσι πᾶν τοὐναντίον ξυμβαίνει.

[1] *Laws* vii. 798 D, τὰ περὶ τοὺς ῥυθμοὺς καὶ πᾶσαν μουσικήν ἐστι τρόπων μιμήματα βελτιόνων καὶ χειρόνων ἀνθρώπων. Similarly dancing *Laws* vii. 814 E.

[2] *Poet.* ii. 2. Here Polygnotus is spoken of as a portrayer of good ἤθη, in vi. 11 he is a good portrayer of ἤθη, ἀγαθὸς ἠθογράφος, as opposed to Zeuxis. Cf. *Pol.* v. (viii.) 5. 1340 a 36, δεῖ μὴ τὰ Παύσωνος θεωρεῖν τοὺς νέους, ἀλλὰ τὰ Πολυγνώτου κἂν εἴ τις ἄλλος τῶν γραφέων ἢ τῶν ἀγαλματοποιῶν ἐστιν ἠθικός.

correspond to purely ethical distinctions. Roughly we may say that idealistic treatment is exemplified in Polygnotus, realistic in Dionysius, and the tendency to caricature in Pauson. His own examples might have led Aristotle to discard the moral formula, and to seek elsewhere the differentiating marks of artistic representation. As it is, his precise thought is not difficult to discover. Obviously, a perfect art does not, in his view, imply characters of faultless virtue. The sketch of the ideal tragic hero in ch. xiii. 3–4 itself precludes such a notion. Another decisive passage is ch. xv. 8. Defective characters—those, for instance, who are irascible or indolent (ὀργίλοι καὶ ῥᾴθυμοι)—may be ennobled (ἐπιεικεῖς ποιεῖν) by poetic treatment. One of the examples given is the Achilles of Homer, whose leading defect is a passionate temperament, and who would, doubtless, be placed among the ὀργίλοι.[1] Such a character, poetically idealised, conforms to the conditions of goodness (χρηστὰ ἤθη) prescribed in this chapter. Even without these express indications we might draw some such inference from a comparison of the phrase μίμησις σπουδαίων (ch. v. 4) applied to epic and tragic poetry, with the description of comedy in ch. v. 1 as a

---

[1] See Bywater, *Journal of Philology*, xiv. 27, p. 48. The words παράδειγμα σκληρότητος are rightly, I think, bracketed by him.

μίμησις φαυλοτέρων μέν, οὐ μέντοι κατὰ πᾶσαν κακίαν,
'an imitation of characters of a lower type, not
however, in the full sense of the word, bad.' The
badness which comedy delineates is not coexten-
sive with moral badness. It is explained to be
that specific form of badness which consists in an
ugliness or deformity of character that is ludicrous.
A similar qualification of the kind of goodness that
is required in the higher forms of poetry, might
naturally be inferred. The phrase μίμησις σπουδαίων
would thus imply a restrictive clause, οὐ μέντοι κατὰ
πᾶσαν ἀρετήν, 'but not, in the full sense of the word,
good.' This missing qualification is, however,
partly supplied by the passages of ch. xiii. and
ch. xv. above referred to.

The result, then, arrived at is briefly this.
According to Aristotle, the characters portrayed by
epic and tragic poetry have their basis in moral
goodness; but the goodness is of the heroic order.
It is quite distinct from plain, unaspiring virtue.
It has nothing in it common or mean. Whatever
be the moral imperfections in the characters, they
are such as impress our imagination, and arouse
the sense of grandeur: we are lifted above the
reality of daily life. To go farther would be to part
company with Aristotle: he would hardly allow that
there may be a dignity, an elevation of character,
which saves even vice from being contemptible,
and brings it under the higher requirements of

art. Had he wished to mark the distinctively
aesthetic quality of characters grand or elevated,
he might have used such expressions as μέγα τι,
or οὐδὲν φαῦλον, or οὐδὲν ἀγεννὲς πράττειν (φρονεῖν).
The grandeur, however, which he demands is a
moral grandeur. Greatness cannot take the place
of goodness. Satan, though he were never 'less
than archangel ruined,' would be admitted into
an epic poem only as one of the rare exceptions
already noted.[1]

Aristotle, in respect to the delineation of
character, is still on the border-land between morals
and aesthetics. Mere goodness does not satisfy
him : something, he feels, must be infused into
it which does not belong to the prosaic world.
But what that is, he does not tell us. He has no
adequate perception of the wide difference that
separates moral and poetical excellence of character.
When he comes to define tragedy, he makes, it
would appear, a step in advance, though at the
cost of logical consistency. In the definition
given in ch. vi., tragedy no longer μιμεῖται σπουδαίους but is a μίμησις πράξεως σπουδαίας. Here
there seems to be a transition to a different sense of
the word σπουδαῖος. Logically, it ought, no doubt,
to bear the same meaning—'good,' 'noble'—as
applied to the tragic action, that it bore in the
previous divisions of poetry as applied to the

[1] See p. 227.

persons whom tragedy represents.[1] But Aristotle imperceptibly glides into the meaning 'serious,' 'elevated,' 'grand,'—a meaning which the word readily admits of in reference to a *thing*, such as a πρᾶξις, though it could not be so used of a *person* without the addition of other words or of a qualifying context. This new shade of meaning, which enters into the definition, is required in order to differentiate the tragic action from the γελοία πρᾶξις of Comedy.[2] Aristotle passes lightly from μιμεῖται σπουδαίους to μίμησις πράξεως σπουδαίας, as if the one expression were merely the equivalent of the other. He can hardly have realised the important bearings of the change by which the word σπουδαῖος is freed from the limited moral reference which attaches to it in ch. ii. If in his observations upon character (τὰ ἤθη) in ch. xv. he had followed out the line of thought which the adjective here suggests as applied to the tragic action, he might have made a notable improvement on his aesthetic theory. In pursuance of this idea, tragedy would have demanded not mere goodness of character (χρηστὰ ἤθη), but a greatness or elevation corresponding to the grandeur of the action.

Before we dismiss the phrase μίμησις σπουδαίων,

[1] Mr. R. P. Hardie in *Mind*, vol. iv. No. 15, argues that this meaning must be retained in the definition.

[2] See p. 241.

we may for a moment glance aside to notice
one curious chapter in its history. The French
critics of the seventeenth and eighteenth centuries
generally took σπουδαῖοι to mean persons of high
rank. So strange a perversion of language is hardly
credible, and yet it admits of easy explanation. A
Roman rule, itself founded on Greek writers subsequent to Aristotle, had prescribed that the fundamental difference between tragedy and comedy is to
be sought in the fact, that kings and heroes are the
actors in tragedy, ordinary citizens in comedy.[1] This
purely outward distinction won acceptance with
many distinguished scholars.[2] When the *Poetics*
came to be received as the guide and canon of
criticism in France, Aristotelian authority was
eagerly sought for this among other literary
traditions. With an entire disregard of linguistic
usage, the phrase μίμησις σπουδαίων was—in default
of any other—seized on as affording the desired
sanction. The Abbé d'Aubignac in his book *La
Pratique du Théâtre*, which long continued to be
the text-book of French dramatic writers, declares

---

[1] The grammarian Diomedes says : 'Tragoedia est heroicae
fortunae in adversis comprehensio, a Theophrasto ita definita est,
τραγῳδία ἐστὶν ἡρωϊκῆς τύχης περίστασις. . . . Comoedia est
privatae civilisque fortunae sine periculo vitae comprehensio, apud
Graecos ita definita, κωμῳδία ἐστὶν ἰδιωτικῶν πραγμάτων ἀκίν-
δυνος περιοχή. . . . Comoedia a tragedia differt, quod in tragoedia
heroes, duces, reges, in comoedia humiles atque privatae personae.'

[2] e.g. Robortelli, Maggi, Scaliger (Spingarn, pp. 63, 69).

that 'tragedy represents the life of princes,' while 'comedy serves to depict the actions of the people.'[1] Dacier goes even to greater lengths in his note on μίμησις σπουδαίων. 'It is not necessary,' he says, 'that the action which affords matter for an Epic poem be illustrious and important in itself; on the contrary, it may be very ordinary or common; but it must be so by the quality of the persons who act. Thus Horace says plainly, "Res gestae regumque ducumque." This is so true that the most notable action of a citizen can never be made the subject of an epic poem, when the most indifferent one of a king or general of an army will be such, and always with success.'[2] In all this misapprehension there is just one grain of solid fact. Aristotle does undoubtedly hold that the chief actors in tragedy ought to be illustrious by birth and position. The narrow and trivial life of obscure persons cannot give scope for a great and significant action, one of tragic consequence. But nowhere

---

[1] *La Pratique du Théâtre* bk. ii. ch. 10, 'La Tragédie représentoit la vie des Princes. . . . La Comédie servoit à dépeindre les actions du peuple.'

[2] Dacier on *Poet.* v. 4, note 17 (Trans. London, 1705). Cf. note 9 on ch. xiii., 'Tragedy, as Epic poem, does not require that the action which it represents should be great and important in itself. It is sufficient that it be tragical, the names of the persons are sufficient to render it magnificent; which for that very reason are all taken from those of the greatest fortune and reputation. The greatness of these eminent men renders the action great, and their reputation makes it credible and possible.'

does he make outward rank the distinguishing feature of tragic as opposed to comic representation. Moral nobility is what he demands; and this—on the French stage, or at least with French critics— is transformed into an inflated dignity, a courtly etiquette and decorum, which seemed proper to high rank. The instance is one of many in which literary critics have wholly confounded the teaching of Aristotle.

But to return from this digression. Aristotle, as our inquiry has shown, was the first who attempted to separate the theory of aesthetics from that of morals. He maintains consistently that the end of poetry is a refined pleasure. In doing so he severs himself decisively from the older and more purely didactic tendency of Greece. But in describing the means to the end, he does not altogether cast off the earlier influence. The aesthetic representation of character he views under ethical lights, and the different types of character he reduces to moral categories. Still he never allows the moral purpose of the poet or the moral effects of his art to take the place of the artistic end. If the poet fails to produce the proper pleasure, he fails in the specific function of his art. He may be good as a teacher, but as a poet or artist he is bad.

Few of Aristotle's successors followed out this way of thinking; and the prevailing Greek tradition that the primary office of poetry is to convey

ethical teaching was carried on through the schools
of Greek rhetoric till it was firmly established in
the Roman world. The Aristotelian doctrine as
it has been handed down to modern times has
again in this instance often taken the tinge of
Roman thought, and been made to combine in
equal measure the *utile* with the *dulce*. Sir
Philip Sidney, for example, who in his *Apologie
for Poetrie* repeatedly states that the end of
poetry is 'delightful teaching,' or 'to teach and
to delight,' has no suspicion that he is following the
Ars Poetica of Horace rather than that of Aristotle.
The view of Sidney was that of the Elizabethan
age in general.[1] It was a new departure when
Dryden wrote in the spirit of Aristotle : 'I am
satisfied if it [verse] cause delight; for delight is
the chief if not the only end of poesy : instruction
can be admitted but in the second place, for poesy
only instructs as it delights.'[2]

[1] This too was the prevailing view at the Renaissance, but
Castelvetro (1570) forms a notable exception. He goes even
beyond Aristotle in maintaining that poetry is intended, not only
to please, but to please even the vulgar mob (see Spingarn, pp.
55–56).

[2] *Defence of an Essay of Dramatic Poetry.*

CHAPTER VI

THE FUNCTION OF TRAGEDY

ARISTOTLE's definition of tragedy [1] runs thus :—
'Tragedy is an imitation of an action that is serious, complete, and of a certain magnitude; in language embellished with each kind of artistic ornament, the several kinds being found in separate parts of the play; in the form of action,[2] not of narrative; through pity and fear effecting the proper *katharsis*, or purgation, of these [3] emotions.'

---

[1] *Poet.* vi. 2, ἔστιν οὖν τραγῳδία μίμησις πράξεως σπουδαίας καὶ τελείας μέγεθος ἐχούσης, ἡδυσμένῳ λόγῳ χωρὶς ἑκάστῳ (codd. ἑκάστου) τῶν εἰδῶν ἐν τοῖς μορίοις, δρώντων καὶ οὐ δι' ἀπαγγελίας, δι' ἐλέου καὶ φόβου περαίνουσα τὴν τῶν τοιούτων παθημάτων κάθαρσιν.

[2] On δρώντων see p. 335, note 2.

[3] τῶν τοιούτων has given rise to much misunderstanding. It is not 'all such emotions' or 'these and suchlike emotions,' but by a frequent and idiomatic use 'the aforesaid emotions,' namely, pity and fear. It is with these, and these only, that tragedy is concerned throughout the *Poetics*. There is probably, as Reinkens (p. 161) says, a delicate reason here for the preference of τῶν τοιούτων over the demonstrative. The ἔλεος and φόβος of the definition, as will be evident in the sequel, are the aesthetic emotions of pity and fear, those which are awakened by the tragic representation. τῶν

240

The 'several kinds of embellishment' are in the next paragraph explained to be verse and song; verse without music being employed in the dialogue, lyrical song in the choral parts. Tragedy is hereby distinguished from Nomic and Dithyrambic poetry, which use the combined embellishments throughout.[1]

From this definition it appears first, that the *genus* of tragedy is Imitation. This it has in common with all the fine arts.

Next, it is differentiated from comedy as being a μίμησις πράξεως σπουδαίας, an imitation of an action that is neither γελοία nor φαύλη, neither ludicrous nor morally trivial. It is concerned with a serious end, namely εὐδαιμονία,[2]—that well-being which is the true end of life. It is a picture of human destiny in all its significance. No one English word completely renders σπουδαίας. The translation ' noble,' which has the merit of applying to the characters as well as to the action, yet suggests too much a purely moral quality, while at the same time it does not adequately bring out the implied antithesis to comedy. *Grave* and *great* —these are the two ideas contained in the word. Many of the older critics, missing the true import

τοιούτων παθημάτων are the emotions of pity and fear which belong to real life. The use of τούτων instead of τοιούτων might have suggested that the feelings were identically the same.

[1] Cf. *Poet.* i. 10.   [2] *Poet.* vi. 9.

R

of σπουδαίας, transfer the meaning which they ought to have found here to the later words, μέγεθος ἐχούσης, of the definition. These—as is plain from Aristotle's explanation in ch. vii.—refer to the actual length of the poem. Addison,[1] who does not stand alone in this view, includes under them the greatness or significance of the action (which is in fact denoted by σπουδαίας) and also the internal length or duration of the action, of which Aristotle here says nothing.

Further, tragedy is differentiated in form from Epic poetry as being dramatic, not narrative.

The remainder of the definition describes the specific effect, the proper function (ἔργον) of tragedy,—namely, to produce a certain kind of *katharsis*. It would be a curious study to collect the many and strange translations that have been given of this definition in the last three hundred years. Almost every word of it has been misinterpreted in one way or another. But after all it contains only two real difficulties. The one lies in the clause concerning the 'several kinds of embellishment.' Fortunately, however, Aristotle has interpreted this for us himself; otherwise it would doubtless have called forth volumes

---

[1] *Spectator* No. 267 : 'Aristotle by the greatness of the action does not only mean that it should be great in its nature but also in its duration, or in other words that it should have a due length in it, as well as what we properly call greatness.'

of criticism.   The other and more fundamental difficulty relates to the meaning of the *katharsis*.[1] Here we seek in vain for any direct aid from the *Poetics*.

A great historic discussion has centred round the phrase.   No passage, probably, in ancient literature has been so frequently handled by commentators, critics, and poets, by men who knew Greek, and by men who knew no Greek. A tradition almost unbroken through centuries found in it a reference to a moral effect which tragedy produces through the 'purification of the passions.'   What the precise effect is, and what are the passions on which tragedy works, was very variously interpreted.   Corneille, Racine,[2] Lessing,

---

[1] Since the first edition of this book was published, a complete account of the uses of the word κάθαρσις has been given by Susemihl and Hicks (*Politics of Aristotle*) in a valuable note, pp. 641–656, 'κάθαρσις as an aesthetic term' being treated pp. 650 ff. In a few details the explanation of the word in its reference to tragedy differs from what will be found in the following pages, but I have not seen reason to alter what had been written.

[2] Racine states his own purpose as a dramatic writer in the Preface to *Phèdre*: 'Ce que je puis assurer c'est que je n'en ai point fait où la vertu soit plus mise en jour que dans celle-ci ; les moindres fautes y sont sévèrement punies : la seule pensée du crime y est regardée avec autant d'horreur que le crime même ; les faiblesses de l'amour y passent pour de vraies faiblesses.   Les passions n'y sont présentées aux yeux que pour montrer tout le désordre dont elles sont cause ; et le vice y est peint partout avec des couleurs qui en font connaître et haïr la difformité.   C'est là proprement le but que tout homme qui travaille pour le public doit se proposer ; et c'est ce que les premiers poètes tragiques avaient en vue sur

each offered different solutions, but all agreed in assuming the purely ethical intention of the drama. Goethe protested; but his own most interesting theory[1] is for linguistic reasons quite impossible, nor does it accord with much else that is contained in the *Poetics*. In 1857 a pamphlet by Jacob Bernays[2] reopened the whole question, and gave a new direction to the argument. His main idea had been forestalled by Italian critics of the Renaissance;[3] afterwards it fell into oblivion; a similar theory was independently struck out by H. Weil in 1847,[4] but it attracted little notice till Bernays set it forth in detail.

toute chose. Leur théâtre était une école où la vertu n'était pas moins bien enseignée que dans les écoles des philosophes. Aussi Aristote a bien voulu donner des règles du poème dramatique ; et Socrate, le plus sage des philosophes, ne dédaignait pas de mettre la main aux tragédies d'Euripide. Il serait à souhaiter que nos ouvrages fussent aussi solides et aussi pleins d'utiles instructions que ceux de ces poètes.'

[1] Published in *Nachlese zu Aristoteles Poetik*, 1826. His translation of the definition is worth recording, if only for its errors. ' Die Tragödie ist die Nachahmung einer bedeutenden und abgeschlossenen Handlung, die eine gewisse Ausdehnung hat und in anmuthiger Sprache vorgetragen wird, und zwar von abgesonderten Gestalten, deren jede ihre eigene Rolle spielt, und nicht erzählungsweise von einem Einzelnen ; nach einem Verlauf aber von Mitleid und Furcht, mit Ausgleichung solcher Leidenschaften ihr Geschäft abschliesst.' The εἴδη of the definition here become the dramatic characters and the μόρια are the parts they play !

[2] Republished in 1880 in the volume *Zwei Abhandlungen über die Aristotelische Theorie des Drama* (Berlin).

[3] See infra, p. 247, note.

[4] In his paper at the Philological Congress of Bâle, 1847,

Bernays, with equal learning and literary skill, maintained that *katharsis* here is a medical metaphor,[1] 'purgation,' and denotes a pathological effect on the soul analogous to the effect of medicine on the body. The thought, as he interpreted it, may be expressed thus. Tragedy excites the emotions of pity and fear—kindred emotions that are in the breasts of all men—and by the act of excitation affords a pleasurable relief. The feelings called forth by the tragic spectacle are not indeed permanently removed, but are quieted for the time, so that the system can fall back upon its normal course. The stage, in fact, provides a harmless and pleasurable outlet for instincts which demand satisfaction, and which can be indulged here more fearlessly than in real life.

Plato, it must be remembered, in his attack upon the drama had said that 'the natural hunger after sorrow and weeping' which is kept under

reprinted in *Verhandlungen der zehnten Versammlung deutscher Philologen in Basel* (pp. 131–141).

[1] The three chief meanings of the word, (1) the medical, (2) the religious or liturgical, 'lustratio' or 'expiatio,' and (3) the moral, 'purificatio,' are sometimes difficult to keep apart. In Plato *Soph.* 230 c the medical metaphor is prominent. Refutation (ἔλεγχος) is a mode of κάθαρσις. Before knowledge can be imparted internal obstacles must be removed (τὰ ἐμποδίζοντα ἐκβαλεῖν). In *Crat.* 405 A doctors and soothsayers both use ἡ κάθαρσις καὶ οἱ καθαρμοί. In *Phaedo* 69 c the medical sense of κάθαρσις shades off into the religious, the transition being effected by the mention of καθαρμός. In *Timaeus* 89 B–C the φαρμακευτικὴ κάθαρσις is discussed.

control in our own calamities, is satisfied and delighted by the poets.[1] ' Poetry feeds and waters the passions instead of starving them.'[2] Through its tearful moods it enfeebles the manly temper; it makes anarchy in the soul by exalting the lower elements over the higher, and by dethroning reason in favour of feeling. Aristotle held that it is not desirable to kill or to starve the emotional part of the soul, and that the regulated indulgence of the feelings serves to maintain the balance of our nature. Tragedy, he would say, is a vent for the particular emotions of pity and fear. In the first instance, it is true, its effect is not to tranquillise but to excite. It excites emotion, however, only to allay it. Pity and fear, artificially stirred, expel the latent pity and fear which we bring with us from real life, or at least, such elements in them as are disquieting. In the pleasurable calm which follows when the passion is spent, an emotional cure has been wrought.[3]

---

[1] *Rep.* x. 606 A, τὸ βίᾳ κατεχόμενον τότε ἐν ταῖς οἰκείαις ξυμφοραῖς καὶ πεπεινηκὸς τοῦ δακρῦσαί τε καὶ ἀποδύρασθαι ἱκανῶς καὶ ἀποπλησθῆναι, φύσει ὂν τοιοῦτον οἷον τούτων ἐπιθυμεῖν, τότ᾽ ἐστὶ τοῦτο τὸ ὑπὸ τῶν ποιητῶν πιμπλάμενον καὶ χαῖρον. Cf. 606 B, λογίζεσθαι γάρ, οἶμαι, ὀλίγοις τισὶ μέτεστιν, ὅτι ἀπολαύειν ἀνάγκη ἀπὸ τῶν ἀλλοτρίων εἰς τὰ οἰκεῖα. θρέψαντα γὰρ ἐν ἐκείνοις ἰσχυρὸν τὸ ἐλεεινὸν οὐ ῥᾴδιον ἐν τοῖς αὑτοῦ πάθεσι κατέχειν.

[2] *Rep.* x. 606 D, τρέφει γὰρ ταῦτα ἄρδουσα, δέον αὐχμεῖν.

[3] Zeller (*Phil. der Gr.*) thinks it unimportant whether the medical or the religious use of the *katharsis* is primarily intended,

It is worth noting, as has been pointed out by Bernays, and before him by Twining, that Milton had already apprehended something of the true import of Aristotle's words. In adopting the pathological theory of the effect of tragedy he was, as has been more recently shown, following in the wake of Italian criticism.[1] In his preface to *Samson Agonistes* he writes :

'Tragedy, as it was anciently composed, hath been ever held the gravest, moralest, and most profitable of all other poems; therefore said by Aristotle to be of power, by raising pity and fear, or terrour, to purge the mind of those and such-like passions; that is to temper or reduce them to just measure with a kind of delight stirred up by reading or seeing those passions well imitated.

as in either case the word bears a sense far removed from the original metaphor. But the distinctive method of relief is different in the two cases. The medical *katharsis* implies relief following upon previous excitation. There is first a ταραχή or κίνησις, then κάθαρσις or ἔκκρισις. This is of vital moment for the argument. If we lose sight of the metaphor, the significance of the process is missed.

[1] Mr. Spingarn in his interesting volume already mentioned, *Literary Criticism in the Renaissance* (New York, 1899), quotes from Minturno, *L' Arte Poetica*, p. 77 (Venice, 1564), the following passage : 'As a physician eradicates, by means of poisonous medicine, the perfervid poison of disease which affects the body, so tragedy purges the mind of its impetuous perturbations by the force of these emotions beautifully expressed in verse.' See also an article by Professor Bywater in *Journal of Philology*, xxvii. 54 (1900), with quotations from Scaino's Italian paraphrase of Aristotle's *Politics* (Rome, 1578).

Nor is Nature herself wanting in her own effects to make good his assertion, for so, in physick, things of melancholick hue and quality are used against melancholy, sour against sour, salt to remove salt humours.' In other words tragedy is a form of homoeopathic treatment, curing emotion by means of an emotion like in kind, but not identical.[1]

Aristotle, it would seem, was led to this remarkable theory by observing the effect of certain melodies upon a form of religious ecstasy, or, as the Greeks said, 'enthusiasm,' such as is rarely seen in this country, and whose proper home is in the East. The persons subject to such transports were regarded as men possessed by a god, and were taken under the care of the priesthood. The treatment prescribed for them was so far homoeopathic in character, that it consisted in applying movement to cure movement, in soothing the internal trouble of the mind by a wild and restless music. The passage in the *Politics*[2] in which Aristotle de-

---

[1] Cf. the closing lines of *Samson Agonistes* :

His servants he, with new acquist
Of true experience, from this great event
With peace and consolation hath dismissed,
And calm of mind, all passion spent.

[2] *Pol.* v. (viii.) 7. 1341 b 32—1342 a 15. For ἐνθουσια-σμός as a morbid state to be cured by music see Aristides Quintilianus (circa 100 A.D.) περὶ μουσικῆς ii. p. 157, quoted and explained in Döring p. 332, cf. p. 261. There the healing process is denoted by καταστέλλεσθαι, ἀπομειλίττεσθαι, ἐκκαθαίρεσθαι.

scribes the operation of these tumultuous melodies is the key to the meaning of *katharsis* in the *Poetics*. Such music is expressly distinguished by Aristotle from the music which has a moral effect or educational value (παιδείας ἕνεκεν). It differs, again, from those forms of music whose end is either relaxation (πρὸς ἀνάπαυσιν) or the higher aesthetic enjoyment (πρὸς διαγωγήν).[1] Its object is *katharsis*. It is a physical stimulus which provides an outlet for religious fervour. Patients, who have been subjected to this process, 'fall back,' to quote Aristotle's phrase, 'into their normal state, as if they had undergone a medical or purgative treatment.'[2] The emotional result is a 'harmless joy.'[3]

The music employed is called a μίμησίς τις (i.e. of the enthusiasm), which shows that the musical κάθαρσις is a kind of homoeopathic cure.

[1] Susemihl (*Pol.*, Susemihl and Hicks pp. 638 ff.) maintains that κάθαρσις is not a distinct end of music, but a means either to διαγωγή or ἀνάπαυσις, and would alter the text of 1341 b 40 accordingly. I hold with Zeller (*Phil. der Gr.*) that a comparison of the two passages *Pol.* v. (viii.) 5. 1339 b 11, and 7. 1341 b 36 leads to the conclusion that Aristotle recognises *four* different uses of music.

[2] *Pol.* v. (viii.) 7. 1342 a 10, καθισταμένους ὥσπερ ἰατρείας τυχόντας καὶ καθάρσεως. The ὥσπερ marks the introduction of the metaphor : ἰατρεία is explained by the more specific term κάθαρσις. καθίστασθαι is also a *verb. prop.* in medicine, either of the patient relapsing into his natural state or of the disease settling down (cf. Döring p. 328). In the same passage of the *Politics* 1342 a 14 the medical metaphor is kept up in κουφίζεσθαι ('obtain relief') μεθ᾽ ἡδονῆς.

[3] *Pol.* v. (viii.) 7. 1342 a 15, ὁμοίως δὲ καὶ τὰ μέλη τὰ

The homoeopathic cure of morbid 'enthusiasm' by means of music, was, it may be incidentally observed, known also to Plato.[1] In a passage of the *Laws*,[2] where he is laying down rules for the management of infants, his advice is that infants should be kept in perpetual motion, and live as if they were always tossing at sea. He proceeds to compare the principle on which religious ecstasy is cured by a strain of impassioned music with the method of nurses, who lull their babies to sleep not by silence but by singing, not by holding them quiet but by rocking them in their arms. Fear, he thinks, is in each case the emotion that has to be subdued,—a fear caused by something that has gone wrong within. In each case the method of cure is the same; an external agitation (κίνησις) is employed to calm and counteract an internal.

καθαρτικὰ παρέχει χαρὰν ἀβλαβῆ τοῖς ἀνθρώποις. Susemihl here accepts Sauppe's emendation πρακτικὰ for καθαρτικὰ (see note ad loc.). But the text may well stand if we regard 1342 a 11–15 (ταὐτὸ δὴ τοῦτο . . . κουφίζεσθαι μεθ' ἡδονῆς) as parenthetic, and as alluding not to the musical κάθαρσις but to the κάθαρσις of ἔλεος and φόβος in tragedy. Then the words ὁμοίως δὲ καὶ τὰ μέλη τὰ καθ. mark the return to the musical κάθαρσις. (Newman, *Pol.* vol. iii. 567, retains καθαρτικά, making the sense, 'cathartic melodies as distinguished from the sacred melodies.') For the phrase ἀβλαβὴς ἡδονή see supra, p. 205, and *Nic. Eth.* vii. 14. 1154 b 4.

[1] In *Rep.* viii. 560 D certain religious rites (probably musical) produce an effect on the soul analogous to that of kathartic medicine on the body : τούτων δέ γέ που κενώσαντες καὶ καθήραντες τὴν τοῦ κατεχομένου τε ὑπ' αὐτῶν καὶ τελουμένου ψυχὴν μεγάλοισι τέλεσι κ.τ.λ.

[2] *Laws* vii. 790–1.

But Plato recognised the principle only as it applied to music and the useful art of nursing. Aristotle, with his generalising faculty and his love of discovering unity in different domains of life, extended the principle to tragedy and hints at even a wider application of it. In the *Politics*, after explaining the action of the musical *katharsis*, he adds that 'those who are liable to pity and fear, and, in general, persons of emotional temperament pass through a like experience ; . . . they all undergo a *katharsis* of some kind and feel a pleasurable relief.'[1]

The whole passage of the *Politics* here referred to is introduced by certain important prefatory words : 'What we mean by *katharsis* we will now state in general terms (ἁπλῶς) ; hereafter we will explain it more clearly (ἐροῦμεν σαφέστερον) in our treatise on Poetry.'[2] But in the *Poetics*, as we have it, the much desired explanation is wanting ;

---

[1] *Pol.* v. (viii.) 7. 1342 a 11, ταὐτὸ δὴ τοῦτο ἀναγκαῖον πάσχειν καὶ τοὺς ἐλεήμονας καὶ τοὺς φοβητικοὺς καὶ τοὺς ὅλως παθητικούς, . . . καὶ πᾶσι γίγνεσθαί τινα κάθαρσιν καὶ κουφίζεσθαι μεθ' ἡδονῆς. Here τινα κάθαρσιν implies that the *katharsis* in all cases is not precisely of the same kind. Hence we see the force of the article in the definition of tragedy, τὴν τῶν τοιούτων παθημάτων κάθαρσιν, *the specific katharsis*, that which is appropriate to these emotions. Nothing but a very dubious interpretation of *Poetics* xxvi. 7 supports the assumption of many commentators that epic poetry excites precisely the same emotions as tragedy.

[2] *Pol.* v. (viii.) 7. 1341 b 39.

there appears to be a gap in the text at this most
critical point. We are therefore driven back upon
the *Politics* itself as our primary authority. The
tone of the passage and particular expressions show
two things plainly—first, that there the term is
consciously metaphorical; secondly, that though its
technical use in medicine was familiar, the metaphorical application of it was novel and needed
elucidation. Moreover, in the words last quoted,
—'all undergo a *katharsis* of some kind,'—it is
pretty plainly implied that the *katharsis* of pity
and fear in tragedy is analogous to, but not identical
with, the *katharsis* of 'enthusiasm.'

Now, Bernays transferred the *katharsis* of the
Politics almost without modification of meaning to
the definition of tragedy. He limited its reference
to the simple idea of an emotional relief, a pleasurable vent for overcharged feeling.[1] This idea, no
doubt, almost exhausts the meaning of the phrase
as it is used in the *Politics*. It also expresses, as

---

[1] Keble's theory of poetry—of the ' vis medica poeticae,' as he
calls it—may well be compared. It is expounded in his *Praelec-
tiones Academicae*, and also in a review of Lockhart's *Life of Scott*,
which has been republished in Keble's *Occasional Papers and
Reviews*. The most important pages of the review are quoted in
Prickard (*Aristotle on the Art of Poetry*), pp. 102 sqq. Dr. Lock
(*Biography of Keble*) sums up the theory thus : ' Poetry is essentially
for him a relief to the poet, a relief for overcharged emotion. It is
the utterance of feelings which struggle for expression, but which
are too deep for perfect expression at all, much more for expression
in the language of daily life.' Having pointed out that Keble's

has been above explained, one important aspect of the tragic *katharsis*. But the word, as taken up by Aristotle into his terminology of art, has probably a further meaning. It expresses not only a fact of psychology or of pathology, but a principle of art. The original metaphor is in itself a guide to the full aesthetic significance of the term. In the medical language of the school of Hippocrates it strictly denotes the removal of a painful or disturbing element from the organism, and hence the purifying of what remains, by the elimination of alien matter.[1] Applying this to tragedy we observe

theory rests mainly on the *Poetics* he adds : 'But Aristotle writes as a critic and is thinking of the effect upon the readers ; Keble, as a poet, dwells primarily on the effect upon the poet, and secondarily on that upon the readers.'

[1] κένωσις in the Hippocratic writings denotes the entire removal of healthy but surplus humours (τῶν οἰκείων ὅταν ὑπερβάλλῃ τῷ πλήθει) ; κάθαρσις the removal of τὰ λυποῦντα and the like,—'of qualitatively alien matter' (τῶν ἀλλοτρίων κατὰ ποιότητα, Galen). Thus Galen xvi. 105, κένωσις ὅταν ἅπαντες οἱ χυμοὶ ὁμοτίμως κενῶνται, κάθαρσις δὲ ὅταν οἱ μοχθηροὶ κατὰ ποιότητα : xvi. 106, ἔστι μὲν οὖν ἡ κάθαρσις τῶν λυπούντων κατὰ ποιότητα κένωσις : cf. [Plat.] "Οροι 415 D, κάθαρσις ἀπόκρισις χειρόνων ἀπὸ βελτιόνων. Plato was familiar with this idea. In *Soph.* 226 D, καθαρμός is the proper name for 'separation' of a certain kind,— τῆς καταλειπούσης μὲν τὸ βέλτιον διακρίσεως, τὸ δὲ χεῖρον ἀποβαλλούσης. Cf. *Rep.* viii. 567 c (of tyrants who make a purge of all the best elements in the state), καλόν γε, ἔφη, καθαρμόν. Ναί, ἦν δ' ἐγώ, τὸν ἐναντίον ἢ οἱ ἰατροὶ τὰ σώματα· οἱ μὲν γὰρ τὸ χείριστον ἀφαιροῦντες λείπουσι τὸ βέλτιστον, ὁ δὲ τοὐναντίον.

καθαίρειν admits of a double construction. It takes—

(i.) An accusative of the disturbing element which is expelled or *purged away* : e.g. τὸ περίττωμα, τὰ λυποῦντα, τὰ

that the feelings of pity and fear in real life contain
a morbid and disturbing element. In the process
of tragic excitation they find relief, and the morbid
element is thrown off. As the tragic action progresses, when the tumult of the mind, first roused,
has afterwards subsided, the lower forms of emotion
are found to have been transmuted into higher and
more refined forms. The painful element in the
pity and fear of reality is purged away; the
emotions themselves are purged. The curative
and tranquillising influence that tragedy exercises
follows as an immediate accompaniment of the
transformation of feeling. Tragedy, then, does

ἀλλότρια. The idea here uppermost is the negative one
of removing a foreign substance.

(ii.) An accusative of the object which is *purged* by this process
of removal : e.g. τὸν ἄνθρωπον, τὸ σῶμα, τὴν ψυχήν, τὰ
παθήματα. The idea here uppermost is the positive one
of purifying and clarifying the organism, organ, or portion
of the system from which the morbid matter is expelled.

Corresponding to this two-fold use of the accusative with the
verb we have a twofold use of the genitive with the noun
κάθαρσις :—

(i.) κάθαρσις τῶν λυπούντων, τοῦ περιττώματος, τῶν ἀλλοτρίων
and the like. To this class belongs the expression in Plato
Phaedo 69 C, κάθαρσις τῶν τοιούτων πάντων (sc. τῶν
ἡδονῶν), ' the purging away of these pleasures,' the pleasures
being regarded as not merely containing a morbid element,
but as being in themselves morbid; cf. Plut. *De Inim.
Util.* 10. 91 F, τῶν παθῶν τούτων ποιούμενος εἰς τοὺς
ἐχθροὺς ἀποκαθάρσεις, 'expending (or discharging) these
feelings upon his enemies' (in order to rid himself from
them).

(ii.) κάθαρσις ('purgation of') τοῦ ἀνθρώπου, τοῦ σώματος, τῶν

more than effect the homoeopathic cure of certain passions. Its function on this view is not merely to provide an outlet for pity and fear, but to provide for them a distinctively aesthetic satisfaction, to purify and clarify them by passing them through the medium of art.

But what is the nature of this clarifying process? Here we have no direct reply from Aristotle. He has, however, left us some few hints, some materials, out of which we may perhaps reconstruct the outlines of his thought.

The idea of *katharsis* implies, as we have seen, the expulsion of a painful and disquieting element, —τὰ λυποῦντα. Now pity and fear in their relation to real life are by Aristotle reckoned among τὰ λυποῦντα. Each of them is, according to the

παθημάτων, where the genitive expresses the person or thing on which the κάθαρσις takes effect.

In the definition of tragedy the genitive seems to fall under (ii.). The κάθαρσις τῶν τοιούτων παθημάτων is 'the purgation or purification of the pity and fear' of real life by the expulsion of the morbid element. This element is—it is argued above—a certain pain or λύπη, which again arises from the selfishness which clings to these emotions in actual life.

The interpretation of Bernays, 'the alleviating discharge of these emotions,' implies that the genitive falls under (i.). According to this interpretation the cure is effected by the total expulsion of the emotions, instead of by their clarification.

The double meaning of the accusative with καθαίρειν is already foreshadowed in Homer, who employs a double accusative, of the thing and of the person : *Iliad* xvi. 667—

εἰ δ' ἄγε νῦν, φίλε Φοῖβε, κελαινεφὲς αἷμα κάθηρον
ἐλθὼν ἐκ βελέων Σαρπηδόνα.

definition in the *Rhetoric*, a form of pain (λύπη τις).
Fear Aristotle defines to be 'a species of pain or
disturbance arising from an impression of impending
evil which is destructive or painful in its nature.'[1]
Moreover, the evil is near not remote, and the
persons threatened are ourselves. Similarly, pity
is 'a sort of pain at an evident evil of a destructive
or painful kind in the case of somebody who does
not deserve it, the evil being one which we might
expect to happen to ourselves or to some of our
friends, and this at a time when it is seen to
be near at hand.'[2] Pity, however, turns into
fear where the object is so nearly related to
us that the suffering seems to be our own.[3]
Thus pity and fear in Aristotle are strictly
correlated feelings. We pity others where under
like circumstances we should fear for ourselves.[4]

---

[1] Welldon's Trans. of *Rhet.* ii. 5. 1382 a 21, ἔστω δὴ φόβος
λύπη τις ἢ ταραχὴ ἐκ φαντασίας μέλλοντος κακοῦ φθαρτικοῦ
ἢ λυπηροῦ.

[2] Ib. ii. 8. 1385 b 13, ἔστω δὴ ἔλεος λύπη τις ἐπὶ φαινομένῳ
κακῷ φθαρτικῷ καὶ λυπηρῷ τοῦ ἀναξίου τυγχάνειν, ὃ κἂν αὐτὸς
προσδοκήσειεν ἂν παθεῖν ἢ τῶν αὐτοῦ τινά, καὶ τοῦτο ὅταν πλησίον
φαίνηται. Cf. 1386 a 28, ἐπεὶ δ' ἐγγὺς φαινόμενα τὰ πάθη ἐλεεινά
ἐστιν, τὰ δὲ μυριοστὸν ἔτος γενόμενα ἢ ἐσόμενα οὔτε ἐλπίζοντες
οὔτε μεμνημένοι ἢ ὅλως οὐκ ἐλεοῦσιν ἢ οὐχ ὁμοίως, κ.τ.λ. Stress
is laid on the object of pity being ἀνάξιος, e.g. in 1386 b 5–16,
Poet. xiii. 2 (infra, p. 259, note).

[3] Ib. ii. 8. 1386 a 17, ἐλεοῦσι δὲ τούς τε γνωρίμους, ἂν μὴ
σφόδρα ἐγγὺς ὦσιν οἰκειότητι· περὶ δὲ τούτους ὥσπερ περὶ αὐτοὺς
μέλλοντας ἔχουσιν.

[4] Ib. ii. 8. 1386 a 27, ὅσα ἐφ' αὑτῶν φοβοῦνται, ταῦτα ἐπ'

Those who are incapable of fear are incapable also of pity.[1]

Thus in psychological analysis fear is the primary emotion from which pity derives its meaning. Its basis is a self-regarding instinct; it springs from the feeling that a similar suffering may happen to ourselves. It has in it a latent and potential fear. But it is a wrong inference to say, as Lessing does,[2] that fear is always an ingredient in pity,— that we fear for ourselves whenever we feel pity for another. The Aristotelian idea simply is that we would fear for ourselves if we were in the position of him who is the object of our pity. The possible fear may never become actual, but the strength of the pity is not thereby impaired. Still the tacit reference to self makes pity, as generally described in the *Rhetoric*, sensibly different from the pure instinct of compassion, the unselfish sympathy with others'

ἄλλων γιγνόμενα ἐλεοῦσιν. ii. 5. 1382 b 26, ὡς δ' ἁπλῶς εἰπεῖν, φοβερά ἐστιν ὅσα ἐφ' ἑτέρων γιγνόμενα ἢ μέλλοντα ἐλεεινά ἐστιν.

[1] *Rhet.* ii. 8. 1385 b 19, διὸ οὔτε οἱ παντελῶς ἀπολωλότες ἐλεοῦσιν· οὐδὲν γὰρ ἂν ἔτι παθεῖν οἴονται, πεπόνθασι γάρ· οὔτε οἱ ὑπερευδαιμονεῖν οἰόμενοι, ἀλλ' ὑβρίζουσιν. Cf. ii. 5. 1383 a 9.

[2] Lessing, *Hamb. Dram.* Trans. (Bohn) pp. 409, 415, 436. The view that the mention of fear in the definition is superfluous, fear being implicit in pity, is strangely inconsistent with the position he takes up against Corneille, that pity and fear are the tragic emotions, pity alone being insufficient.

distress, which most modern writers understand by pity.[1]

The conditions of dramatic representation, and above all the combined appeal which tragedy makes to both feelings, will considerably modify the emotions as they are known in actual reality. Pity in itself undergoes no essential change. It has still for its object the misfortunes of 'one who is undeserving' (ὁ ἀνάξιος); which phrase, as interpreted by Aristotle (*Poet.* ch. xiii.), means not a wholly innocent sufferer, but rather a man who meets with sufferings beyond his deserts. The emotion of fear is profoundly altered when it is transferred from the real to the imaginative world. It is no longer the direct apprehension of misfortune impending over our own life. It is not caused by the actual approach of danger. It

---

[1] Cf. Mendelssohn, 'Pity is a complex emotion composed of love for an object and displeasure caused by its misery.' Schopenhauer held pity to be at the root of all true morality. Aristotle himself in the *Rhetoric* marks a distinction between the disinterested and generous ἔλεος of the young and the self-regarding ἔλεος of the old: ii. 12. 1389 b 8, the young are ἐλεητικοὶ διὰ τὸ πάντας χρηστοὺς καὶ βελτίους ὑπολαμβάνειν . . . ὥστε ἀνάξια πάσχειν ὑπολαμβάνουσιν αὐτούς. ii. 13. 1390 a 19, ἐλεητικοὶ δὲ καὶ οἱ γέροντές εἰσιν, ἀλλ᾽ οὐ· διὰ ταὐτὸ τοῖς νέοις· οἱ μὲν γὰρ διὰ φιλανθρωπίαν, οἱ δὲ δι᾽ ἀσθένειαν· πάντα γὰρ οἴονται ἐγγὺς εἶναι αὐτοῖς παθεῖν. For a similar disinterested compassion compare the striking lines of Euripides, *Electra* 294-5·—

ἔνεστι δ᾽ οἶκτος ἀμαθίᾳ μὲν οὐδαμοῦ
σοφοῖσι δ᾽ ἀνδρῶν.

is the sympathetic shudder we feel for a hero whose character in its essentials resembles our own.[1]

[1] *Poet.* xiii. 2, . . . οὔτε ἔλεον οὔτε φόβον, ὁ μὲν γὰρ περὶ τὸν ἀνάξιόν ἐστιν δυστυχοῦντα, ὁ δὲ περὶ τὸν ὅμοιον, ἔλεος μὲν περὶ τὸν ἀνάξιον, φόβος δὲ περὶ τὸν ὅμοιον. I now take this passage in its obvious grammatical sense, ' we feel pity for τὸν ἀνάξιον (cf. quotations from *Rhetoric*, p. 256 note 2); we feel fear for τὸν ὅμοιον.' At different moments of a play pity or fear will be uppermost according as the course of the action brings home to us more vividly the undeserved nature of the suffering or the moral resemblance between ourselves and the hero.

Thus the φόβος of tragedy is not, like the φόβος of the *Rhetoric* and of real life, a fear for ourselves. But the fact that fear is inspired by the sufferings of ὁ ὅμοιος indicates that even tragic fear is in the last analysis traced back psychologically to a self-regarding instinct. The awakening of fear as distinct from mere pity depends on the close identification of the hero and ourselves.

In Ed. 2 I inclined to the view that the φόβος of tragedy, like the φόβος of real life, is *primarily* fear for ourselves. On that assumption περί must bear a different sense in the two clauses : ' we feel pity for τὸν ἀνάξιον : we feel fear *in connexion with* τὸν ὅμοιον,' i.e. his sufferings awaken a fear for ourselves who share his humanity. The change of meaning is undeniably harsh, though certain considerations were offered which mitigate the difficulty.

Some distinguished scholars have explained the difference between tragic fear and pity otherwise. Tragic fear, they maintain, is the fear felt for the hero while the misfortune is still impending ; pity, on the other hand, is awakened by events in the present or the past. The reasons against reducing the difference merely to one of time are :—

(1) Fear in Aristotle is not distinguished from pity by a reference to future time. In *Rhet.* ii. 5. 1382 b 26, quoted p. 256 note 4, μέλλοντα shows that we may pity a man for what is about to happen. Cf. also *Rhet.* ii. 8. 1386 a 34, ἢ ὡς μέλλον ἢ ὡς γεγονός.

(2) If pity and fear in tragedy are only two sides of the same feeling, why distinguish them as sharply as is done in *Poet.* xi. 4 (ἢ ἔλεον ἢ φόβον) : xiv. 3 (ποῖα οὖν δεινὰ ἢ ποῖα οἰκτρὰ φαίνεται ;) ?

The tragic sufferer is a man like ourselves
(ὅμοιος);[1] and on this inner likeness the effect of
tragedy, as described in the *Poetics*, mainly hinges.
Without it our complete sympathy would not be
enlisted. The resemblance on which Aristotle insists
is one of moral character. His hero (*Poet.* ch. xiii) is
not a man of flawless perfection, nor yet one of consummate villainy; by which we must not understand
that he has merely average or mediocre qualities.
He rises, indeed, above the common level in moral
elevation and dignity, but he is not free from
frailties and imperfections.[2] His must be a rich
and full humanity, composed of elements which
other men possess, but blended more harmoniously
or of more potent quality. So much human
nature must there be in him that we are able in

And why again insist, as Aristotle does, on the *combined* effect?
In any play with a tragic ending, in which the incidents work up
towards a catastrophe, pity at the event implies, on this theory, a
preceding fear : the separate mention of fear might be dispensed with.

(3) Pity, says Aristotle, is περὶ τὸν ἀνάξιον, fear περὶ τὸν
ὅμοιον. But why should the mere distinction of time make a
distinction of character necessary? Why, that is, must the hero
be ἀνάξιος if we are to feel for him in present misfortune, but
ὅμοιος if we are to feel for him under impending calamity?

[1] In *Poet.* xiii. 2 (see last note) φόβος is περὶ τὸν ὅμοιον, while
ἔλεος is περὶ τὸν ἀνάξιον. In *Rhet.* ii. 8. 1386 a 24, τοὺς ὁμοίους
ἐλεοῦσιν κατὰ ἡλικίαν, κατὰ ἤθη, κατὰ ἕξεις, κατὰ ἀξιώματα, κατὰ
γένη, the reason being added that such similarity of conditions
suggests fear for ourselves. It may be noted that the 'likeness' of
the *Rhetoric* includes various external forms of resemblance which
are outside the scope of *Poet.* xiii.

[2] See infra, ch. viii.

some sense to identify ourselves with him, to make
his misfortunes our own. At the same time he is
raised above us in external dignity and station.
He is a prince or famous man who falls from a
height of greatness. Apart from the impressive
effect of the contrast so presented, there is a gain
in the hero being placed at an ideal distance from
the spectator. We are not confronted with outward conditions of life too like our own. The
pressure of immediate reality is removed; we are
not painfully reminded of the cares of our own
material existence. We have here part of the
refining process which the tragic emotions undergo within the region of art. They are disengaged
from the petty interests of self, and are on the
way to being universalised.

The tragic fear, though modified in passing
under the conditions of art, is not any languid
emotion. It differs, indeed, from the crushing
apprehension of personal disaster. In reading or
witnessing the *Oedipus Tyrannus* we are not
possessed with a fear that we may be placed in
circumstances similar to those of Oedipus, or be
overtaken by the same calamities.[1] Yet a thrill
runs through us, a shudder of horror or of vague

---

[1] Corneille (Discours ii. *De la Tragédie*) argues from the
absence of any such dread that the *Oedipus Tyrannus* excites pity
only, and not fear. But if fear is rightly understood, it is *par
excellence* a tragedy of fear.

foreboding.¹ The feeling is immediate and un-
reflective. The tension of mind, the agonised
expectation with which we await the impending
catastrophe, springs from our sympathy with the
hero in whose existence we have for the time
merged our own.² The events as they pass before
us seem almost as if we were directly concerned.
We are brought into a mood in which we feel that
we too are liable to suffering.³ Yet the object of
dread is not a definite evil threatening us at close
quarters. In the spectacle of another's errors or
misfortunes, in the shocks and blows of circum-
stance, we read the 'doubtful doom of human
kind.' The vividness with which the imagination
pictures unrealised calamity produces the same
intensity of impression as if the danger were at
hand.⁴ The true tragic fear becomes an almost

¹ *Poet.* xiv. 1, δεῖ γὰρ καὶ ἄνευ τοῦ ὁρᾶν οὕτω συνεστάναι τὸν
μῦθον, ὥστε τὸν ἀκούοντα τὰ πράγματα γινόμενα καὶ φρίττειν
καὶ ἐλεεῖν ἐκ τῶν συμβαινόντων· ἅπερ ἂν πάθοι τις ἀκούων τὸν
τοῦ Οἰδίπου μῦθον. Cf. Plat. *Rep.* iii. 387 c, ὅσα . . . φρίττειν
δὴ ποιεῖ . . . τοὺς ἀκούοντας (of epic stories).

² Cf. Plat. *Rep.* x. 605 D, ἐνδόντες ἡμᾶς αὐτοὺς ἑπόμεθα ξυμ-
πάσχοντες.

³ Cf. *Rhet.* ii. 5. 1383 a 8, ὥστε δεῖ τοιούτους παρασκευάζειν,
ὅταν ᾖ βέλτιον τὸ φοβεῖσθαι αὐτούς, ὅτι τοιοῦτοί εἰσιν οἷοι
παθεῖν· καὶ γὰρ ἄλλοι μείζους ἔπαθον.

⁴ This fact as the result of scenic representation is noted by
Aristotle with regard to ἔλεος, *Rhet.* ii. 8. 1386 a 31, ἀνάγκη
τοὺς συναπεργαζομένους σχήμασι καὶ φωναῖς καὶ ἐσθῆσι (αἰσθήσει
Aᶜ) καὶ ὅλως ἐν ὑποκρίσει ἐλεεινοτέρους εἶναι· ἐγγὺς γὰρ
ποιοῦσι φαίνεσθαι τὸ κακὸν πρὸ ὀμμάτων ποιοῦντες, ἢ ὡς

impersonal emotion, attaching itself not so much to this or that particular incident, as to the general course of the action which is for us an image of human destiny. We are thrilled with awe at the greatness of the issues thus unfolded, and with the moral inevitableness of the result. In this sense of awe the emotions of fear and pity are blended.

We can now see that the essential tragic effect depends on maintaining the intimate alliance between pity and fear. According to Aristotle, not pity alone should be evoked by tragedy, as many moderns have held;[1] not pity *or* fear, for which Corneille argued;[2] not pity and 'admiration,' which is the modification under which the Aristotelian

μέλλον ἢ ὡς γεγονός. (For τοὺς συναπ. σχήμ. cf. *Poet.* xvii. 1.) It may be remarked that there is no allusion in the *Rhetoric* to φόβος as awakened in the drama.

[1] e.g. Schiller in his essay *On Tragic Art.* Elsewhere in his letters and other writings he sometimes speaks of fear as well as pity; but his fear is not the Aristotelian fear; it is merely the apprehension felt while the terrible event is still in the future, a fear which becomes pity after the event.

In ancient tragedy fear was a powerful and necessary factor. In modern tragedy—with the exception of Shakespeare—pity predominates over fear. In the eighteenth century fear was almost entirely eliminated.

[2] Corneille, Discours ii. *De la Tragédie.* He thinks he is supported by Aristotle in this view. ' Il suffit selon lui (Aristote) de l'un des deux pour faire cette purgation, avec cette différence toutefois, que la pitié n'y peut arriver sans la crainte, et que la crainte peut y parvenir sans la pitié.' But, as has been already shown, there may be pity without fear in the Aristotelian sense.

phrase finds currency in the Elizabethan writers.[1]
The requirement of Aristotle is pity *and* fear.[2]   He
would no doubt allow that in some tragedies the
primary and predominant impression is fear, in
others pity. He would probably go farther and say
that an inferior tragedy may excite one only of the
two emotions generally called tragic.[3]   But the full
tragic effect requires the union of the two, nor can

---

[1] e.g. Sir Philip Sidney, *An Apologie for Poetrie* : ' The high and
excellent Tragedy . . . that with stirring the affects of admiration
and commiseration teacheth the uncertainty of the world. . . .'

[2] The twofold emotion is recognised in Plato, *Phaedr.* 268 c,
τί δ' εἰ Σοφοκλεῖ αὖ προσελθὼν καὶ Εὐριπίδῃ τις λέγοι, ὡς
ἐπίσταται περὶ σμικροῦ πράγματος ῥήσεις παμμήκεις ποιεῖν καὶ
περὶ μεγάλου πάνυ σμικράς, ὅταν τε βούληται οἰκτράς, καὶ
τοὐναντίον αὖ φοβερὰς καὶ ἀπειλητικάς κ.τ.λ.   *Ion* 535 E,
καθορῶ γὰρ ἑκάστοτε αὐτοὺς ἄνωθεν ἀπὸ τοῦ βήματος κλαίοντάς
τε καὶ δεινὸν ἐμβλέποντας καὶ συνθαμβοῦντας τοῖς λεγομένοις.
In *Rep.* iii. 387 B–D, pity and fear are both mentioned among the
effects produced by ' Homer and the other poets,' pity being caused
by sympathy with others who experience τὰ φοβερά.   In *Rep.* x.
605 D – 606 B pity alone is specified as awakened by ' Homer or
one of the tragedians.'

[3] In the passages where ' pity or fear ' occurs instead of
' pity and fear ' the disjunctive particle retains its proper force.
In *Poet.* xi. 4 the reference is to the effect of a special kind of
ἀναγνώρισις combined with περιπέτεια rather than to the total
impression of the tragedy : ἡ γὰρ τοιαύτη ἀναγνώρισις καὶ
περιπέτεια ἢ ἔλεον ἕξει ἢ φόβον, οἵων πράξεων ἡ τραγῳδία
μίμησις ὑπόκειται.   Again in xiii. 2 we read, οὐ γὰρ φοβερὸν
οὐδὲ ἐλεεινὸν τοῦτο: οὔτε γὰρ φιλάνθρωπον οὔτε ἐλεεινὸν οὔτε
φοβερόν ἐστι: οὔτε ἔλεον οὔτε φόβον (ἔχοι ἄν): οὔτε ἐλεεινὸν
οὔτε φοβερὸν ἔσται τὸ συμβαῖνον: i.e. none of the plots here
referred to has a single element of tragedy, much less can the full
tragic effect be thus produced.

the distinctive function of tragedy as *katharsis* be discharged otherwise.

In the phrase of the anonymous fragment, ' On Comedy,'[1] which appears to contain some genuine Aristotelian tradition, ' tragedy seeks to blend fear with pity in due proportion' (ἡ τραγῳδία συμμετρίαν θέλει ἔχειν τοῦ φόβου). Pity, as Bernays explains, through its kinship with fear, is preserved from eccentricity and sentimentalism. Fear, through its alliance with pity, is divested of a narrow selfishness, of the vulgar terror which is inspired by personal danger.[2] A self-absorbed anxiety or alarm makes us incapable of sympathy with others. In this sense ' fear casts out pity.'[3] Tragic fear, though it may send an inward shudder through the blood, does not paralyse the mind or stun the

---

[1] Printed by Vahlen and Susemihl at the end of their editions of the *Poetics*, and commented on in detail by Bernays, pp. 142 sqq.

[2] Voltaire quotes with approval the observation of Saint-Evremont that in French tragedy tenderness takes the place of pity and surprise the place of fear. ' It cannot be denied,' he says, ' that Saint-Evremont has put his finger on the secret sore of the French theatre.' The idea of fear, again, was frequently that of mere terror. Thus in France in the seventeenth century the conception of the tragic had come to be the union of the sentimental and the horrible.

[3] *Rhet.* ii. 8. 1386 a 21, τὸ γὰρ δεινὸν ἕτερον τοῦ ἐλεεινοῦ καὶ ἐκκρουστικὸν τοῦ ἐλέου, added as a comment on the story told in Herod. iii. 14. Cf. ii. 8. 1385 b 33, οὐ γὰρ ἐλεοῦσιν οἱ ἐκπεπληγμένοι διὰ τὸ εἶναι πρὸς τῷ οἰκείῳ πάθει. *King Lear*, Act v. Sc. 3, ' This judgment of the heavens, that makes us tremble, | Touches us not with pity.'

sense, as does the direct vision of some impending calamity. And the reason is that this fear, unlike the fear of common reality, is based on an imaginative union with another's life. The spectator is lifted out of himself. He becomes one with the tragic sufferer, and through him with humanity at large. One effect of the drama, said Plato, is that through it a man becomes many, instead of one; it makes him lose his proper personality in a pantomimic instinct, and so prove false to himself. Aristotle might reply: True; he passes out of himself, but it is through the enlarging power of sympathy. He forgets his own petty sufferings. He quits the narrow sphere of the individual. He identifies himself with the fate of mankind.

We are here brought back to Aristotle's theory of poetry as a representation of the universal. Tragedy exemplifies with concentrated power this highest function of the poetic art. The characters it depicts, the actions and fortunes of the persons with whom it acquaints us, possess a typical and universal value. The artistic unity of plot, binding together the several parts of the play in close inward coherence, reveals the law of human destiny, the causes and effects of suffering. The incidents which thrill us are intensified in their effect, when to the shock of surprise is added the discovery that each thing as it has happened could

not be otherwise; it stands in organic relation to
what has gone before. There is a combination of
the inevitable and the unexpected.[1] Pity and fear
awakened in connexion with these larger aspects
of human suffering, and kept in close alliance with
one another, become universalised emotions. What
is purely personal and self-regarding drops away.
The spectator who is brought face to face with
grander sufferings than his own experiences a
sympathetic ecstasy, or lifting out of himself. It
is precisely in this transport of feeling, which
carries a man beyond his individual self, that the
distinctive tragic pleasure resides. Pity and fear
are purged of the impure element which clings to
them in life. In the glow of tragic excitement
these feelings are so transformed that the net
result is a noble emotional satisfaction.

The *katharsis*, viewed as a refining process,
may have primarily implied no more to Aristotle
than the expulsion of the disturbing element,
namely, the pain,[2] which enters into pity and fear
when aroused by real objects. The mere fact of
such an expulsion would have supplied him with

---

[1] *Poet.* ix. 11, where the point lies in the union of παρὰ τὴν
δόξαν with δι' ἄλληλα.

[2] Cf. Plut. *Symp. Qu.* iii. 8 (in reference to the musical *katharsis*),
ὥσπερ ἡ θρηνῳδία καὶ ὁ ἐπιτήδειος αὐλὸς ἐν ἀρχῇ πάθος κινεῖ καὶ
δάκρυον ἐκβάλλει, προάγων δὲ τὴν ψυχὴν εἰς οἶκτον οὕτω κατὰ
μικρὸν ἐξαιρεῖ καὶ ἀναλίσκει τὸ λυπητικόν—a passage
which is also instructive as to the *kathartic* method generally.

a point of argument against Plato, in addition to the main line of reply above indicated.[1] In the *Philebus* Plato had described the mixed (μιχθεῖσαι) or impure (ἀκάθαρτοι) pleasures as those which have in them an alloy of pain; and the pleasure of tragedy was stated to be of the mixed order.[2] The Aristotelian theory asserts that the emotions on which tragedy works do indeed in real life contain a large admixture of pain, but that by artistic treatment the painful element is expelled or overpowered.

In the foregoing pages, however, we have carried the analysis a step farther, and shown how and why the pain gives way to pleasure. The sting of the pain, the disquiet and unrest, arise from the selfish element which in the world of reality clings to these emotions. The pain is expelled when the taint of egoism is removed. If it is objected that the notion of universalising the emotions and ridding them of an intrusive element that belongs to the sphere of the accidental and individual, is a modern conception, which we have no warrant for attributing to Aristotle, we may reply that if this is not what Aristotle meant, it is at least the

[1] See pp. 245–6.

[2] *Phil.* 50 B, μηνύει δὴ νῦν ὁ λόγος ἡμῖν ἐν θρήνοις τε καὶ ἐν τραγῳδίαις, μὴ τοῖς δράμασι μόνον ἀλλὰ τῇ τοῦ βίου ξυμπάσῃ τραγῳδίᾳ καὶ κωμῳδίᾳ, λύπας ἡδοναῖς ἅμα κεράννυσθαι, καὶ ἐν ἄλλοις δὴ μυρίοις. Cf. 48 A, τάς γε τραγικὰς θεωρήσεις, ὅταν ἅμα χαίροντες κλάωσι.

natural outcome of his doctrine; to this conclusion his general theory of poetry points.

Let us assume, then, that the tragic *katharsis* involves not only the idea of an emotional relief, but the further idea of the purifying of the emotions so relieved. In accepting this interpretation we do not ascribe to tragedy a direct moral purpose and influence. Tragedy, according to the definition, acts on the feelings, not on the will. It does not make men better, though it removes certain hindrances to virtue. The refining of passion under temporary and artificial excitement is still far distant from moral improvement. Aristotle would probably admit that indirectly the drama has a moral influence in enabling the emotional system to throw off some perilous stuff, certain elements of feeling, which, if left to themselves, might develop dangerous energy and impede the free play of those vital functions on which the exercise of virtue depends. The excitation of noble emotions will probably in time exert an effect upon the will. But whatever may be the indirect effect of the repeated operation of the *katharsis*, we may confidently say that Aristotle in his definition of tragedy is thinking, not of any such remote result, but of the immediate end of the art, of the aesthetic function it fulfils.

It is only under certain conditions of art that

the homoeopathic cure of pity and fear by similar emotions is possible. Fear cannot be combined with the proper measure of pity unless the subject-matter admits of being universalised. The dramatic action must be so significant, and its meaning capable of such extension, that through it we can discern the higher laws which rule the world. The private life of an individual, tragic as it may be in its inner quality, has never been made the subject of the highest tragedy. Its consequences are not of far-reaching importance; it does not move the imagination with sufficient power. Within the limited circle of a *bourgeois* society a great action is hardly capable of being unfolded. A parochial drama, like that of Ibsen, where the hero struggles against the cramping conditions of his normal life, sometimes with all the ardour of aspiring hope, more often in the spirit of egoistic self-assertion which mistakes the measure of the individual's powers, can hardly rise to tragic dignity. We are conscious of a too narrow stage, of a confined outlook, and of squalid motives underlying even conduct which is invested with a certain air of grandeur. The play moves on the flat levels of existence. The characters are unequal to the task imposed on them; and though we may find room for human pity in witnessing failure and foiled hopes, still it is commonplace and gloomy failure. No one can question the skill in dramatic

construction and the stirring interest of Ibsen's
plays, but the depressing sense of the trivial cannot
be shaken off, and the action always retains traces
of an inherent littleness which hinders the awakening of tragic fear,—still more of that solemnity and
awe which is the final feeling left by genuine
tragedy.   Some quality of greatness in the situation
as well as in the characters appears to be all but
indispensable, if we are to be raised above the
individual suffering and experience a calming
instead of a disquieting feeling at the close.   The
tragic *katharsis* requires that suffering shall be
exhibited in one of its comprehensive aspects ; that
the deeds and fortunes of the actors shall attach
themselves to larger issues, and the spectator himself be lifted above the special case and brought
face to face with universal law and the divine plan
of the world.

In order that an emotion may be not only
excited but also allayed,—that the tumult of the
mind may be resolved into a pleasurable calm,—
the emotion stirred by a fictitious representation
must divest itself of its purely selfish and material
elements, and become part of a new order of things.
It is perhaps for this reason that love in itself
is hardly a tragic motive.   The more exclusive and
self-absorbed a passion is, the more does it resist
kathartic treatment.   The feelings excited must
have their basis in the permanent and objective

realities of life, and be independent of individual caprice or sentiment. In the ordinary novel the passion of love in its egoistic and self-centred interest does not admit of being generalised, or its story enlarged into a typical and independent action. The rare cases where a love story is truly tragic go to prove the point which is here enforced. In *Romeo and Juliet* the tragedy does not lie merely in the unhappy ending of a tale of true love. Certain other conditions, beyond those which contribute to give a dramatic interest, are required to produce the tragic effect. There is the feud of the two houses, whose high place in the commonwealth makes their enmity an affair of public concern. The lovers in their new-found rapture act in defiance of all external obligations. The elemental force and depth of their passion bring them into collision with the fabric of the society to which they belong. Their tragic doom quickly closes in upon them. Yet even in death the consequences of their act extend beyond the sphere of the individual. Over the grave of their love the two houses are reconciled.

Tragedy, as it has been here explained, satisfies a universal human need. The fear and pity on and through which it operates are not, as some have maintained, rare and abnormal emotions. All men, as Aristotle says,[1] are susceptible to them,

[1] *Pol.* v. (viii.) 7. 1342 a 5–7.

some persons in an overpowering measure. For the modern, as for the ancient world, they are still among the primary instincts; always present, if below the surface, and ready to be called into activity.[1] The Greeks, from temperament, circumstances, and religious beliefs, may have been more sensitive to their influence than we are, and more likely to suffer from them in a morbid form. Greek tragedy, indeed, in its beginnings was but a wild religious excitement, a bacchic ecstasy. This aimless ecstasy was brought under artistic law. It was ennobled by objects worthy of an ideal emotion. The poets found out how the transport of human pity and human fear might, under the excitation of art, be dissolved in joy, and the pain escape in the purified tide of human sympathy.

[1] Cf. *Some Aspects of the Greek Genius*, Ed. 3, pp. 154–5.

CHAPTER VII

'UNITY of plot does not,' says Aristotle,[1] 'as some persons think, consist in the unity of the hero. For infinitely various are the incidents in one man's life which cannot be reduced to unity; and so, too, there are many actions of one man out of which we cannot make one action. Hence the error, as it appears, of all poets who have composed a Heracleid, a Theseid, or other poems of the kind. They imagine that as Heracles was one man, the story of Heracles must also be a unity.' Such is the principle laid down for tragedy in ch. viii., and Homer is there held up as the true model even to the tragedian. Precisely the same principle is affirmed of epic poetry in ch. xxiii., where it is added that unity of time, like unity of person, does not of itself bind events into a unity.[2] Not only epics like the *Achilleid* of Statius offend against this fundamental principle, but also many modern dramas in which the life and character of the hero become

---

[1] *Poet.* viii. 1.   [2] *Poet.* xxiii. 1–4.

the ultimate motive, and a biographical or historical interest takes the place of the dramatic interest.

The first requirement of a tragedy is Unity of Action.[1] Unity in Aristotle is the principle of limit, without which an object loses itself in the ἄπειρον, the region of the undefined, the indeterminate, the accidental. By means of unity the plot becomes individual and also intelligible. The greater the unity, the more perfect will it be as a concrete and individual thing; at the same time it will gain in universality and typical quality.[2]

The Unity of the tragic action is, again, an organic unity, an inward principle which reveals itself in the form of an outward whole.[3] It is opposed indeed to plurality, but not opposed to the idea of manifoldness and variety; for simple as it is in one sense, it admits of all the complexity of vital phenomena. The whole (ὅλον) in which it is manifested is complete (τέλειον)[4] in its parts, the

---

[1] For the meaning of πρᾶξις, 'action,' see pp. 123 and 334 sqq.

[2] In *Prob.* xviii. 9. 017 b 8 sqq., the pleasure derived from a Unity is ultimately resolved into the fact that it is γνωριμώτερον : διὰ τί ποτε τῶν ἱστοριῶν ἥδιον ἀκούομεν τῶν περὶ ἓν συνεστηκυιῶν ἢ τῶν περὶ πολλὰ πραγματευομένων ; ἢ διότι τοῖς γνωριμωτέροις μᾶλλον προσέχομεν καὶ ἥδιον αὐτῶν ἀκούομεν· γνωριμώτερον δέ ἐστι τὸ ὡρισμένον τοῦ ἀορίστου. τὸ μὲν οὖν ἓν ὥρισται, τὰ δὲ πολλὰ τοῦ ἀπείρου μετέχει.

[3] *Poet.* ch. vii. (τὸ ὅλον), ch. viii. (τὸ ἕν): supra pp. 186 sqq.

[4] In the definition of tragedy (*Poet.* vi. 2) we have τελείας πράξεως, in vii. 2 τελείας καὶ ὅλης πράξεως. So in xxiii. 1 epic

parts themselves being arranged in a fixed order
(τάξις),[1] and structurally related so that none can
be removed, none transposed, without disturbing
the organism.[2] Within the single and complete
action which constitutes the unity of a tragedy,
the successive incidents are connected together
by an inward and causal bond,—by the law of
necessary and probable sequence on which Aristotle
is never tired of insisting.

Again, a certain magnitude (μέγεθος) is indispensable for the harmonious evolution of a whole
such as is here described. This is frequently
affirmed by Aristotle. As a biological law it
applies to the healthy life and growth of all
organic structures.[3] It is also an artistic law,

poetry is περὶ μίαν πρᾶξιν ὅλην καὶ τελείαν. A perfect ὅλον is
necessarily τέλειον. In *Phys.* iii. 6. 207 a 7 sqq. ὅλον and τέλειον
are opposed to ἄπειρον, and the two words declared to be almost
equivalent in meaning : ἄπειρον μὲν οὖν ἐστὶν οὗ κατὰ ποσὸν
λαμβάνουσιν ἀεί τι λαβεῖν ἔστιν ἔξω. οὗ δὲ μηδὲν ἔξω, τοῦτ᾽
ἐστὶ τέλειον καὶ ὅλον· οὕτω γὰρ ὁριζόμεθα τὸ ὅλον, οὗ μηθὲν
ἄπεστιν, οἷον ἄνθρωπον ὅλον ἢ κιβωτόν : ib. 13, ὅλον δὲ καὶ
τέλειον ἢ τὸ αὐτὸ πάμπαν ἢ σύνεγγυς τὴν φύσιν ἐστίν. Plato,
Parm. 157 D, ἑνός τινος, ὃ καλοῦμεν ὅλον, ἐξ ἁπάντων ἓν τέλειον
γεγονός, τούτου μόριον ἂν τὸ μόριον εἴη.

    [1] Cf. Plat. *Gorg.* 503 E, (every craftsman and artist) εἰς τάξιν
τινὰ ἕκαστος ἕκαστον τίθησιν ὃ ἂν τιθῇ, καὶ προσαναγκάζει τὸ
ἕτερον τῷ ἑτέρῳ πρέπον τε εἶναι καὶ ἁρμόττειν, ἕως ἂν τὸ ἅπαν
σύστηται τεταγμένον τε καὶ κεκοσμημένον πρᾶγμα.

    [2] *Poet.* viii. 4, μετατιθεμένου τινὸς μέρους ἢ ἀφαιρουμένου δια-
φέρεσθαι (? διαφορεῖσθαι or διαφθείρεσθαι) καὶ κινεῖσθαι τὸ ὅλον.

    [3] *De Anim.* ii. 4. 416 a 16, τῶν δὲ φύσει συνισταμένων πάντων
ἐστὶ πέρας καὶ λόγος μεγέθους τε καὶ αὐξήσεως : de Gen. Anim.

expressing one of the first conditions of organic beauty.[1] In this latter sense it is emphasised in chapter vii. of the *Poetics*. An object is unfit for artistic representation if it is infinitely large or infinitesimally small.[2] On this principle a whole such as the Trojan war, 'though it has a beginning and an end,' is too vast in its compass even for epic treatment; it cannot be grasped by the mind, and incurs the risk attaching to any πολυμερὴς πρᾶξις, of becoming a series of detached scenes or incidents.[3]

Aristotle wisely avoids attempting to lay down any very precise rules as to the possible length to which a play may be extended. What he does say on the subject is marked by much sobriety and good sense. He rejects as inartistic any reference to the outward and accidental conditions of stage representation.[4] He falls back on the law of beauty as

ii. 6. 745 a 5, ἔστι γάρ τι πᾶσι τοῖς ζῴοις πέρας τοῦ μεγέθους. The same principle applies to a πόλις, *Pol.* iv. (vii.) 4. 1326 a 35, ἀλλ' ἔστι τι καὶ πόλεσι μεγέθους μέτρον, ὥσπερ καὶ τῶν ἄλλων πάντων, ζῴων φυτῶν ὀργάνων. *Pol.* viii. (v.) 3. 1302 b 34, ὥσπερ σῶμα ἐκ μερῶν σύγκειται καὶ δεῖ αὐξάνεσθαι ἀνάλογον, ἵνα μένῃ συμμετρία, . . . οὕτω καὶ πόλις κ.τ.λ.

[1] *Poet.* vii. 4, ἔτι δ' ἐπεὶ τὸ καλὸν καὶ ζῷον καὶ ἅπαν πρᾶγμα ὃ συνέστηκεν ἐκ τινῶν οὐ μόνον ταῦτα τεταγμένα δεῖ ἔχειν ἀλλὰ καὶ μέγεθος ὑπάρχειν μὴ τὸ τυχόν κ.τ.λ. Cf. ib. 7, ἀεὶ μὲν ὁ μείζων (sc. μῦθος) μέχρι τοῦ σύνδηλος εἶναι καλλίων ἐστὶ κατὰ τὸ μέγεθος. *Pol.* iv. (vii.) 4. 1326 a 34, διὸ καὶ πόλιν ἧς μετὰ μεγέθους ὁ λεχθεὶς ὅρος ὑπάρχει, ταύτην εἶναι καλλίστην ἀναγκαῖον.

[2] *Poet.* vii. 4–5 : supra, p. 187.

[3] *Poet.* xxiii. 3.

[4] *Poet.* vii. 6, τοῦ μήκους ὅρος <ὁ> μὲν πρὸς τοὺς ἀγῶνας καὶ τὴν αἴσθησιν οὐ τῆς τέχνης ἐστίν.

governing a work of art, and—intimately related
to this—on men's normal powers of memory and
enjoyment. The whole, he says, must be of such
dimensions that the memory or mind's eye can
embrace and retain it.¹ The more truly artistic
principle, however, is that which is stated in
ch. vii. 7. A play should be of a magnitude
sufficient to allow room for the natural development of the story. The action must evolve itself
freely and fully, and the decisive change of fortune
come about through the causal sequence of events.²

This rule holds good of the two varieties of
plot that are afterwards distinguished,—of the
ἁπλῆ πρᾶξις, where the action proceeds on a simple
and undeviating course from start to finish ; and
of the πεπλεγμένη πρᾶξις—preferred by Aristotle
as intensifying the tragic emotions—where the
catastrophe is worked out by the surprises of
Recognition (ἀναγνώρισις) and Reversal of the Situation (περιπέτεια);³ these surprises, however, being
themselves woven into the tissue of the plot,⁴ and

---

¹ With εὐμνημόνευτον (ch. vii. 5) as a limit of μέγεθος in
the tragic μῦθος cf. xxiii. 3, εὐσύνοπτος, and xxiv. 3, δύνασθαι
γὰρ δεῖ συνορᾶσθαι τὴν ἀρχὴν καὶ τὸ τέλος in regard to epic
poetry.

² Poet. vii. 7, ὡς δὲ ἁπλῶς διορίσαντας εἰπεῖν, ἐν ὅσῳ μεγέθει
κατὰ τὸ εἰκὸς ἢ τὸ ἀναγκαῖον ἐφεξῆς γιγνομένων συμβαίνει εἰς
εὐτυχίαν ἐκ δυστυχίας ἢ ἐξ εὐτυχίας εἰς δυστυχίαν μεταβάλλειν,
ἱκανὸς ὅρος ἐστὶν τοῦ μεγέθους.

³ Poet. x. 1–2. For περιπέτεια see xi. 1 and infra, pp. 329–31.

⁴ Ib. x. 3, ταῦτα δὲ δεῖ γίνεσθαι ἐξ αὐτῆς τῆς συστάσεως τοῦ

discovered in the light of the event to be the inevitable, though unexpected, consequences of all that has preceded.[1] The λύσις, the unravelling or *Dénouement* of the plot, must, as we are told, in every case 'arise out of the plot itself,'[2] not by recourse to the *Deus ex Machina* or to the play of accident—a warning the need of which is proved by the whole history of the stage. 'What did she die of?' was asked concerning one of the characters in a bad tragedy. 'Of what? of the fifth act,' was the reply. Lessing, who tells the story, adds[3] that 'in very truth the fifth act is an ugly evil disease that carries off many a one to whom the first four acts promised a longer life.'

Let us now look a little more closely into Aristotle's conception of a 'whole,' as the term is applied to the tragic action.

'A whole,' he says, 'is that which has a beginning, a middle, and an end'; and each of these terms is then defined. 'A beginning is that which does not itself follow anything by causal necessity,

μύθου, . . . διαφέρει γὰρ πολὺ τὸ γίγνεσθαι τάδε διὰ τάδε ἢ μετὰ τάδε.

[1] *Poet.* ix. 11.

[2] *Poet.* xv. 7, φανερὸν οὖν ὅτι καὶ τὰς λύσεις τῶν μύθων ἐξ αὐτοῦ δεῖ τοῦ μύθου συμβαίνειν κ.τ.λ. Cf. the censure passed ch. xvi. 4 on the mode in which Orestes is discovered by Iphigenia in Eur. *I. T.*, ἐκεῖνος δὲ αὐτὸς λέγει ἃ βούλεται ὁ ποιητὴς ἀλλ' οὐχ ὁ μῦθος.

[3] Lessing, *Hamb. Dram.*, Trans. (Bohn) p. 238.

but after which something naturally is or comes to be. An end, on the contrary, is that which itself naturally follows some other thing, either by necessity, or as a rule, but has nothing following it. A middle is that which follows something as some other thing follows it.'[1] Some difficulties have been felt with respect to these definitions. How, it is said, can a beginning be causally unconnected with what precedes? Do the opening scenes of a tragedy stand apart from the rest of the hero's career? Is nothing implied as to his previous history?

The answer would appear to be of this kind. The beginning of a drama is, no doubt, the natural sequel of something else. Still it must not carry us back in thought to all that has gone before. Antecedent events do not thrust themselves on us in an unending series. Certain facts are necessarily given. We do not trace each of these facts back

---

[1] *Poet.* vii. 3, ὅλον δέ ἐστιν τὸ ἔχον ἀρχὴν καὶ μέσον καὶ τελευτήν. ἀρχὴ δέ ἐστιν ὃ αὐτὸ μὲν μὴ ἐξ ἀνάγκης μετ' ἄλλο ἐστίν, μετ' ἐκεῖνο δ' ἕτερον πέφυκεν εἶναι ἢ γίνεσθαι· τελευτὴ δὲ τοὐναντίον ὃ αὐτὸ μετ' ἄλλο πέφυκεν εἶναι ἢ ἐξ ἀνάγκης ἢ ὡς ἐπὶ τὸ πολύ, μετὰ δὲ τοῦτο ἄλλο οὐδέν· μέσον δὲ ὃ καὶ αὐτὸ μετ' ἄλλο καὶ μετ' ἐκεῖνο ἕτερον. Cf. Plat. *Parm.* 145 A, τί δέ; ὅλον ὂν οὐκ ἀρχὴν ἂν ἔχοι καὶ μέσον καὶ τελευτήν; ἢ οἷόν τέ τι ὅλον εἶναι ἄνευ τριῶν τούτων; so 153 C. *Sophist* 244 E, εἰ τοίνυν ὅλον ἐστίν, . . . τοιοῦτόν γε ὂν τὸ ὂν μέσον τε καὶ ἔσχατα ἔχει, ταῦτα δὲ ἔχον πᾶσα ἀνάγκη μέρη ἔχειν. The opposite holds good of τὸ ἄπειρον: *Phileb.* 31 B, ἡδονὴ δὲ ἄπειρός τε αὐτὴ καὶ τοῦ μήτε ἀρχὴν μήτε μέσα μήτε τέλος ἐν αὐτῷ ἀφ' ἑαυτοῦ ἔχοντος . . . γένους.

to its origin, or follow the chain of cause and effect *ad infinitum.*[1] If we did, the drama would become an endless retrograde movement. A play must begin at some definite point, and at some definite point it must end. It is for the poet to see that the action is complete in itself, and that neither the beginning nor the end is arbitrarily chosen. Within the dramatic action, a strict sequence of cause and effect is prescribed; but the causal chain must not be indefinitely extended outwards.

The definition of the 'middle' as 'that which follows something as some other thing follows it,' looks at first sight mere tautology: but the context shows that the word 'follows' here marks a causal, not a purely temporal sequence. The idea is that

---

[1] So Teichmüller (*Arist. Forsch.* i. 54, 250) rightly, in defending the reading μὴ ἐξ ἀνάγκης in the definition of ἀρχή against the proposed transposition ἐξ ἀνάγκης μή. The latter reading, 'that which necessarily does not follow something else,' would, as he says, describe the *absolute* beginning, the πρῶτον κινοῦν, whereas Aristotle here wishes to denote a *relative* beginning, that which follows other things in time, but not as a necessary consequence.

He adds, however, that the reason Aristotle insists on this relative beginning is that tragedy is within the sphere of freedom: it must be begun by an act of free will. It seems most unlikely that anything of the sort is in Aristotle's mind. On the other hand, it is true that the Greek tragedians do generally make the action begin at a point where the human will has free play. This is a striking feature in Sophocles' treatment of the legends. Dark or superhuman forces may be at work in the antecedents of the play, but within the tragedy there is human will in action. The *Ajax*, the *Philoctetes*, the *Oedipus Tyrannus*, and the *Oedipus Coloneus* are examples.

the 'middle' unlike the 'beginning' stands in causal relation to what goes before, and unlike the 'end' is causally connected with what follows. There is no attempt to mark at what point in the development of the play the 'middle' is to be placed. The purpose of the definitions is to exclude beginnings which require something to precede them, endings which do not conclude the action, and middles which stand alone, unconnected either with the beginning or the end. We have here an emphatic condemnation of that kind of plot which Aristotle calls ' epeisodic' (ἐπεισοδιώδης), where the scenes follow one another without the inward connexion of the εἰκός or ἀναγκαῖον.[1] A succession of stirring scenes does not make a tragedy; and it is just this truth that Euripides is apt to forget when, instead of creating a well-articulated whole, he often delights to substitute pathetic effects, striking situations, rapid contrasts and surprises.

These definitions, however, like so many in the *Poetics*, have reference to the ideal tragedy; they are not to be taken as a rule to which all Greek plays conform. This will account for the inconsistency between the account here given of the ' beginning,' and the account in ch. xviii. of the Complication (δέσις) and *Dénouement* (λύσις) of the tragic plot. The Complication is that group

[1] *Poet*. ix. 10. Cf. p. 158 note 1.

of events which precedes the decisive turn of
fortune ; the *Dénouement* is that group of events
which follows it. In strictness, and according to
the definition of ch. vii., the 'beginning' of the
play should be also the 'beginning' of the Complication. But the Complication, according to
ch. xviii., frequently includes τὰ ἔξωθεν,[1]—certain
incidents external to the action proper, but presupposed in the drama and affecting the development of the piece. With plays before him like the
Oedipus Tyrannus and the *Ajax*, Aristotle even
at the cost of slight inconsistency admits such
external incidents to form part of the dramatic
entanglement. It is in some measure owing to
this practice of the Greek theatre that an ancient
tragedy often resembles the concluding acts of a
modern play. It begins almost at the climax:
the action proper is highly compressed and concentrated, and forms the last moment of a larger
action hastening to its close.[2]

If the analytical method of Aristotle in ch. vi.,
and his artificial isolation of the several elements

---

[1] *Poet.* xviii. 1, τὰ μὲν ἔξωθεν καὶ ἔνια τῶν ἔσωθεν πολλάκις ἡ
δέσις, τὸ δὲ λοιπὸν ἡ λύσις (where, however, Ueberweg's transposition, τὰ μὲν ἔξωθεν πολλάκις καὶ ἔνια τῶν ἔσωθεν ἡ δέσις, if
not absolutely necessary, gives the more natural order of the words).

[2] Cf. Dryden, *Essay of Dramatic Poesy*, 'The Ancients . . . set
the audience, as it were, at the post where the race is to be con-
cluded ; and, saving them the tedious expectation of seeing the
poet set out and ride the beginning of the course, you behold him
not till he is in sight of the goal, and just upon you.'

of tragedy, are in themselves liable to mislead the reader, the rules of chapters vii. and viii. ought to correct any erroneous impression that may arise. The thought that here stands out above all others is that of the organic structure of the drama. Further, it becomes apparent that the recurring phrase of the *Poetics*, σύστασις (or σύνθεσις) τῶν πραγμάτων, does not denote a mechanical piecing together of incidents, but a vital union of the parts.[1] But, it may be asked, how is the organic unity revealed? From what point of view can we most clearly realise it?

If we have rightly apprehended the general tenor of Aristotle's teaching in the *Poetics*, unity—he would say—is manifested mainly in two ways. First, in the causal connexion that binds together the several parts of a play,—the thoughts, the emotions, the decisions of the will, the external events being inextricably interwoven. Secondly, in the fact that the whole series of events, with all the moral forces that are brought into collision, are directed to a single end. The action as it advances converges on a definite point. The thread of purpose running through it becomes more marked. All minor effects are subordinated to the sense of an ever-growing unity. The end is linked to the beginning with inevitable certainty, and in the end we discern the meaning of the

[1] Cf. p. 347.

whole — τὸ τέλος μέγιστον ἁπάντων.[1] In this powerful and concentrated impression lies the supreme test of unity.

Aristotle's conception of the unity of plan essential to the drama could not be much better summed up than in the following extract from Lowell:[2]—'In a play we not only expect a succession of scenes, but that each scene should lead, by a logic more or less stringent, if not to the next, at any rate to something that is to follow, and that all should contribute their fraction of impulse towards the inevitable catastrophe. That is to say, the structure should be organic, with a necessary and harmonious connexion and relation of parts, and not merely mechanical, with an arbitrary or haphazard joining of one part to another. It is in the former sense alone that any production can be called a work of art.'

The general law of unity laid down in the *Poetics* for an epic poem is almost the same as for the drama;[3] but the drama forms a more compact and serried whole. Its events are in more direct relation with the development of character; its incidents are never incidents and nothing more. The sequence of the parts is more inevitable—

---

[1] *Poet.* vi. 10.

[2] J. R. Lowell, *The Old English Dramatists*, p. 55.

[3] In the *Poetics* the epic is treated chiefly from the point of view of the drama ; in Dryden's dramatic criticism the converse holds good.

morally more inevitable—than in a story where the external facts and events have an independent value of their own. And though the modern drama, unlike the ancient, aspires to a certain epic fulness of treatment, it cannot violate the determining conditions of dramatic form.

The epic, being of wider compass, can admit many episodes, which serve to fill in the pauses of the action, or diversify the interest.[1] They give what Aristotle calls ποικιλία,[2] embellishment and variety to the narrative. The epic moreover advances slowly, and introduces 'retarding' incidents,— incidents by which the *Dénouement* is delayed, and the mental strain for the time relieved, only to be intensified again when the climax comes. Further, owing to the number of its minor actions, the epic, while keeping its essential unity, contains the plots of many tragedies; in the phrase of Aristotle, it is πολύμυθος :[3] whereas the drama rejects this multiplicity of incidents; it is of closer tissue, pressing forward to an end which controls its entire structure. By the very conditions also of dramatic representation a play cannot, except through the

---

[1] *Poet.* xxiii. 3, ἐπεισοδίοις οἷς διαλαμβάνει (cf. *Lat.* 'distinguit') τὴν ποίησιν. xxiv. 4, τὸ μεταβάλλειν τὸν ἀκούοντα καὶ ἐπεισοδιοῦν ἀνομοίοις ἐπεισοδίοις.

[2] *Poet.* xxiii. 3.

[3] *Poet.* xviii. 4, χρὴ δὲ ὅπερ εἴρηται πολλάκις μεμνῆσθαι καὶ μὴ ποιεῖν ἐποποιικὸν σύστημα τραγῳδίαν. ἐποποιικὸν δὲ λέγω τὸ πολύμυθον κ.τ.λ.

mouth of messengers or by similar means, place before us other than successive events. The epic, by virtue of its narrative form, can describe actions that are simultaneous.[1] Thus the *Odyssey*, after a long interval, resumes the main story, which had been left in suspense; simultaneous and collateral incidents are narrated with much fulness of detail, and the scattered threads bound together in the unity of a single and accelerating action.

The action, then, of the drama is concentrated, while that of the epic is large and manifold. The primary difference of form is here a governing fact in the development of the two varieties of poetry. The epic is a story of the past, the drama a representation in the present. The epic story-teller can take his time; his imagination travels backward to a remote distance and there expatiates at will. He surveys the events of a past which is already a closed book. If he happens to be the rhapsodist of an early society, he and his audience alike have time immeasurable at their command, he to tell, and they to listen. 'Behold,' says King Alcinous in the *Odyssey*, 'the night is of great length unspeakable, and the time for sleep in the hall is not yet; tell me therefore of those wondrous

---

[1] *Poet.* xxiv. 4, ἔχει δὲ . . . πολύ τι ἡ ἐποποιία ἴδιον διὰ τὸ ἐν μὲν τῇ τραγῳδίᾳ μὴ ἐνδέχεσθαι ἅμα πραττόμενα πολλὰ μέρη μιμεῖσθαι ἀλλὰ τὸ ἐπὶ τῆς σκηνῆς καὶ τῶν ὑποκριτῶν μέρος μόνον· ἐν δὲ τῇ ἐποποιίᾳ διὰ τὸ διήγησιν εἶναι ἔστι πολλὰ μέρη ἅμα ποιεῖν περαινόμενα.

deeds. I could abide even till the bright dawn, so
long as thou couldst endure to rehearse me these
woes of thine in the hall.'[1] That is the true temper
of the epic audience. They will listen through the
night, and next day desire to take up the tale again.

The conditions of the drama are the opposite of
all this. The spectacle of an action evolving itself
in the present is very different from the leisurely
recital of an event that has happened in the past.
The impressions are more vivid in proportion to
their nearness. Nay, so vivid do they become that
the spectator, living in the present, becomes almost
one with the hero whose fortunes he follows. He
is impatient to see the sequel : he cannot listen to
long stories, to adventures unconnected with that
in which the central interest lies. The action which
rivets his attention is hastening towards its goal.
By the very fact that the dramatic struggle and
catastrophe take place before his eyes, the action
gains a rapidity, partly dramatic, partly lyric, that
is alien to the epic poem.

The only dramatic Unity enjoined by Aristotle
is Unity of Action. It is strange that this should
still need to be repeated. So inveterate, however,
is a literary tradition, once it has been established
under the sanction of high authority, that we still
find the 'Three Unities' spoken of in popular
writings as a rule of the *Poetics*.

---

[1] *Odyss.* xi. 373–6.

It may be interesting here to cast a rapid glance over the history of this famous literary superstition.[1] The doctrine of the 'Unity of Time,' or as it was sometimes called the 'Unity of the Day,' rests on one passage in the *Poetics*,[2] and one only.

[1] For the early history of this doctrine see Breitinger, *Les Unités d'Aristote avant le Cid de Corneille* (Genève, 1879); and for its history in France, Ad. Ebert, *Entwickelungsgeschichte der französische Tragödie, vornehmlich im 16. Jahrhundert* (Gotha, 1856).

[2] *Poet.* v. 4, ἔτι δὲ τῷ μήκει, <ἐπεὶ> ἡ μὲν (sc. ἡ τραγῳδία) ὅτι μάλιστα πειρᾶται ὑπὸ μίαν περίοδον ἡλίου εἶναι ἢ μικρὸν ἐξαλλάττειν, ἡ δὲ ἐποποιία ἀόριστος τῷ χρόνῳ, καὶ τούτῳ διαφέρει· καίτοι τὸ πρῶτον ὁμοίως ἐν ταῖς τραγῳδίαις τοῦτο ἐποίουν καὶ ἐν τοῖς ἔπεσιν.

Teichmüller (*Arist. Forsch.* pp. 206 ff.) attempts to show not only that μῆκος here is the external length of the poem, but also that χρόνος is the actual time taken in recitation (or representation), as distinct from the ideal or imaginary time over which the action extends. He seems to prove his case with respect to μῆκος, which invariably in the *Poetics* means external length. But his view of χρόνος is open apparently to fatal objections, the chief of which are these :—(1) μίαν περίοδον ἡλίου can hardly express the day of twelve hours. The word περίοδος as applied to a heavenly body always means its *full orbit*, its motion from a given starting-point back again to the same point. This periphrasis, instead of the simple phrase μίαν ἡμέραν, seems expressly designed to indicate that the day of twenty-four hours—ἡμέρα together with νύξ—is meant. (2) As has been shown by Ribbeck, *Rhein. Mus.* 24, p. 135, the parenthetical remark, τὸ πρῶτον ὁμοίως ἐν ταῖς τραγῳδίαις τοῦτο ἐποίουν καὶ ἐν τοῖς ἔπεσιν, tells strongly against Teichmüller. The reference must be to the imaginary time of the action *in* the play itself. (3) τραγῳδία throughout the *Poetics* is used for tragedy as a distinct species of poetry, or for a particular tragedy,—never for the tragic performance including a tetralogy. (4) μάλιστα πειρᾶται loses almost all point if the χρόνος is external time, and

υ

'Epic poetry and tragedy differ, again, in their length : for tragedy endeavours, as far as possible, to confine itself to a single revolution of the sun, or but slightly to exceed this limit; whereas the epic action has no limits of time.' We have here a rough generalisation as to the practice of the Greek stage. The imaginary time of the dramatic action is limited, as far as may be, to the day of twenty-four hours. The practice, however, did not always exist. In the earlier days of tragedy, as the next sentence shows, the time - limit was ignored in the tragic no less than in the epic action.

No strict rule is here laid down. A certain historic fact is recorded,—a prevailing, but not an invariable usage. The effort of tragedy was in this direction, though the result could not always be achieved. Even in the developed Attic drama several exceptions to the practice are to be found.

if ὑπὸ μίαν . . . εἶναι instead of its natural sense 'fall within,' 'be comprised within,' is forced to mean 'occupy,' or 'fill up,' twelve hours of daylight.

The translation adopted in the text follows Ueberweg's explanation. μῆκος is (with Teichmüller) referred to the actual length of the poem, but χρόνος to the internal time of the action. The difference in the length of a poem is made to depend on a difference in the time occupied by the action. Roughly speaking, such a relation generally exists, at least in the drama. But it is far from being a strict rule.

In forming this conclusion on a passage which is still not without difficulty, I have had the advantage of some correspondence with Prof. Bywater.

In the *Eumenides* months or years elapse between the opening of the play and the next scene. The *Trachiniae* of Sophocles and the *Supplices* of Euripides afford other and striking instances of the violation of the so - called rule. In the *Agamemnon*, even if a definite interval of days cannot be assumed between the fire - signals announcing the fall of Troy, and the return of Agamemnon, at any rate the conditions of time are disregarded and the march of events is imaginatively accelerated.[1]

As for the ' Unity of Place,' this too was a stage-practice, generally observed in the Greek drama but sometimes neglected, more especially in comedy: it is nowhere even hinted at in the *Poetics*, and, as a rule of art, has been deduced by the critics from the Unity of Time.[2]

[1] On the time-question in the *Agamemnon* see an article by Prof. Lewis Campbell in the *Classical Review*, vol. iv. 303–5. On the general question of ' The Unity of Time ' see Verrall, *Ion of Eurip.* Intr. pp. xlviii ff. (Cambridge Press).

[2] The formal recognition of the *Unity of Place* as a third Unity dates from Castelvetro's first edition of the *Poetics* in 1570 ; see an article by H. Breitinger in *Revue Critique* 1879, ii. pp. 478–80. In the same article two other points are noted : (1) that Castelvetro adopts the theory put forward in the *Poetik* published 1561 from the remains of J. C. Scaliger, identifying the time of the action with that of the representation ; (2) that Sir Philip Sidney in his *Apologie for Poetrie*, written soon after 1580 and published in 1595, derived from Castelvetro many of the arguments and examples by which he maintains his vigorous defence of the Three Unities.

See also Spingarn p. 99, ' In fact, Castelvetro specifically says

There are several very obvious reasons for the general observance of the minor Unities in Greek tragedy.   The simple and highly concentrated movement of a Greek play seldom demanded, or even permitted, a change of place or intervals between the scenes.   Such breaks would, as a rule, have been liable to disturb the impression of the unity of the whole.   Moreover, as has been often remarked, the Chorus formed an ideal bond of union between the separate parts of the action. Lessing suggests[1] that the limitations of time and place were necessary in order that the Chorus might not seem to be kept too long away from their homes.   But if once we realise the painful fact that these worthy men are kept standing, it may be for twenty-four hours, fasting and in one place, our distress will not be perceptibly augmented if the action is prolonged to thirty-six or forty-eight hours.   Still, it is true that the constant presence of the same group of actors in a theatre where there was no drop-scene, no division into Acts, did naturally lead to the representation of a continuous and unbroken action.

From this point of view the presence of the Chorus tended towards Unity of Place and Unity of Time.   From another point of view the Chorus

that the unity of action is not essential to the drama, but is merely made expedient by the requirements of time and place.'

[1] *Hamb. Dram.* Trans. (Bohn) p. 369.

releases us from the captivity of time. The interval
covered by a choral ode is one whose value is just
what the poet chooses to make it. While the time
occupied by the dialogue has a relation more or
less exact to real time, the choral lyrics suspend
the outward action of the play, and carry us still
farther away from the world of reality. What
happens in the interval cannot be measured by
any ordinary reckoning; it is much or little as the
needs of the piece demand. A change of place
directly obtrudes itself on the senses, but time is
only what it appears to the mind. The imagination
travels easily over many hours; and in the Greek
drama the time that elapses during the songs of
the Chorus is entirely idealised.

In interpreting the passage of the *Poetics*
above quoted (ch. v. 4), the earlier critics dealt
very loosely with the Greek. πειρᾶται ἡ τραγῳδία,
says Aristotle. Corneille and d'Aubignac translate
πειρᾶται by *doit*, and thereby convert the general
statement of fact at once into a rule. Successive
commentators repeated the error. But the stress
of the controversy gathered round another point.
What is the meaning of the phrase μίαν περίοδον
ἡλίου, ' a single revolution of the sun '?[1] Is it the
day of twenty-four hours or the day of twelve
hours? The Italian critics were divided on this

---

[1] See p. 289 note 2.

question ; so too were the French.   Corneille [1]
declared in favour of twenty - four hours ; but
proposed, by a stretch of the rule, to allow thirty
hours ; and even this limit he thought hampering.
He wavers curiously between the true poetic view
as to the ideal management of time, and the
principle of poetic deception so widely held by
his contemporaries, that the more exact the reproduction of the conditions of reality, the better
the art.

At one moment he says that, if the representation lasts two hours, the dramatic action ought
to be the same length, that the resemblance may
be perfect.   If, however, the action cannot with
due regard to probability be compressed into two
hours, he would allow it to run to four or six or
ten hours, but not much beyond the twenty-four.
Might it not have occurred to him that long before
the extreme limit of twenty-four or thirty hours
was reached, the principle of a life-like imitation of
reality would have been surrendered ?   No sooner,
however, has he enunciated the rule than his
instincts as a poet get the upper hand, and he
writes : 'Above all I would leave the length of the
action to the imagination of the hearers, and never
determine the time, if the subject does not require
it. . . . What need is there to mark at the opening

---

[1] Corneille, Discours iii. *Des Trois Unités.*

of the play that the sun is rising, that it is noon at the third act, and sunset at the end of the last ?'

Dacier[1] disputes the view that the 'single revolution of the sun' means a day of twenty-four hours. He holds it to be monstrous and against common sense ; 'it would ruin the verisimilitude.' He fixes twelve hours as the extreme limit of the dramatic action, but these may be either in the night or in the day, or half in one and half in the other.[2] In the perfect tragedy—and here he agrees with Corneille—the time of the action and of the representation should coincide. He roundly asserts that this was an indispensable law of Greek tragedy,[3] though this statement is afterwards qualified. If, owing to the nature of the subject, the poet cannot observe the rule of strict equivalence, he may have recourse to 'verisimilitude'; and this is stated to be the Aristotelian principle : 'Aristotle supplied the defect of necessity by probability.'[4] Thus the law of the εἰκός and

[1] Dacier on Aristotle's *Poetics*, ch. v. note 21, Trans. (London 1705).

[2] Cf. d'Aubignac's translation of ἢ μικρὸν ἐξαλλάττειν, 'ou do changer un peu ce temps,' i.e. to change from day to night or from night to day.

[3] Dacier on *Poetics*, ch. vii. note 14.

[4] Dacier on *Poetics*, ch. vii. note 18. Here the ἀναγκαῖον of Aristotle becomes the exact equivalence of the time of the action with the time of the representation : the εἰκός becomes the verisimilitude which in default of such equivalence ' will cheat the audience, who will not pry so narrowly as to mind what is behind the scenes, provided there be nothing too extravagant.'

ἀναγκαῖον in the *Poetics* degenerates into a device
which may lead the audience to imagine that the
scene on the stage is a facsimile of real life. The
fallacious principle that the dramatic imitation is
meant to be in some sense a deception,[1] is at the
basis of all these strange reasonings as to the possible
equivalence between real and imaginary time. The
idea exists in Corneille.[2] It is pushed to its
extreme by Dacier and Batteux. Even Voltaire
commits himself to the absurd position that 'if
the poet represents a conspiracy and makes the
action to last fourteen days, he must account to me
for all that takes place in those fourteen days.'[3]

[1] 'It is false that any representation is mistaken for reality ;
that any dramatic fable, in its materiality, was ever credible, or
for a single moment was ever credited.'—Dr. Johnson, *Preface to
Shakspeare.*

[2] With regard to Unity of Place Corneille says : 'Cela
aiderait à tromper l'auditeur, qui ne voyant rien qui lui marquât
la diversité des lieux, ne s'en apercevrait pas, à moins d'une
reflexion malicieuse et critique, dont il y en a peu qui soient
capables' (Disc. iii.).

[3] So Dacier on *Poetics*, ch. xviii. note 3 : 'Mr. Corneille is
satisfied that the audience should know why the actors go out of
the place where the scene is laid ; but he does not think it
necessary to know what they do during the intervals, neither that
't is required that the actors should do anything during the
intervals, but is persuaded that they may sleep then, if they please,
and not break the continuity of the action. We find just the
contrary according to Aristotle's principles, and that it ceases to be
a tragedy when 't is so, for this would certainly ruin all the probability, if the audience did not know what the actors were doing
during the intervals ; and if the actors have nothing to do, pray
what does the audience stay for ? 't is very odd to expect the

Unity of Place was generally held to follow as a corollary from Unity of Time.[1] Corneille, the first French poet who rigorously observes the rule, admits that he finds no such precept in Aristotle.[2] In defending it he is driven to desperate shifts, which end in a kind of compromise. He points out that the moderns are met by a difficulty the ancients did not encounter. The Greeks could make their kings meet and speak in public. In France such a familiarity was impossible; royal personages could not be brought forth from the seclusion of their chambers; nor could private confidences be exchanged anywhere but in the private apartments of the several characters. He would, therefore, admit some extension of the rule. He would allow a change of scene, provided that

---

sequel of an action, when the actors have nothing more to do, and to be interested in a thing, which the actors are so little concerned in, that they may go to sleep.' It is needless to say, there is not a trace of all this in Aristotle.

[1] Voltaire derives it from Unity of Action on the strangely illogical ground that 'no one action can go on in several places at once.' But surely a single action can go on in several places *successively*.

[2] Others who had never read the *Poetics* were not slow to assert that all the Unities are there enjoined. Frederick the Great (on *German Literature*) ridicules the plays of Shakespeare as ridiculous farces, worthy of the savages of Canada; they offend against all the rules of the stage. 'For these rules are not arbitrary; you will find them in the *Poetics* of Aristotle, where Unity of Place, Unity of Time, and Unity of Interest are pre-scribed as the only means of making tragedy interesting.'

the action represented took place within a single
town, and that the scene was not shifted in the
same act. Again, the place (an abstract *lieu théâtral*)
must be alluded to only under its general name—
Paris, Rome, or the like—and the stage decoration
must remain unaltered so far as this local area is
concerned.[1]

Such were the anxious and minute contrivances
which a great poet devised to enable the imagination
to do its proper work. The principle, as Batteux
carefully explained, was that if the scene of the
action is changed while the spectator remains in
one place, he will be reminded that he is assisting
at an unreal performance ; the imitation will be so
far defective.

Far better—we feel—in the interests of the
dramatic art was the practice of the Shakespearian
theatre,—the bare stage without movable scenery,
and the frank surrender of all attempt to cheat the
senses. The poet simply invoked the aid of the
imagination to carry his hearers through space and
time ; to

> 'digest
> The abuse of distance, . . .'
> 'jumping o'er times,
> Turning the accomplishment of many years
> Into an hour-glass.'

---

[1] Dryden, *Essay of Dramatic Poesy*, speaks of the 'regular
French play' in which 'the street, the window, the houses and
the closet, are made to walk about, and the persons to stand still.'

The problem of the 'Unities' cannot, indeed, have presented itself to Aristotle in its modern lights. But even if he had known what was to be written on the subject, he would, doubtless, have taken his stand no less decisively on the fundamental Unity of Action, and refrained from laying down any binding rules for change of scene or lapse of time. If Unity of Action is preserved, the other Unities will take care of themselves. Unity of Action is indeed in danger of being impaired by marked discontinuity of place or time. There are Spanish dramas in which the hero is born in Act i., and appears again on the scene as an old man at the close of the play. The missing spaces are almost of necessity filled in by the undramatic expedient of narrating what has occurred in the intervals. Yet even here all depends on the art of the dramatist. Years may elapse between successive acts without the unity being destroyed, as we see from *The Winter's Tale*.

After all, the drama is not possible without a certain idealisation of place and time. If the poet has once succeeded in transporting us to a far-off land and a distant age—to ancient Rome or Athens —we are not inclined to quarrel with him as to the number of hours or days over which the dramatic action extends. We do not ask at the end of each act, what the hour is by poet's time; and, should we seek to discover it from indications in the play,

our curiosity will for the most part be baffled.
There is no calendar for such a reckoning, no table
of equivalent hours in the real and the ideal world.
It is part of the poet's art to make us forget all
time ; and, if in his company we lose count of
months and years, we do not cry out against the
impossibility.   For, on the one hand, the imagination is not to be cheated by puerile devices into
the belief that its world is the world of reality :
on the other, we can hardly place any limit on the
demands to which it will respond, if only these
demands are made by one who knows how.   Shakespeare deals freely, and as he will, with place and
time ; yet he is generally nearer to the doctrine of
the *Poetics* than those who fancied they wrote in
strict accordance with the rules of that treatise.

French poets and writers on aesthetics did not
derive their dramatic rules directly from the Greek
models on which the *Poetics* of Aristotle is based.
The genius of Rome was more congenial to them
than that of Greece.   Seneca, rather than Aeschylus
or Sophocles, was the teacher of Corneille and Racine,
and even Molière's comedy was powerfully affected
by Plautus and Terence.   The French, having learnt
their three Unities from Roman writers, then sought
to discover for them Aristotelian authority.   They
committed a further and graver error.   Instead of
resting the minor Unities of Time and Place on
Unity of Action, they subordinated Unity of Action

to the observance of the other rules. The result not unfrequently was to compress into a space of twelve or twenty-four hours a crowded sequence of incidents and a series of mental conflicts which needed a fuller development. The natural course of the action was cut short, and the inner consistency of character violated. A similar result followed from the scrupulous precautions taken to avoid a change of scene. The characters, instead of finding their way to the place where dramatic motives would have taken them, were compelled to go elsewhere, lest they should violate the Unities. The external rule was thus observed, but at the cost of that inward logic of character and events which is prescribed by the *Poetics*. The failures and successes of the modern stage alike prove the truth of the Aristotelian principle, that Unity of Action is the higher and controlling law of the drama. The Unities of Time and Place, so far as they can claim any artistic importance, are of secondary and purely derivative value.

CHAPTER VIII

WITH the exception of the definition of tragedy itself, probably no passage in the *Poetics* has given rise to so much criticism as the description of the ideal tragic hero in ch. xiii. The qualities requisite to such a character are here deduced from the primary fact that the function of tragedy is to produce the *katharsis* of pity and fear; pity being felt for a person who, if not wholly innocent, meets with suffering beyond his deserts; fear being awakened when the sufferer is a man of like nature with ourselves.[1] Tragic character must be exhibited through the medium of a plot which has the capacity of giving full satisfaction to these emotions. Certain types, therefore, of character and certain forms of catastrophe are at once excluded, as failing either in whole or in part to produce the tragic effect.

In the first place, the spectacle of a man

---

[1] See pp. 260 ff.

eminently good¹ undergoing the change from prosperous to adverse fortune awakens neither pity nor
fear. It shocks or repels us (μιαρόν ἐστιν). Next,
and utterly devoid of tragic quality, is the representation of the bad man who experiences the
contrary change from distress to prosperity. Pity
and fear are here alike wanting. Even the sense
of justice (τὸ φιλάνθρωπον)² is unsatisfied. The
impression left by such a spectacle is, indeed, the

¹ The ἐπιεικής of *Poet.* xiii. 2 is from the context to be identified
with ὁ ἀρετῇ διαφέρων καὶ δικαιοσύνῃ of § 3.

² Vahlen here (ch. xiii. 2) takes τὸ φιλάνθρωπον in its ordinary
sense, as human sympathy with suffering, even if the suffering be
deserved and the sympathy, therefore, fall short of ἔλεος. But the
comparison of ch. xviii. 6 suggests a more special meaning. The
outwitting of the clever rogue and the defeat of the brave villain
are there given as instances of τὸ φιλάνθρωπον. It appears to
denote that which gratifies the moral sense, which produces a
feeling of satisfied justice. So it is taken by Zeller, Susemihl and
others. Properly it is a sympathetic human feeling; and this
may be evoked either by the sight of suffering (merited or unmerited), or by the punishment of the evil-doer. In *Rhet.* ii. 9.
1386 b 26 sympathy with unmerited suffering—namely, ἔλεος—
has as its other side the sense of satisfaction over merited misfortune—what is here called τὸ φιλάνθρωπον. ὁ μὲν γὰρ λυπού-
μενος ἐπὶ τοῖς ἀναξίως κακοπραγοῦσιν ἡσθήσεται ἢ ἄλυπος ἔσται
ἐπὶ τοῖς ἐναντίως κακοπραγοῦσιν· οἷον τοὺς πατραλοίας καὶ
μιαιφόνους, ὅταν τύχωσι τιμωρίας, οὐδεὶς ἂν λυπηθείη χρηστός·
δεῖ γὰρ χαίρειν ἐπὶ τοῖς τοιούτοις. Dr. Lock has given me an
interesting illustration of φιλάνθρωπον in the meaning here
assigned to it from the Book of Wisdom i. 6, φιλάνθρωπον γὰρ
πνεῦμα σοφία καὶ οὐκ ἀθωώσει τὸν βλάσφημον.

With φιλάνθρωπον, 'satisfying to human feeling,' may be compared the later use of the word (common e.g. in Plutarch), of
'pleasing,' 'gratifying,' in a more general way.

exact opposite of ἔλεος, 'pity': it is that which
the Greeks denoted by νέμεσις, the righteous anger
or moral indignation excited by undeserved good
fortune.[1] Again, there is the overthrow of the
utter villain (ὁ σφόδρα πονηρός),—a catastrophe
that satisfies the moral sense, but is lacking in the
higher and distinctively tragic qualities. Lastly,
Aristotle mentions the case which in his view
answers all the requirements of art. It is that of
a man who morally stands midway between the
two extremes. He is not eminently good or just,
though he leans to the side of goodness.[2] He is
involved in misfortune, not, however, as the result
of deliberate vice, but through some great flaw of
character or fatal error in conduct.[3] He is, moreover, illustrious in rank and fortune; the chief
motive, no doubt, for this requirement being that
the signal nature of the catastrophe may be more
strikingly exhibited.

Another possible case remains, though it is not
among those here enumerated. The good man
may be represented as passing from adversity to
prosperity. On Aristotle's principles this would

[1] *Rhet.* ii. 9. 1386 b 9, ἀντίκειται δὲ τῷ ἐλεεῖν μάλιστα μὲν ὃ
καλοῦσι νεμεσᾶν· τῷ γὰρ λυπεῖσθαι ἐπὶ ταῖς ἀναξίαις κακο-
πραγίαις ἀντικείμενόν ἐστι τρόπον τινὰ καὶ ἀπὸ τοῦ αὐτοῦ ἤθους
τὸ λυπεῖσθαι ἐπὶ ταῖς ἀναξίαις εὐπραγίαις.

[2] *Poet.* xiii. 4, βελτίονος μᾶλλον ἢ χείρονος.

[3] *Poet.* xiii. 3, μήτε διὰ κακίαν καὶ μοχθηρίαν μεταβάλλων εἰς
τὴν δυστυχίαν ἀλλὰ δι᾽ ἁμαρτίαν τινά. xiii. 4, μὴ διὰ μοχθηρίαν
ἀλλὰ δι᾽ ἁμαρτίαν μεγάλην.

fail to produce the proper tragic effect; for, though in the course of the action we may be profoundly moved by the spectacle of threatened ruin, the total impression is alien to tragedy. The 'happy ending,' frequent as it is in Greek and in all dramatic literature, comes under the same general censure as attaches to a plot with a double thread of interest and a double catastrophe,—prosperity for the good, misfortune for the bad.[1] Aristotle observes that 'owing to the weakness of the audience' a play so constructed generally passes as the best.[2] The effect is that of τὸ φιλάνθρωπον

[1] *Poet.* xiii. 7, δευτέρα δ' ἡ πρώτη λεγομένη ὑπὸ τινῶν ἐστιν [σύστασις] ἡ διπλῆν τε τὴν σύστασιν ἔχουσα, καθάπερ ἡ 'Οδύσσεια, καὶ τελευτῶσα ἐξ ἐναντίας τοῖς βελτίοσι καὶ χείροσιν.

[2] *Poet.* xiii. 7, δοκεῖ δὲ εἶναι πρώτη διὰ τὴν τῶν θεάτρων ἀσθένειαν. Cf. Twining ii. 116, 'Chaucer's monk had the true Aristotelic idea of Tragedy :—

> Tragedie is to sayn a certain storie,
> As olde books maken us memorie,
> Of him that stood in great prosperitee,
> And is yfallen out of high degree
> In to miserie, and endeth wretchedly.

But the knight and the host were among the θεαταὶ ἀσθενεῖς :

> Ho ! quod the knight, good sire, no more of this :
> That ye have said is ynough ywis,
> And mochel more ; for litel heviness
> Is right enough to mochel folk, I gesse.
> I say for me, it is a gret disese,
> Wher as men have ben in gret welth and ese,
> To heren of hir soden fall, alas !
> And the contrary is joye and gret solas,
> As when a man has ben in poure estat,
> And climbeth up, and wexeth fortunat,

X

above mentioned : reward and punishment are in
exact correspondence with desert. He himself

> And ther abideth in prosperitee ;
> Swiche thing is gladsom, as it thinketh me,
> And of swiche thing were goodly for to telle.'

The Aristotelian view is maintained in *Spectator* No. 40, *Tatler*
No. 82. On the other hand cf. Dryden, Dedication of the *Spanish
Friar* : ' It is not so trivial an undertaking to make a tragedy end
happily ; for 't is more difficult to save than 't is to kill. The
dagger and the cup of poison are always in readiness ; but to
bring the action to the last extremity, and then by probable means
to recover all, will require the art and judgment of a writer and
cost him many a pang in the performance.'

Dr. Johnson gives expression to the extreme view of 'poetical
justice' in his criticism of *King Lear* (vol. ii. 164–5). 'Shakspeare has suffered the virtue of Cordelia to perish in a just cause,
contrary to the natural idea of justice, to the hope of the reader,
and what is yet more strange, to the faith of chronicles. Yet this
conduct is justified by the Spectator, who blames Tate for giving
Cordelia success and happiness in his alteration, and declares that,
in his opinion, the tragedy has lost half its beauty. Dennis has
remarked, whether justly or not, that to secure the favourable
reception of Cato, the town was poisoned with much false and
abominable criticism, and that endeavours had been used to discredit
and decry poetical justice. A play in which the wicked prosper,
and the virtuous miscarry, may doubtless be good, because it is
a just representation of the events of human life : but since all
reasonable beings naturally love justice, I cannot easily be persuaded, that the observation of justice makes a play worse ; or that
if other excellences are equal, the audience will not always rise
the better pleased for the triumph of persecuted virtue. In the
present case the public has decided. Cordelia from the time of
Tate has always retired with victory and felicity. And if my
sensations could add anything to the general suffrage, I might relate,
I was many years ago so shocked by Cordelia's death, that I know
not whether I ever endured again to read the last scenes of the
play till I undertook to revise them as an editor.'

regards the pleasure hence derived as proper rather to comedy, where all discords are reconciled, the bitterest foes part as friends, 'no one slays or is slain' : [1]—or, as Goethe in a similar context puts it, 'no one dies, every one is married.'

The stress laid in this chapter on the unhappy ending is the key to the striking phrase in which Euripides, faulty as he may perhaps be in dramatic structure, is pronounced to be 'still the most tragic of poets.' [2] The saying must be read along with

[1] *Poet.* xiii. 8. Cf. Schol. on Eurip. *Orest.* p. 347 (Dind.), ἡ κατάληξις τῆς τραγῳδίας ἢ εἰς θρῆνον ἢ εἰς πάθος καταλύει, ἡ δὲ τῆς κωμῳδίας εἰς σπονδὰς καὶ διαλλαγάς, ὅθεν ὁρᾶται τόδε τὸ δρᾶμα κωμικῇ καταλήξει χρησάμενον· διαλλαγαὶ γὰρ πρὸς Μενέλαον καὶ Ὀρέστην. Arg. to *Alcest.* p. 87. 9 (Dind.), τὸ δὲ δρᾶμά ἐστι σατυρικώτερον, ὅτι εἰς χαρὰν καὶ ἡδονὴν καταστρέφει· παρὰ τοῖς τραγικοῖς ἐκβάλλεται ὡς ἀνοίκεια τῆς τραγικῆς ποιήσεως ὅ τε Ὀρέστης καὶ ἡ Ἄλκηστις ὡς ἐκ συμφορᾶς μὲν ἀρχόμενα, εἰς εὐδαιμονίαν δὲ καὶ χαρὰν λήξαντα. ἔστι δὲ μᾶλλον κωμῳδίας ἐχόμενα. Cf. Dante, *Epist.* x. 10.

[2] *Poet.* xiii. 6, ὁ Εὐριπίδης εἰ καὶ τὰ ἄλλα μὴ εὖ οἰκονομεῖ, ἀλλὰ τραγικώτατός γε τῶν ποιητῶν φαίνεται. The praise is here further limited by the previous remark that the effectiveness of such tragedies depends partly on stage representation : ἐπὶ γὰρ τῶν σκηνῶν καὶ τῶν ἀγώνων τραγικώταται αἱ τοιαῦται φαίνονται, ἂν κατορθωθῶσιν.

The 'powerful tragic effect' on the stage (τραγικώταται φαίνονται, τραγικώτατός γε φαίνεται) is a serious reservation for Aristotle to make, for he requires a good tragedy to produce its proper effect merely by reading, ch. xiv. 1. See Susemihl (Introd. p. 29), who also compares the use of τραγικός in a somewhat restricted sense in the two other passages where it occurs in the *Poetics*,—xiv. 7, τό τε γὰρ μιαρὸν ἔχει, καὶ οὐ τραγικόν· ἀπαθὲς γάρ (where τραγικόν implies tragic disaster), and xviii. 5 (applied to Agathon), τραγικὸν γὰρ τοῦτο καὶ φιλάνθρωπον. Its limitation in the latter

certain limiting expressions in the context, and
in other passages of the *Poetics*. But whatever
deductions may have to be made from the force of
the phrase, the estimate of Euripides here given is
directly connected[1] by Aristotle with the preference
of the poet for the true tragic ending.

Reverting now to the several types of excluded
characters, we may consider Aristotle's conclusions
more in detail. First, the ἐπιεικής or perfectly
blameless character is deemed unfit to be a tragic
hero on the ground that wholly unmerited suffering causes repulsion, not fear or pity. Why, we
may ask, not pity? Surely we feel pity for one
who is in the highest sense ἀνάξιος, an innocent
sufferer? In reply it has been sometimes said that
such persons themselves despise the pain of suffering; they enjoy so much inward consolation that
they have no need of our sympathy. 'Si vis me
flere dolendum est primum ipsi tibi.' This may
appear a cynical reflexion, though it can be so

---

passage is very remarkable in connexion with φιλάνθρωπον. The
discomfiture of the wicked man, there spoken of, does not answer
to the true tragic idea ; it merely 'satisfies the moral sense'; so
that τραγικόν can hardly mean much more than strikingly
dramatic. In ch. xiii. 6 the chief thought is the *pathetic* and
moving power of Euripides. Cf. *Probl.* xviii. 6. 918 a 10, διὰ τί ἡ
παρακαταλογὴ ἐν ταῖς ᾠδαῖς τραγικόν ; where παθητικόν in the
next line is used as an equivalent. In Plato, *Rep.* x. 602 B, τούς τε
τῆς τραγικῆς ποιήσεως ἀπτομένους ἐν ἰαμβείοις καὶ ἐν ἔπεσι, the
word includes the sad narratives of epic poetry as well as of tragedy.

[1] *Poet.* xiii. 6, διὸ καί κ.τ.λ.

put as to convey a real truth. The pity we feel for outward misfortune may be sunk in our admiration for the courage with which it is borne. Aristotle's answer, however, would probably be different. He too would say that pity is expelled by a stronger feeling; as in the *Rhetoric* 'terror tends to drive out pity.'[1] But the mention here of τὸ μιαρόν suggests that the sense of outraged justice would displace the softer emotions. Lessing, agreeing with Aristotle on the main point, takes occasion to enforce his own favourite theory— not Aristotelian—which attributes a direct moral purpose to tragedy. He speaks of the 'mere thought in itself so terrible, that there should be human beings who can be wretched without any guilt of their own.'[2]

The unqualified rejection of such a theme as unsuited to tragedy may well surprise us. Aristotle had not to go beyond the Greek stage to find a guiltless heroine whose death does not shock the moral sense. Nothing but a misplaced ingenuity, or a resolve at all costs to import a moral lesson into the drama, can discover in Antigone any fault or failing which entailed on her suffering as its due penalty. She was so placed that she had to choose between contending duties; but who can doubt that she chose aright? She sacrificed the

---

[1] *Rhet.* ii. 8. 1386 a 21, quoted supra, p. 265.
[2] Lessing, *Hamb. Dram.* Trans. (Bohn) p. 435.

lower duty to the higher; and if, in so doing, her conduct fell short of formal perfection, the defect lay in the inherent one-sidedness of all human action in an imperfect world.　Hers was a 'sinless crime,'[1] nor could Aristotle on his own principles call her other than ἐπιεικής, 'good' in the fullest sense of the word.

Yet his reluctance to admit a perfect character to the place of the protagonist has been almost justified by the history of the tragic drama.　Such a character has been rarely chosen, and still more rarely has been successful.　But the reason assigned in this passage does not appear to be the true one.　Blameless goodness has seldom the quality needed to make it dramatically interesting. It wants the motive power which leads to decisive acts of will, which impels others to action and produces a collision of forces.　Dramatic character implies some self-assertive energy.　It is not a rounded or perfect whole; it realises itself within a limited sphere, and presses forward passionately in a single direction.　It has generally a touch of egoism, by which it exercises a controlling influence over circumstances or over the wills of minor characters that are grouped around it. Goodness, on the other hand, with its unselfish, self-effacing tendency, is apt to be immobile and uncombative.　In refusing to strike back it brings

---

[1] Soph. *Ant.* 74, ὅσια πανουργήσασ'.

the action to a standstill. Even where it has no lack of strong initiative, its impersonal ardour in the cause of right has not the same dramatic fascination as the spectacle of human weakness or passion doing battle with the fate it has brought upon itself.

Mazzini conceived the idea of a new drama in which man shall no longer appear as a rebel against the laws of existence, or the victim of an external struggle with his own nature, but as the ally of Providence, co-operating with the powers of good in that secular conflict whose drama is the history of the world. We may doubt whether such a drama can in the true sense be tragic. The death of the martyr—of the hero who leads a forlorn hope—of the benefactor of mankind who bears suffering with unflinching fortitude, and through suffering achieves moral victory—fills us with emotions of wonder and admiration ; but it can hardly produce the thrill of fear or tragic awe, which Aristotle rightly felt to be an indispensable factor in true tragedy.[1] The reason perhaps is that tragedy, in its pure idea, shows us a mortal will engaged in an unequal struggle with destiny, whether that destiny be represented by the forces within or without the mind. The conflict reaches

[1] Corneille (Discours ii. *De la Tragédie*) objects to banishing martyrs from the stage, and adduces his own Polyeucte in support of his view—a very doubtful example.

its tragic issue when the individual perishes, but through his ruin the disturbed order of the world is restored and the moral forces re-assert their sway. The death of the martyr presents to us not the defeat, but the victory of the individual; the issue of a conflict in which the individual is ranged on the same side as the higher powers, and the sense of suffering consequently lost in that of moral triumph.

The next case is that of the bad man who is raised from adverse to prosperous fortune. This, says Aristotle, is most alien to the spirit of tragedy. No one will dispute the observation; though we cannot adopt Dacier's reason for accepting it. 'There is nothing more opposed to the refining of the passions than the prosperity of the wicked; instead of correcting, it nourishes and strengthens them; for who would take the trouble to get rid of his vices, if they made him happy?'[1] Good fortune following upon a course of bad actions is frequent enough in life; none the less it is to be rigorously excluded from tragic and, indeed, from all art. It may excite a lively sense of impending terror, though even this is denied by Aristotle. It certainly awakens no pity, and—we may add with Aristotle—it offends the sense of justice. Even granting that art must touch us through our aesthetic sensibility, and has nothing directly

[1] Dacier on *Poetics*, ch. xiii. Trans. (London, 1705).

to do with the sense of justice, the aesthetic effect itself will be one of pain and disquiet; the doubt and disturbance which arise from the spectacle of real life will be reproduced and perhaps intensified. In the drama our view of the universe needs to be harmonised, not confused; we expect to find the connexion of cause and effect in a form that satisfies the rational faculty. To suspend the operation of the moral law by the triumph of wickedness is to introduce the reign of caprice or blind chance.

The overthrow of signal villainy is next set aside by Aristotle as unsuited to tragedy,—in spite, as he expressly says, of the satisfaction it offers to the moral sense. We cannot feel pity when the suffering is deserved; we cannot feel fear when the sufferer is so far removed in nature from ourselves. Here again the judgment of Aristotle, if tested by concrete examples, receives on the whole striking confirmation. Yet this is precisely one of the cases where the inadequacy of his rules is most apparent. The limitation of view arises from applying a purely ethical instead of an aesthetic standard to dramatic character. Crime as crime has, it is true, no place in art; it is common, it is ugly. But crime may be presented in another light. Wickedness on a grand scale, resolute and intellectual, may raise the criminal above the commonplace and invest him with a sort of dignity. There is something terrible and sublime in mere will-power working its evil way, dominating its surroundings with a superhuman energy. The wreck of such power excites in us a certain tragic sympathy; not indeed the genuine pity which is inspired by unmerited suffering, but a sense of loss and regret over the waste or misuse of gifts so splendid.

It needs, however, the genius of a Shakespeare to portray this potent and commanding villainy. It was a perilous task to concentrate the whole interest of a play round a character such as Richard III.; and we may doubt whether Shakespeare himself would have ventured on it in the maturer period of his genius. The ancient drama offers nothing comparable to this great experiment —no such embodiment of an entirely depraved will, loveless and unhuman, fashioning all things with relentless adaptation to its own ends, yet standing sufficiently aloof from life to jest over it with savage humour. The wickedness of Richard III. is on a different level from that of Iago. In Iago we have no heroic criminal, but a plotter of a meaner order, in whom the faculty of intrigue amounts almost to genius; coldly diabolical, more malignant even than Richard, and delighting in evil for its own sake. Richard, equally devoid of moral scruple, and glorying in his ' naked villainy,' is yet a prince with royal purposes and an insight into affairs. His masterpieces of crime are forged by intellect and carried out with artistic finish and completeness. The moral sense is kept half in abeyance up to the close of such a drama. The badness of the man is almost lost in the sense of power. Tragic pity there cannot be for the protagonist; hardly even for his victims; terror and grandeur leave little room for any gentler feelings.

There is a certain 'contradiction,' Schiller observes,[1] 'between the aesthetic and the moral judgment.' 'Theft, for example, is a thing absolutely base . . . it is always an indelible brand stamped upon the thief, and aesthetically speaking he will always remain a base object. On this point taste is even less forgiving than morality, and its tribunal is more severe. . . . According to this view a man who robs would always be an object to be rejected by the poet who wishes to present serious pictures. But suppose this man is at the same time a murderer, he is even more to be condemned than before by the moral law. But in the aesthetic judgment he is raised one degree higher. . . . He who abases himself by a vile action can to a certain extent be raised by a crime, and can be thus reinstated in our aesthetic estimation. . . . In presence of a deep and horrible crime we no longer think of the quality but of

---

[1] Schiller's *Aesthotical Essays*, p. 251 (Bell and Sons).

the awful consequences of the action. . . . Directly
we begin to tremble, all the delicacies of taste are
reduced to silence. . . . In a word, the base element
disappears in the terrible.'

Aristotle does not appear to have been alive
to this effect of art. Still it must not be inferred
from this passage, nor again from ch. xv.,[1] that all
artistic portraiture of moral depravity is forbidden.
The Menelaus of Euripides is twice cited as an
example of character 'gratuitously bad,'[2] a phrase
which implies that there may be a badness that is
required by the dramatic motive and the structure
of a play.[3] It will fall under the wider law which
demands the light and shade of contrasted characters,
—characters either standing out against one another
in strong relief, or each forming the complement of
the other. Thus we have such pairs as Antigone
and Ismene, Odysseus and Neoptolemus, Lear and
Gloucester, Hamlet and Laertes, Brutus and Antony.
The principle once admitted will allow of the utmost
divergence of ethical type. Aristotle admits the
principle, but in a cursory and parenthetic manner,
nor does he seem to have been aware of its range
and significance.

We now come to the ideal protagonist of tragedy,
as sketched in this chapter. He is composed of
mixed elements, by no means supremely good, but
a man 'like ourselves' (ὅμοιος). The expression, if

[1] *Poet.* xv. 1–2, 8.   [2] *Poet.* xv. 5, xxv. 19.   [3] See p. 227.

taken alone, might seem to describe a person of
mediocre virtue and average powers. But Aristotle
must not be read in detached sections; and the
comparison of ch. ii. and ch. xv. with our passage
shows us that this character, while it has its basis
in reality, transcends it by a certain moral elevation.[1] We could wish that Aristotle had gone
farther and said explicitly that in power, even
more than in virtue, the tragic hero must be raised
above the ordinary level; that he must possess a
deeper vein of feeling, or heightened powers of
intellect or will; that the morally trivial, rather
than the morally bad, is fatal to tragic effect. As
it is, we arrive at the result that the tragic hero is
a man of noble nature, like ourselves in elemental
feelings and emotions; idealised, indeed, but with
so large a share of our common humanity as to
enlist our eager interest and sympathy. He falls
from a position of lofty eminence; and the disaster
that wrecks his life may be traced not to deliberate
wickedness, but to some great error or frailty.

This last expression is not free from difficulty,
and has been variously interpreted. The word
ἁμαρτία by usage admits of various shades of meaning. As a synonym of ἁμάρτημα and as applied to
a single act,[2] it denotes an error due to inadequate

---

[1] See p. 233.

[2] e.g. Aesch. *Prom.* 8,   τοιᾶσδέ τοι
ἁμαρτίας σφὲ δεῖ θεοῖς δοῦναι δίκην.

knowledge of particular circumstances. According
to strict usage we should add the qualification, that
the circumstances are such as might have been
known.[1] Thus it would cover any error of judgment arising from a hasty or careless view of the
special case ; an error which in some degree is
morally culpable, as it might have been avoided.
Error of this kind has the highest claim to pity
or consideration.[2] But ἁμαρτία is also more laxly
applied to an error due to unavoidable ignorance,
for which the more proper term is ἀτύχημα, 'misfortune.'[3] In either case, however, the error is
unintentional; it arises from want of knowledge ;
and its moral quality will depend on whether
the individual is himself responsible for his
ignorance.

Distinct from this, but still limited in its reference to a single act, is the moral ἁμαρτία proper,
a fault or error where the act is conscious and

---

[1] *Eth. Nic.* v. 8. 1135 b 16, ὅταν μὲν οὖν παραλόγως ἡ βλάβη
γένηται, ἀτύχημα· ὅταν δὲ μὴ παραλόγως, ἄνευ δὲ κακίας, ἁμάρτημα
(ἁμαρτάνει μὲν γὰρ ὅταν ἡ ἀρχὴ ἐν αὐτῷ ᾖ τῆς αἰτίας, ἀτυχεῖ δ'
ὅταν ἔξωθεν)· ὅταν δὲ εἰδὼς μὲν μὴ προβουλεύσας δέ, ἀδίκημα.
Cf. *Rhet.* 1. 13. 1374 b 6.

[2] *Eth. Nic.* iii. 2. 1110 b 33, ἡ καθ᾽ ἕκαστα (ἄγνοια), ἐν οἷς
καὶ περὶ ἃ ἡ πρᾶξις· ἐν τούτοις γὰρ καὶ ἔλεος καὶ συγγνώμη· ὁ
γὰρ τούτων τι ἀγνοῶν ἀκουσίως πράττει. iii. 1. 1109 b 31, ἐπὶ
δὲ τοῖς ἀκουσίοις συγγνώμης (γινομένης).

[3] In *Eth. Nic.* v. 8. 1135 b 12 τὰ μετ᾽ ἀγνοίας ἁμαρτήματα
include (a) ἃ ἀγνοῶν τις πράττει = ἁμαρτήματα proper, (b) ἃ δι᾽
ἄγνοιάν τις πράττει = ἀτυχήματα.

intentional, but not deliberate. Such are acts committed in anger or passion.[1]

Lastly, the word may denote a defect of character, distinct on the one hand from an isolated error or fault, and, on the other, from the vice which has its seat in a depraved will. This use, though rarer, is still Aristotelian.[2] Under this head would be included any human frailty or moral weakness, a flaw of character that is not tainted by a vicious purpose. In our passage there is much to be said in favour of the last sense, as it is here brought into relation with other words of purely moral significance, words moreover which describe not an isolated act,[3] but a more permanent state.

[1] In *Eth. Nic.* v. 8. 1135 b 22 such an act is called an ἀδίκημα, but the agent is not ἄδικος : ταῦτα γὰρ βλάπτοντες καὶ ἁμαρτά-νοντες ἀδικοῦσι μέν, καὶ ἀδικήματά ἐστιν, οὐ μέντοι πω ἄδικοι διὰ ταῦτα οὐδὲ πονηροί. . . . διὸ καλῶς τὰ ἐκ θυμοῦ οὐκ ἐκ προνοίας κρίνεται. But in *Eth. Nic.* iii. 1. 1110 b 6 the man who acts in anger or drunkenness acts ἀγνοῶν or οὐκ εἰδώς, though not δι' ἄγνοιαν : the acts, therefore, are ἁμαρτήματα.

[2] Thus ἁμαρτία is opposed to κακία : *Eth. Nic.* vii. 4. 1148 a 2, ἡ μὲν γὰρ ἀκρασία ψέγεται οὐχ ὡς ἁμαρτία μόνον ἀλλὰ καὶ ὡς κακία τις ἢ ἁπλῶς οὖσα ἢ κατά τι μέρος. But ἁμαρτία is sometimes used loosely as a euphemistic phrase for the vicious state of the ἄδικοι who act from ἡ καθόλου ἄγνοια or ἡ ἐν τῇ προαιρέσει ἄγνοια : *Eth. Nic.* iii. 1. 1110 b 29, διὰ τὴν τοιαύτην ἁμαρτίαν ἄδικοι καὶ ὅλως κακοὶ γίνονται.

[3] *Poet.* xiii. 3, ὁ μήτε ἀρετῇ διαφέρων καὶ δικαιοσύνῃ, μήτε διὰ κακίαν καὶ μοχθηρίαν μεταβάλλων εἰς τὴν δυστυχίαν : xiii. 4, μὴ διὰ μοχθηρίαν ἀλλὰ δι' ἁμαρτίαν μεγάλην. It must be owned, however, that μεγάλη is not a natural adjective to apply to a mental quality or a flaw in conduct.

On the other hand, there are many indications
in the *Poetics* that the *Oedipus Tyrannus* of
Sophocles is Aristotle's ideal play.   Now Oedipus,
though of a hasty and impulsive temperament,
with something too of proud self-assertion, cannot,
broadly speaking, be said to have owed his ruin
to any striking moral defect.   His character was
not the determining factor in his fortunes.   He, if
any man, was in a genuine sense the victim of
circumstances.   In slaying Laius he was probably
in some degree morally culpable.   But the act
was done certainly after provocation, and possibly
in self-defence.[1] His life was a chain of errors,
the most fatal of all being the marriage with his
mother.   All minor acts of ignorance culminated
here; and yet it was a purely unconscious offence
to which no kind of blame attached.   If Oedipus
is the person who suggested to Aristotle the
formula of this chapter, we can hardly limit the
word to its moral meaning, as marking either a
defect of character or a single passionate or
inconsiderate act.   ἁμαρτία may well include the
three meanings above mentioned, which in English
cannot be covered by a single term.[2] The larger
sense, if it may be assumed, will add to the

---

[1] *Oed. Col.* 992.

[2] For ἁμαρτία, ἁμαρτάνω in successive lines shifting from the
sense of voluntary to involuntary wrong-doing cf. *Oed. Col.*
966 sqq.——

profound significance of Aristotle's remark. A single great error, whether morally culpable or not; a single great defect in a character otherwise noble,—each and all of these may carry with them the tragic issues of life and death.

In any case no sharp distinction can be drawn between moral and purely intellectual error, least of all by a philosopher who laid as much stress as Aristotle did on right knowledge as an element in conduct. A moral error easily shades off into a mere defect of judgment. But that mere defect may work as potently as crime. Good intentions do not make actions right. The lofty disinterestedness of Brutus cannot atone for his want of practical insight. In the scheme of the universe a wholly unconscious error violates the law of perfection; it disturbs the moral order of the world. Distinctions of motive—the moral guilt or purity of the agent—are not here in question. So too in tragedy those are doomed who innocently err no less than those who sin consciously. Nay, the tragic irony sometimes lies precisely herein, that owing to some inherent frailty or flaw—it may be human short-sightedness, it may be some error of blood or judgment—the very virtues of a man hurry him

ἐπεὶ καθ' αὑτόν γ' οὐκ ἂν ἐξεύροις ἐμοὶ
ἁμαρτίας ὄνειδος οὐδέν, ἀνθ' ὅτου
τάδ' εἰς ἐμαυτὸν τοὺς ἐμούς θ' ἡμάρτανον.

The first ἁμαρτία is a conscious sin which might have brought on him involuntary guilt as a divinely sent expiation.

Y

forward to his ruin.   Othello in the modern drama,
Oedipus in the ancient—widely as they differ in
moral guilt—are the two most conspicuous examples
of ruin wrought by characters, noble indeed, but
not without defects, acting in the dark, and, as it
seemed, for the best.

We should probably be putting too great a
pressure on the words of Aristotle and should go
beyond his intention, if we sought to include under
the rule of ch. xiii. such a character as Macbeth.
Still the thought of our passage lends itself easily
to this enlargement of the meaning.   Macbeth
does not start with criminal purpose.   In its
original quality his nature was not devoid of
nobility.   But with him the ἁμαρτία, the primal
defect, is the taint of ambition, which under the
promptings of a stronger character than his own
and a will of inflexible force works in him as a
subtle poison.   In a case such as this, tragic fear
is heightened into awe, as we trace the growth of
a mastering passion, which beginning in a fault
or frailty enlarges itself in its successive stages,
till the first false step has issued in crime, and
crime has engendered fresh crime.   It is of the
essence of a great tragedy to bring together the
beginning and the end ; to show the one implicit
in the other.   The intervening process disappears ;
the causal chain so unites the whole that the first
ἁμαρτία bears the weight of the tragic result.

Aristotle's theory of the tragic character has suggested two divergent lines of criticism. On the one hand it is urged, that the rule δι' ἁμαρτίαν leaves no room for a 'true tragic collision.' The fate of the hero is determined by forces outside the control of the human will. A mere error, due to the inherent limitations of man's faculties, brings ruin. Thus, it is said, the highest form of tragedy in which character is destiny, is at once excluded. Nothing is left but the drama of an external fate.

This objection assumes that the tragic ἁμαρτία is in truth no more than an ἀτύχημα, a mere accident, a misadventure, the circumstances being such that reason and foresight are unavailing. Now, even if the word, as here used, were so limited, a collision of forces such as is essential to the drama would not be wanting. If a man is so placed that he is at war with the forces outside him—either the forces of the universe, the fixed conditions of existence, the inevitable laws of life, which constitute 'Fate'; or the forces that reside in other wills that cross and thwart his own—the result may be a tragic conflict. The ancient drama is chiefly, though by no means exclusively, the representation of a conflict thus unwittingly begun, however much purpose may be involved in its later stages. The spectacle of a man struggling with his fate affords ample scope for the display of will-power and ethical qualities. The *Oedipus Tyrannus* portrays a tragic conflict none the less moving because the original error which leads to the catastrophe springs from the necessary blindness and infirmity of human nature.

But if we yield the main contention of these critics and admit that a ' true tragic collision ' is one in which character and passion determine destiny ; in which the individual by an act of will enters on a conflict where the forces enlisted on either side are chiefly moral forces, Aristotle's phrase, if we have rightly interpreted it, will still include the most interesting and significant of such cases. The great frailty will then be a moral frailty. The resulting collision will in general be one of two kinds. Either the individual from levity or passion violates a known right, encroaches on a sphere not his own, and provokes a conflict which reacts on his character and culminates in tragic disaster : or the collision will be one between internal moral forces, the scene of the conflict being the heart of man. Hence we get the struggles of conscience, the wavering purpose, the divided will,—dramatic motives rarely found in the older Greek tragedians, but which with Euripides entered into the domain of the drama and thenceforth held an assured place. The objection, therefore, to this extent appears to be invalid. At the same time, as already indicated,

Aristotle's doctrine is in a measure defective. It fails to take account of two exceptional types of tragedy,—that which exhibits the antagonism between a pure will and a disjointed world, or between a grand but criminal purpose and the higher moral forces with which it is confronted.

Another class of critics have been reluctant under any circumstances to disallow the authority of Aristotle. It was gravely observed by Roger Bacon that 'Aristotle hath the same authority in philosophy that the Apostle Paul hath in divinity.' After the Renaissance the general intellectual sovereignty already wielded by Aristotle was extended, especially in France, to the whole field of literature. Every well constructed tragedy, ancient or modern, was supposed to square with the rules of the *Poetics*. When the facts of literary history refused to adjust themselves to the text, the meaning of the text was strained or explained away, till the original rules were not unfrequently forced to bear the very sense they were designed to exclude. So far was the infallibility of Aristotle carried that on one occasion Dacier makes short work with an Italian commentator, who had ventured to find an inconsistency between a passage of the *Poetics* and the words of Holy Writ. He brushes the objection aside with a simple *reductio ad absurdum*. 'As if Divinity and the Holy Scriptures could ever be contrary to the sentiments

of Nature on which Aristotle founds his judgments.'[1]
Methods of interpretation were applied to the
Poetics with which we are more familiar in Biblical
criticism. The words of Aristotle were explained
and defended by just those expedients that have
been resorted to in support of the verbal interpretation of Scripture.

Corneille was one of the adepts in the art of
adding glosses and saving clauses to the Aristotelian
text. Though he has left many luminous statements
of the principles of poetry, his work as an expositor
is too often inspired by the desire to reconcile
Aristotelian rules with plays of his own, which had
been written before he had become acquainted
with the *Poetics*. A single instance—one of those
quoted by Lessing—will show his easy method of
harmonising difficulties. Character, we are told
in the *Poetics* (ch. xv.), must be χρηστά, ' good ' :—
the word can bear no other than the moral meaning. Corneille, seeing that this requirement, taken
rigidly, would condemn a large number of admirable
plays, surmises that what Aristotle demands is
'the brilliant or elevated character of a virtuous
or criminal habit.'[2] He instances his own Cleopatra,
a heroine who is ' extremely wicked '; ' there is no
murder from which she shrinks.' 'But all her
crimes are connected with a certain grandeur of

---

[1] Dacier on *Poetics*, ch. xiii. note 1, Trans.

[2] Corneille, Discours i. *Du Poème Dramatique.*

soul, which has in it something so elevated, that while we condemn her actions, we must still admire the source whence they flow.'

In itself this criticism is on the right track; but not as an explanation of the Aristotelian χρηστὰ ἤθη. It is what Aristotle ought to have said, not what he says. As Lessing observes,[1] Aristotle's 'goodness' must on this view be 'of a sort that agrees with moral badness as well as with moral goodness.' In a similar spirit of mistaken loyalty to Aristotle and in similar defiance of linguistic usage, other commentators, — Bossu, Dacier, Metastasio—persuaded themselves that χρηστὰ ἤθη could mean 'well marked' characters, in this way rescuing the word from its objectionable moral limitations.[2] Lessing here, while avoiding these errors of interpretation and retaining the plain meaning of the words, does so on grounds which are wholly un-Aristotelian. 'Corneille,' he says, 'could not have had a more pernicious idea' than that vice may be ennobled by aesthetic treatment. 'If we carry it out there is an end to all truth, and all delusion, to all moral benefit of tragedy. . . . What folly to desire to deter by the unhappy consequences of vice if we conceal its

[1] Lessing, Hamb. Dram. Trans. (Bohn) p. 437.

[2] Cf. Dryden, Preface to Troilus and Cressida (where he is evidently summarising Poet. ch. xv.), 'first they [the manners] must be apparent; that is, in every character of the play some inclinations of the person must appear.'

inner ugliness.' He is still under the influence of
his great assumption, that the immediate business
of tragedy is to make men better.

There is another method by which the authority
of Aristotle has been vindicated. Plays have been
brought into harmony with his supposed rules at
the cost of manifest violence done to the poems
themselves. Shakespeare has not escaped this
vice of interpretation. Gervinus dominated, as it
would seem, by the idea of a moral ἁμαρτία is
inclined to find some culpable error wherever
there is tragic ruin. Such an error is proved to
be the cause, or partial cause, of the misfortune
that ensues not merely to the protagonist, but also
to the subordinate dramatic characters. He discovers a 'poetic justice' in the death of Duncan,
whose unwary security led him to accept the
hospitality of Macbeth; in the death of Cordelia,
whose want of 'wise and prudent foresight' places
her in contrast with Edgar, and justifies the
difference between her fate and his; in the death
of Desdemona, who is guilty of 'dangerous inter-
cession on behalf of Cassio,' and 'falls into sin
through innocence and goodness.'

Setting aside these strange perversions of
criticism, we may well believe that Aristotle
would have felt some surprise at being assumed to
have laid down a binding code of poetical rules
for all time and place. The contrast, is, indeed, a

curious one between his own tentative manner and
the dogmatic conclusions based on what he has
written. He feels his way, he tacitly corrects or
supplements what he has previously said; with a
careless ease he throws out suggestions, without
guarding against misconception. He little thought
of the far-reaching meaning that would one day be
attached to each stray utterance. It is not merely
the fragmentary form of the *Poetics* and the gaps
and errors in the text that should warn us against
straining the significance of isolated expressions.
Aristotle's own manner is allusive and incomplete.
He does not write with the fear of other critics
before his eyes. He assumes an audience already
familiar with the general drift of his thought, able
to fill in what is unsaid and to place his rules in
proper light and perspective.

In this very chapter he proposes at the outset
to sketch the plan of the *ideal* tragedy.[1] It is
of the type technically known in the *Poetics* as
'complex' ($\pi\epsilon\pi\lambda\epsilon\gamma\mu\acute{\epsilon}\nu\eta$), not simple ($\acute{a}\pi\lambda\acute{r}$). The
'complex' tragedy is one in which the Change
of Fortune ($\mu\epsilon\tau\acute{a}\beta\alpha\sigma\iota\varsigma$) is combined with Reversal
of the Situation ($\pi\epsilon\rho\iota\pi\acute{\epsilon}\tau\epsilon\iota\alpha$) or with Recognition
($\acute{a}\nu\alpha\gamma\nu\acute{\omega}\rho\iota\sigma\iota\varsigma$), or with both.[2] Much misconcep-

---

[1] *Poet.* xiii. 2, $\tau\grave{\eta}\nu$ $\sigma\acute{\upsilon}\nu\theta\epsilon\sigma\iota\nu$ . . . $\tau\hat{\eta}s$ $\kappa\alpha\lambda\lambda\acute{\iota}\sigma\tau\eta s$ $\tau\rho\alpha\gamma\psi\delta\acute{\iota}\alpha s$.

[2] *Poet.* x. 2. The precise meaning of $\pi\epsilon\rho\iota\pi\acute{\epsilon}\tau\epsilon\iota\alpha$ is a matter of
some controversy. The old rendering 'Reversal of Fortune' can
hardly now be maintained. In Ed. 3 I translated the word
'Reversal of Intention,' accepting the view put forward by Vahlen

tion might have been avoided had it been
noted that Aristotle is here determining not
in his *Beiträge zu Aristoteles' Poetik* and further elucidated by
Dr. Lock in an interesting article in the *Classical Review*, vol. ix.
pp. 251–253. According to that view περιπέτεια is any event in
which the intention of one of the agents is overruled to produce
an effect the opposite of that which is intended (*Poet.* xi. 1, ἡ εἰς
τὸ ἐναντίον τῶν πραττομένων μεταβολή). Professor Bywater,
however (*Festschrift Theodor Gomperz dargebracht zum siebzigsten
Geburtstage*, Wien, 1902, pp. 164 ff.), urges strong reasons against
attaching so technical and limited a meaning to the term. He
argues that τὰ πραττόμενα of the definition 'would naturally
denote no more than the incidents taking place in a certain scene';
that the meaning assigned to the word by Vahlen is 'more
artificial than an ordinary stage-term can bear'; that it goes
beyond the definition and 'depends too much on an accident of
expression in Aristotle's account of περιπέτεια in the *Oedipus
Tyrannus*' (ἐλθὼν ὡς εὐφρανῶν τὸν Οἰδίπουν καὶ ἀπαλλάξων τοῦ
πρὸς τὴν μητέρα φόβου κ.τ.λ.)—where the *intention* ascribed to
the Messenger is not fully warranted by the play itself; and that
it is very difficult to reconcile this meaning with the description
in the *Poetics* of the great scene in the *Lynceus*. He holds that
περιπέτεια was only meant to designate *a complete change of situation
in the course of a single scene*;—thus τῶν πραττομένων in the
definition will be governed by μεταβολή rather than by εἰς τὸ
ἐναντίον. The term περιπέτεια will nevertheless remain distinct
from the term μετάβασις, as denoting a striking change occurring
in the course of the general movement (μετάβασις) leading up to
the crisis of a play.

I agree in the main with this contention; but would add that
περιπέτεια as defined by Aristotle presents, I think, a sharper and
less vague idea than is conveyed by any such phrase as 'Complete
Change of the Situation,' or 'Reversal of the Situation,' though
we may be driven to this rendering for a want of a nearer
equivalent. The tragic περιπέτεια in ch. xi. 1 suggests, if I
mistake not, a series of incidents or a train of action (τὰ
πραττόμενα) tending to bring about a certain end but resulting
in something wholly different. The situation, as it were, turns

what is *good* in tragic art, but what is *best*; he is describing the ideal tragedy, with the ideal upon the agent who is attempting to deal with it,—swings round and catches him in the recoil. It may be noted that among τὰ ἐλεεινά enumerated in *Rhet.* ii. 8. 1386 a 12 is τὸ ὅθεν προσῆκεν ἀγαθόν τι ὑπάρξαι, κακόν τι συμβῆναι.

'Reversal of *Intention*' will not, then, be of the essence of περιπέτεια. On the other hand, it may enter as an element into the case and heighten the dramatic effect. The instances, therefore, adduced by Dr. Lock—the story of Shylock in the *Merchant of Venice*, of Adrastus in Herodotus, of Haman and Mordecai in the book of Esther, of Joseph and his brethren—though not entirely typical, are yet apposite illustrations. Furthermore, Dr. Lock remarks that 'περιπέτεια is to actions what irony is to language. In the latter case, words are caught up by circumstances and charged with a fuller meaning than the speaker meant; in the former, deeds are equally caught up out of his grasp and charged with a meaning the very opposite of that which the agent meant.' This statement appears to need similar qualification. Every περιπέτεια does not come under this description; but an overruled intention, with the new significance thereby added to the event, is one of the special forms which περιπέτεια may assume. It is worth observing that περιπέτεια so modified sometimes approaches nearly to what is known in modern criticism as the 'Irony of Destiny.'

Apart, however, from the meaning of περιπέτεια as defined in ch. xi. 1, Aristotle also uses the word in a more lax and popular sense for the mere development or evolution of incident out of incident. Mr. Prickard has called my attention to a passage in *de Hist. Anim.* viii. 2. 590 b 13, where περιπέτεια is applied to the *turn of incident* by which the polypus eats the crab, the crab eats the conger, and the conger eats the polypus. In this looser sense I take the phrase ἐκ περιπετείας (*Poet.* xvi. 3), which is used of the recognition of Odysseus by his nurse (*Odyss.* xix. 396 ff.), as opposed to an ἀναγνώρισις πίστεως ἕνεκα (i.e. with the deliberate intention to convince). The interpretation 'accidentally' offered by Dr. Lock differs but slightly from this; he compares the usage of the word in Polybius for 'an accident,' or 'a disaster.'

hero to correspond. The way in which other types
of plot and character are dismissed is, no doubt,
too sweeping, too summary, and partakes of the
same exaggeration as certain remarks in ch. vi.
about the subordinate place of character in the
drama.[1] It is, however, a feature of Aristotle's
manner, especially in his more popular treatises,
to set aside the less preferred of two alternatives
in words which imply unqualified rejection. The
ideal tragedy, as here sketched by him, is one
which will excite pity and fear in no ordinary
combination, but these two emotions heightened
to their utmost capacity under the conditions of
the most perfect art. We cannot infer that he
would condemn as utterly bad all that did not
come up to these requirements. There may be an
inferior, but still an interesting tragedy, in which
the union of the terrible and the pathetic does not
answer to the full tragic idea. The play will fall
short — so Aristotle would probably say—in a
greater or less degree of perfection, but it does
not cease to be tragedy.

When due weight has been given to these considerations, the formula here proposed for the
character of the tragic hero will still remain incomplete and inadequate. Yet—as is often the case
with Aristotle's sayings—it contains a profound
truth, and a capacity for adaptation beyond what

[1] See pp. 343 ff.

was immediately present to the mind of the writer. He insists on the conditions above specified as requisite if we would merge our own personality in the creation of the poet. No 'faultily faultless' hero, any more than a consummate villain, can inspire so vital a sympathy as the hero whose weakness and whose strength alike bring him within the range of our common humanity. Modern literature, and above all the Shakespearian drama, while proving that the formula of Aristotle is too rigid, have also revealed new meanings in the idea of the tragic ἁμαρτία. Its dramatic possibilities have been enlarged and deepened. In Hamlet, Othello, Lear, Macbeth, Coriolanus, we have the ruin of noble natures through some defect of character. In infinitely various ways it has been shown that the most dramatic of motives is the process by which a frailty or flaw of nature grows and expands till it culminates in tragic disaster.

CHAPTER IX

PLOT AND CHARACTER IN TRAGEDY

OF the six elements into which Aristotle analyses a tragedy,[1] plot ($\mu\hat{v}\theta os$) holds the first place. Next in order is placed *ēthos* ($\hat{\eta}\theta os$), and then *dianoia* ($\delta\iota\acute{a}\nu o\iota a$). Each of these terms needs some explanation.

Plot in the drama, in its fullest sense, is the artistic equivalent of 'action' in real life.[2] We have already observed[3] that 'action' ($\pi\rho\hat{a}\xi\iota s$) in Aristotle is not a purely external act, but an inward process which works outward, the expression of a man's rational personality. Sometimes it is used for 'action' or 'doing' in its strict and limited sense; sometimes for that side of right conduct ($\epsilon\dot{v}\pi\rho a\xi\acute{\iota}a$) in which doing is only one element, though the most important. Again, it can denote 'faring' as well as 'doing': hence, in the drama, where 'action' is represented by the plot, it must

---

[1] *Poet.* vi., $\ddot{o}\psi\iota s$, $\mu\epsilon\lambda o\pi o\iota\acute{\iota}a$, $\lambda\acute{\epsilon}\xi\iota s$, $\mu\hat{v}\theta os$, $\hat{\eta}\theta os$, $\delta\iota\acute{a}\nu o\iota a$.
[2] *Poet.* vi. 6, $\ddot{\epsilon}\sigma\tau\iota\nu$ $\delta\grave{\eta}$ $\tau\hat{\eta}s$ $\mu\grave{\epsilon}\nu$ $\pi\rho\acute{a}\xi\epsilon\omega s$ $\acute{o}$ $\mu\hat{v}\theta os$ $\acute{\eta}$ $\mu\acute{\iota}\mu\eta\sigma\iota s$.
[3] See p. 123.

include outward fortune and misfortune (εὐτυχία and δυστυχία). Again, it is used by Aristotle of the processes of the mental life;[1] and lastly, in some contexts it is almost synonymous with πάθη.

The πρᾶξις of the drama has primary reference to that kind of action which, while springing from the inward power of will, manifests itself in external doing. The very word ' drama ' indicates this idea. The verb (δρᾶν), from which the noun comes, is the strongest of the words used to express the notion of *doing*; it marks an activity exhibited in outward and energetic form.[2] In the drama the characters are not described, they enact their own story and so reveal themselves. We know them not from what we are told of them, but by their *performance* before our eyes.[3] Without action in this sense a poem

---

[1] *Pol.* iv. (vii.) 3. 1325 b 16, ἀλλὰ τὸν πρακτικὸν (βίον) οὐκ ἀναγκαῖον εἶναι πρὸς ἑτέρους, καθάπερ οἴονταί τινες, οὐδὲ τὰς διανοίας εἶναι μόνον ταύτας πρακτικὰς τὰς τῶν ἀποβαινόντων χάριν γινομένας ἐκ τοῦ πράττειν, ἀλλὰ πολὺ μᾶλλον τὰς αὐτοτελεῖς καὶ τὰς αὐτῶν ἕνεκεν θεωρίας καὶ διανοήσεις. ἡ γὰρ εὐπραξία τέλος, ὥστε καὶ πρᾶξίς τις· μάλιστα δὲ πράττειν λέγομεν κυρίως καὶ τῶν ἐξωτερικῶν πράξεων τοὺς ταῖς διανοίαις ἀρχιτέκτονας.

[2] δρώντων καὶ οὐ δι' ἀπαγγελίας are the words of the definition of tragedy. So (of Sophocles and Aristophanes) *Poet.* iii. 2, πράττοντας γὰρ μιμοῦνται καὶ δρῶντας ἄμφω. Cf. the frequent antithesis of δρᾶν and πάσχειν, and the adj. δραστήριος.

[3] Cf. the spectacular use of δρᾶν, e.g. τὰ δρώμενα Ἐλευσῖνι.

would be not a bad drama, but no drama at all. The form might be epic or lyric, it would not be dramatic.

But this does not exhaust the idea of πρᾶξις as understood by Aristotle. Among the reasons he gives for the pre-eminent place assigned to the plot, one is of fundamental importance. Tragedy, he explains, is an imitation of an action which is an image of human life,—of its supreme welfare or misery; human life itself consisting in a mode of action, not in a mere quality of mind [1]—in a form of moral energy or activity, which has a profoundly inward as well as an outward side. The plot or πρᾶξις of the drama reproduces this most significant mode of action; it does not stop short at strenuous doing. Still less is it a representation of purely outward fortune or misfortune. The words used by Aristotle are not μίμησις εὐτυχίας καὶ δυστυχίας, but μίμησις πράξεως καὶ βίου. The former phrase would be too external, too superficial to sum up

---

[1] *Poet.* vi. 9, ἡ γὰρ τραγῳδία μίμησίς ἐστιν οὐκ ἀνθρώπων ἀλλὰ πράξεως καὶ βίου· <ὁ δὲ βίος> ἐν πράξει ἐστὶν καὶ τὸ τέλος πρᾶξίς τις ἐστίν, οὐ ποιότης. (For the reading see Crit. Notes.) With the last words cf. *Pol.* iv. (vii.) 3. 1325 b 21 (quoted note 1, p. 335): *Phys.* ii. 6. 197 b 2, διὸ καὶ ἀνάγκη περὶ τὰ πρακτὰ εἶναι τὴν τύχην· σημεῖον δ' ὅτι δοκεῖ ἤτοι ταὐτὸν εἶναι τῇ εὐδαιμονίᾳ ἡ εὐτυχία ἢ ἐγγύς, ἡ δ' εὐδαιμονία πρᾶξίς τις· εὐπραξία γάρ. Plato had already observed that all imitative art imitates 'men in action,' *Rep.* x. 603 c, πράττοντας, φαμέν, ἀνθρώπους μιμεῖται ἡ μιμητικὴ βιαίους ἢ ἑκουσίας πράξεις καὶ ἐκ τοῦ πράττειν ἢ εὖ οἰομένους ἢ κακῶς πεπραγέναι.

the essence and meaning of a tragedy as a whole, though it is through the outward turns of fortune that the catastrophe is brought about; these are the medium by which the inner sense of the action is revealed.

The plot, then, contains the kernel of that 'action' which it is the business of tragedy to represent. The word 'action,' as is evident from what has been said, requires to be interpreted with much latitude of meaning. It embraces not only the deeds, the incidents, the situations, but also the mental processes, and the motives which under-lie the outward events or which result from them.[1] It is the compendious expression for all these forces working together towards a definite end.

Next we come to *ēthos* and *dianoia*. In their aesthetic application these present some difficulties. Aristotle appears, indeed, to bestow unusual pains on elucidating their meaning, for he gives at least two definitions or interpretations of each in ch. vi., which again are supplemented by the observations of ch. xv. regarding *ēthos*, and of ch. xix. regarding *dianoia*.[2] Yet a clear and consistent view

---

[1] Cf. Dryden, *Essay of Dramatic Poesy*, 'Every alteration or crossing of a design, every new-sprung passion, and turn of it, is a part of the action, and much the noblest, except we conceive nothing to be action till they come to blows.'

[2] Mr. R. P. Hardie (*Mind*, vol. iv. No. 15) observes that while the expression or imitation of the πρᾶξις is called the μῦθος, there are no special words for the μίμησις of ἦθος and of διάνοια, and

cannot be extracted from ch. vi. in the form in
which we have it; and this fact, taken in conjunction with the multiplicity of definitions, has
afforded some ground for suspecting that there

hence both are ambiguously used, (1) as implied in the visible
πρᾶξις, (2) as = μίμησις τοῦ ἤθους and μίμησις τῆς διανοίας,
where a certain amount of λόγος is required to make clear to
the audience what is going on in the minds of the agents, without
which knowledge the πρᾶξις cannot be rightly understood.

The dramatic ἦθος is defined in the following passages :—

(i.) *Poet.* vi. 6, τὰ δὲ ἤθη (λέγω), καθ᾽ ὃ ποιούς τινας εἶναί
φαμεν τοὺς πράττοντας : cf. vi. 10, εἰσὶν δὲ κατὰ μὲν
τὰ ἤθη ποιοί τινες. These passages are both somewhat
inconsistent with vi. 5, where the character of persons
(ποιοί τινες) is said to be determined not by ἦθος alone,
but by ἦθος and διάνοια.

(ii.) *Poet.* vi. 17 (where ἦθος is in the second sense above
mentioned, = μίμησις τοῦ ἤθους), ἔστιν δὲ ἦθος μὲν τὸ
τοιοῦτον ὃ δηλοῖ τὴν προαίρεσιν ὁποῖά τις [προ]αιρεῖται
ἢ φεύγει· διόπερ οὐκ ἔχουσιν ἦθος τῶν λόγων ἐν οἷς
οὐκ ἔστι δῆλον ἢ ἐν οἷς μηδ᾽ ὅλως ἔστιν ὅ τι [προ]αιρεῖ-
ται ἢ φεύγει ὁ λέγων. (For the reading see Crit. Notes.)
In this context the reference is to the dramatic λόγοι
which express (a) ἦθος, (b) διάνοιαν. Cf. the rule for
rhetorical λόγοι in *Rhet.* iii. 16. 1417 a 15, ἠθικὴν δὲ
χρὴ τὴν διήγησιν εἶναι. ἔσται δὲ τοῦτο, ἂν εἰδῶμεν
τί ἦθος ποιεῖ. ἓν μὲν δὴ τὸ προαίρεσιν δηλοῦν, ποιὸν
δὲ τὸ ἦθος τῷ ποιὰν ταύτην· ἡ δὲ προαίρεσις ποιὰ τῷ
τέλει.

(iii.) *Poet.* xv. 1, where ἦθος is expressed by any λόγος or
πρᾶξις that manifests moral purpose : ἕξει δὲ ἦθος μὲν
ἐὰν ὥσπερ ἐλέχθη ποιῇ φανερὸν ὁ λόγος ἢ ἡ πρᾶξις
προαίρεσίν τινα, χρηστὸν δὲ ἐὰν χρηστήν.

(On the different uses of ἦθος in the *Rhetoric* see Cope's Introduction pp. 108 ff.)

The dramatic διάνοια is thus explained :—

(i.) *Poet.* vi. 6, διάνοιαν δέ, ἐν ὅσοις λέγοντες ἀποδεικνύασίν τι

may be both omissions and interpolations in the text. In what follows we will confine ourselves to certain broad conclusions, though even these may not all pass unchallenged.

The term *ēthos* is generally translated ' character,'

ἢ καὶ ἀποφαίνονται γνώμην. A γνώμη is a general maxim, and ἀποφαίνεσθαι, ' enunciate,' a *verbum proprium* in connexion with it : so καθόλου τι ἀποφαίνονται in § 17. A γνώμη, though usually a *moral* maxim, exhibits διάνοια rather than ἦθος, probably because it is thought of as the starting-point or conclusion of an argument. See the use of γνῶμαι in *Rhet.* ii. 21. 1395 b 14 as rhetorical enthymemes. There, however, they are said to give an *ethical* character to speeches.

(ii.) *Poet.* vi. 15, τρίτον δὲ ἡ διάνοια· τοῦτο δέ ἐστιν τὸ λέγειν δύνασθαι τὰ ἐνόντα καὶ τὰ ἁρμόττοντα.

Poet. vi. 17, διάνοια δέ, ἐν οἷς ἀποδεικνύουσί τι ὡς ἔστιν ἢ ὡς οὐκ ἔστιν ἢ καθόλου τι ἀποφαίνονται. Here, as in vi. 6, διάνοια = μίμησις τῆς διανοίας, the subject to ἀποδεικνύουσι being the dramatic characters.

(iii.) xix. 1–2, ἔστι δὲ κατὰ τὴν διάνοιαν ταῦτα, ὅσα ὑπὸ τοῦ λόγου δεῖ παρασκευασθῆναι. μέρη δὲ τούτων τό τε ἀποδεικνύναι καὶ τὸ λύειν καὶ τὸ πάθη παρασκευάζειν, οἷον ἔλεον ἢ φόβον ἢ ὀργὴν καὶ ὅσα τοιαῦτα, καὶ ἔτι μέγεθος καὶ μικρότητας. Here διάνοια as manifested in dramatic λόγοι is brought within the domain of Rhetoric (τὰ μὲν οὖν περὶ τὴν διάνοιαν ἐν τοῖς περὶ ῥητορικῆς κείσθω).

Finsler (p. 79) is, I think, right in referring the phrase τὸ πάθη παρασκευάζειν to the emotional effects which the *dramatis personae* produce on one another by their λόγοι, not (as commonly interpreted) to the excitation of feeling in the minds of the audience. It may be observed that the πάθη mentioned are not only ἔλεος and φόβος but also ὀργὴ καὶ ὅσα τοιαῦτα.

Mr. R. P. Hardie (l.c.) approaches to this view, but takes the phrase in the sense of 'supply (to the spectators) the πάθη of οἱ λέγοντες,'—a sense which παρασκευάζειν could hardly bear.

and in many contexts this is its natural English
equivalent. But if we would speak of character
in its widest sense, as including all that reveals
a man's personal and inner self—his intellectual
powers no less than the will and the emotions—
we go beyond the meaning of the Aristotelian
ēthos. In the *Poetics*, *ēthos* and *dianoia* are each
one side of character; they are two distinct factors
which unite to constitute the concrete and living
person. Character in its most comprehensive
sense depends on these two elements, which, again,
are declared to be the causes of action, and to
determine its quality.[1] *Ēthos*, as explained by
Aristotle, is the moral element in character. It
reveals a certain state or direction of the will. It
is an expression of moral purpose, of the permanent
disposition and tendencies, the tone and sentiment
of the individual. *Dianoia* is the thought, the
intellectual element, which is implied in all rational
conduct, through which alone *ēthos* can find outward expression, and which is separable from *ēthos*
only by a process of abstraction.

When we pass to the dramatic *ēthos* and *dianoia*,

---

[1] *Poet.* vi. 5, πράττεται δὲ ὑπὸ τινῶν πραττόντων, οὓς ἀνάγκη
ποιούς τινας εἶναι κατά τε τὸ ἦθος καὶ τὴν διάνοιαν (διὰ γὰρ
τούτων καὶ τὰς πράξεις εἶναί φαμεν ποιάς τινας, πέφυκεν δὲ αἴτια
δύο τῶν πράξεων εἶναι, διάνοιαν καὶ ἦθος . . .). Cf. *Eth. Nic.* vi. 2.
1139 a 34, εὐπραξία γὰρ καὶ τὸ ἐναντίον ἐν πράξει ἄνευ διανοίας
καὶ ἤθους οὐκ ἔστιν. But in *Poet.* vi. 6 and 10 it is more
loosely said that we are ποιοί τινες κατὰ τὰ ἤθη.

we find that *ēthos* reveals itself both in the speeches
and in the actions of the dramatic characters in a
manner corresponding to the twofold manifestations
of *ēthos* in real life.[1]   But we observe with surprise
that *ēthos* as revealed in action is but lightly touched
on.   Still more surprising is it that though *dianoia*
in real life is stated to be one of the two causes
of action, there is no express recognition of it as
similarly manifested in the drama.   The reason of
the omission may possibly be that action is treated

[1] Note 2, p. 337.   Mr. Bosanquet in his acute observations on
plot and character-drawing (*History of Aesthetic*, pp. 70 ff.) argues
against ἦθος being taken to mean 'character in the sense in which
character is understood to-day, to be the object of artistic portraiture
in Shakespeare or Thackeray.'   The remarks in the text bear out
this contention, though from another point of view.   It is more
difficult to agree entirely with his view that ἦθος in the *Poetics*
is something merely 'typical and generic,' 'as we say good or bad
character,' a certain type of disposition or moral temperament
without the more individual traits.   We may indeed readily admit
that the subtlety and delicacy of modern character-drawing did not
present themselves to Aristotle's mind, more simple and elementary
qualities formed the basis of dramatic character as he understood
it.   But it appears pretty certain that he thought of *individual*
portraiture, and not merely of the delineation of a moral type.
This seems to follow if only from the rules about τὰ ἤθη in ch. xv.,
especially from the requirement that the law of necessity or probability, prescribed for the plot, shall apply also to the speeches
and actions of the dramatic persons (§§ 5–6).   This inner rationality
surely demands a strong basis of individual character.

   Mr. R. P. Hardie (l.c.) similarly observes in reference to ch. xiii.,
where ἦθος is discussed in reference to μῦθος, that 'the drift of the
whole passage implies that ἦθος does not necessarily mean to
Aristotle a simple generic type, but that its complexity is precisely
on a level with the complexity of the plot.'

in the *Poetics* as a separate and independent element of tragedy, and kept distinct as far as possible from the other elements. This is, indeed, one of the inconveniences arising from the highly analytic method of Aristotle in dealing with the organic parts of an artistic whole, as also with the phenomena of life. It is a method that tends to divert our attention from the interlacing union of the parts and from their final synthesis. Be the cause what it may, explicit mention is made in our text of the dramatic *dianoia* as embodied only in speech not in action.

In the dramatic dialogue, the persons who converse do not discuss abstract truth such as the problems of mathematics;[1] they desire to explain their own doings and influence others. The two elements, *ēthos* and *dianoia*, may indeed be found side by side in one and the same discourse; but even so, there is an appreciable difference between them. Wherever moral choice, or a determination of the will is manifested, there *ēthos* appears.[2]

---

[1] Cf. *Poet.* vi. 17, διόπερ οὐκ ἔχουσιν ἦθος τῶν λόγων ἐν οἷς οὐκ ἔστι δῆλον ἢ ἐν οἷς μηδ' ὅλως ἔστιν ὅ τι [προ]αιρεῖται ἢ φεύγει ὁ λέγων, with *Rhet.* iii. 16. 1417 a 18, διὰ τοῦτο οὐκ ἔχουσιν οἱ μαθηματικοὶ λόγοι ἤθη ὅτι οὐδὲ προαίρεσιν.

[2] Inferior writers attempted, it would seem, to make ethical monologues take the place of a well constructed plot. *Poet.* vi. 12, ἔτι ἐάν τις ἐφεξῆς θῇ ῥήσεις ἠθικὰς καὶ λέξει καὶ διανοίᾳ εὖ πεποιημένας, οὐ ποιήσει ὃ ἦν τῆς τραγῳδίας ἔργον. Cf. Plat. *Phaedr.* 268 c—269 A, where such ῥήσεις are reckoned among τὰ πρὸ τραγῳδίας, 'the preliminaries of tragedy,' not as τὰ τραγικά.

Under *dianoia* are included the intellectual reflexions of the speaker; the proof of his own
statements, the disproof of those of his opponents,
his general maxims concerning life and conduct,
as elicited by the action and forming part of a
train of reasoning. The emphasis laid by Aristotle
on this dialectical *dianoia* is doubtless connected
with the decisive influence exercised by political
debate and forensic pleading on the Greek theatre,
the ἀγών of the ecclesia or of the law-courts being
reproduced in the ἀγών of the drama.

A few sentences of cardinal importance as to
plot and character, from ch. vi. 9–11, must here be
quoted : 'Tragedy is an imitation, not of men, but
of an action and of life, and life consists in action,
and its end is a mode of action, not a quality.
Now character determines men's qualities, but it is
by their actions that they are happy or the reverse.
Dramatic action, therefore, is not with a view to
the representation of character : character comes in
as subsidiary to the actions. Hence the incidents
and the plot are the end of a tragedy ; and the end
is the chief thing of all. Again, without action
there cannot be a tragedy ; there may be without
character.' The eager insistence with which
Aristotle maintains the subordination of *ēthos* to
plot[1] leads him into a certain exaggeration of state-

---

[1] *Poet.* vi. 10, οὔκουν ὅπως τὰ ἤθη μιμήσωνται πράττουσιν,
ἀλλὰ τὰ ἤθη συμπαραλαμβάνουσιν διὰ τὰς πράξεις: vi. 15,

ment. The two elements are set against one another in sharp and impossible opposition. 'Without action there cannot be a tragedy; there may be without ēthē.'[1] Clearly, this last remark cannot be pressed in a perfectly literal sense.[2] The meaning intended probably is, that there may be a

ἔστιν τε (ὁ μῦθος) μίμησις πράξεως καὶ διὰ ταύτην μάλιστα τῶν πραττόντων.

[1] *Poet.* vi. 11, ἔτι ἄνευ μὲν πράξεως οὐκ ἂν γένοιτο τραγῳδία, ἄνευ δὲ ἠθῶν γένοιτ' ἄν. There is a similar exaggeration also in the following sentence, αἱ γὰρ τῶν νέων τῶν πλείστων ἀήθεις τραγῳδίαι εἰσίν, and again in ἡ δὲ Ζεύξιδος γραφὴ οὐδὲν ἔχει ἦθος.

[2] In discussing the place of character and plot in the drama confusion is frequently caused by an ambiguity in the use of the words, such as indeed we are conscious of also in the use of the corresponding words in the *Poetics.* In the popular antithesis of the two terms 'character' has not its full dramatic value, and instead of signifying 'characters producing an action,' it stands for an abstract impression of character left on our minds by the reading of a play. Similarly 'plot' is regarded as the 'story' in a play, viewed in abstraction from the special nature of the persons; and, in particular, denotes a complication exciting wonder or suspense,—an idea, however, which is not necessarily present in the word μῦθος. In this sense a play with a weak 'plot' but good 'character-drawing' is undramatic, though it tells us something about human nature. On the cther hand a play with a strong 'plot' and weak delineation of 'character' may tell us almost nothing about human nature, and yet may be dramatic. (It is more doubtful whether it can ever be tragic.) From this point of view it may be said that you can have a drama without 'character,' but not without 'plot.'

'Plot' in the full sense of the word is the 'action' (in the large Greek meaning of πρᾶξις), and includes not only the circumstances and incidents which form the main part of 'plot' as popularly conceived, but also 'character' in the full dramatic sense of

tragedy in which the moral character of the individual agents is so weakly portrayed as to be of
no account in the evolution of the action.   The
persons may be mere types, or marked only by
class characteristics, or lacking in those distinctive
qualities out of which dramatic action grows.[1]   The
next sentence adds by way of corroboration that
'the tragedies of most of our modern poets are
devoid of character.' The later tragedians attempted,
it would seem, by an ingenious mechanism of plot
to make up for their want of skill in character-
drawing.   The other side of the antithesis above
quoted cannot be disputed : ' Without action there
cannot be a tragedy' ; for action is the *differentia*
of drama, and must ever remain the primary and
controlling principle.   The illustration from painting

'characters producing an action.'   An antithesis, therefore, between
'character' and 'plot,' thus understood, is obviously impossible.

On these grounds, we may say that 'character,' in the popular
sense, exists for the sake of the 'action' ; but 'character' in the
full sense cannot correctly be said to exist for the sake of the 'action.'
What is meant in the latter instance is rather, that, dramatically,
the significance of the 'characters' arises from their place in the
'action.'

[1] Mr. Bosanquet (*History of Aesthetic*, p. 73) explains Aristotle's
meaning a little differently.   'He may not have been contrasting
the plot, as a mere puzzle and solution, with the portrayal of
individual human character, but he may rather have intended to
oppose the man as revealed in action, or in speech which contributes to the march of incident, with monologue or conversation
simply intended to emphasise this or that type of disposition in
the interlocutors' (cf. supra, p. 342, note 2).

in ch. vi. 15, which has been subjected to some
strained interpretations, throws further light on the
reason why *ēthos* holds a position subsidiary to the
plot or action. 'The most beautiful colours, laid on
confusedly, will not give as much pleasure as the
chalk outline of a portrait.'[1]   Here the outlined
sketch corresponds to the outline of plot. *Ēthos*
divorced from plot is like a daub of beautiful
colour, which apart from form gives little pleasure.
The plot is the groundwork, the design, through
the medium of which *ēthos* derives its meaning and
dramatic value.

The whole gist of the argument is finally summed
up thus : 'The plot is the first principle, and, as it
were, the soul of a tragedy.'[2]   The analogy here indicated goes deeper than might at once be apparent
from the English words.   The precise point of the
comparison depends on the relation in which the
soul stands to the body in the Aristotelian philosophy.[3]   A play is a kind of living organism.   Its
animating principle is the plot.   As in the animal
and vegetable world the soul or principle of life is
the primary and moving force, the ἀρχή from which

---

[1] *Poet.* vi. 15, εἰ γάρ τις ἐναλείψειε τοῖς καλλίστοις φαρμάκοις χύδην, οὐκ ἂν ὁμοίως εὐφράνειεν καὶ λευκογραφήσας εἰκόνα.

[2] *Poet.* vi. 14, ἀρχὴ μὲν οὖν καὶ οἷον ψυχὴ ὁ μῦθος τῆς
τραγῳδίας.

[3] See *de Anim.* ii. 4. 415 b 7–21, where the soul is explained
to be the efficient cause, the formal cause, and the final cause of
the body.

the development of the organism proceeds, so it is
with the plot in tragedy.[1]   Round this nucleus the
parts grow and group themselves.   It is the origin
of movement, the starting-point and basis of the
play.   Without it the play could not exist.   It is
the plot, again, which gives to the play its inner
meaning and reality, as the soul does to the body.
To the plot we look in order to learn what the play
means ;   here lies its essence, its true significance.
Lastly, the plot is 'the end of a tragedy'[2] as well
as the beginning.   Through the plot the intention
of the play is realised.   The distinctive emotional
effect which the incidents are designed to produce
is inherent in the artistic structure of the whole.
Above all, it is the plot that contains those
Reversals of the Situation (περιπέτειαι)[3] and other
decisive moments, which most powerfully awaken
tragic feeling and excite the pleasure appropriate
to tragedy.

[1] The constant use of συνιστάναι in the biological treatises of
Aristotle should be compared with its meaning in the *Poetics* as
applied to the formation and organic structure of a tragedy.   *De
Gen. Anim.* ii. 1. 733 b 20, ἧς (γονῆς) εἰσελθούσης τὰ ζῷα συν-
ίσταται καὶ λαμβάνει τὴν οἰκείαν μορφήν.   ii. 4. 739 b 33, ὅταν
δὲ συστῇ τὸ κύημα ἤδη . . . iii. 2. 753 b 3, γίγνεται τροφὴ τοῖς
συνισταμένοις ζῴοις.   So σύστασις : *de Gen. Anim.* ii. 6. 744 b
28, ἡ μὲν οὖν τῶν ὀστῶν φύσις ἐν τῇ πρώτῃ συστάσει γίγνεται
τῶν μορίων : cf. *de Part. Anim.* ii. 1. 646 a 20 sqq.   *De Caelo* ii. 6.
288 b 16, ὅλη γὰρ ἴσως σύστασις τῶν ζῴων ἐκ τοιούτων συνέστηκεν
ἃ διαφέρει τοῖς οἰκείοις τόποις.

[2] *Poet.* vi. 10, ὁ μῦθος τέλος τῆς τραγῳδίας.

[3] See p. 329, note 2.

Aristotle's doctrine of the primary importance of action or plot has been disputed by many modern critics. Plot, it is argued, is a mere external framework, a piece of mechanism designed to illustrate the working of character. Character is in thought prior to action and is implied in it. Events have no meaning, no interest, except so far as they are supposed to proceed from will. Action is defined, expressed, interpreted by character. The question, however, which this chapter of the *Poetics* raises is not whether one element can in logical analysis be shown ultimately to contain the other; we have rather to ask which of the two is the more fundamental as regards the artistic conception and dramatic structure of a play. We will therefore inquire shortly what in its simplest analysis is meant by the drama,—what it is that constitutes dramatic action.

Action, as has been shown, is the first artistic necessity of a play, the controlling condition of its existence. But mere action is not enough; an isolated deed, however terrible, however pathetic, has not in it the dramatic quality. Action, to be dramatic, must be exhibited in its development and in its results ; it must stand in reciprocal and causal relation to certain mental states. We desire to see the feelings out of which it grows, the motive force of will which carries it to its conclusion ; and, again, to trace the effect of the deed accomplished upon the mind of the doer,—the emotions there generated as they become in turn new factors of action, and as they react thereby on the other dramatic characters. The drama, therefore, is will or emotion in action.

Further, the dramatic action forms a complete whole : it is a coherent series of events, standing in organic relation to one another and bound together by the law of cause and effect.   The internal centre, the pivot round which the whole system turns, is the plot.   The characters are dramatic only so far as they are grouped round this centre, and work in with the movement of events towards an appointed end.   Free and self-determined though they are, they exercise their freedom within a sphere which is prescribed by this primary condition of dramatic art.   They reveal their personality not in all its fulness, but to such an extent as the natural course of the action may require.   The situation and the circumstances in which they are placed, the other wills with which they come into collision, are precisely those which are best fitted to search out their weak places, to elicit their energy and exhibit it in action.

But the drama not only implies emotion expressing itself in a complete and significant action and tending towards a certain end ; it also implies a conflict.   We may even modify Aristotle's phrase and say, that the dramatic conflict, not the mere plot, is 'the soul of a tragedy.'   In every drama

there is a collision of forces. Man is imprisoned
within the limits of the actual. Outside him is a
necessity which restricts his freedom, a superior power
with which his will frequently collides. Again, there
is the inward discord of his own divided will ; and,
further, the struggle with other human wills which
obstruct his own. The delineation of character is
determined by the fact that a dramatic conflict of
some kind has to be represented, and by the relation
in which the several antagonistic forces stand to the
plot as a whole. But while conflict is the soul of the
drama, every conflict is not dramatic. In real life,
as Aristotle points out,[1] all action does not manifest
itself in external acts ; there is a silent activity of
speculative thought which in the highest sense may
be called action, though it never utters itself in deed.
But the action of the drama cannot consist in an
inward activity that does not pass beyond the
region of thought or emotion. Even where the
main interest is centred in the internal conflict, this
conflict must have its outward as well as its inward
side : it must manifest itself in individual acts, in
concrete relations with the world outside ; it must
bring the agent into collision with other personalities.
We therefore exclude from the province of the drama
purely mental conflicts—action and reaction within
the mind itself—such as are the solitary struggles
of the ascetic, the artist, the thinker. These are

[1] *Pol.* iv. (vii.) 3. 1325 b 16–23 (quoted p. 335, note 1).

dramatic only when they are brought into a plot which gives them significance, and by which they become links in a chain of great events.

Only certain kinds of character, therefore, are capable of dramatic treatment.[1] Character on its passive side, character expressing itself in passionate emotion and nothing more, is fit for lyrical poetry, but not for the drama. As action is the first necessity of the drama, so dramatic character has in it some vital and spontaneous force which can make and mould circumstances, which sets obstacles aside. It is of the battling, energetic type. The emotions must harden into will and the will express itself in deed. Much more rarely, as in Hamlet, can character become dramatic by an intellectual and masterly inactivity which offers resistance to the motives that prompt ordinary men to action. Events are then brought about, not by the free energy of will, but by acts, as it were, of arrested volition, by forces such as operate in the world of dreamland. There is in Hamlet a strenuous inaction, a *not-acting*, which is in itself a form of

---

[1] 'It is quite possible that Aristotle detected a tendency in the tragedy of his day which he held dangerous to the vitality of drama—the tendency to the merely statuesque, to motionless life. If so, his over-statement of the case for the other side was nothing less than a piece of practical wisdom. Even to-day this drama of motionless life beguiles some men to heresy ; M. Maeterlinck makes it his ideal in his " Static Theatre," the very negation of all drama.'—*Times Literary Supplement* 23rd May, 1902

action.   Characters such as this are not purely passive, they have an originating and resisting force of their own.   Most, however, of Shakespeare's characters, like the heroes of the Greek drama, are strong and dominant natures, they are of a militant quality of mind.   They put their whole selves, their whole force of thinking and of willing, into what they do.   Nothing is more wonderful than the resistless impulse, the magnificent energy of will, with which a Macbeth or a Richard III. goes to meet his doom.

Plot, then, is not, as is sometimes said, a mere external, an accident of the inner life.   In the action of the drama character is defined and revealed.   The conception of the plot as a whole must be present in embryo to the poet's mind prior to the evolution of the parts ; the characters will grow and shape themselves out of the dramatic situation in conformity with the main design.   In maintaining, however, that plot is the first essential of the drama, it is not implied that the plot must be complicated, that a difficult skein is tangled in order to excite curiosity, and unravelled again to relieve the feelings so excited.   Neither in Aeschylus nor in Sophocles has plot for its own sake become a motive.   Not even in the *Oedipus Tyrannus*, where the threads are more elaborately tangled and the texture of the plot is woven closer than in any other Greek tragedy, is dramatic complication an end in itself.   The

normal Greek tragedy is singularly simple in
structure. We do not find, as in *King Lear*
and elsewhere in the Shakespearian drama, two
concurrent actions which are skilfully interwoven
in order to lead up to a tragic end. Some of the
greatest Greek plays are not only devoid of in-
tricate plot, but present an unchanging situation.
In the *Prometheus* there is no outward movement,
the main situation is at the end what it was at
the beginning : the mental attitude of the hero is
fixed and immovable, while a series of interlocutors
come and go. We see before us the conflict of two
superhuman wills, neither of which can yield to
the other. Yet the dialogue is not mere conversation. Each speech of Prometheus is a step in the
action ; each word he utters is equivalent to a
deed ; it is the authentic voice of will which rises
superior to physical bondage. The play is action
throughout,—action none the less real because
it consists not in outward doing. The reproach
of want of movement which has been brought
against the *Prometheus* has been also urged
against Milton's *Samson Agonistes*. It is a drama,
says Dr. Johnson, ' in which the intermediate parts
have neither cause nor consequence, neither hasten
nor retard the catastrophe.' Here again, however,
a somewhat similar criticism is applicable. The
speeches of Samson form an integral part of the
action. The will-power which utters itself in

2 A

dialogue is translated into deed, and culminates in a tragic catastrophe, as soon as the outward constraints are removed.

We must hold, then, with Aristotle that plot or action is the primary element in the artistic structure of the drama. But the case also presents another side, which is lightly touched by him, and which deserves to be made more prominent. Briefly stated it is this. The action which springs out of character, and reflects character, alone satisfies the higher dramatic conditions.

Here there is a marked difference between epic and dramatic poetry. The epic poem relates a great and complete action which attaches itself to the fortunes of a people, or to the destiny of mankind, and sums up the life of a period. The story and the deeds of those who pass across its wide canvas are linked with the larger movement of which the men themselves are but a part. The particular action rests upon forces outside itself. The hero is swept into the tide of events. The hairbreadth escapes, the surprises, the episodes, the marvellous incidents of epic story, only partly depend on the spontaneous energy of the hero.

The tragic drama, on the other hand, represents the destiny of the individual man. Action and character are here more closely intertwined. Even if the connexion cannot be traced in every detail,

it is generally manifest when we look to the whole
tenor of the play.   The action is the product of
the characters and of the circumstances in which
they are placed.   It is but seldom that outward
circumstances are entirely dominant over the forces
of the spirit.   If it is true that 'things outward
do draw the inward quality after them,' it is
no less true in tragedy that things inward draw
the outward after them.   The outer and the
inner world are here in nearer correspondence and
equivalence than in any other form of poetry.   The
element of chance is all but eliminated.   An inner
bond of probability or necessity binds events
together.   This inevitable sequence of cause and
effect is the link that character forges as it
expresses itself in action.   A man's deeds become
external to him; his character dogs and pursues
him as a thing apart.   The fate that overtakes the
hero is no alien thing, but his own self recoiling
upon him for good or evil.   'Man's character,'
as Heraclitus said, 'is his destiny' ($\check{\eta}\theta o\varsigma$ $\dot{a}\nu\theta\rho\acute{\omega}\pi\varphi$
$\delta a\acute{\iota}\mu\omega\nu$).   To this vital relation between action and
character is due the artistically compacted plot,
the central unity of a tragedy.   If, as Aristotle
says, tragedy is a picture of life, it is of life
rounded off, more complete, more significant, than
any ordinary human life; revealing in itself the
eternal law of things, summing up as in a typical
example the story of human vicissitudes.

The dissent from Aristotle's doctrine that plot is the primary element in tragedy, is sometimes expressed in a modified form. Plot, it is admitted, was the primary element in the ancient drama; but, it is urged, the ancient drama was a drama of destiny; it obliterated character, while in the modern drama action is subordinate to character. Such is the view that De Quincey maintains. Man, he says, being the 'puppet of fate could not with any effect display what we call a character'; for the will which is 'the central pivot of character was obliterated, thwarted, cancelled by the dark fatalism which brooded over the Grecian stage.' 'Powerful and elaborate character . . . would have been wasted, nay would have been defeated and interrupted by the blind agencies of fate.' Hence, as he argues, the Greek drama presents grand situations but no complex motives; statuesque groups of tragic figures, but little play of human passion; 'no struggle internal or external.'

It is strange that the Greeks of all people, and Aeschylus of all poets, should have been accused of depriving man of free agency and making him the victim of a blind fate. The central lesson of the Aeschylean drama is that man is the master of his own destiny: nowhere is his spiritual freedom more vigorously asserted.[1]

[1] See *Some Aspects of the Greek Genius*, pp. 108 ff. Ed. 3.

The retribution which overtakes him is not in-
flicted at the hands of cruel or jealous powers.   It
is the justice of the gods, who punish him for
rebellion against their laws.   In ancient tragedy,
the supernatural forces that order man's outward
fortunes are, it is true, more visible than in the
modern drama, but character is not obliterated, nor
free personality effaced.   The tragic action is no
mere series of external incidents; it is a struggle
of moral forces, the resultant of contending wills,
though a supreme necessity may guide the movement of events to unexpected issues.   Plot does
not overpower character; it is the very medium
through which character is discerned, the touch-
stone by which its powers are tested.

Yet there is a certain sense in which we may
say that the modern drama lays increased stress
on the delineation of individual character.   On
the Greek stage the development of character was
impeded by the unpliable material with which the
tragedian had to work.   By consecrated usage he
was confined to a circle of legends whose main
outlines were already fixed.   These had come
down from a remote past and bore traces of the
rude times which had given them birth.   The
heroic legends of Greece were woven into the
texture of national life: they appealed to the
people by many associations, by local worships
and familiar representations of art.   Epic story,

however, had in it elements which the purer and
more reflective morality of the Periclean age was
constrained to reject. The traditional legends had
to be adapted, as best they might, to the new
ethical ideals.

In carrying out this task the poets were limited
by the possibilities of the plot. The great facts of
the legends could not be set aside. The audience,
familiar with their own heroic history, were not
prepared for bold surprises. So far as the delineation of character itself was concerned, the utmost
freedom of invention was allowed; the same
dramatist might in successive tragedies exhibit
a single person under various and inconsistent
types of character. The point at which ethical
portraiture was hampered was when the dramatic
persons had to be fitted harmoniously into the
framework of a particular plot. The details of
the story might vary within wide limits, but the
end was a thing given; and in the drama the end
cannot but dominate the structure of the whole,—
incidents and character alike. The weakness of
the *Dénouement*, as compared with the complication, of many Greek tragedies is the direct result
of the controlling tradition of the plot.

Though the poets handled the myths freely,
often transforming the inner spirit and meaning
of the tale, yet they could not quite overcome
the inherent difficulties presented by the problem.

Aeschylus and Sophocles succeeded in deepening
and humanising the archaic stories, and in liberat-
ing the characters from the influence of the past.
But in Euripides the strain has become too great.
The tissue of the material yields ; the old and the
new world start asunder, the actions done belong-
ing to the older order of things, the characters
portrayed being the children of the poet's own
generation.

The freedom of the Greek poet in delineating
character was thus restricted by the choice of
subject-matter.   Add to this another consideration.   The themes usually handled were simple in
outline, the main issues were clear and free from
the disturbing accidents of individuality.   In the
legends selected the working of the eternal laws
which govern human life could be visibly discerned.   The dramatic characters were of corresponding simplicity.   Their personality was seized
by the immediate intuition of the poet at some
decisive moment of action.   A small portion was
carved out of their career, illustrating human life
in one of its typical aspects.   Aeschylus, at once
poet and prophet, sets forth in dramatic form the
conflict between opposing principles,—between the
implacable vengeance of an early age and the
mercy which tempers justice, as in the *Eumenides* :
or again, as in the *Prometheus*, he takes us back
to a far-off past, and depicts the strife between

two antagonists, each of them divine, who are
representative of different dispensations, and hints
at a future harmony, when divine Might should no
longer be divorced from Wisdom and Benevolence.
Sophocles, too, brings rival principles into collision.
In the *Antigone* the divine and the human law stand
opposed, and the religious duty towards the family
triumphs over the claims of civic obedience.   In
the *Philoctetes*, the instincts of natural truthfulness
finally carry the day against diplomatic falsehood
for the public good.

Greek Tragedy, in its most characteristic
examples, dramatises not the mere story of
human calamities, but the play of great principles, the struggle between contending moral
forces.   The heroes are themselves the concrete
embodiment of these forces.   Religion, the State,
the Family,—these were to a Greek the higher
and enduring realities, the ideal ends for which he
lived.   Hence in the Greek drama, patriotism,
wifely or sisterly devotion, all those elementary
emotions which cluster round home and country,
are the motives which chiefly impel to action and
call forth the ardour of self-sacrifice.   Seldom, at
least in the older tragedians, do passions purely
personal animate these tragic heroes : they are free
from inward discord and self-contradiction : the
ends they pursue are objective and rest on a
belief in the abiding reality of the social organism.

The characters hereby gain universal meaning and validity: they are not of their own age and country only, but can claim kinship with mankind.

The modern drama introduces us into another world of poetic emotion. A richer and more varied inner life is opened up. The sense of personality is deepened. Even the idiosyncrasies of human nature become material to the dramatist. In Shakespeare character assumes inexhaustible variety. Its aspects are for ever changing, discordant elements meet and are blended. The contradictions do not easily yield to psychological analysis; we seek to explain them, but we find ourselves dealing only with abstractions. Not until the persons enact their story before us, and are seen in the plenitude of organic life, do we feel that they are possible and real creations. The discovery of unsuspected depths in human nature has brought into prominence the subjective side of ethical portraiture and subjective modes of viewing life. Love, honour, ambition, jealousy are the prevailing motives of modern tragedy; and among these love, the most exclusive of all the passions, dominates all other motives.

Shakespeare in deepening the subjective personality of man does not, however, lose sight of the objective ends of life and of the corresponding phases of character. Between these two sides of human experience he maintains a just balance. The par-

ticular emotions he stamps, as did the Greeks, with
the impress of the universal. Nor does he permit
the dramatised action to become subservient to the
portrayal of individual character. Other poets, who
have explored, though less profoundly, the recesses
of human nature, and reproduced the rarer and
more abnormal states of feeling, have been unable
to rise above the pathological study of man,—a
study as dangerous as it is fascinating to the
dramatist. Indeed the conscious analysis of character and motive, even where the study of morbid
conditions is not added, has marred the dramatic
effect of many modern productions. Goethe with
all his poetic genius did not surmount this danger.
His reflective, emotional characters, who view life
through the medium of individual feeling, seldom
have the energy of will requisite to carry out a
tragic action. They are described by the mouth of
others, they express themselves in lyrical utter-
ances of incomparable beauty. But the result
is that where Shakespeare would have given us
historical dramas, Goethe gives only dramatic
biographies. And, in general, the modern introspective habit, the psychological interest felt in
character, has produced many dramatic lyrics, but
few dramas.

The increased emphasis attaching to individual
portraiture is seen again in the tendency of the
romantic drama to exhibit character in growth, in

each successive stage of its evolution. A Greek
tragedy takes a few significant scenes out of the
hero's life; these are bound together by a causal
chain and constitute a single and impressive action.
Much that the moderns would include in the play
itself is placed outside the drama, and forms a
groundwork of circumstances, antecedent to the
action but necessary to explain it. Frequently the
whole action of a Greek drama would form merely
the climax of a modern play. The Greek custom
of representing four dramas in a day placed a
natural limit on the length of each play and on
the range of the action. The romantic drama aimed
at a more comprehensive representation; a single
play in its scope and compass approached to the
dimensions of a Trilogy. Sir Philip Sidney gently
ridicules the quickened pace with which time is compelled to move, in order to condense into a few hours
the events of as many years. 'Now of time they
are more liberall, for ordinary it is that two young
Princes fall in love. After many traverces, she is
got with childe, delivered of a faire boy, he is
lost, groweth a man, falls in love, and is ready
to get another child, and all this in two hours'
space.'

The dramatic theme is frequently enlarged in
modern tragedy so that the entire process may be
traced from the moment when a deed lies dormant
as a germ in the mind, till it has matured into action

and unfolded itself in all its consequences. As the period embraced by the action is extended, and the relations with the outer world become more complex, it is only natural that the characters should expand in new directions and undergo essential changes. A wider range was here opened up for dramatic portraiture. It was not, of course, an untried region of art. The Greeks had exhibited character as moulded by the plot and developed under pressure from without, or through impulses which operated from within. Indeed every drama must, in some measure, show the play and counter-play of those forces which rule the outer and the inner world. The process by which feeling is consolidated into a deed cannot but leave its mark on the mind of the agent. Antigone suffers the natural reaction from high-strained emotion. Neoptolemus becomes a changed person in the progress of the action, though the change is merely to restore him to his true self, which for the moment he had lost. Even Prometheus, grand in his immobility, is in some sense worked upon by the persons and the scenes which pass before him. His will, unconquerable from the first, expresses itself in tones still more defiant at the close.

In all these instances we have character in process of becoming. Wherever, in short, an action grows and expands according to dramatic laws, character, or at least feeling, must move in concert

with it. But the extent to which growth and
movement in the character accompany the march
of the action is very various. The ancient stage
furnishes us with no such complete instance of
character-development as we have, for example, in
Macbeth. It is the peculiar delight of the moderns
to follow the course of such an evolution, to be
present at the determining moment of a man's
career, to watch the dawning of a passion, the
shaping of a purpose, and to pursue the deed to
its final accomplishment. We desire not only to
know what a man was, and how he came to be it,
but to be shown each step in the process, each link
in the chain; and we are the more interested if we
find that the gradual course of the dramatic movement has wrought a complete change in the original
character. In this sense we may admit that the
modern drama has brought the delineation of
character into new and stronger relief.

But when we have taken into account all the
minor variations of structure which the modern
drama has undergone; when we have allowed for
the greater complexity of the plot, the greater prominence given to the more subjective and individual
aspects of character, the deeper interest taken in the
unfolding of character and in its manifold developments; yet plot and character, in their essential
relation, still hold the place sketched for them in
the *Poetics*, and assigned to them on the Greek

stage.   Plot is artistically the first necessity of the
drama.   For the drama, in its true idea, is a poetical
representation of a complete and typical action,
whose lines converge on a determined end ; which
evolves itself out of human emotion and human
will in such a manner that action and character
are each in turn the outcome of the other.

Such a drama was the creation of Greece, and of
all her creations perhaps the greatest.   Epic and lyric
poetry have everywhere sprung up independently.
Dramatic spectacles, religious or secular, are found
in every country, and at all periods of civilisation.
Dramatic narratives, such as the *Book of Job*,
dramatic lyrics, such as the *Song of Solomon*, are
among the forms of composition which meet us in
the Old Testament.   Lyrical dramas, which in their
constituent elements recall the first beginnings of
the Greek drama, have existed in China and Japan.
India has produced vast poems which pass under the
name of dramas, wanting, however, both the unity
of action and the spiritual freedom which the drama
proper implies.   The Greek drama is the harmonious
fusion of two elements which never before had been
perfectly blended.   Lyrical in its origin, epic in the
nature of its materials, it is at once an expression
of passionate feeling and the story of an action ; it
embodies emotion, but an emotion which grows into
will and issues in deeds.   If the lyrical utterance of
feeling had remained the dominant, as it was the

original, element in a Greek tragedy, it would have been left for some other people to create the tragic drama. As it was, the Greeks fixed unalterably its distinctive form and the artistic principle of its structure.

CHAPTER X

THE GENERALISING POWER OF COMEDY

POETRY, we say—following Aristotle—is an expression of the universal element in human life; or, in equivalent modern phrase, it idealises life. Now the word 'idealise' has two senses, which have given rise to some confusion. Writers on aesthetics generally mean by it the representation of an object in its permanent and essential aspects, in a form that answers to its true idea; disengaged from the passing accidents that cling to individuality, and from disturbing influences that obscure the type. What is local or transient is either omitted or reduced to subordinate rank; the particular is enlarged till it broadens out into the human and the universal. In this sense 'the ideal' is 'the universal' of the *Poetics*. But there is another and more popular use of the term, by which an idealised representation implies not only an absence of disturbing influences in the manifestation of the idea, but a positive accession of what is beautiful. The object is seized in some

happy and characteristic moment, its lines of grace
or strength are more firmly drawn, its beauty is
heightened, its significance increased, while the
likeness to the original is retained.   The two senses
of the word coincide in the higher regions of art.
When the subject-matter of artistic representation
already possesses a grandeur or dignity of its own,
its dominant characteristics will become more
salient by the suppression of accidental features,
and the ideal form that results will have added
elements of beauty.   The leading characters in
tragedy, while true to human nature, stand out
above the common man in stature and nobility,
just as, by the art of the portrait-painter, a likeness
is reproduced and yet idealised.[1]   In the very act
of eliminating the accidental a higher beauty and
perfection are discovered than was manifested in
the world of reality.   Tragedy, therefore, in the
persons of its heroes combines both kinds of
idealisation; it universalises, and in so doing it
embellishes.

Idealised portraiture does not, as has been
already observed,[2] consist in presenting characters
of flawless virtue.   Aristotle's tragic hero, as
delineated in the *Poetics* (ch. xiii.), is by no means
free from faults or failings.   The instance, again,

---

[1] *Poet.* xv. 8, ἀποδιδόντες τὴν ἰδίαν μορφὴν ὁμοίους ποιοῦντες
καλλίους γράφουσιν.

[2] p. 232.

of Achilles as a poetic type of character, who in
spite of defects has a moral nobility entitling him
to rank as ideal, shows that the idealising process,
as understood by Aristotle, does not imply the
omission of all defects.[1]   In general it may be said
that some particular quality or group of qualities
must be thrown into relief; some commanding
faculty heightened, provided that in so doing the
equipoise of character which constitutes a typical
human being is not disturbed.   The ideal is that
which is raised above the trivial and accidental ;
by virtue of a universal element which answers to
the true idea of the object it transcends the limitations of the individual.   Even vicious characters
are not entirely excluded from tragedy on Aristotle's theory,[2] though the villain may not hold the
position of protagonist.   The saying attributed to
Sophocles, αὐτὸς μὲν οἵους δεῖ ποιεῖν, Εὐριπίδην δὲ
οἷοι εἰσί, does not bear the interpretation sometimes
assigned to it, that the characters of Sophocles are
patterns of heroic goodness, while those of Euripides are the men and women of real life.[3]   The

---

[1] Poet. xv. 8.   [2] pp. 227 and 316.

[3] Poet. xxv. 6, πρὸς δὲ τούτοις ἐὰν ἐπιτιμᾶται ὅτι οὐκ ἀληθῆ,
ἀλλ' ἴσως <ὡς> δεῖ—οἷον καὶ Σοφοκλῆς ἔφη αὐτὸς μὲν οἵους δεῖ
ποιεῖν, Εὐριπίδην δὲ οἷοι εἰσίν—ταύτῃ λυτέον.   There is some
doubt as to the literal rendering of the words αὐτὸς μὲν οἵους δεῖ
ποιεῖν.   Vahlen and most editors understand εἶναι with οἵους δεῖ,
'men as they should be,' whereas strict grammar undoubtedly
requires us to understand ποιεῖν, 'men as the poet should repre-

meaning is that the characters of Sophocles answer
to the higher dramatic requirements; they are
typical of universal human nature in its deeper
and abiding aspects; they are ideal, but ideally
human; whereas Euripides reproduced personal
idiosyncrasies and the trivial features of everyday
reality.

Objection may be taken to the distinction
drawn between the two meanings of the word
'idealise,' on the ground that they run into one
another and fundamentally mean the same thing.
It may be urged that so far as an object assumes
its universal form, ridding itself of non-essentials,
it will stand out in perfect beauty; for all ugliness,
all imperfection, all evil itself, is an accident
of nature, a derangement and disturbance by
which things fall short of their true idea.   To

sent them,' 'men as they ought to be drawn.'   In the first edition
I inclined to the latter view.

The general context, however, and the equivalent phrases in
this chapter (οἷα εἶναι δεῖ § 1, <ὡς> δεῖ § 6, βέλτιον § 7, πρὸς
τὸ βέλτιον § 17) point strongly to the first interpretation.   It
has in its favour this further fact (as is justly observed by Mr.
R. C. Seaton, *Classical Review*, vol. xi. No. 6), that the saying of
Sophocles is thus couched in a less arrogant form.   Accepting
this view we must explain οἵους δεῖ (and similarly <ὡς> δεῖ § 6)
as a kind of shorthand expression used, with more than Aristotelian
brevity and disregard of grammar, to denote the ideal in poetry.

Even if εἶναι is to be understood with δεῖ, the δεῖ will still be
the 'ought' of aesthetic obligation, not the moral 'ought.'   It has
been previously shown, however, that the aesthetic ideal of character
in the *Poetics* implies a high, though not a perfect morality.

represent the universal would thus in its ultimate analysis imply the representation of the object in the noblest and fairest forms in which it can clothe itself according to artistic laws. Comedy, which concerns itself with the follies and foibles, the flaws and imperfections of mankind, cannot on this reasoning idealise or universalise its object.

Now, it may or may not be that evil or imperfection can be shown to be a necessary and ultimate element in the universe; but the point seems to be one for philosophy to discuss, not for art to assume. Art, when it seeks to give a comprehensive picture of human life, must accept such flaws as belong to the normal constitution of man. At what precise point imperfections are to be regarded as accidental, abnormal, irregular; as presenting so marked a deviation from the type as to be unworthy of lasting embodiment in art, is a problem whose answer will vary at different stages of history, and will admit of different applications according to the particular art that is in question. Certain imperfections, however, will probably always be looked on as permanent features of our common humanity. With these defects comedy amuses itself, discovering the inconsistencies which underlie life and character, and exhibiting evil not as it is in its essential nature, but as a thing to be laughed at rather than hated. Thus limiting its range of vision, comedy is able to

give artistic expression to certain types of character
which can hardly find a place in serious art.

Again, it must not be forgotten that the individual character, considered by itself, is not the
same as this character considered in its place in the
drama.   A character universalised may, if regarded
alone, still be 'ugly,' and yet it may contribute to
the beauty of the whole.   In that sense we can
continue to call it 'ugly' only by a kind of abstraction.   Or to put it otherwise,—evil regarded in its
essential nature may be ugly; but, shown in the
action of the comedy to be nugatory and ridiculous,
it ceases to be ugly ; it is an element in a fact which
is beautiful.

Aristotle draws no distinction between the universality which is proper to tragedy and comedy
respectively.   Each of these, as a branch of the
poetic art, embodies the type rather than the individual, and to this extent they have a common
function.

An Athenian of the fifth century would hardly
have singled out comedy as an example of poetic
generalisation.   The large admixture of personal
satire in the old Attic comedy would rather have
suggested the view that the main ingredient in
comic mirth is the malicious pleasure afforded by
the discomfiture of another.   And, in fact, Plato,
in the subtle analysis he gives in the *Philebus*[1] of

[1] *Philebus* pp. 48–50.

the emotions excited by comedy, proceeds on some
such assumption. The pleasure of the ludicrous
springs, he says, from the sight of another's misfortune, the misfortune, however, being a kind of
self-ignorance that is powerless to inflict hurt. A
certain malice is here of the essence of comic enjoyment. Inadequate as this may be, if taken as a
complete account of the ludicrous, it nevertheless
shows a profound insight into some of the chief
artistic modes of its manifestation. Plato antici-
pates, but goes deeper than Hobbes, whose well-
known words are worth recalling : ' The passion of
laughter is nothing else but a sudden glory, arising
from a sudden conception of some eminency in
ourselves, by comparison of the infirmity of others
or with our own formerly.'

The laughter that has in it a malicious element
and implies in some sense the abasement of another, does not satisfy Aristotle's conception of the
idea of the ludicrous. His definition in the *Poetics*[1]
carries the analysis a step farther than it had been
carried by Plato. ' The ludicrous,' he says, ' consists in some defect or ugliness which is not painful
or destructive. To take an obvious example, the
comic mask is ugly and distorted, but does not
imply pain.' The phrase ' not painful or destruc-

---

[1] *Poet.* v. 1, τὸ γὰρ γελοῖόν ἐστιν ἁμάρτημά τι καὶ αἶσχος
ἀνώδυνον καὶ οὐ φθαρτικόν, οἶον εὐθὺς τὸ γελοῖον πρόσωπον
αἰσχρόν τι καὶ διεστραμμένον ἄνευ ὀδύνης.

tive'—either, that is, to the object of laughter, or
sympathetically to the subject—is a remarkable
contribution to the idea under discussion. Still
more significant is the omission of malice, which
to Plato had seemed an essential ingredient.

The pleasure, therefore, of the pure ludicrous is
not to be explained, as some tell us to-day, by
the disinterested delight of primitive man in the
infliction of suffering. It does not consist in a
gratified feeling of malignity, softened indeed by
civilisation, but ultimately to be resolved into a
kind of savage mirth. A good joke becomes, indeed,
a little more pungent if it is seasoned with malice,
but, even without the malice, laughter may be pro-
voked. And, according to Aristotle, the quality
that provokes laughter is a certain 'ugliness,' a
'defect' or 'deformity.' These words, primarily
applicable to the physically ugly, the dispropor-
tionate, the unsymmetrical, will include the frailties,
follies, and infirmities of human nature, as distinguished from its graver vices or crimes. Further,
taking account of the elements which enter into the
idea of beauty in Aristotle, we shall probably not
unduly strain the meaning of the expression, if we
extend it to embrace the incongruities, absurdities,
or cross-purposes of life, its blunders and discords,
its imperfect correspondences and adjustments, and
that in matters intellectual as well as moral.

Aristotle's definition is indeed still wanting in

exactness; for though the ludicrous is always incongruous, yet the incongruous (even limited as it
is here) is not always ludicrous. Incongruity, in
order to be ludicrous, requires a transition, a change
of mood, resulting in the discovery either of an
unexpected resemblance where there was unlikeness,
or of an unexpected unlikeness where there was resemblance. There is always a blending of contrasted
feelings. The pleasure of the ludicrous thus arises
from the shock of surprise at a painless incongruity.
It sometimes allies itself with malice, sometimes
with sympathy, and sometimes again is detached
from both. For our present purpose, however, it is
enough to note that, although Aristotle's definition
is hardly complete, it has the merit of recognising
the pure ludicrous, which is awakened by the perception of incongruity and provokes no malignant
or triumphant laughter. The definition harmonises
well with his exclusion of personal satire and galling
caricature from genuine comedy, and with his
theory of the generalising power of poetry.

Indeed, Aristotle selects comedy as a salient
illustration of what he means by the representation
of the universal.[1] If I understand him aright he

---

[1] *Poet.* ix. 4–5, οὗ (sc. τοῦ καθόλου) στοχάζεται ἡ ποίησις
ὀνόματα ἐπιτιθεμένη . . . ἐπὶ μὲν οὖν τῆς κωμῳδίας ἤδη τοῦτο
δῆλον γέγονεν· συστήσαντες γὰρ τὸν μῦθον διὰ τῶν εἰκότων οὐ
(οὕτω MSS.) τὰ τυχόντα ὀνόματα ὑποτιθέασιν, καὶ οὐχ ὥσπερ οἱ
ἰαμβοποιοὶ περὶ τὸν καθ' ἕκαστον ποιοῦσιν.

I have ventured to admit into the text my conjecture οὐ

points to the tendency shown in comedy to discard
the use of historical names and adopt names which
are suggestive of character or occupation or 'humours.'
It was part of the effort, which, as he says, poetry
makes to express the universal. The name had
only to be heard in order that the type to which
the person belonged might be recognised; much in

(or οὐχὶ) τὰ τυχόντα for οὕτω τὰ τυχόντα of the MSS.: 'the plot
is first constructed; then *characteristic* or *appropriate* names are
affixed.' (For οὐ τὰ τυχ. cf. *Poet.* vii. 4, xxvi. 7, *Pol.* v. (viii.) 5. 1339
b 32, οὐ τὴν τυχοῦσαν ἡδονήν.) The Arabic version which has a
negative ('nequaquam,' Margoliouth) instead of οὕτω supports the
correction. By a similar error in this very chapter, ix. 2. 1451
a 37, A^c gives οὕτω where the apographa rightly read οὐ τό.

The thought of the passage will, with the correction, be of this
kind : 'It is at this universality that poetry aims when she attaches
names to the characters, i.e. when instead of adopting historical
names (γενόμενα ὀνόματα) she gives names of her own invention
(cf. § 6 πεποιημένα). The names in that case are expressive ; they
indicate that the person is not an individual but a type. This
generalising tendency, which has been counteracted in tragedy, has
become apparent in the development of comedy.' Plato in the
Cratylus pp. 392–5 goes far beyond this. By a series of fanciful
etymologies he professes to discover an inner correspondence
between the names of various tragic heroes and their characters or
fortunes.

It is not quite clear whether the reference in ἤδη τοῦτο δῆλον
γέγονεν is to the comedy of Aristotle's own day or is meant to
include all the developed forms of comedy. The contrast drawn
between the practice of οἱ ἰαμβοποιοί (cf. v. 3, Κράτης . . . ἀφέμενος
τῆς ἰαμβικῆς ἰδέας) and the new tendency points rather to the
wider reference. Since comedy passed beyond the lampooning
stage, the movement towards generalisation has been perceptible.

The significant names of Greek Comedy fall into at least two
classes :

(1) Names, etymologically significant, such as Dicaeopolis, Euelpides,

the same way as in the New Comedy the Boor, the
Parasite, and other types were known on the stage
by their familiar masks. It may be added that
not the names only of the characters, but the
extant titles of plays composed by writers of the
Middle Comedy, imply the same effort after
generalisation. They remind us of the character-

Peithetaerus, Pheidippides in the Aristophanic comedy, coexisting
side by side with real names (Socrates, Cleon, etc.), which were a
survival of the ἰαμβικὴ ἰδέα. On this model probably Plautus
coined his Bombomachides, Polymachaeroplagides, Pyrgopolyneices
(cf. also Αἱρησιτείχης in Diphylus) and the like. Of a tamer
kind but still of the same class are the names of soldiers of fortune
in Menander, Thrasonides (in the Μισούμενος), Bias (in the Κόλαξ),
Polemon (in the Περικειρόμενος), and Thrasyleon.
(2) Names which, being appropriated by usage to certain parts,
designated occupation or condition, e.g. Ξανθίας, Μανᾶς (in Phere-
crates, Alexis, etc. as well as in Aristophanes), Πυρρίας, Μανία,
all slave-names. Similarly in Plautus, many of the names of
meretrices, Philematium, Glycerium, Palaestra, etc., come pretty
certainly from writers of the New Comedy. Such names were
employed in ordinary life, to judge from Athenaeus (xiii. 583 D
ff.). Again, Plautus and Terence agree in using Chremes, Calli-
demides, Cratinus, Demipho, etc. for senes, and Charinus, Pamphilus
for adulescentes.

In Plautus the number of names etymologically significant
and appropriate largely preponderates over the non-significant ;
in Terence the proportion is the other way. In arguing back
from the usage of Plautus and Terence to Greek originals much
caution has to be observed. In Plautus, for instance, there are
some five hundred names which have a Greek appearance (Rassow,
De Plauti substantivis, Leipzig, 1881), but many of these are of a
mongrel formation. Terence's names are for the most part good
Attic names and were probably more or less associated with stock
characters in the New Comedy. Unfortunately the fragments of
Attic Comedy (Middle and New) furnish us with a very scanty

sketches of Theophrastus. Such are 'the Peevish man' (ὁ Δύσκολος), 'the Fault-finder' (ὁ Μεμψίμοιρος), 'the Busybody' (ὁ Πολυπράγμων), 'the Boor' (ὁ Ἄγροικος), 'the Hermit' (ὁ Μονότροπος). Other pieces again bear the name of a profession or occupation, as 'the Boxer' (ὁ Πύκτης), 'the Charioteer' (ὁ Ἡνίοχος), 'the Soldier' (ὁ Στρατιώτης), 'the Painter' (ὁ Ζωγράφος); and others are called after a people,—'the Thessalians,' 'the Thebans,' 'the Corinthians,'—and may be assumed, incidentally at least, to portray or satirise national characteristics.

In various places Aristotle indicates the distinction between comedy proper, which playfully

supply of names on which to rest our conclusions. The Γεωργός of Menander contains no names etymologically appropriate to the characters, though Δᾶος and Σύρος are stock slaves' names, familiar to us from Terence.

The following passage from Donatus on Ter. *Ad.* 1, which well illustrates οὐ τὰ τυχόντα ὀνόματα of the first class above mentioned : 'nomina personarum, in comoediis dumtaxat, *habere debent rationem et etymologiam* ; etenim absurdum est comicum aperte argumenta confingere, vel nomen personae incongruum dare, vel officium quod sit a nomine diversum.'

If the MSS. reading is retained the passage will run thus :—' In the case of comedy this is already clear : the writers first construct their plots . . . and then, and not till then (οὕτω), affix such names as first come to hand ' (τὰ τυχόντα ὀνόματα being opposed to τὰ γενόμενα ὀνόματα). The names are given at haphazard ; they are not as in primitive comedy and tragedy tied down to any historical personage,—not limited by association with any known individual ; and this fact serves to bring out the generality of the action. The connexion between τὰ τυχόντα and the καθόλου on this interpretation is somewhat forced, though not impossible.

touches the faults and foibles of humanity, and
personal satire (ἡ ἰαμβικὴ ἰδέα)[1] or invective
(λοιδορία). The one kind of composition is a
representation of the universal, the other of the
particular. He does not expressly mention
Aristophanes in this connexion; but in the *Ethics*,
the old political comedy of Athens is contrasted
with the Middle Comedy as employing coarse or
abusive language (αἰσχρολογία), instead of delicate
innuendo (ὑπόνοια).[2] Aristotle himself manifestly
prefers the comedy from which personalities are
banished and which presents generalised types of
character in conformity with the fundamental laws
of poetry.

It is doubtful whether Aristotle had any perception of the genius and imaginative power of
Aristophanes. The characters of the Aristophanic
drama are not fairly judged if they are thought of
simply as historical individuals, who are subjected
to a merciless caricature. Socrates, Cleon, Euripides are types which represent certain movements
in philosophy, politics, and poetry. They are

---

[1] *Poet.* v. 3.

[2] *Eth. Nic.* iv. 8. 1128 a 22, ἴδοι δ' ἄν τις καὶ ἐκ τῶν
κωμῳδιῶν τῶν παλαιῶν καὶ τῶν καινῶν· τοῖς μὲν γὰρ ἦν γελοῖον
ἡ αἰσχρολογία, τοῖς δὲ μᾶλλον ἡ ὑπόνοια. Cf. frag. περὶ
κωμῳδίας (Cramer *Anecd.*): διαφέρει ἡ κωμῳδία τῆς λοιδορίας,
ἐπεὶ ἡ μὲν λοιδορία ἀπαρακαλύπτως τὰ προσόντα κακὰ διέξεισιν,
ἡ δὲ δεῖται τῆς καλουμένης ἐμφάσεως: where ἐμφάσεως = the
Aristotelian ὑπονοίας.

labelled with historic names; a few obvious traits
are borrowed which recall the well-known personalities; but the dramatic personages are in no
sense the men who are known to us from history.
Such poetic truth as they possess is derived simply
from their typical quality.   It is not, indeed, in the
manner of Aristophanes to attempt any faithful
portraiture of life or character.   His imagination
works by giving embodiment to what is abstract.
His love of bold personification is in part inherited
from his predecessors on the Attic stage : Cratinus
had introduced Laws (Νόμοι) and Riches (Πλοῦτοι)
as his choruses.   But Aristophanes goes farther;
he seems to think through materialised ideas.   He
personifies the Just and the Unjust Logic, and
brings them before us as lawcourt disputants; he
incarnates a metaphor such as the philosopher 'in
the clouds,' the jurymen with waspish temper,
mankind with their airy hopes.   The same bent
of mind leads him to give a concrete form to the
forces and tendencies of the age, and to embody
them in actual persons.   A play of Aristophanes
is a dramatised debate, an ἀγών, in which the
persons represent opposing principles; for in form
the piece is always combative, though the fight
may be but a mock fight.   These principles are
brought into collision and worked out to their
most irrational conclusions, little regard being paid
to the coherence of the parts and still less to

propriety of character. The Aristophanic comedy, having transported real persons into a world where the conditions of reality are neglected, strips them of all that is truly individual and distinctive, it invests them with the attributes of a class or makes them representative of an idea.

In the Middle Comedy and still more in the New Comedy we observe a change in the manner of poetic generalisation. We quit the fantastic world of Aristophanes with its audacious allegories and grotesque types of character. There is now a closer study of real life and a finer delineation of motive. The action by degrees gains strength and consistency, till, like that of tragedy, it has a beginning, a middle, and an end. Character and action become more intimately united. The typical follies and failings of mankind are woven into a plot, in which moral probability takes the place of the arbitrary sequence of loosely connected scenes and incidents. The broad characteristics of humanity receive a more faithful, if a more prosaic rendering. Moreover, the great ideas of Hellenism disengage themselves from local and accidental influences and make their appeal to a universal human sentiment. In Aristotle's day the movement here described was but partially developed. He did not live to see the master-pieces of Menander, which were the poetic em-bodiment of his own theory. The Middle Comedy which suggested to him his ideal had not indeed altogether dropped the element of personal satire ; it merely replaced the invective formerly levelled against public men by a gentle raillery of poets and philosophers. Still Aristotle discerned accurately the direction in which comedy was travelling, and not improbably contributed by his reasoned principles and precepts to carry forward the literary movement already initiated.

We have seen that in the *Poetics* (ch. ix.) he draws no distinction between the generalisation proper to tragedy and comedy respectively. It is an important omission, though in a treatise so incomplete as the *Poetics*, in which we have a bare fragment of the section devoted to comedy, we are hardly warranted in assuming that he saw no difference in this respect between the two forms of poetry. Yet critics give ingenious reasons for what they conceive to be the orthodox Aristotelian view. Lessing, to whom Aristotle's authority was that of a lawgiver in art,[1] and who admits that he considers the *Poetics* 'as infallible as the *Elements of Euclid*,' having once satisfied himself that Aristotle had pronounced upon the matter in dispute, enforces at length the conclusion that the characters in comedy are 'general,' precisely

[1] This tradition goes back to Scaliger (1561): see Spingarn, page 141, 'Aristoteles imperator noster, omnium bonarum artium dictator perpetuus.' (Scaliger, *Poet.* vii. ii. 1.)

in the same sense as those of tragedy.[1] He con-
troverts the saying of Diderot that 'comedy has
species, tragedy has individuals,' and the similar
observation of Hurd that 'comedy makes all
characters general, tragedy particular.'[2]

But, surely, there is a real distinction between
the generalisation of tragedy and of comedy, though
it is not exactly expressed in the sayings above
quoted. Comedy looking at a single aspect of
life, at the follies, the imperfections, the inconsistencies of men, withdraws its attention from the
graver issues which concern the end of conduct.
It takes those moments when life appears to be
idle and distorted, a thing of vanity and nothing-
ness; it brings out its negative side, its inherent
limitations; it exhibits situations in which the
sense of the ideal is lost under an outward gaiety,
or its realisation wholly frustrated. It does not
detach the essentials of life from the unreal appearances; and, though some elements of tragic
earnestness may underlie the representation, comedy
cannot, while remaining within its own strict limits,
present, as tragedy does, a rounded and complete
action, an image of universal human nature. In
respect of character-drawing, its usual method—so
far as it maintains itself as a distinct artistic type
—is to embody a dominant characteristic or a lead-

---

[1] Lessing, *Hamb. Dram.* pp. 458–470.
[2] ib. p. 468.

ing passion, so that the single attribute becomes
the man.

A character so created, exhibiting an ideal of
covetousness, misanthropy, or whatever the quality
may be, almost of necessity runs to caricature. It
is framed on lines of impossible simplicity. The
single quality, which in nature is organically related
to other impulses and powers, is isolated and exaggerated. The process is one of abstraction, and
corresponds to an original one-sidedness in the
comic view of life. Even Molière in *Tartuffe* and
Alceste portrays abstract qualities rather than
living men. Not that comedy in its generalising
effort suppresses particulars. No detail is too
trivial for it, no utterance too momentary, no desires
too purely egoistic, if only they can be made to
serve the general effect; but the details it
accentuates are of a different kind from those which
tragedy admits. In the passing and unreal appearances of life it finds everywhere material for
mirth. In a sense it individualises everything, no
less truly than in another sense it generalises all.
What it can rarely achieve as a purely sportive
activity is to combine these two aspects in ethical
portraiture.

The line that severs tragedy and comedy is not,
indeed, so sharply drawn by modern dramatic art
as it was in the ancient world ; and characters have
been created in which the serious and the comic

element interpenetrate one another. By the close alliance of sympathy with humour—an alliance which was still imperfect in antiquity—the most far-reaching results have been produced affecting the range and meaning of the ludicrous. Humour, enriched by sympathy, directs its observation to the more serious realities of life. It looks below the surface, it rediscovers the hidden incongruities and deeper discords to which use and wont have deadened our perception. It finds everywhere the material both for laughter and tears ; and pathos henceforth becomes the companion of humour. The humorist does not, like the satirist, stand apart from men in fancied superiority. He recognises his own kinship with the humanity which provokes him to mirth. He sees around him shattered ideals ; he observes the irony of destiny ; he is aware of discords and imperfections, but accepts them all with playful acquiescence, and is saddened and amused in turn. Humour is the meeting-point of tragedy and comedy ; and the saying of Socrates in the *Symposium* has in great measure been justified, that the genius of tragedy and of comedy is the same.[1]

It is chiefly through humour of the deeper sort that modern comedy has acquired its generalising power. To the humorist there is no such thing

---

[1] Plato, *Sympos.* 223 D, τοῦ αὐτοῦ ἀνδρὸς εἶναι κωμῳδίαν καὶ τραγῳδίαν ἐπίστασθαι ποιεῖν.

as individual folly, but only folly universal in a
world of fools.   Humour annihilates the finite.
As Coleridge says, 'The little is made great and
the great little, in order to destroy both, because
all is equal in contrast with the infinite.'   Uncle
Toby, in *Tristram Shandy*, with his campaigns and
his fortresses, is an epitome of the follies of mankind.   In the greatest creations of humour, such as
Don Quixote, we have a summary of the contradictions of human life, of the disproportion between
the idea and the fact, between soul and body,
between the brilliant day-dream and the waking
reality.

This universalising power of humour is not, indeed, unknown in ancient literature.   The *Birds* of
Aristophanes is a splendid example to the contrary.
But if we restrict our attention, as we have chiefly
done here, to the portraiture of character that is
individual while at the same time it is universal,
we are at once aware of a distinction.   Don Quixote
and Sancho are living and breathing beings ; each
is a tissue of contradictions, yet each is a true
personality.   The actors in an Aristophanic
play are transparent caricatures.   In these half-
grotesque impersonations the individual is entirely
subordinated to the type ; and not here only, but
also—so far as we can judge—in the more minute
and realistic art of the New Comedy, where differences of age, sex, family relationship, or social

condition are carefully delineated, coexisting, however, with strongly marked features of a common
humanity.   Greek tragedy, on the other hand, like
all tragedy of the highest order, combines in one
harmonious representation the individual and the
universal.   Whereas comedy tends to merge the
individual in the type, tragedy manifests the
type through the individual.   In brief, it may be
said that comedy, in its unmixed sportive form,
creates personified ideals, tragedy creates idealised
persons.

CHAPTER XI

IT is characteristic of Aristotle's method that he starts from concrete facts, and that his rules are in the main a generalisation from these facts. He is, in the first instance, a Greek summing up Greek experience. The treasure-house of Greek art and poetry lay open before him ; a vast body of literature, lost to us, was in his hands. He looked back upon the past, conscious, it would seem, that the great creative era was closed, and that in the highest regions, at least, of artistic composition the Greek genius had reached the summit of its powers. The time was ripe for criticism to take a survey of the whole field of poetic literature. Aristotle approaches the subject as the historian of poetry, but his generalising faculty impels him to seek the law in the facts, and from the observed effects of different kinds of poetry to penetrate to the essential character of each. If his rules have proved in most cases to be not merely rules of Greek art but principles of art, it is because first, the Greek poets contain so much that appeals to universal human nature, and because next, Aristotle was able from the mass of literature before him to disengage and to formulate this universal element. The laws that he discovers are those which were already impressed on the chief productions of the Greek genius.

We can hardly claim, as has been sometimes done for Aristotle, that he rose above the traditions and limitations of the Hellenic mind, and took up the attitude of the purely human or cosmopolitan spectator. On some points, doubtless, he expresses opinions which contradict the current ideas of his age. He admits that in certain cases the tragic poet may take entirely fictitious subjects instead of the well-known legends.[1] He holds that metre, which was popularly thought to be the most essential element of poetry, is in truth the least essential, if indeed it is essential at all.[2] He leaves it at least an open question whether the drama may not still admit of new developments.[3] But in general it remains true that Greek experience was the starting-point and basis of his theory, though that experience had to be sifted, condensed, and interpreted before any coherent doctrine of poetry could be framed or judgment be passed on individual authors. Aristotle does not accept even the greater tragedians as all of equal authority, or all their works as alike canons of art; and it is a mistake to assume that the

[1] *Poet.* ix. 8.   [2] pp. 141 ff.   [3] *Poet.* iv. 11.

precepts of the *Poetics* must, if there is no indication to the contrary, harmonise with the practice of
Aeschylus, Sophocles, and Euripides, if not of minor
writers also.   His rules are based on a discriminating
and selective principle, and imply some criterion for
judging of artistic excellence.

The principles of art as laid down by Aristotle
faithfully reflect the Greek genius in the exclusion
of certain tendencies to which other nations have
yielded.   First, pure realism is forbidden ; that is,
the literal and prosaic imitation which reaches perfection in a jugglery of the senses by which the copy
is mistaken for the original.   In the decay of Greek
art this kind of ingenuity came into vogue, but it
never found favour in the best times.   Even the
custom of setting up votive statues of athletes who
had been thrice victors in the games did not lead to
a realism such as in Egypt was the outcome of the
practice which secured the immortality of a dead
man through the material support of a portrait
statue.   Next, pure symbolism is forbidden,—those
fantastic shapes which attracted the imagination of
Oriental nations, and which were known to the
Greeks themselves in the arts of Egypt and Assyria.
The body of a lion with the head of a man and the
wings and feathers of a bird was an attempt to
render abstract attributes in forms which do not
correspond with the idea.   Instead of the concrete
image of a living organism the result is an impossible

compound, which in transcending nature violates nature's laws. The *Odyssey*, on the other hand, with its impossible adventures by sea and land, its magic ship, its enchanted islands, its men transformed into swine, its vision of the world below, is constructed according to the laws of poetic truth. The whole is a faithful representation of human life and action, the irrational elements (τὰ ἄλογα) being but accessories that do not disturb the main impression. They are presented to the imagination with such vividness and coherence that the impossible becomes plausible, the fiction looks like truth.

That these principles were arrived at after due observation of Oriental art is very improbable. Familiar as Aristotle must have been with the external characteristics of this art and with specimens of Greek workmanship which had been moulded under its influence, there is no express allusion to Eastern works of art in his writings. The omission is not explained simply by saying that he did not set himself the task of writing a treatise on sculpture, and that his sole concern was with poetry. For, had he given serious thought to the plastic art of the East, as he certainly did to that of his own country, some trace of it would probably have been found in his writings; just as his observation of Greek models led him to drop many detached remarks on painting and sculpture. To learn a barbarous tongue, however, was so uncongenial to a Greek that even the all-acquisitive mind of Aristotle was content to remain ignorant of every literature but his own ; and it may similarly have seemed a waste of labour to study the symbolism of a barbarous art.[1] Oriental art on the face of it was not a rational and intelligent creation ; it had no counterpart in the world of reality.

The Greek imagination of the classical age is under the strict control of reason, it is limited by a sense of measure and a faculty of self-restraint. It does not like the Oriental run riot in its own prodigal wealth. We are always conscious of a reserve of power, a temperate strength which knows

---

[1] It is strange how little notice the Greeks took of symbolical art. Dion Chrysostom (circa A.D. 100), Ὀλυμπ. Or. xii. 404 R, in a speech put into the mouth of Phidias defends the plastic art of Greece, which expresses the divine nature in human form. The human body serves indeed as a symbol of the invisible, but it is a nobler symbolism than that of the barbarians, who in animal shapes discover the divine image. Philostratus Vit. Apoll. vi. 19 discusses the point at greater length. Apollonius is here supporting the method of Greek sculpture as contrasted with the grotesque forms under which the gods were represented in Egypt (ἄτοπα καὶ γελοῖα θεῶν εἴδη). Thespesion, with whom he is conversing, argues that the wisdom of the Egyptians is shown chiefly in this, that they give up the daring attempt directly to reproduce the deity, and by symbol and allegory produce a more impressive effect : σοφὸν γὰρ εἴπερ τι Αἰγυπτίων καὶ τὸ μὴ θρασύνεσθαι ἐς τὰ τῶν θεῶν εἴδη, ξυμβολικὰ δὲ αὐτὰ ποιεῖσθαι καὶ ὑπονοούμενα, καὶ γὰρ ἂν καὶ σεμνότερα οὕτω φαίνοιτο. To which Apollonius replies that the effect would have been still more impressive if instead of fashioning a dog or goat or ibis they had offered no visible representation, and left it to the imagination, which is a better artist, to give form and shape to the divinity.

its own resources and employs them without effort
and without ostentation.   The poet, the historian,
the artist, each of them could do much more if he
chose, but he does not care to dazzle us.   He is
bent on seeing truly, on seeing harmoniously, and
on expressing what he sees.   The materials on
which his imagination works are fused and combined according to the laws of what is possible,
reasonable, natural.   Greek mythology as it has
come to us in literature bears on it this mark
of reasonableness.   Traces indeed there are of an
earlier type,—rude and unassimilated elements,
flaws which have been left untouched by the
shaping hand of the poet or by the constructive
genius of the race.   But compare Greek mythology
with that of other nations, and we cannot but
wonder at its freedom from the extravagant and
grotesque.   The Greeks in creating their gods in
their own likeness followed that imperious instinct
of their nature which required that every product
of their minds should be a harmonious and intelligible creation, not a thing half in the world,
half out of it, no hybrid compound of symbolic
attributes.

To watch the formation of the Homeric Olympus
is to see the Greek mind working in its own
artistic fashion.   The several tribes,—Achaeans,
Argives, Minyae, and a host of others,—have each
their local gods and goddesses, uncharacterised,

unspecialised, save by the vague omnipotence of godhead. With the victory of dominant races and the fusion of cults there came a redistribution of functions and attributes that might have issued in unmeaning chaos or in bare abstractions. Not so with the Greeks. From the motley assemblage of tribal divinities the Homeric gods stand out clear and calm as their own statues. The gods of other nations may be but the expression of the people's practical needs, or the abstracted utterance of their thought. The gods of the Greeks are fashioned by a race of artists in accordance with nature, but completing and transcending her. The mythologist notes how in the assignment of their spheres and duties all that is non-essential is eliminated. Attributes which a god already has in common with other gods fall out. The Homeric Olympus is a great gathering of living type-forms whose image henceforth haunted the imagination of the race.

It would not be true to say that the lighter play of fancy is excluded from the literature and mythology of the Greeks. Few nations have taken more delight in weaving airy and poetic fictions apart from all reality, made out of nothing and ending nowhere. Almost all the Greek poets have something of this national taste. It breaks out at moments even in the prose-writers, in Herodotus or Plato. In one domain, that of comedy, fancy seems at first sight to reign supreme and uncontrolled. It obeys its own laws and revels in its own absurdities. It turns the world upside down, and men and gods follow its bidding. The poet yields in thorough abandonment to the spirit of the festival, he leads the orgy and shares its madness and intoxication. No sooner is he launched on his course than he is carried wherever an exuberant poetic fancy and a gift of inextinguishable laughter lead him. The transitions from jest to earnest are as quick as thought. Whole scenes follow one another in which no single word can be taken seriously. Yet even comedy has its lucid intervals, or rather in its madness there is a method. In its wildest freaks there is some underlying reason, some intelligible drift and purpose. The fantastic licence, however, of comedy stands alone in Greek literature. In other departments fancy is much more restrained, more reserved. It breaks through as a sudden and transient light, as gleams that come and go, it does not disturb the serenity of thought.

The Greeks themselves were accustomed to speak of poetic genius as a form of madness, an inspired enthusiasm. It is the doctrine of Plato in the *Ion*, in the *Phaedrus*, in the *Symposium*. Even Aristotle, who sometimes writes as if the faculty of the logician were enough to construct

a poem, says 'poetry is a thing inspired.'[1] Elsewhere he more accurately distinguishes two classes
of poets,—the man of flexible genius who can take
the impress of each character in turn, and the
man of fine frenzy, who is lifted out of his
proper self, and loses his own personality.[2] In
another place we read of a poet who never composed so well as when he was in 'ecstasy' or
delirium;[3] but of these compositions no specimens

[1] *Rhet.* iii. 7. 1408 b 19, ἔνθεον γὰρ ἡ ποίησις.

[2] *Poet.* xvii. 2, διὸ εὐφυοῦς ἡ ποιητική ἐστιν ἢ μανικοῦ· τούτων
γὰρ οἱ μὲν εὔπλαστοι οἱ δὲ ἐκστατικοί εἰσιν. The reading
ἐκστατικοί is found in one MS. : the others have ἐξεταστικοί.
The correspondence of the two clauses is beyond doubt best
maintained by reading ἐκστατικοί. Then, οἱ μέν, i.e. the εὐφυεῖς,
are εὔπλαστοι : the finely gifted natures, poets who have the
versatility of genius, can take the mould of other characters :
whereas οἱ δέ, i.e. the μανικοί, are ἐκστατικοί. If we keep
ἐξεταστικοί, οἱ μέν will refer to μανικοί, οἱ δέ to εὐφυεῖς. By
ἐξεταστικοί will be meant a fine instinct of criticism, an artistic
judgment, a delicate power of seizing resemblances and differences.
In favour of this it may be argued that the εὐφυής has the special
gift of a fine critical faculty : cf. *Eth. Nic.* iii. 5. 1114 b 6, ἀλλὰ
φῦναι δεῖ ὥσπερ ὄψιν ἔχοντα, ᾗ κρινεῖ καλῶς . . . καὶ ἔστιν
εὐφυὴς ᾧ τοῦτο καλῶς πέφυκεν. But in either case the εὐφυής
has a more conscious and critical faculty than the μανικός. The
Arabic version, which at first seemed undecipherable, is now found
to afford unquestionable confirmation of ἐκστατικοί : see Preface,
p. xxvi.

As a curious instance of perverted criticism, it is worth
mentioning that Dryden (following Rapin), *Preface to Troilus and
Cressida*, wished to read εὐφυοῦς οὐ μανικοῦ, lest the 'madness of
poetry' should be justified from the authority of Aristotle.

[3] *Probl.* xxx. 1. 954 a 38, Μαρακὸς δὲ ὁ Συρακούσιος καὶ
ἀμείνων ἦν ποιητὴς ὅτ' ἐκσταίη.

survive. Of the great poets of Greece, however, we can say with certainty that whatever was the exact nature of their madness, inspiration, ecstasy —call it what you will—they never released themselves from the sovereignty of reason. Capricious and inconsequent they were not. Their imaginative creations even in their most fantastic forms obeyed a hidden law.

Lamb's essay on 'The Sanity of True Genius' may be illustrated from Greek poetry as fitly as from Shakespeare. 'So far from the position holding true that great wit (or genius, in our modern way of speaking) has a necessary alliance with insanity, the greatest wits, on the contrary, will ever be found to be the sanest writers. . . . But the true poet dreams being awake. He is not possessed by his subject, but has dominion over it. . . . Where he seems most to recede from humanity he will be found the truest to it. From beyond the scope of Nature if he summon possible existences, he subjugates them to the law of her consistency. He is beautifully loyal to that sovereign directress, even when he appears most to betray and desert her.' The perfect sanity of the Greek genius is intimately connected with its universality. For is not insanity a kind of disordered individualism? The madman is an egoist; he takes his own fancies as the measure of all things. He does not correct his impressions, or compare them with those of others, or bring them into harmony with external fact. The test of a man's sanity is the relation in which his mind stands to the universal. We call a man sane when his ideas not only form a coherent whole in themselves, but fit in with the laws and facts of the outer world and with the universal human reason. Is not all this in keeping with Aristotle's theory that the effort of poetry is towards the universal; that it represents the permanent possibilities of human nature, the essentials rather than the accidents? The poet does not on the one hand create at random or by guesswork, nor yet does he merely record what has happened. He tells what may happen according to laws of internal probability or necessity. The sequence of poetry is not the empirical sequence of fact but the logical or conceivable sequence of ideas; it eliminates chance and discovers unity and significance in characters and events.

All great poetry and art fulfil this law of universality, but none perhaps so perfectly as the poetry and art of the Greeks. Take a single instance,—the delineation of female character in Greek poetry. The heroines of Homer and of the tragedians are broadly and unmistakably human. In real life woman is less individual than man; she runs less into idiosyncrasies, she conforms rather to the general type. This however, it may be said, is owing to the deference she pays to the conventional rules of society ; it is due to artificial causes that do not reach to the foundations of character. But an inwardly eccentric woman is also rare. Go below the surface and you find that with all outward marks of difference, whether of fashion or of manner, and in spite of a caprice that has become proverbial, female character can be reduced to certain elemental types of womanhood. These essential types are few. Maiden, wife, mother, daughter, sister, — here are the great determining relations of life. They form the groundwork of character. Accident may modify character, circumstances may stamp it with a particular expression, and bring into relief this or that dominant feature. But there remains an ideal mould in which the type is cast. Once the deeper springs of feeling are moved, circumstances are thrust aside, and a woman's action may almost with certainty be predicted.

The superiority of the Greeks over all but the very greatest of the moderns in portraying female character, is probably due to their power of seizing and expressing the universal side of human nature —that side which is primary and fundamental in woman. They 'follow,' as Coleridge says of Shakespeare, 'the main march of the human affections.' The vulgar and obtrusive elements of personality are cast off, and in proportion as the characters are divested of what is purely individual, do they gain in interest and elevation. Penelope, Nausicaa, Andromache, Antigone, Iphigenia, are beings far less complex than the heroines of a dozen novels that come out now in a single year. Their beauty and truth lie precisely in their typical humanity. Nor, in gaining universal significance, do the women of Greek literature fade into abstract types. The finer shades of character are not excluded by the simplicity with which the main lines are drawn. In discarding what is accidental their individuality is not obliterated but deepened and enriched; for it is not disordered emotion or perplexity of motive that makes a character poetical, but power of will or power of love. Attentive study of such a poetic creation as Antigone reveals innumerable subtle traits illustrative of the general principle of Greek art by which the utmost variety of detail is admitted, if only it contributes to the total impression and is subject to a controlling unity of design.

For many centuries the standing quarrel of Greek literature had been between the poets and the philosophers. Poetry, said the philosophers, is all fiction, and immoral fiction too; philosophy seeks the good and the true. Plato, inheriting the ancient dislike of the wise men towards poetry, banished the poets from his ideal republic. Aristotle would heal the strife. He discovers a meeting-point of poetry and philosophy in the relation in which they stand to the universal. We should have been glad if he had explained his conception of the exact difference between them; clearly, he did not intend to merge poetry in philosophy. Following the lines of his general theory we can assert thus much,—that poetry is akin to philosophy in so far as it aims at expressing the universal; but that, unlike philosophy, it employs the medium of sensuous and imaginative form. In this sense poetry is a concrete philosophy, 'a criticism of life' and of the universe. This is completely true only of the higher imaginative creations, of such poems as those of Homer, Aeschylus, Shakespeare, Dante. In them there is an interpretation of man and of life and of the world; a connected scheme and view of things not systematised or consciously unfolded, but latent, underlying the poet's thought and essential to the unity of the poem. Poets, too, even of an inferior order, who, like Wordsworth, are capable of presenting truly, if not the whole of life, yet certain definite aspects of it in imaginative form, are in their own way philosophers. They embody a consistent and harmonious wisdom of their own.

Between poetry and philosophy there had been an ancient feud. It was otherwise with poetry and history. Here at first there was no opposition.

'Poetry,' says Bacon, 'is feigned history'; much of
the poetry of the Greeks might be called authentic
history,—true not in precision of detail or in the
record of personal adventures, but in its indication
of the larger outlines of events and its embodiment
in ideal form of the past deeds of the race. Aristotle himself speaks of the myths as history ; the
incidents they narrate are facts (τὰ γενόμενα); the
names of their heroes are 'historical' (γενόμενα
ὀνόματα) as opposed to fictitious (πεποιημένα) names.[1]
In this sense Greek tragedy was historical, but its
facts were drawn not from recent history or con-
temporaneous events. The tragedian was the suc-
cessor of the epic poet, who was himself the earliest
historian of the Greek race and the keeper of its
archives. Homer, it is true, is not to us as he was
to the Greeks the minute and literal chronicler of
the Trojan war. We may smile when we think of
his lines being quoted and accepted as evidence in
the settlement of an international claim. Yet the
Homeric poems are still historical documents of the
highest value ; and that not merely as reflecting
the life of the poet's age, the sentiments and
manners of the heroic society of which he formed
a part, but also as preserving the popular traditions
of Greece. Not many years ago it was the fashion
to speak of the legendary history of Greece as
legend and nothing more. Art and archaeology are

----

[1] *Poet.* ix. 6–7 : supra, pp. 168–170.

every day adding fresh testimony as to its substantial truth. Explorations and excavations are
restoring the traditional points of contact between
Greece and Asia Minor. Famous dynasties which
not long since had been resolved into sun-myths
again stand out as historical realities. Troy,
Tiryns, Mycenae rest on sure foundations; their
past greatness, their lines of princes, their relations with outside states, are not the dreams
of poetic imagination. The kernel of truth, which
was thought to be non-existent or indiscoverable,
is being extracted by the new appliances of the
historical method.

The Hellenic people, in short, are found to have
perpetuated their history with marvellous fidelity
through popular myth. Myth was the unwritten
literature of an early people whose instinctive
language was poetry. It was at once their philosophy and their history. It enshrined their unconscious theories of life, their reflexions upon things
human and divine. It recorded all that they knew
about their own past, about their cities and families,
the geographical movements of their tribes and the
exploits of their ancestors. Myth to the Greeks was
not simply what we mean by legend. Aristotle
observes that the poet is none the less a poet or
maker though the incidents of his poem should
chance to be actual events; for some actual events
have that internal stamp of the probable or possible

which makes them the subject-matter of poetry.[1]
Such were the 'actual events' recorded in myth.
They lay ready to the poet's hand as an anonymous
work, touched by the imagination of an artistic race,
many of them hardly needing to be recast from the
poetic mould in which they lay.   Truth and fiction
were here fused together, and the collective whole
was heroic history.   This was the idealising
medium through which the past became poetical;
it afforded that imaginative remoteness which
enabled the hearers to escape from present realities.   It lifted them into a higher sphere of
existence where the distractions of the present
were forgotten in the thrilling stories of an age
which, though distant, appealed to them by many
associations.   The Athenians fined Phrynichus for
his *Capture of Miletus* not because the event it
represented was historical instead of mythical, but
because it was recent and painful history.   As the
fairy-land of fancy was to Spenser

'The world's sweet inn from pain and wearisome turmoil,'

so the Greeks looked to poetry as a refuge from the
miseries and toilsomeness of life.   The comic poet
Timocles in explaining the effect of tragedy gives
expression to the common sentiment of Greece.
'The mind, made to forget its own sufferings and

---

[1] *Poet.* ix. 9.

touched with the charm of ancther's woe, carries away instruction and delight.'[1]

Greek poetry and art with true historic sense did not take the present as an isolated point, but projected it into the past, whose half-effaced outlines were restored by the imagination. Myth was the golden link which bound together the generations. The odes of Pindar are a case in point. The poet, starting from the individual victor in the games, raises the interest above the personal level and beyond the special occasion, by giving historical perspective and background to the event. The victor's fortunes are connected with the annals of his house, with the trials and triumphs of the past. Nor does the poet stop at the deeds of ancestors. The mention of a common ancestor—of a Heracles—will transport him from Lacedaemon to Thessaly. He passes outside the family and the city and

---

[1] Timocles Διονυσιάζουσαι : Meineke, *Com. Frag.* ii. 800 :

ὁ γὰρ νοῦς τῶν ἰδίων λήθην λαβὼν
πρὸς ἀλλοτρίῳ τε ψυχαγωγηθεὶς πάθει
μεθ᾽ ἡδονῆς ἀπῆλθε παιδευθεὶς ἅμα.

Cf. Hesiod, *Theog.* 98–103 :

εἰ γάρ τις καὶ πένθος ἔχων νεοκηδέϊ θυμῷ
ἄζηται κραδίην ἀκαχήμενος, αὐτὰρ ἀοιδὸς
Μουσάων θεράπων κλεῖα προτέρων ἀνθρώπων
ὑμνήσῃ, μάκαράς τε θεοὺς οἳ Ὄλυμπον ἔχουσιν,
αἶψ᾽ ὅ γε δυσφρονέων ἐπιλήθεται, οὐδέ τι κηδέων
μέμνηται· ταχέως δὲ παρέτραπε δῶρα θεάων.

Iambl. *de Mysteriis*, i. 11, p. 39, διὰ δὴ τοῦτο ἔν τε κωμῳδίᾳ καὶ τραγῳδίᾳ ἀλλότρια πάθη θεωροῦντες ἵσταμεν τὰ οἰκεῖα πάθη.

sweeps with rapid glance from colony to mother-city, from city to country, from the personal to the Panhellenic interest. Thus the ode is more than an occasional poem, and the theme as it is unfolded acquires a larger meaning. 'The victor is trans-figured into a glorious personification of his race, and the present is reflected, magnified, illuminated in the mirror of the mythic past.'[1] The ode rises by clear ascents from the individual to the universal.

It is this that constitutes Greek idealism. The world of reality and the world of imagination were not for the Greeks separate spheres which stood apart; the breath of poetry kindled the facts of experience and the traditions of the past. The ideal in Greek art was not the opposite of the real, but rather its fulfilment and perfection. Each sprang out of the same soil; the one was the full-blown flower of which the other was the germ.

[1] Gildersleeve, *Pindar*, Intr. p. xviii.

INDEX I

[The references here given are to the Essays only.]

409

INDEX II

[The references here given are to the Preface and the Essays only.]

412

INDEX III

[Passages of Greek Authors referred to in the Critical Notes or in the Essays.]

[1] Under ARISTOTLE are included works which, though not genuine, have been reckoned among the Aristotelian writings.

416

THE END

A CATALOG OF SELECTED
DOVER BOOKS
IN ALL FIELDS OF INTEREST

A CATALOG OF SELECTED DOVER
BOOKS IN ALL FIELDS OF INTEREST

100 BEST-LOVED POEMS, Edited by Philip Smith. "The Passionate Shepherd to His Love," "Shall I compare thee to a summer's day?" "Death, be not proud," "The Raven," "The Road Not Taken," plus works by Blake, Wordsworth, Byron, Shelley, Keats, many others. 96pp. 5³⁄₁₆ x 8¼. 0-486-28553-7

100 SMALL HOUSES OF THE THIRTIES, Brown-Blodgett Company. Exterior photographs and floor plans for 100 charming structures. Illustrations of models accompanied by descriptions of interiors, color schemes, closet space, and other amenities. 200 illustrations. 112pp. 8⅜ x 11. 0-486-44131-8

1000 TURN-OF-THE-CENTURY HOUSES: With Illustrations and Floor Plans, Herbert C. Chivers. Reproduced from a rare edition, this showcase of homes ranges from cottages and bungalows to sprawling mansions. Each house is meticulously illustrated and accompanied by complete floor plans. 256pp. 9⅜ x 12¼. 0-486-45596-3

101 GREAT AMERICAN POEMS, Edited by The American Poetry & Literacy Project. Rich treasury of verse from the 19th and 20th centuries includes works by Edgar Allan Poe, Robert Frost, Walt Whitman, Langston Hughes, Emily Dickinson, T. S. Eliot, other notables. 96pp. 5³⁄₁₆ x 8¼. 0-486-40158-8

101 GREAT SAMURAI PRINTS, Utagawa Kuniyoshi. Kuniyoshi was a master of the warrior woodblock print — and these 18th-century illustrations represent the pinnacle of his craft. Full-color portraits of renowned Japanese samurais pulse with movement, passion, and remarkably fine detail. 112pp. 8⅜ x 11. 0-486-46523-3

ABC OF BALLET, Janet Grosser. Clearly worded, abundantly illustrated little guide defines basic ballet-related terms: arabesque, battement, pas de chat, relevé, sissonne, many others. Pronunciation guide included. Excellent primer. 48pp. 4³⁄₁₆ x 5¾. 0-486-40871-X

ACCESSORIES OF DRESS: An Illustrated Encyclopedia, Katherine Lester and Bess Viola Oerke. Illustrations of hats, veils, wigs, cravats, shawls, shoes, gloves, and other accessories enhance an engaging commentary that reveals the humor and charm of the many-sided story of accessorized apparel. 644 figures and 59 plates. 608pp. 6⅛ x 9¼. 0-486-43378-1

ADVENTURES OF HUCKLEBERRY FINN, Mark Twain. Join Huck and Jim as their boyhood adventures along the Mississippi River lead them into a world of excitement, danger, and self-discovery. Humorous narrative, lyrical descriptions of the Mississippi valley, and memorable characters. 224pp. 5³⁄₁₆ x 8¼. 0-486-28061-6

ALICE STARMORE'S BOOK OF FAIR ISLE KNITTING, Alice Starmore. A noted designer from the region of Scotland's Fair Isle explores the history and techniques of this distinctive, stranded-color knitting style and provides copious illustrated instructions for 14 original knitwear designs. 208pp. 8⅜ x 10⅞. 0-486-47218-3

Browse over 9,000 books at www.doverpublications.com

ALICE'S ADVENTURES IN WONDERLAND, Lewis Carroll. Beloved classic about a little girl lost in a topsy-turvy land and her encounters with the White Rabbit, March Hare, Mad Hatter, Cheshire Cat, and other delightfully improbable characters. 42 illustrations by Sir John Tenniel. 96pp. 5%6 x 8¼. 0-486-27543-4

AMERICA'S LIGHTHOUSES: An Illustrated History, Francis Ross Holland. Profusely illustrated fact-filled survey of American lighthouses since 1716. Over 200 stations — East, Gulf, and West coasts, Great Lakes, Hawaii, Alaska, Puerto Rico, the Virgin Islands, and the Mississippi and St. Lawrence Rivers. 240pp. 8 x 10¾. 0-486-25576-X

AN ENCYCLOPEDIA OF THE VIOLIN, Alberto Bachmann. Translated by Frederick H. Martens. Introduction by Eugene Ysaye. First published in 1925, this renowned reference remains unsurpassed as a source of essential information, from construction and evolution to repertoire and technique. Includes a glossary and 73 illustrations. 496pp. 6⅛ x 9¼. 0-486-46618-3

ANIMALS: 1,419 Copyright-Free Illustrations of Mammals, Birds, Fish, Insects, etc., Selected by Jim Harter. Selected for its visual impact and ease of use, this outstanding collection of wood engravings presents over 1,000 species of animals in extremely lifelike poses. Includes mammals, birds, reptiles, amphibians, fish, insects, and other invertebrates. 284pp. 9 x 12. 0-486-23766-4

THE ANNALS, Tacitus. Translated by Alfred John Church and William Jackson Brodribb. This vital chronicle of Imperial Rome, written by the era's great historian, spans A.D. 14-68 and paints incisive psychological portraits of major figures, from Tiberius to Nero. 416pp. 5%6 x 8¼. 0-486-45236-0

ANTIGONE, Sophocles. Filled with passionate speeches and sensitive probing of moral and philosophical issues, this powerful and often-performed Greek drama reveals the grim fate that befalls the children of Oedipus. Footnotes. 64pp. 5%6 x 8 ¼. 0-486-27804-2

ART DECO DECORATIVE PATTERNS IN FULL COLOR, Christian Stoll. Reprinted from a rare 1910 portfolio, 160 sensuous and exotic images depict a breathtaking array of florals, geometrics, and abstracts — all elegant in their stark simplicity. 64pp. 8⅜ x 11. 0-486-44862-2

THE ARTHUR RACKHAM TREASURY: 86 Full-Color Illustrations, Arthur Rackham. Selected and Edited by Jeff A. Menges. A stunning treasury of 86 full-page plates span the famed English artist's career, from Rip Van Winkle (1905) to masterworks such as Undine, A Midsummer Night's Dream, and Wind in the Willows (1939). 96pp. 8⅜ x 11. 0-486-44685-9

THE AUTHENTIC GILBERT & SULLIVAN SONGBOOK, W. S. Gilbert and A. S. Sullivan. The most comprehensive collection available, this songbook includes selections from every one of Gilbert and Sullivan's light operas. Ninety-two numbers are presented uncut and unedited, and in their original keys. 410pp. 9 x 12. 0-486-23482-7

THE AWAKENING, Kate Chopin. First published in 1899, this controversial novel of a New Orleans wife's search for love outside a stifling marriage shocked readers. Today, it remains a first-rate narrative with superb characterization. New introductory Note. 128pp. 5%6 x 8¼. 0-486-27786-0

BASIC DRAWING, Louis Priscilla. Beginning with perspective, this commonsense manual progresses to the figure in movement, light and shade, anatomy, drapery, composition, trees and landscape, and outdoor sketching. Black-and-white illustrations throughout. 128pp. 8⅜ x 11. 0-486-45815-6

Browse over 9,000 books at www.doverpublications.com

THE BATTLES THAT CHANGED HISTORY, Fletcher Pratt. Historian profiles 16 crucial conflicts, ancient to modern, that changed the course of Western civilization. Gripping accounts of battles led by Alexander the Great, Joan of Arc, Ulysses S. Grant, other commanders. 27 maps. 352pp. 5⅜ x 8½. 0-486-41129-X

BEETHOVEN'S LETTERS, Ludwig van Beethoven. Edited by Dr. A. C. Kalischer. Features 457 letters to fellow musicians, friends, greats, patrons, and literary men. Reveals musical thoughts, quirks of personality, insights, and daily events. Includes 15 plates. 410pp. 5⅜ x 8½. 0-486-22769-3

BERNICE BOBS HER HAIR AND OTHER STORIES, F. Scott Fitzgerald. This brilliant anthology includes 6 of Fitzgerald's most popular stories: "The Diamond as Big as the Ritz," the title tale, "The Offshore Pirate," "The Ice Palace," "The Jelly Bean," and "May Day." 176pp. 5⅜ x 8½. 0-486-47049-0

BESLER'S BOOK OF FLOWERS AND PLANTS: 73 Full-Color Plates from Hortus Eystettensis, 1613, Basilius Besler. Here is a selection of magnificent plates from the *Hortus Eystettensis,* which vividly illustrated and identified the plants, flowers, and trees that thrived in the legendary German garden at Eichstätt. 80pp. 8⅜ x 11. 0-486-46005-3

THE BOOK OF KELLS, Edited by Blanche Cirker. Painstakingly reproduced from a rare facsimile edition, this volume contains full-page decorations, portraits, illustrations, plus a sampling of textual leaves with exquisite calligraphy and ornamentation. 32 full-color illustrations. 32pp. 9⅜ x 12¼. 0-486-24345-1

THE BOOK OF THE CROSSBOW: With an Additional Section on Catapults and Other Siege Engines, Ralph Payne-Gallwey. Fascinating study traces history and use of crossbow as military and sporting weapon, from Middle Ages to modern times. Also covers related weapons: balistas, catapults, Turkish bows, more. Over 240 illustrations. 400pp. 7¼ x 10⅛. 0-486-28720-3

THE BUNGALOW BOOK: Floor Plans and Photos of 112 Houses, 1910, Henry L. Wilson. Here are 112 of the most popular and economic blueprints of the early 20th century — plus an illustration or photograph of each completed house. A wonderful time capsule that still offers a wealth of valuable insights. 160pp. 8⅜ x 11. 0-486-45104-6

THE CALL OF THE WILD, Jack London. A classic novel of adventure, drawn from London's own experiences as a Klondike adventurer, relating the story of a heroic dog caught in the brutal life of the Alaska Gold Rush. Note. 64pp. 5³⁄₁₆ x 8¼. 0-486-26472-6

CANDIDE, Voltaire. Edited by Francois-Marie Arouet. One of the world's great satires since its first publication in 1759. Witty, caustic skewering of romance, science, philosophy, religion, government — nearly all human ideals and institutions. 112pp. 5³⁄₁₆ x 8¼. 0-486-26689-3

CELEBRATED IN THEIR TIME: Photographic Portraits from the George Grantham Bain Collection, Edited by Amy Pastan. With an Introduction by Michael Carlebach. Remarkable portrait gallery features 112 rare images of Albert Einstein, Charlie Chaplin, the Wright Brothers, Henry Ford, and other luminaries from the worlds of politics, art, entertainment, and industry. 128pp. 8⅜ x 11. 0-486-46754-6

CHARIOTS FOR APOLLO: The NASA History of Manned Lunar Spacecraft to 1969, Courtney G. Brooks, James M. Grimwood, and Loyd S. Swenson, Jr. This illustrated history by a trio of experts is the definitive reference on the Apollo spacecraft and lunar modules. It traces the vehicles' design, development, and operation in space. More than 100 photographs and illustrations. 576pp. 6¾ x 9¼. 0-486-46756-2

Browse over 9,000 books at www.doverpublications.com

A CHRISTMAS CAROL, Charles Dickens. This engrossing tale relates Ebenezer Scrooge's ghostly journeys through Christmases past, present, and future and his ultimate transformation from a harsh and grasping old miser to a charitable and compassionate human being. 80pp. 5³⁄₁₆ x 8¼. 0-486-26865-9

COMMON SENSE, Thomas Paine. First published in January of 1776, this highly influential landmark document clearly and persuasively argued for American separation from Great Britain and paved the way for the Declaration of Independence. 64pp. 5³⁄₁₆ x 8¼. 0-486-29602-4

THE COMPLETE SHORT STORIES OF OSCAR WILDE, Oscar Wilde. Complete texts of "The Happy Prince and Other Tales," "A House of Pomegranates," "Lord Arthur Savile's Crime and Other Stories," "Poems in Prose," and "The Portrait of Mr. W. H." 208pp. 5³⁄₁₆ x 8¼. 0-486-45216-6

COMPLETE SONNETS, William Shakespeare. Over 150 exquisite poems deal with love, friendship, the tyranny of time, beauty's evanescence, death, and other themes in language of remarkable power, precision, and beauty. Glossary of archaic terms. 80pp. 5³⁄₁₆ x 8¼. 0-486-26686-9

THE COUNT OF MONTE CRISTO: Abridged Edition, Alexandre Dumas. Falsely accused of treason, Edmond Dantès is imprisoned in the bleak Chateau d'If. After a hair-raising escape, he launches an elaborate plot to extract a bitter revenge against those who betrayed him. 448pp. 5³⁄₁₆ x 8¼. 0-486-45643-9

CRAFTSMAN BUNGALOWS: Designs from the Pacific Northwest, Yoho & Merritt. This reprint of a rare catalog, showcasing the charming simplicity and cozy style of Craftsman bungalows, is filled with photos of completed homes, plus floor plans and estimated costs. An indispensable resource for architects, historians, and illustrators. 112pp. 10 x 7. 0-486-46875-5

CRAFTSMAN BUNGALOWS: 59 Homes from "The Craftsman," Edited by Gustav Stickley. Best and most attractive designs from Arts and Crafts Movement publication — 1903–1916 — includes sketches, photographs of homes, floor plans, descriptive text. 128pp. 8¼ x 11. 0-486-25829-7

CRIME AND PUNISHMENT, Fyodor Dostoyevsky. Translated by Constance Garnett. Supreme masterpiece tells the story of Raskolnikov, a student tormented by his own thoughts after he murders an old woman. Overwhelmed by guilt and terror, he confesses and goes to prison. 480pp. 5³⁄₁₆ x 8¼. 0-486-41587-2

THE DECLARATION OF INDEPENDENCE AND OTHER GREAT DOCUMENTS OF AMERICAN HISTORY: 1775-1865, Edited by John Grafton. Thirteen compelling and influential documents: Henry's "Give Me Liberty or Give Me Death," Declaration of Independence, The Constitution, Washington's First Inaugural Address, The Monroe Doctrine, The Emancipation Proclamation, Gettysburg Address, more. 64pp. 5³⁄₁₆ x 8¼. 0-486-41124-9

THE DESERT AND THE SOWN: Travels in Palestine and Syria, Gertrude Bell. "The female Lawrence of Arabia," Gertrude Bell wrote captivating, perceptive accounts of her travels in the Middle East. This intriguing narrative, accompanied by 160 photos, traces her 1905 sojourn in Lebanon, Syria, and Palestine. 368pp. 5⅜ x 8½. 0-486-46876-3

A DOLL'S HOUSE, Henrik Ibsen. Ibsen's best-known play displays his genius for realistic prose drama. An expression of women's rights, the play climaxes when the central character, Nora, rejects a smothering marriage and life in "a doll's house." 80pp. 5³⁄₁₆ x 8¼. 0-486-27062-9

Browse over 9,000 books at www.doverpublications.com

DOOMED SHIPS: Great Ocean Liner Disasters, William H. Miller, Jr. Nearly 200 photographs, many from private collections, highlight tales of some of the vessels whose pleasure cruises ended in catastrophe: the *Morro Castle, Normandie, Andrea Doria, Europa,* and many others. 128pp. 8⅞ x 11¼. 0-486-45366-9

THE DORÉ BIBLE ILLUSTRATIONS, Gustave Doré. Detailed plates from the Bible: the Creation scenes, Adam and Eve, horrifying visions of the Flood, the battle sequences with their monumental crowds, depictions of the life of Jesus, 241 plates in all. 241pp. 9 x 12. 0-486-23004-X

DRAWING DRAPERY FROM HEAD TO TOE, Cliff Young. Expert guidance on how to draw shirts, pants, skirts, gloves, hats, and coats on the human figure, including folds in relation to the body, pull and crush, action folds, creases, more. Over 200 drawings. 48pp. 8¼ x 11. 0-486-45591-2

DUBLINERS, James Joyce. A fine and accessible introduction to the work of one of the 20th century's most influential writers, this collection features 15 tales, including a masterpiece of the short-story genre, "The Dead." 160pp. 5³⁄₁₆ x 8¼. 0-486-26870-5

EASY-TO-MAKE POP-UPS, Joan Irvine. Illustrated by Barbara Reid. Dozens of wonderful ideas for three-dimensional paper fun — from holiday greeting cards with moving parts to a pop-up menagerie. Easy-to-follow, illustrated instructions for more than 30 projects. 299 black-and-white illustrations. 96pp. 8⅜ x 11. 0-486-44622-0

EASY-TO-MAKE STORYBOOK DOLLS: A "Novel" Approach to Cloth Dollmaking, Sherralyn St. Clair. Favorite fictional characters come alive in this unique beginner's dollmaking guide. Includes patterns for Pollyanna, Dorothy from *The Wonderful Wizard of Oz*, Mary of *The Secret Garden*, plus easy-to-follow instructions, 263 black-and-white illustrations, and an 8-page color insert. 112pp. 8¼ x 11. 0-486-47360-0

EINSTEIN'S ESSAYS IN SCIENCE, Albert Einstein. Speeches and essays in accessible, everyday language profile influential physicists such as Niels Bohr and Isaac Newton. They also explore areas of physics to which the author made major contributions. 128pp. 5 x 8. 0-486-47011-3

EL DORADO: Further Adventures of the Scarlet Pimpernel, Baroness Orczy. A popular sequel to *The Scarlet Pimpernel,* this suspenseful story recounts the Pimpernel's attempts to rescue the Dauphin from imprisonment during the French Revolution. An irresistible blend of intrigue, period detail, and vibrant characterizations. 352pp. 5³⁄₁₆ x 8¼. 0-486-44026-5

ELEGANT SMALL HOMES OF THE TWENTIES: 99 Designs from a Competition, Chicago Tribune. Nearly 100 designs for five- and six-room houses feature New England and Southern colonials, Normandy cottages, stately Italianate dwellings, and other fascinating snapshots of American domestic architecture of the 1920s. 112pp. 9 x 12. 0-486-46910-7

THE ELEMENTS OF STYLE: The Original Edition, William Strunk, Jr. This is the book that generations of writers have relied upon for timeless advice on grammar, diction, syntax, and other essentials. In concise terms, it identifies the principal requirements of proper style and common errors. 64pp. 5⅜ x 8½. 0-486-44798-7

THE ELUSIVE PIMPERNEL, Baroness Orczy. Robespierre's revolutionaries find their wicked schemes thwarted by the heroic Pimpernel — Sir Percival Blakeney. In this thrilling sequel, Chauvelin devises a plot to eliminate the Pimpernel and his wife. 272pp. 5³⁄₁₆ x 8¼. 0-486-45464-9

Browse over 9,000 books at www.doverpublications.com

AN ENCYCLOPEDIA OF BATTLES: Accounts of Over 1,560 Battles from 1479 B.C. to the Present, David Eggenberger. Essential details of every major battle in recorded history from the first battle of Megiddo in 1479 B.C. to Grenada in 1984. List of battle maps. 99 illustrations. 544pp. 6½ x 9¼. 0-486-24913-1

ENCYCLOPEDIA OF EMBROIDERY STITCHES, INCLUDING CREWEL, Marion Nichols. Precise explanations and instructions, clearly illustrated, on how to work chain, back, cross, knotted, woven stitches, and many more — 178 in all, including Cable Outline, Whipped Satin, and Eyelet Buttonhole. Over 1400 illustrations. 219pp. 8⅜ x 11¼. 0-486-22929-7

ENTER JEEVES: 15 Early Stories, P. G. Wodehouse. Splendid collection contains first 8 stories featuring Bertie Wooster, the deliciously dim aristocrat and Jeeves, his brainy, imperturbable manservant. Also, the complete Reggie Pepper (Bertie's prototype) series. 288pp. 5⅜ x 8½. 0-486-29717-9

ERIC SLOANE'S AMERICA: Paintings in Oil, Michael Wigley. With a Foreword by Mimi Sloane. Eric Sloane's evocative oils of America's landscape and material culture shimmer with immense historical and nostalgic appeal. This original hardcover collection gathers nearly a hundred of his finest paintings, with subjects ranging from New England to the American Southwest. 128pp. 10⅝ x 9. 0-486-46525-X

ETHAN FROME, Edith Wharton. Classic story of wasted lives, set against a bleak New England background. Superbly delineated characters in a hauntingly grim tale of thwarted love. Considered by many to be Wharton's masterpiece. 96pp. 5³⁄₁₆ x 8 ¼. 0-486-26690-7

THE EVERLASTING MAN, G. K. Chesterton. Chesterton's view of Christianity — as a blend of philosophy and mythology, satisfying intellect and spirit — applies to his brilliant book, which appeals to readers' heads as well as their hearts. 288pp. 5⅜ x 8½. 0-486-46036-3

THE FIELD AND FOREST HANDY BOOK, Daniel Beard. Written by a co-founder of the Boy Scouts, this appealing guide offers illustrated instructions for building kites, birdhouses, boats, igloos, and other fun projects, plus numerous helpful tips for campers. 448pp. 5³⁄₁₆ x 8¼. 0-486-46191-2

FINDING YOUR WAY WITHOUT MAP OR COMPASS, Harold Gatty. Useful, instructive manual shows would-be explorers, hikers, bikers, scouts, sailors, and survivalists how to find their way outdoors by observing animals, weather patterns, shifting sands, and other elements of nature. 288pp. 5⅜ x 8½. 0-486-40613-X

FIRST FRENCH READER: A Beginner's Dual-Language Book, Edited and Translated by Stanley Appelbaum. This anthology introduces 50 legendary writers — Voltaire, Balzac, Baudelaire, Proust, more — through passages from *The Red and the Black, Les Misérables, Madame Bovary,* and other classics. Original French text plus English translation on facing pages. 240pp. 5⅜ x 8½. 0-486-46178-5

FIRST GERMAN READER: A Beginner's Dual-Language Book, Edited by Harry Steinhauer. Specially chosen for their power to evoke German life and culture, these short, simple readings include poems, stories, essays, and anecdotes by Goethe, Hesse, Heine, Schiller, and others. 224pp. 5⅜ x 8½. 0-486-46179-3

FIRST SPANISH READER: A Beginner's Dual-Language Book, Angel Flores. Delightful stories, other material based on works of Don Juan Manuel, Luis Taboada, Ricardo Palma, other noted writers. Complete faithful English translations on facing pages. Exercises. 176pp. 5⅜ x 8½. 0-486-25810-6

Browse over 9,000 books at www.doverpublications.com

FIVE ACRES AND INDEPENDENCE, Maurice G. Kains. Great back-to-the-land classic explains basics of self-sufficient farming. The one book to get. 95 illustrations. 397pp. 5⅜ x 8½. 0-486-20974-1

FLAGG'S SMALL HOUSES: Their Economic Design and Construction, 1922, Ernest Flagg. Although most famous for his skyscrapers, Flagg was also a proponent of the well-designed single-family dwelling. His classic treatise features innovations that save space, materials, and cost. 526 illustrations. 160pp. 9⅜ x 12¼.
0-486-45197-6

FLATLAND: A Romance of Many Dimensions, Edwin A. Abbott. Classic of science (and mathematical) fiction — charmingly illustrated by the author — describes the adventures of A. Square, a resident of Flatland, in Spaceland (three dimensions), Lineland (one dimension), and Pointland (no dimensions). 96pp. 5³⁄₁₆ x 8¼.
0-486-27263-X

FRANKENSTEIN, Mary Shelley. The story of Victor Frankenstein's monstrous creation and the havoc it caused has enthralled generations of readers and inspired countless writers of horror and suspense. With the author's own 1831 introduction. 176pp. 5³⁄₁₆ x 8¼. 0-486-28211-2

THE GARGOYLE BOOK: 572 Examples from Gothic Architecture, Lester Burbank Bridaham. Dispelling the conventional wisdom that French Gothic architectural flourishes were born of despair or gloom, Bridaham reveals the whimsical nature of these creations and the ingenious artisans who made them. 572 illustrations. 224pp. 8⅜ x 11. 0-486-44754-5

THE GIFT OF THE MAGI AND OTHER SHORT STORIES, O. Henry. Sixteen captivating stories by one of America's most popular storytellers. Included are such classics as "The Gift of the Magi," "The Last Leaf," and "The Ransom of Red Chief." Publisher's Note. 96pp. 5³⁄₁₆ x 8¼. 0-486-27061-0

THE GOETHE TREASURY: Selected Prose and Poetry, Johann Wolfgang von Goethe. Edited, Selected, and with an Introduction by Thomas Mann. In addition to his lyric poetry, Goethe wrote travel sketches, autobiographical studies, essays, letters, and proverbs in rhyme and prose. This collection presents outstanding examples from each genre. 368pp. 5⅜ x 8½. 0-486-44780-4

GREAT EXPECTATIONS, Charles Dickens. Orphaned Pip is apprenticed to the dirty work of the forge but dreams of becoming a gentleman — and one day finds himself in possession of "great expectations." Dickens' finest novel. 400pp. 5³⁄₁₆ x 8¼.
0-486-41586-4

GREAT WRITERS ON THE ART OF FICTION: From Mark Twain to Joyce Carol Oates, Edited by James Daley. An indispensable source of advice and inspiration, this anthology features essays by Henry James, Kate Chopin, Willa Cather, Sinclair Lewis, Jack London, Raymond Chandler, Raymond Carver, Eudora Welty, and Kurt Vonnegut, Jr. 192pp. 5⅜ x 8½. 0-486-45128-3

HAMLET, William Shakespeare. The quintessential Shakespearean tragedy, whose highly charged confrontations and anguished soliloquies probe depths of human feeling rarely sounded in any art. Reprinted from an authoritative British edition complete with illuminating footnotes. 128pp. 5³⁄₁₆ x 8¼. 0-486-27278-8

THE HAUNTED HOUSE, Charles Dickens. A Yuletide gathering in an eerie country retreat provides the backdrop for Dickens and his friends — including Elizabeth Gaskell and Wilkie Collins — who take turns spinning supernatural yarns. 144pp. 5⅜ x 8½. 0-486-46309-5

HEART OF DARKNESS, Joseph Conrad. Dark allegory of a journey up the Congo River and the narrator's encounter with the mysterious Mr. Kurtz. Masterly blend of adventure, character study, psychological penetration. For many, Conrad's finest, most enigmatic story. 80pp. 5³⁄₁₆ x 8¼. 0-486-26464-5

HENSON AT THE NORTH POLE, Matthew A. Henson. This thrilling memoir by the heroic African-American who was Peary's companion through two decades of Arctic exploration recounts a tale of danger, courage, and determination. "Fascinating and exciting." — *Commonweal.* 128pp. 5⅜ x 8½. 0-486-45472-X

HISTORIC COSTUMES AND HOW TO MAKE THEM, Mary Fernald and E. Shenton. Practical, informative guidebook shows how to create everything from short tunics worn by Saxon men in the fifth century to a lady's bustle dress of the late 1800s. 81 illustrations. 176pp. 5⅜ x 8½. 0-486-44906-8

THE HOUND OF THE BASKERVILLES, Arthur Conan Doyle. A deadly curse in the form of a legendary ferocious beast continues to claim its victims from the Baskerville family until Holmes and Watson intervene. Often called the best detective story ever written. 128pp. 5³⁄₁₆ x 8¼. 0-486-28214-7

THE HOUSE BEHIND THE CEDARS, Charles W. Chesnutt. Originally published in 1900, this groundbreaking novel by a distinguished African-American author recounts the drama of a brother and sister who "pass for white" during the dangerous days of Reconstruction. 208pp. 5⅜ x 8½. 0-486-46144-0

THE HUMAN FIGURE IN MOTION, Eadweard Muybridge. The 4,789 photographs in this definitive selection show the human figure — models almost all undraped — engaged in over 160 different types of action: running, climbing stairs, etc. 390pp. 7⅞ x 10⅝. 0-486-20204-6

THE IMPORTANCE OF BEING EARNEST, Oscar Wilde. Wilde's witty and buoyant comedy of manners, filled with some of literature's most famous epigrams, reprinted from an authoritative British edition. Considered Wilde's most perfect work. 64pp. 5³⁄₁₆ x 8¼. 0-486-26478-5

THE INFERNO, Dante Alighieri. Translated and with notes by Henry Wadsworth Longfellow. The first stop on Dante's famous journey from Hell to Purgatory to Paradise, this 14th-century allegorical poem blends vivid and shocking imagery with graceful lyricism. Translated by the beloved 19th-century poet, Henry Wadsworth Longfellow. 256pp. 5³⁄₁₆ x 8¼. 0-486-44288-8

JANE EYRE, Charlotte Brontë. Written in 1847, *Jane Eyre* tells the tale of an orphan girl's progress from the custody of cruel relatives to an oppressive boarding school and its culmination in a troubled career as a governess. 448pp. 5³⁄₁₆ x 8¼.
0-486-42449-9

JAPANESE WOODBLOCK FLOWER PRINTS, Tanigami Kônan. Extraordinary collection of Japanese woodblock prints by a well-known artist features 120 plates in brilliant color. Realistic images from a rare edition include daffodils, tulips, and other familiar and unusual flowers. 128pp. 11 x 8¼. 0-486-46442-3

JEWELRY MAKING AND DESIGN, Augustus F. Rose and Antonio Cirino. Professional secrets of jewelry making are revealed in a thorough, practical guide. Over 200 illustrations. 306pp. 5⅜ x 8½. 0-486-21750-7

JULIUS CAESAR, William Shakespeare. Great tragedy based on Plutarch's account of the lives of Brutus, Julius Caesar and Mark Antony. Evil plotting, ringing oratory, high tragedy with Shakespeare's incomparable insight, dramatic power. Explanatory footnotes. 96pp. 5³⁄₁₆ x 8¼. 0-486-26876-4

CATALOG OF DOVER BOOKS

THE JUNGLE, Upton Sinclair. 1906 bestseller shockingly reveals intolerable labor practices and working conditions in the Chicago stockyards as it tells the grim story of a Slavic family that emigrates to America full of optimism but soon faces despair. 320pp. 5³⁄₁₆ x 8¼. 0-486-41923-1

THE KINGDOM OF GOD IS WITHIN YOU, Leo Tolstoy. The soul-searching book that inspired Gandhi to embrace the concept of passive resistance, Tolstoy's 1894 polemic clearly outlines a radical, well-reasoned revision of traditional Christian thinking. 352pp. 5³⁄₁₆ x 8¼. 0-486-45138-0

THE LADY OR THE TIGER?: and Other Logic Puzzles, Raymond M. Smullyan. Created by a renowned puzzle master, these whimsically themed challenges involve paradoxes about probability, time, and change; metapuzzles; and self-referentiality. Nineteen chapters advance in difficulty from relatively simple to highly complex. 1982 edition. 240pp. 5⅜ x 8½. 0-486-47027-X

LEAVES OF GRASS: The Original 1855 Edition, Walt Whitman. Whitman's immortal collection includes some of the greatest poems of modern times, including his masterpiece, "Song of Myself." Shattering standard conventions, it stands as an unabashed celebration of body and nature. 128pp. 5³⁄₁₆ x 8¼. 0-486-45676-5

LES MISÉRABLES, Victor Hugo. Translated by Charles E. Wilbour. Abridged by James K. Robinson. A convict's heroic struggle for justice and redemption plays out against a fiery backdrop of the Napoleonic wars. This edition features the excellent original translation and a sensitive abridgment. 304pp. 6⅛ x 9¼. 0-486-45789-3

LILITH: A Romance, George MacDonald. In this novel by the father of fantasy literature, a man travels through time to meet Adam and Eve and to explore humanity's fall from grace and ultimate redemption. 240pp. 5⅜ x 8½. 0-486-46818-6

THE LOST LANGUAGE OF SYMBOLISM, Harold Bayley. This remarkable book reveals the hidden meaning behind familiar images and words, from the origins of Santa Claus to the fleur-de-lys, drawing from mythology, folklore, religious texts, and fairy tales. 1,418 illustrations. 784pp. 5⅜ x 8½. 0-486-44787-1

MACBETH, William Shakespeare. A Scottish nobleman murders the king in order to succeed to the throne. Tortured by his conscience and fearful of discovery, he becomes tangled in a web of treachery and deceit that ultimately spells his doom. 96pp. 5³⁄₁₆ x 8¼. 0-486-27802-6

MAKING AUTHENTIC CRAFTSMAN FURNITURE: Instructions and Plans for 62 Projects, Gustav Stickley. Make authentic reproductions of handsome, functional, durable furniture: tables, chairs, wall cabinets, desks, a hall tree, and more. Construction plans with drawings, schematics, dimensions, and lumber specs reprinted from 1900s The Craftsman magazine. 128pp. 8⅛ x 11. 0-486-25000-8

MATHEMATICS FOR THE NONMATHEMATICIAN, Morris Kline. Erudite and entertaining overview follows development of mathematics from ancient Greeks to present. Topics include logic and mathematics, the fundamental concept, differential calculus, probability theory, much more. Exercises and problems. 641pp. 5⅜ x 8½. 0-486-24823-2

MEMOIRS OF AN ARABIAN PRINCESS FROM ZANZIBAR, Emily Ruete. This 19th-century autobiography offers a rare inside look at the society surrounding a sultan's palace. A real-life princess in exile recalls her vanished world of harems, slave trading, and court intrigues. 288pp. 5⅜ x 8½. 0-486-47121-7

Browse over 9,000 books at www.doverpublications.com

THE METAMORPHOSIS AND OTHER STORIES, Franz Kafka. Excellent new English translations of title story (considered by many critics Kafka's most perfect work), plus "The Judgment," "In the Penal Colony," "A Country Doctor," and "A Report to an Academy." Note. 96pp. 5³⁄₁₆ x 8¼. 0-486-29030-1

MICROSCOPIC ART FORMS FROM THE PLANT WORLD, R. Anheisser. From undulating curves to complex geometrics, a world of fascinating images abound in this classic, illustrated survey of microscopic plants. Features 400 detailed illustrations of nature's minute but magnificent handiwork. The accompanying CD-ROM includes all of the images in the book. 128pp. 9 x 9. 0-486-46013-4

A MIDSUMMER NIGHT'S DREAM, William Shakespeare. Among the most popular of Shakespeare's comedies, this enchanting play humorously celebrates the vagaries of love as it focuses upon the intertwined romances of several pairs of lovers. Explanatory footnotes. 80pp. 5³⁄₁₆ x 8¼. 0-486-27067-X

THE MONEY CHANGERS, Upton Sinclair. Originally published in 1908, this cautionary novel from the author of The Jungle explores corruption within the American system as a group of power brokers joins forces for personal gain, triggering a crash on Wall Street. 192pp. 5⅜ x 8½. 0-486-46917-4

THE MOST POPULAR HOMES OF THE TWENTIES, William A. Radford. With a New Introduction by Daniel D. Reiff. Based on a rare 1925 catalog, this architectural showcase features floor plans, construction details, and photos of 26 homes, plus articles on entrances, porches, garages, and more. 250 illustrations, 21 color plates. 176pp. 8⅜ x 11. 0-486-47028-8

MY 66 YEARS IN THE BIG LEAGUES, Connie Mack. With a New Introduction by Rich Westcott. A Founding Father of modern baseball, Mack holds the record for most wins — and losses — by a major league manager. Enhanced by 70 photographs, his warmhearted autobiography is populated by many legends of the game. 288pp. 5⅜ x 8½. 0-486-47184-5

NARRATIVE OF THE LIFE OF FREDERICK DOUGLASS, Frederick Douglass. Douglass's graphic depictions of slavery, harrowing escape to freedom, and life as a newspaper editor, eloquent orator, and impassioned abolitionist. 96pp. 5³⁄₁₆ x 8¼. 0-486-28499-9

THE NIGHTLESS CITY: Geisha and Courtesan Life in Old Tokyo, J. E. de Becker. This unsurpassed study from 100 years ago ventured into Tokyo's red-light district to survey geisha and courtesan life and offer meticulous descriptions of training, dress, social hierarchy, and erotic practices. 49 black and white illustrations; 2 maps. 496pp. 5⅜ x 8½. 0-486-45563-7

THE ODYSSEY, Homer. Excellent prose translation of ancient epic recounts adventures of the homeward-bound Odysseus. Fantastic cast of gods, giants, cannibals, sirens, other supernatural creatures — true classic of Western literature. 256pp. 5³⁄₁₆ x 8¼. 0-486-40654-7

OEDIPUS REX, Sophocles. Landmark of Western drama concerns the catastrophe that ensues when King Oedipus discovers he has inadvertently killed his father and married his mother. Masterly construction, dramatic irony. Explanatory footnotes. 64pp. 5³⁄₁₆ x 8¼. 0-486-26877-2

ONCE UPON A TIME: The Way America Was, Eric Sloane. Nostalgic text and drawings brim with gentle philosophies and descriptions of how we used to live — self-sufficiently — on the land, in homes, and among the things built by hand. 44 line illustrations. 64pp. 8⅜ x 11. 0-486-44411-2